A Poet's Sourceboo

A Poet's Sourcebook

Writings about Poetry,
from the Ancient World to the Present

Selected and with an introduction by

Dawn Potter

Autumn House Press

PITTSBURGH

"Autumn House" and "Autumn House Press" are registered trademarks owned by Autumn House Press, a nonprofit corporation whose mission is the publication and promotion of poetry and other fine literature.

Autumn House Press receives state arts funding support through a grant from the Pennsylvania Council on the Arts, a state agency funded by the Commonwealth of Pennsylvania, and the National Endowment for the Arts, a federal agency.

ISBN 978-1-932870-77-0
Library of Congress Control Number: 2012950210

Both in his writings, and still more in his tremendous conversational mono-logues, which transfixed almost everyone who listened to them, Coleridge explored the Kantian insight: "The universe was a cosmic web," as he put it, "woven by God and held together by the crossed strands of attractive and repulsive forces." . . . "What," he wrote to [his friend] Tom Poole, "what if the vital force which I sent from my arm into the stone as I flung it in the air and skimmed it upon the water—what if even that did not perish?" Coleridge had thus stumbled upon what was to become the Principle of the Conservation of Energy.

It was one of the great merits of . . . [science pioneers Humphry] Davy and [Michael] Faraday that they were prepared to read and listen to the poets.

Paul Johnson
The Birth of the Modern: World Society, 1815–1830

Contents

Contents by Theme and Author

Introduction

"How far we are going to read a poet when we can read about a poet is a problem to lay before biographers," wrote Virginia Woolf, in a not entirely complimentary essay about Elizabeth Barrett Browning's novel-poem *Aurora Leigh*. Yet as Woolf well knew, the back story offers its own illuminations; and "we may suspect that Elizabeth Barrett was inspired by a flash of true genius when she rushed into the drawing-room and said that here, where we live and work, is the true place for the poet."

As I sifted among my choices for this anthology, I found myself returning again and again to Woolf's remarks. Why do we hover between reading a poet and reading about a poet? How does poetry come from where we live and work? And how does poetry reach into the broader purviews of art, science, politics, economics, and other human endeavors, while also drawing on those disciplines as its own creative source? These are questions that poets, and the watchers of poets, have been pondering for millennia; and if there is any overarching theme to *A Poet's Sourcebook*, it lingers within those perplexities.

Neither a craft handbook nor a theory manual, this anthology is merely one reader's record of the long human need to make poetry. For no matter how distant in time those individuals have become, reading about that need, in both their own words and the words of others, keeps our relationship with them intimate and immediate. Suetonius explains Virgil's revision process; Sir Philip Sidney argues with Aristotle; Emily Brontë peels potatoes and creates an imaginary country; Phillis Wheatley tries on John Milton's syntax for size; Walt Whitman invents a manifesto for a poetic tribe that doesn't yet exist; Audre Lorde sings the body electric; Jack Wiler rants about high school; ten-year-old Ethan Richard complains that poetry "always spouts the truth you don't want other people to hear in public."

In her novel *Daniel Deronda*, George Eliot writes:

> A human life, I think, should be well rooted in some spot of a native land, where it may get the love of tender kinship for the face of the earth, for the labours men go forth to, for the sounds and accents that haunt it, for whatever will give that early home a familiar unmistakable difference amid the future widening of knowledge: a spot where the definiteness of early memories may be inwrought with affection, and kindly acquaintance with all neighbours, even to the dogs and

donkeys, may spread not by sentimental effort and reflection, but as a sweet habit of the blood.

As I worked on this anthology, I became increasingly aware of my "tender kinship" for these writers, past and present, distant and near, who are, in some deep ancient way, my flesh and bones. The native land we share is poetry, and the very act of choosing these particular voices from among all the other voices of history was like embarking alongside them on a voyage to our collective home. Yet at the same time I was discovering how personal any such compendium must be; how, despite all efforts at universality, it ends up reflecting its editor's obsessions and limitations.

What can we do but be ourselves? That, too, is a question that poets continue to ask century after century – from Lao Tzu to Ovid, from Sappho to Sor Juana, from Mikhail Yurievich Lermontov to Gregory Corso, from Toi Derricotte to Garth Greenwell. Nonetheless, as a collector, I have tried to be various. I have included many different types of writing – essays, journal entries, letters, interviews, scripts, poems – and I have done my best to feature a swath of voices, though many intriguing works of literature have yet to appear in a reliable English translation. The vagaries of reprint permission have also limited the book's scope – sometimes for reasons of cost or authorial policy but often because I was unable to forge a trail to the rights holder.

I organized the book chronologically by each writer's date of birth, and a separate table of contents lists a few of the thematic links I noted among the excerpts. Occasionally my name appears as editor alongside a nineteenth-century translation of a classical work; but except for Benjamin Jowett's version of Plato's *Republic*, where I added paragraph breaks to the dialogue, all of my changes simply clarify punctuation or spelling.

Many people offered conversation, support, and advice as I worked on this anthology. In particular, I want to thank Richard Potter and Baron Wormser for sharing stacks of books and lists of resources; Teresa Carson, Jay Franzel, and Thomas Rayfiel for conversations about writers that matter to them; Jo Dexter for emergency T. S. Eliot aid; Mike Walker for suggestions about younger writers to include; and Ruth Harlow for help with reprint permission. Thanks also to the staff at Abbott Memorial Library in Dexter, Maine, for managing to spirit so many obscure tomes up to the north woods. But my greatest thanks goes to Michael Simms, founder and editor-in-chief of Autumn House Press, who, out of the blue, offered me the chance to create this book. I will be forever amazed and grateful.

Homer

Although Homer is the central figure of ancient Greek literature, no one knows anything about the man himself – including whether or not he actually existed. According to tradition, he is the author of the Iliad, *the* Odyssey, *and several lesser-known works that date between the seventh and ninth centuries* B.C.E. *Among those works are the Homeric hymns, thirty-four poems that may or may not have been composed by the poet or poets who composed some version of the* Iliad *or the* Odyssey. *Lyrical, mysterious, and eloquent, the hymns open a window into a time when myth was not yet metaphor but a physical and emotional bond between humanity and the unknown – a sensation that, for poets, the act of creation can still evoke.*

Homeric Hymn 25: To the Muses and Apollo

translated by Hugh G. Evelyn-White

I will begin with the Muses and Apollo and Zeus. For it is through the Muses and Apollo that there are singers upon the earth and players upon the lyre; but kings are from Zeus. Happy is he whom the Muses love: sweet flows speech from his lips.

Hail, children of Zeus! Give honour to my song! And now I will remember you and another song also.

Lao Tzu

(circa 604 B.C.E.)

*According to one version of his legend, the philosopher Lao Tzu was fathered
by a shooting star and stayed in his mother's womb for sixty-two years un-
til she leaned against a plum tree and he was born, fully grown and white
haired. Traditionally he is considered to be the author of the* Tao Te Ching,
*the key text of Taoism, which stands, with Confucianism, as one of China's
two great religious and philosophical systems. Yet his influence has extended
much farther. As translator Witter Bynner observes, "twenty-five centuries be-
fore Whitman, he knew the value of loafing and inviting one's soul; and the
American poet, whether or not consciously, has been in many ways one of the
Chinese poet's more eminent Western disciples." In the following brief chapter
from the* Tao Te Ching, *Lao Tzu celebrates the poetic mind – its willingness to
court ambiguity and to thrive on what others might call aimlessness.*

from *Tao Te Ching*

translated by Witter Bynner

Chapter 20

Leave off fine learning! End the nuisance
Of saying yes to this and perhaps to that,
Distinctions with how little difference!
Categorical this, categorical that,
What slightest use are they!
If one man leads, another must follow,
How silly that is and how false!
Yet conventional men lead an easy life
With all their days feast-days,
A constant spring visit to the Tall Tower,
While I am a simpleton, a do-nothing,
Not big enough yet to raise a hand,
Not grown enough to smile,
A homeless, worthless waif.
Men of the world have a surplus of goods,
While I am left out, owning nothing.

What a booby I must be
Not to know my way round,
What a fool!
The average man is so crisp and confident
That I ought to be miserable
Going on and on like the sea,
Drifting nowhere.
All these people are making their mark in the world,
While I, pig-headed, awkward,
Different from the rest,
Am only a glorious infant still nursing at the breast.

The Book of Genesis

Genesis is the first book of both the Christian Old Testament and the Hebrew Torah, with the Hebrew text dating back to the sixth century B.C.E. In the following excerpt, we read the tale of Jacob, third patriarch of the Hebrew people, who has tricked his older brother Esau out of his patrimony. On his return to Canaan, in fear for his life and his family, Jacob meets a mysterious man and wrestles with him. This simple yet ambiguous incident has captured the imagination of poets as varied as Rilke and Dickinson, demonstrating that even our oldest tales may continue to inspire remarkably different poetic reactions; and see page 145 for Thomas Wentworth Higginson's discussion of the tale's influence on the work of African-American spiritual singers.

Chapter 32: Jacob Fears Esau; Wrestles with an Angel

King James Version (1611)

And Jacob went on his way, and the angels of God met him.

And when Jacob saw them, he said, This is God's host: and he called the name of that place Mahanaim.

And Jacob sent messengers before him to Esau his brother unto the land of Seir, the country of Edom.

And he commanded them, saying, Thus shall ye speak unto my lord Esau; Thy servant Jacob saith thus, I have sojourned with Laban [his father-in-law and uncle], and stayed there until now:

And I have oxen, and asses, flocks, and menservants, and womenservants: and I have sent to tell my lord, that I may find grace in thy sight.

And the messengers returned to Jacob, saying, We came to thy brother Esau, and also he cometh to meet thee, and four hundred men with him.

Then Jacob was greatly afraid and distressed: and he divided the people that was with him, and the flocks, and herds, and the camels, into two bands;

And said, If Esau come to the one company, and smite it, then the other company which is left shall escape.

And Jacob said, O God of my father Abraham, and God of my father Isaac, the Lord which saidst unto me, Return unto thy country, and to thy kindred, and I will deal well with thee:

I am not worthy of the least of all the mercies, and of all the truth, which thou hast shewed unto thy servant; for with my staff I passed over this Jordan; and now I am become two bands.

Deliver me, I pray thee, from the hand of my brother, from the hand of Esau: for I fear him, lest he will come and smite me, and the mother with the children.

And thou saidst, I will surely do thee good, and make thy seed as the sand of the sea, which cannot be numbered for multitude.

And he lodged there that same night; and took of that which came to his hand a present for Esau his brother;

Two hundred she goats, and twenty he goats, two hundred ewes, and twenty rams,

Thirty milch camels with their colts, forty kine, and ten bulls, twenty she asses, and ten foals.

And he delivered them into the hand of his servants, every drove by themselves; and said unto his servants, Pass over before me, and put a space betwixt drove and drove.

And he commanded the foremost, saying, When Esau my brother meeteth thee, and asketh thee, saying, Whose art thou? and whither goest thou? and whose are these before thee?

Then thou shalt say, They be thy servant Jacob's; it is a present sent unto my lord Esau: and, behold, also he is behind us.

And so commanded he the second, and the third, and all that followed the droves, saying, On this manner shall ye speak unto Esau, when ye find him.

And say ye moreover, Behold, thy servant Jacob is behind us. For he said, I will appease him with the present that goeth before me, and afterward I will see his face; peradventure he will accept of me.

So went the present over before him: and himself lodged that night in the company.

And he rose up that night, and took his two wives, and his two womenservants, and his eleven sons, and passed over the ford Jabbok.

And he took them, and sent them over the brook, and sent over that he had.

And Jacob was left alone; and there wrestled a man with him until the breaking of the day.

And when he saw that he prevailed not against him, he touched the hollow of his thigh; and the hollow of Jacob's thigh was out of joint, as he wrestled with him.

And he said, Let me go, for the day breaketh. And he said, I will not let thee go, except thou bless me.

And he said unto him, What is thy name? And he said, Jacob.

And he said, Thy name shall be called no more Jacob, but Israel: for as a prince hast thou power with God and with men, and hast prevailed.

And Jacob asked him, and said, Tell me, I pray thee, thy name. And he said, Wherefore is it that thou dost ask after my name? And he blessed him there.

And Jacob called the name of the place Peniel: for I have seen God face to face, and my life is preserved.

And as he passed over Penuel the sun rose upon him, and he halted upon his thigh.

Therefore the children of Israel eat not of the sinew which shrank, which is upon the hollow of the thigh, unto this day: because he touched the hollow of Jacob's thigh in the sinew that shrank.

Sappho

(circa 615–circa 550 B.C.E.)

Sappho is not only the most famous female poet of antiquity but one of the best-known lyric poets of all time. According to the few historical details available, she was a native of the island of Lesbos, where she married a wealthy man and had a daughter. She also seems to have run a school for young women that was connected in some way to the cult of Aphrodite and Eros. Through at least the third century B.C.E., Sappho's work was widely available; and the ancient Greeks and Romans celebrated her as a great poet. Plato is said to have called her "the tenth muse," and Ovid promoted her legend in his poem "Sappho to Phaon." Although very little of her work survives today, its lyrical intensity continues to compel poets to respond to her voice. Catullus, Sir Philip Sidney, Lord Tennyson, T. S. Eliot, William Carlos Williams, and Robert Lowell all have very different – and very personal – translations of the following fragment.

Fragment 31

translated by Sir Philip Sidney

My muse, what ails this ardour?
Mine eys be dym, my lymbs shake,
My voice is hoarse, my throte scorcht,
My tong to this roofe cleaves,
My fancy amazde, my thoughtes dull'd,
My head doth ake, my life faints
My sowle begins to take leave,
So greate a passion all feele,
To think a soare so deadly
I should so rashly ripp up.

Plato

(circa 427–circa 348 B.C.E.)

Plato was a Greek philosopher. A student of Socrates, he devoted his writing life to recording his mentor's teachings and arguments, nearly always in the form of dialogues between Socrates and a student. In the following extract from The Republic, *Socrates is talking to Plato's brother Glaucon about whether or not poets belong in the ideal state; and as the poet-reader soon discovers, the answer is not favorable. In Socrates' view, poetry is not only "an outrage on the understanding," but it "feeds and waters the passions and desires . . . instead of ruling them." The only way to avoid such dangers, according to the master, is to expel all poets from the republic. Both Sidney (in the sixteenth century) and Shelley (in the nineteenth century) wrote long, impassioned defenses in response to elements of the dialogue; and in the twentieth century, writers as varied as Auden and Rich continued to worry the Platonic bone.*

from *The Republic*

translated by Benjamin Jowett, edited by Dawn Potter

from Book 10

"Many things pleased me in the order of our State, but there was nothing which I liked better than the regulation about poetry. The division of the soul throws a new light on our exclusion of imitation. I do not mind telling you in confidence that all poetry is an outrage on the understanding, unless the hearers have that balm of knowledge which heals error. I have loved Homer ever since I was a boy, and even now he appears to me to be the great master of tragic poetry. But much as I love the man, I love truth more, and therefore I must speak out: and first of all, will you explain what is imitation, for really I do not understand?"

"How likely then that I should understand!"

"That might very well be, for the duller often sees better than the keener eye."

"True, but in your presence I can hardly venture to say what I think."

"Then suppose that we begin in our old fashion, with the doctrine of universals. Let us assume the existence of beds and tables. There is one idea of a bed, or of a table, which the maker of each had in his mind when making them; he did not make the ideas of beds and tables, but he made beds and tables according to the ideas. And is there not a maker of the works of all workmen, who makes not only vessels but plants and animals, himself, the earth and heaven, and things in heaven and under the earth? He makes the Gods also."

"He must be a wizard indeed!"

"But do you not see that there is a sense in which you could do the same? You have only to take a mirror, and catch the reflection of the sun, and the earth, or anything else – there now you have made them."

"Yes, but only in appearance."

"Exactly so; and the painter is such a creator as you are with the mirror, and he is even more unreal than the carpenter; although neither the carpenter nor any other artist can be supposed to make the absolute bed."

"Not if philosophers may be believed."

"Nor need we wonder that his bed has but an imperfect relation to the truth. Reflect: here are three beds; one in nature, which is made by God; another, which is made by the carpenter; and the third, by the painter. God only made one, nor could he have made more than one; for if there had been two, there would always have been a third – more absolute and abstract than either, under which they would have been included. We may therefore conceive God to be the natural maker of the bed, and in a lower sense the carpenter is also the maker; but the painter is rather the imitator of what the other two make; he has to do with a creation which is thrice removed from reality. And the tragic poet is an imitator, and, like every other imitator, is thrice removed from the king and from the truth. The painter imitates not the original bed, but the bed made by the carpenter. And this, without being really different, appears to be different, and has many points of view, of which only one is caught by the painter, who represents everything because he represents a piece of everything, and that piece an image. And he can paint any other artist, although he knows nothing of their arts; and this with sufficient skill to deceive children or simple people. Suppose now that somebody came to us and told us how he had met a man who knew all that everybody knows, and better than anybody. Should we not infer him to be a simpleton who, having no discernment of truth and falsehood, had met with a wizard or enchanter, whom he fancied to be all-wise? And when we hear persons saying that Homer and the tragedians know all the arts and all the virtues, must we not infer that they are under a similar delusion? They do not see that the poets are imitators, and that their creations are only imitations."

"Very true."

"But if a person could create as well as imitate, he would rather leave some permanent work and not an imitation only; he would rather be the receiver than the giver of praise."

"Yes, for then he would have more honor and advantage."

"Let us now interrogate Homer and the poets. Friend Homer, say I to him, I am not going to ask you about medicine, or any art to which your poems incidentally refer, but about their main subjects – war, military tactics, politics. If you are only twice and not thrice removed from the truth – not an imitator or an image-maker, please to inform us what good you have ever done to mankind? Is there any city which professes to have received laws from you, as Sicily and Italy have from Charondas, Sparta from Lycurgus, Athens from Solon? Or was any war ever carried on by your counsels? Or is any invention attributed to you, as there is to Thales and Anacharsis? Or is there any Homeric way of life, such as the Pythagorean was, in which you instructed men, and which is called after you?"

"No, indeed; and Creophylus (Flesh-child) was even more unfortunate in his breeding than he was in his name, if, as tradition says, Homer in his lifetime was allowed by him and his other friends to starve."

"Yes, but could this ever have happened if Homer had really been the educator of Hellas? Would he not have had many devoted followers? If Protagoras and Prodicus can persuade their contemporaries that no one can manage house or State without them, is it likely that Homer and Hesiod would have been allowed to go about as beggars – I mean if they had really been able to do the world any good? Would not men have compelled them to stay where they were, or have followed them about in order to get education? But they did not; and therefore we may infer that Homer and all the poets are only imitators, who do but imitate the appearances of things. For as a painter by a knowledge of figure and color can paint a cobbler without any practice in cobbling, so the poet can delineate any art in the colors of language, and give harmony and rhythm to the cobbler and also to the general; and you know how mere narration, when deprived of the ornaments of meter, is like a face which has lost the beauty of youth and never had any other. Once more, the imitator has no knowledge of reality, but only of appearance. The painter paints, and the artificer makes a bridle and reins, but neither understands the use of them; the knowledge of this is confined to the horseman, and so of other things. Thus we have three arts: one of use, another of invention, a third of imitation; and the user furnishes the rule to the two others. The flute player will know the good and bad flute, and the maker will put faith in him; but the imitator will neither know nor have faith – neither science nor true opinion can be ascribed to him. Imitation, then, is devoid of knowledge, being only a kind of play or sport, and the tragic and epic poets are imitators in the highest degree.

"And now let us enquire, what is the faculty in man which answers to imitation. Allow me to explain my meaning. Objects are differently seen when in the water and when out of the water, when near and when at a distance; and the painter or juggler makes use of this variation to impose upon us. And the art of measuring and weighing and calculating comes in to save our bewildered minds from the power of appearance; for, as we were saying, two contrary opinions of the same about the same and at the same time cannot both of them be true. But which of them is true is determined by the art of calculation; and this is allied to the better faculty in the soul, as the arts of imitation are to the worse. And the same holds of the ear as well as of the eye, of poetry as well as painting. The imitation is of actions voluntary or involuntary, in which there is an expectation of a good or bad result, and present experience of pleasure and pain. But is a man in harmony with himself when he is the subject of these conflicting influences? Is there not rather a contradiction in him? Let me further ask whether he is more likely to control sorrow when he is alone or when he is in company."

"In the latter case."

"Feeling would lead him to indulge his sorrow, but reason and law control him and enjoin patience since he cannot know whether his affliction is good or evil; and no human thing is of any great consequence while sorrow is certainly a hindrance to good counsel. For when we stumble, we should not, like children, make an uproar; we should take the measures which reason prescribes, not raising a lament, but finding a cure. And the better part of us is ready to follow reason, while the irrational principle is full of sorrow and distraction at the recollection of our troubles. Unfortunately, however, this latter furnishes the chief materials of the imitative arts. Whereas reason is ever in repose and cannot easily be displayed, especially to a mixed multitude who have no experience of her. Thus the poet is like the painter in two ways: first he paints an inferior degree of truth, and secondly, he is concerned with an inferior part of the soul. He indulges the feelings, while he enfeebles the reason; and we refuse to allow him to have authority over the mind of man, for he has no measure of greater and less and is a maker of images and very far gone from truth.

"But we have not yet mentioned the heaviest count in the indictment – the power which poetry has of injuriously exciting the feelings. When we hear some passage in which a hero laments his sufferings at tedious length, you know that we sympathize with him and praise the poet; and yet in our own sorrows such an exhibition of feeling is regarded as effeminate and unmanly (Ion). Now, ought a man to feel pleasure in seeing another do what he hates and abominates in himself? Is he not giving way to a sentiment which in his own case he would control? He is off his guard because the sorrow is another's; and he thinks that he may indulge his feelings without disgrace and will be the gainer by the pleasure. But the inevitable consequence is that he who begins by weeping at the sorrows of others will end by weeping at his own. The same is true of comedy: you may often laugh at buffoonery which you would be ashamed to utter, and the love of coarse merriment on the stage will at last turn you into a buffoon at home. Poetry feeds and waters the passions and desires; she lets them rule instead of ruling them. And therefore, when we hear the encomiasts of Homer affirming that he is the educator of Hellas and that all life should be regulated by his precepts, we may allow the excellence of their intentions and agree with them in thinking Homer a great poet and tragedian. But we shall continue to prohibit all poetry which goes beyond hymns to the Gods and praises of famous men. Not pleasure and pain, but law and reason shall rule in our State.

"These are our grounds for expelling poetry; but lest she should charge us with discourtesy, let us also make an apology to her. We will remind her that there is an ancient quarrel between poetry and philosophy, of which there are many traces in the writings of the poets, such as the saying of 'the she-dog, yelping at her mistress,' and 'the philosophers who are ready to circumvent Zeus,' and 'the philosophers who are paupers.' Nevertheless we bear her no ill-will and will gladly allow her to return upon condition that she makes a defense of herself in verse; and her supporters who are not poets may speak in prose. We confess her charms; but if she cannot show that she is useful as well as delightful, like rational lovers, we must renounce our love, though endeared to us by early associations. Having come to years of discretion, we know that poetry is not truth and that a man should be careful how he introduces her to that state or constitution which he himself is; for there is a mighty issue at stake – no less than the good or evil of a human soul. And it is not worthwhile to forsake justice and virtue for the attractions of poetry, any more than for the sake of honor or wealth."

Aristotle (384–322 B.C.E.)

The Greek philosopher Aristotle was one of Plato's students, and his treatise
The Poetics *has been called the world's first extant work of literary criti-*
cism. In the following extract from The Poetics, *Aristotle considers the poet's*
role as an imitator of reality, reminding us that our "vehicle of expression is
language" and that both poets and critics must concentrate on the details of
language rather than our own preconceptions before passing judgment on a
work of imagination.

from *The Poetics*

translated by Samuel H. Butcher, edited by Dawn Potter

Book 25

With respect to critical difficulties and their solutions, the number and na-
ture of the sources from which they may be drawn may be thus exhibited.
The poet, being an imitator, like a painter or any other artist, must of ne-
cessity imitate one of three objects: things as they were or are, things as
they are said or thought to be, or things as they ought to be. The vehicle
of expression is language – either current terms or, it may be, rare words
or metaphors. There are also many modifications of language, which we
concede to the poets. Add to this, that the standard of correctness is not
the same in poetry and politics, any more than in poetry and any other art.

Within the art of poetry itself there are two kinds of faults: those which
touch its essence, and those which are accidental. If a poet has chosen to
imitate something but has imitated it incorrectly through want of capac-
ity, the error is inherent in the poetry. But if the failure is due to a wrong
choice – if he has represented a horse as throwing out both his off legs at
once or introduced technical inaccuracies in medicine, for example, or in
any other art – the error is not essential to the poetry. These are the points
of view from which we should consider and answer the objections raised
by the critics.

First as to matters which concern the poet's own art. If he describes the
impossible, he is guilty of an error; but the error may be justified if the end

of the art be thereby attained (the end being that already mentioned) – if, that is, the effect of this or any other part of the poem is thus rendered more striking. A case in point is the pursuit of Hector [in the *Iliad*]. If, however, the end might have been as well, or better, attained without violating the special rules of the poetic art, the error is not justified; for every kind of error should, if possible, be avoided. Again, does the error touch the essentials of the poetic art or some accident of it? For example, not to know that a hind has no horns is a less serious matter than to paint it inartistically.

Further, if it be objected that the description is not true to fact, the poet may perhaps reply, "But the objects are as they ought to be," just as Sophocles said that he drew men as they ought to be, Euripides as they are. In this way the objection may be met. If, however, the representation be of neither kind, the poet may answer, "This is how men say the thing is." This applies also to tales about the gods. It may well be that these stories are not higher than fact nor yet true to fact: they are, very possibly, what Xenophanes says of them. [Xenophanes was a poet and philosopher who argued against the prevailing assumption that the gods had human characteristics.] But anyhow, this is what is said. Again, a description may be not be better than the truth but simply the fact at the time, as in the passage about the arms [in the *Iliad*]: "Upright upon their butt-ends stood the spears." This was the custom then, as it now is among the Illyrians. Again, in examining whether what has been said or done by someone is poetically right or not, we must not look merely to the particular act or saying and ask whether it is poetically good or bad. We must also consider by whom it is said or done, to whom, when, by what means, or for what end; whether, for instance, it be to secure a greater good or avert a greater evil.

Other difficulties may be resolved by due regard to the usage of language. We may note a rare word, as in *oureas men proton*, "the mules first he killed," where the poet perhaps employs *oureas* not in the sense of "mules" but of "sentinels." So, again, of Dolon: "ill-favored indeed he was to look upon." It is not meant that his body was ill-shaped but that his face was ugly; for the Cretans use the word *eueides*, "well-flavored," to denote a fair face. Again, *zoroteron de keraie*, "mix the drink livelier," does not mean "mix it stronger," as for hard drinkers, but "mix it quicker." Sometimes an expression is metaphorical, as "Now all gods and men were sleeping through the night," while at the same time the poet says, "Often indeed as he turned his gaze to the Trojan plain, he marveled at the sound of flutes and pipes." "All" is here used metaphorically for "many," "all" being a species of "many." So in the verse "alone she hath no part," *oie*, "alone," is metaphorical; for the best known may be called the only one. Again, the solution may depend upon accent or breathing. Thus [the scholar] Hippias of Thasos solved the difficulties in the lines *didomen (didomen) de hoi*, and *to men hou (ou) kata-puthetai ombro*. Or again, the question may be solved by punctuation, as in Empedocles: "Of a sudden things became mortal that before had learnt to be immortal, and things unmixed before mixed." Or again, by ambiguity of meaning, as *parocheken de pleo nux*, where the word *pleo* is ambiguous. Or by the usage of language. Thus any mixed drink is called *oinos*, "wine." Hence Ganymede is said "to pour the wine to Zeus," though the gods do not drink wine. So, too, workers in iron are called *chalkeas*, or "workers in bronze." This, however, may also be taken as a metaphor. Again, when a word seems to involve some inconsistency of meaning, we should consider how many senses it may bear in the particular passage. For example, with "there was stayed the spear of bronze," we should ask in how many ways we may take "was stayed." The true mode of interpretation is the precise opposite of what [Plato's brother] Glaucon mentions. Critics, he says, jump at certain groundless conclusions; they pass adverse judgment and then proceed to reason on it; and, assuming that the poet has said whatever they happen to think, find fault if a thing is inconsistent with their own fancy. The question about Icarius [father-in-law of Odysseus] has been treated in this fashion. The critics imagine he was a Lacedaemonian. They think it strange, therefore, that Telemachus should not have met him when he went to Lacedaemon. But the Cephallenian story may perhaps be the true one. They allege that Odysseus took a wife from among themselves, and that her father was Icadius, not Icarius. It is merely a mistake, then, that gives plausibility to the objection.

In general, the impossible must be justified by reference to artistic requirements, or to the higher reality, or to received opinion. With respect to the requirements of art, a probable impossibility is to be preferred to a thing improbable and yet possible. Again, it may be impossible that there should be men such as Zeuxis painted. "Yes," we say, "but the impossible is the higher thing, for the ideal type must surpass the reality." To justify the irrational, we appeal to what is commonly said to be. In addition to which we urge that the irrational sometimes does not violate reason, just as "it is probable that a thing may happen contrary to probability." Things that sound contradictory should be examined by the same rules as in dialectical refutation: whether the same thing is meant, in the same relation, and in the same sense. We should therefore solve the question by reference to what the poet says himself or to what is tacitly assumed by a person of intelligence. The element of the irrational and, similarly, depravity of character are justly censured when there is no inner necessity for introducing them. Such is the irrational element in the introduction of Aegeus by Euripides and the badness of Menelaus in the *Oresteia*. Thus, there are five sources from which critical objections are drawn. Things are censured either as impossible, or irrational, or morally hurtful, or contradictory, or contrary to artistic correctness. The answers should be sought under the twelve heads above mentioned.

Horace (65–8 B.C.E.)

Horace was a Roman lyric poet and satirist. Although his verse was metrically accomplished, his style was purposefully informal. He preferred to use every-day language, even slang, and his tone was casual and conversational. Thus, even though the Ars Poetica *is an instructional treatise, its manner is much lighter than, say, Aristotle's* Poetics. *Poet Ben Jonson was its first English translator, and Lord Byron's "Hints from Horace" (see page 91) updates the Roman poet's precepts for nineteenth-century readers.*

Horace's works are filled with personal references, and the following extract in-cludes several names that would have been familiar to his audience. Choerilus was Alexander the Great's court poet. The Ars Poetica *was dedicated "to the Pisos, father and sons"; the father was a Roman senator and consul. Messala was a Roman general, famous as an orator. Cascellius was a Roman jurist, and Maecius was a Roman theater critic and censor.*

from *Ars Poetica*

translated by John Conington

Keep near to truth in a fictitious piece,
Nor treat belief as matter of caprice.
If on a child you make a vampire sup,
It must not be alive when she's ripped up.
Dry seniors scout an uninstructive strain;
Young lordlings treat grave verse with tall disdain:
But he who, mixing grave and gay, can teach
And yet give pleasure, gains a vote from each:
His works enrich the vendor, cross the sea,
And hand the author down to late posterity.

Some faults may claim forgiveness: for the lyre
Not always gives the note that we desire;
We ask a flat; a sharp is its reply;
And the best bow will sometimes shoot awry.

But when I meet with beauties thickly sown,
A blot or two I readily condone,
Such as may trickle from a careless pen,
Or pass unwatched: for authors are but men.
What then? the copyist who keeps stumbling still
At the same word had best lay down his quill:
The harp-player, who for ever wounds the ear
With the same discord, makes the audience jeer:
So the poor dolt who's often in the wrong
I rank with Choerilus, that dunce of song,
Who, should he ever "deviate into sense,"
Moves but fresh laughter at his own expense:
While e'en good Homer may deserve a tap,
If, as he does, he drop his head and nap.
Yet, when a work is long, 'twere somewhat hard
To blame a drowsy moment in a bard.

Some poems, like some paintings, take the eye
Best at a distance, some when looked at nigh.
One loves the shade; one would be seen in light,
And boldly challenges the keenest sight:
One pleases straightway; one, when it has passed
Ten times before the mind, will please at last.

Hope of the Pisos! trained by such a sire,
And wise yourself, small schooling you require;
Yet take this lesson home; some things admit
A moderate point of merit, e'en in wit.
There's yonder counsellor; he cannot reach
Messala's stately altitudes of speech,
He cannot plumb Cascellius' depth of lore,
Yet he's employed, and makes a decent score:
But gods, and men, and booksellers agree
To place their ban on middling poetry.
At a great feast an ill-toned instrument,
A sour conserve, or an unfragrant scent
Offends the taste: 'tis reason that it should;
We do without such things, or have them good:
Just so with verse; you seek but to delight;
If by an inch you fail, you fail outright.

He who knows nought of games abstains from all,
Nor tries his hand at quoit, or hoop, or ball,
Lest the thronged circle, witnessing the play,
Should laugh outright, with none to say them nay:
He who knows nought of verses needs must try
To write them ne'ertheless. "Why not?" men cry:
"Free, gently born, unblemished and correct,
His means a knight's, what more can folks expect?"
But you, my friend, at least have sense and grace;
You will not fly in queen Minerva's face
In action or in word. Suppose some day
You should take courage and compose a lay,
Entrust it first to Maecius' critic ears,
Your sire's and mine, and keep it back nine years.
What's kept at home you cancel by a stroke:
What's sent abroad you never can revoke.

Ovid (43 B.C.E.–circa A.D. 17)

Although the Roman poet Ovid was educated as a lawyer, he turned to poetry as a young man and eventually achieved spectacular success with the Ars Amatoria, *a set of dramatic monologues in the form of erotic love letters. But his public career came to an abrupt end in 8* A.D., *when Emperor Augustus banished him to Tomis, a tiny village on the northern coast of the Black Sea in what is now Romania. The nature of his crime is still unclear: in his autobiographical lament,* Tristia, *Ovid merely referred to* carmen et error – *a poem and a mistake.*

The following excerpt is from his Epistulae ex Ponto *(Letters from the Black Sea), which describe his misery in exile and beg for clemency. Literature in exile has a long history, and Ovid's plight has resonated with many writers – among them the Russian poet Pushkin, exiled to Odessa in 1821, who wrote "To Ovid" as a response to a shared sense of despair. But Ovid's distress also speaks to the many poets who have suffered from the anguish of creation itself—the knowledge that art can be a burden as much as a gift and that a poet, even in misery, cannot escape from poetry.*

---

from *Epistulae ex Ponto: Letter to Cotta Maximus*

translated by Arthur Leslie Wheeler

from Book 1, Letter 5

Why then do I write, you wonder? I too wonder, and with you I often ask what I seek from it. Or do the people say true that poets are not sane and am I the strongest proof of this maxim, I, who though so many times deceived by the barrenness of the soil, persist in sowing my seed in ground that ruins me? Clearly each man shows a passion for his own pursuits, taking pleasure in devoting time to his familiar art. The wounded gladiator forswears the fight, yet forgetting his former wound he dons his arms. The shipwrecked man declares that he will have nothing to do with the waves of the sea, yet plies the oar in the water in which but recently he swam. In the same way I continually hold to a profitless pursuit, returning to the goddesses whom I would I had not worshipped.

Suetonius

(circa 75–circa 150)

Suetonius was a Roman historian, who today is remembered primarily for De Vita Caesareum, *a series of biographies about twelve Roman rulers. The following extract is from* De Poetis, *a parallel biographical series about poets, only fragments of which still exist. One of them, "The Life of Virgil," offers a brief biography of the Roman poet Virgil (70–19 B.C.E.), the greatest epic poet after Homer and most famous as the author of the* Aeneid. *In the course of recounting Virgil's accomplishments, Suetonius veers into a description of the poet's process of revision – an approach that may sound eerily familiar.*

from *The Life of Virgil*

translated by John C. Rolfe, edited by Dawn Potter

When Virgil was writing the *Georgics*, it is said to have been his custom to dictate each day a large number of verses which he had composed in the morning and then to spend the rest of the day in reducing them to a very small number, wittily remarking that he fashioned his poem after the manner of a she-bear, and gradually licked it into shape. In the case of the *Aeneid*, after writing a first draft in prose and dividing it into twelve books, he proceeded to turn into verse one part after another, taking them up just as he fancied, in no particular order. And that he might not check the flow of his thought, he left some things unfinished and, so to speak, bolstered others up with very slight words, which, as he jocosely used to say, were put in like props, to support the structure until the solid columns should arrive.

Badi al-Zaman al-Hamadhani

(967–1007)

Born in Hamadhan, in what is now Iran, Badi al-Zaman al-Hamadhani was an itinerant scholar who is remembered today for his maqamat, *or prose episodes, told from the point of view of a traveling scholar, Isa ibn Hisham. In each* maqama, *Hisham meets the glib-tongued trickster Abul-Fath al-Iskanderi, whose speech often takes mysterious poetic form. In one of those episodes, "The Maqama of Poetry," Hisham and his traveling companions are quoting poems and discussing their difficulties when the enigmatic Iskanderi appears and instantly outdoes them all.*

from *The Maqama of Poetry*

translated by W. J. Prendergast

Tell me what verse is that, half of which elevates and half repels? And what verse is it the whole of which slaps? And what verse is that half of which is angry and half jests? And what verse is it the whole of which is mangy? And what verse is that the last foot of whose first half fights, and the final foot of whose second half conciliates? What verse is that whose whole is scorpions? What verse is that which is unseemly in original intent but can be made proper by punctuation? What verse is that whose tears cease not to flow? What verse is that all of which runs away except its foot? What verse is that whose subject is not known? What verse is that which is longer than its fellow, as though it were not of its kind?

What verse is that which cannot be dissolved, and whose soil cannot be dug? What verse is that half of which is perfect and half clothes? What verse is that whose number cannot be counted? What verse is that which shows thee what pleases? What verse is that which the world cannot contain? What verse is that half of which laughs and half feels pain? What verse is that if its branch be shaken, its beauty departs? What verse is that if we collect it together, its meaning is gone? What verse is that if we set it at liberty, we cause it to go astray? What verse is that whose honey is poison? What verse is that whose praise is censure? What verse is that whose expression is sweet, but underlying it there is grief? What verse is that whose dissolving is binding up, and the whole of it is paid down? What verse is that half of which is prolongation and half rejection? What verse is that half of which is elevation and its elevation is a slap? What verse is that whose expulsion is eulogy, but whose converse is censure? What verse is that which, in a visitation, is a prayer for the time of peril? What verse is that which the sheep eat when they please?

What verse is that which when it hits the head, smashes the teeth? What verse is that which extends till it reaches six pounds? What verse is it that stood up, then fell down and went to sleep? What verse is it that wished to decrease, but increased? What verse is it that was about to go and then returned? What verse destroyed Iraq? What verse conquered Basra? What verse is it that melted under torture?

What verse grew old before adolescence? What verse is it that returned before the appointed time? What verse is it that alighted and then passed away? What verse is it that was tightly twisted and then became strong? What verse is that, which was adjusted till it became rectified? What verse is that which is swifter than [seventh-century poet] Tirimmah's arrow? What verse is it that issued from their eyes? What verse is it that contracted, and then sufficed to fill the world? What verse is it that returned and excited pain? What verse is that half of which is gold and the remainder tail? What verse is that some of which is darkness and some of which is wine? What verse is that whose subject is converted into the object, and whose understanding is made to be understood? What verse is that the whole of which is inviolate? What two verses are like a string of camels? What verse is it that descends from above? What verse is that whose prognostication is ominous? What verse is that whose end flees but whose beginning seeks? What verse is that whose beginning gives, but whose end plunders?

Li Ch'ing Chao (circa 1084–circa 1151)

Li Ch'ing Chao was born in Shandong Province into a family of well-known scholars and government officials. For a girl of her time, she received an excellent education, and she began writing both poetry and prose at an early age. In about 1101 Li married, a relationship she chronicled as intense and lively. But in 1127 Jurchen tartars invaded from the north, and the Sung dynasty fell. During the turmoil, Li's library was burnt, and her husband died. Li spent the rest of her life as an exile in the south.

Today Li Ch'ing Chao is ranked as one of China's greatest poets. Essayist and translator Eliot Weinberger calls Rexroth's renderings of her poems "masterworks of remembered passion," and Rexroth himself aligns her with two women poets of the Renaissance, Gaspara Stampa and Louise Labé – all of them poets of tenderness and heartbreak, all forerunners of what evolved, in the twentieth century, into confessional poetry.

Alone in the Night

translated by Kenneth Rexroth

The warm rain and pure wind
Have just freed the willows from
The ice. As I watch the peach trees,
Spring rises from my heart and blooms on
My cheeks. My mind is unsteady,
As if I were drunk. I try
To write a poem in which
My tears will flow together
With your tears. My rouge is stale.
My hairpins are too heavy.
I throw myself across my
Gold cushions, wrapped in my lonely
Doubled quilt, and crush the phoenixes
In my headdress. Alone, deep
In bitter loneliness, without
Even a good dream, I lie,
Trimming the lamp in the passing night.

Marie de France (late twelfth century)

Marie de France's Lais, *a set of twelve verse narratives based on Breton legends, are key texts in the literature of chivalry and courtly love and were among the first writings to mention King Arthur and his court. They have influenced poets from Spenser to Keats, and their coupling of the Celtic supernatural with the formalized code of chivalry has been a primary influence on the conventions of European fairy-tale literature.*

In the following extract from the Lais, *Marie speaks directly to the reader and defends her right to be a writer. Given that we have so few extant works by medieval women, it is easy to imagine why a woman poet might feel the need to justify her verse. But in this case she is also justifying the importance of preserving a regional culture – the pre-Christian, pre-Roman heritage of Celtic Brittany.*

Priscian, mentioned in the prologue, was a Latin grammarian; and the king to whom Marie dedicates her work was probably Henry II of England.

from the *Lais*

translated by Robert Hanning and Joan Ferrante

Prologue
Whoever has received knowledge
and eloquence in speech from God
should not be silent or secretive
but demonstrate it willingly.
When a great good is widely heard of,
then, and only then, does it bloom,
and when that good is praised by many,
it has spread its blossoms.
The custom among the ancients –
as Priscian testifies –
was to speak quite obscurely
in the books they wrote,

so that those who were to come after
and study them
might gloss the letter
and supply its significance from their own wisdom.
Philosophers knew this,
they understood among themselves
that the more time they spent,
the more subtle their minds would become
and the better they would know how to keep themselves
from whatever was to be avoided.
He who would keep himself from vice
should study and understand
and begin a weighty work
by which he might keep vice at a distance,
and free himself from great sorrow.
That's why I began to think
about composing some good stories
and translating from Latin to Romance;
but that was not to bring me fame:
too many others have done it.
Then I thought of the *lais* I'd heard.
I did not doubt, indeed I knew well,
that those who first began them
and sent them forth
composed them in order to preserve
adventures they had heard.
I have heard many told;
and I don't want to neglect or forget them.
To put them into word and rhyme
I've often stayed awake.

In your honor, noble King,
who are so brave and courteous,
repository of all joys
in whose heart all goodness takes root,
I undertook to assemble these *lais*
to compose and recount them in rhyme.
In my heart I thought and determined,
sire, that I would present them to you.

If it pleases you to receive them,
you will give me great joy;
I shall be happy forever.
Do not think me presumptuous
if I dare present them to you.
Now hear how they begin.

Dante Alighieri

Dante's three-part epic poem, the Commedia *(The Divine Comedy), was the first major literary work written entirely in Italian. It traces the poet's imagined journey through hell (Inferno), purgatory (Purgatorio), and heaven (Paradiso) under the guidance of Roman poet Virgil. Dante's choice of Virgil as a guide reveals how a poet can simultaneously acknowledge both modesty and ambition. By linking himself to Virgil, who had linked himself to Homer, Dante was boldly aligning himself with the two greatest poets of antiquity. Yet his attitude to Virgil is unfailingly humble: the relationship Dante imagines is one of student to mentor, apprentice to master.*

The nineteenth-century poet Henry Wadsworth Longfellow was Dante's first American translator. He began the work after the loss of his much-loved second wife, who burned to death in a household accident. The image of the grieving translator who is following Dante and Virgil word by word into the Inferno *adds yet another link to the chain of influence that binds poets to their forebears.*

In the following extract, Virgil refers to "sub Julio," meaning that he was born during the reign of Julius Caesar. Anchises was the father of Aeneas, subject of Virgil's Aeneid. *Ilion is an alternate name for the city of Troy. The meaning of "Feltro and Feltro" is unclear;* feltro *translates as "felt cloth," but many translators have assumed that Dante used the repeated words as place names. Camilla, Euryalus, Turnus, and Nisus are all characters in the* Aeneid.

from the *Inferno*

translated by Henry Wadsworth Longfellow

Canto 1
Midway upon the journey of our life
I found myself within a forest dark,
For the straightforward pathway had been lost.

Ah me! how hard a thing it is to say
What was this forest savage, rough, and stern,
Which in the very thought renews the fear.

So bitter is it, death is little more;
But of the good to treat, which there I found,
Speak will I of the other things I saw there.

I cannot well repeat how there I entered,
So full was I of slumber at the moment
In which I had abandoned the true way.

But after I had reached a mountain's foot,
At that point where the valley terminated,
Which had with consternation pierced my heart,

Upward I looked, and I beheld its shoulders,
Vested already with that planet's rays
Which leadeth others right by every road.

Then was the fear a little quieted
That in my heart's lake had endured throughout
The night, which I had passed so piteously.

And even as he, who, with distressful breath,
Forth issued from the sea upon the shore,
Turns to the water perilous and gazes;

So did my soul, that still was fleeing onward,
Turn itself back to re-behold the pass
Which never yet a living person left.

After my weary body I had rested,
The way resumed I on the desert slope,
So that the firm foot ever was the lower.

And lo! almost where the ascent began,
A panther light and swift exceedingly,
Which with a spotted skin was covered o'er!

And never moved she from before my face,
Nay, rather did impede so much my way,
That many times I to return had turned.

The time was the beginning of the morning,
And up the sun was mounting with those stars
That with him were, what time the Love Divine

At first in motion set those beauteous things;
So were to me occasion of good hope,
The variegated skin of that wild beast,

The hour of time, and the delicious season;
But not so much, that did not give me fear
A lion's aspect which appeared to me.

He seemed as if against me he were coming
With head uplifted, and with ravenous hunger,
So that it seemed the air was afraid of him;

And a she-wolf, that with all hungerings
Seemed to be laden in her meagreness,
And many folk has caused to live forlorn!

She brought upon me so much heaviness,
With the affright that from her aspect came,
That I the hope relinquished of the height.

And as he is who willingly acquires,
And the time comes that causes him to lose,
Who weeps in all his thoughts and is despondent,

E'en such made me that beast withouten peace,
Which, coming on against me by degrees
Thrust me back thither where the sun is silent.

While I was rushing downward to the lowland,
Before mine eyes did one present himself,
Who seemed from long-continued silence hoarse.

When I beheld him in the desert vast,
"Have pity on me," unto him I cried,
"Whiche'er thou art, or shade or real man!"

He answered me: "Not man; man once I was,
And both my parents were of Lombardy,
And Mantuans by country both of them.

'Sub Julio' was I born, though it was late,
And lived at Rome under the good Augustus,
During the time of false and lying gods.

A poet was I, and I sang that just
Son of Anchises, who came forth from Troy,
After that Ilion the superb was burned.

But thou, why goest thou back to such annoyance?
Why climb'st thou not the Mount Delectable,
Which is the source and cause of every joy?"

"Now, art thou that Virgilius and that fountain
Which spreads abroad so wide a river of speech?"
I made response to him with bashful forehead.

"O, of the other poets honour and light,
Avail me the long study and great love
That have impelled me to explore thy volume!

Thou art my master, and my author thou,
Thou art alone the one from whom I took
The beautiful style that has done honour to me.

Behold the beast, for which I have turned back;
Do thou protect me from her, famous Sage,
For she doth make my veins and pulses tremble."

"Thee it behoves to take another road,"
Responded he, when he beheld me weeping,
"If from this savage place thou wouldst escape;

Because this beast, at which thou criest out,
Suffers not any one to pass her way,
But so doth harass him, that she destroys him;

And has a nature so malign and ruthless,
That never doth she glut her greedy will,
And after food is hungrier than before.

Many the animals with whom she weds,
And more they shall be still, until the Greyhound
Comes, who shall make her perish in her pain.

He shall not feed on either earth or pelf,
But upon wisdom, and on love and virtue;
'Twixt Feltro and Feltro shall his nation be;

Of that low Italy shall he be the saviour,
On whose account the maid Camilla died,
Euryalus, Turnus, Nisus, of their wounds;

Through every city shall he hunt her down,
Until he shall have driven her back to Hell,
There from whence envy first did let her loose.

Therefore I think and judge it for thy best
Thou follow me, and I will be thy guide,
And lead thee hence through the eternal place,

Where thou shalt hear the desperate lamentations,
Shalt see the ancient spirits disconsolate,
Who cry out each one for the second death;

And thou shalt see those who contented are
Within the fire, because they hope to come,
Whene'er it may be, to the blessed people;

To whom, then, if thou wishest to ascend,
A soul shall be for that than I more worthy;
With her at my departure I will leave thee;

Because that Emperor, who reigns above,
In that I was rebellious to his law,
Wills that through me none come into his city.

He governs everywhere, and there he reigns;
There is his city and his lofty throne;
O happy he whom thereto he elects!"

And I to him: "Poet, I thee entreat,
By that same God whom thou didst never know,
So that I may escape this woe and worse,

Thou wouldst conduct me there where thou hast said,
That I may see the portal of Saint Peter,
And those thou makest so disconsolate."

Then he moved on, and I behind him followed.

Francesco Petrarch

(1304–1374)

As one of the world's first serious classical scholars, Francesco Petrarch is some-
times called the father of Renaissance humanism. But in his own time, he was
also celebrated as a poet, and he became the first writer since antiquity to be
crowned poet laureate in Rome. His influence on English literature was pro-
found. By the fourteenth century, Geoffrey Chaucer was borrowing Petrarch's
work for both The Canterbury Tales and Troilus and Criseyde; and Sir
Thomas Wyatt's sixteenth-century experiments with the Petrarchan sonnet
changed the course of English lyric poetry forever.

In the following extract from a letter to the Abbot of Saint Benigno, Petrarch
begins by speaking to his friend about his obsessive work habits and then
unexpectedly shifts to a comic anecdote about the contagions of poetry. His
comment about "Deucalion's stones" refers to the Greek creation myth in
which Deucalion, son of Prometheus, throws stones behind his shoulder; the
stones then turn into men. Africa was an epic poem, written in Latin, about
the Roman general Scipio Africanus; and "the Satirist" refers to the poet Juve-
nal, who wrote satires about life in first-century Rome.

from *Letter to the Abbot of Saint Benigno*

translated by James Harvey Robinson, edited by Dawn Potter

Strangely enough I long to write, but do not know what or to whom. This
inexorable passion has such a hold upon me that pen, ink, and paper, and
work prolonged far into the night, are more to my liking than repose and
sleep. In short, I find myself always in a sad and languishing state when I
am not writing, and, anomalous though it seems, I labor when I rest, and
find my rest in labor. My mind is hard as rock, and you might well think
that it really sprang from one of Deucalion's stones. Let this tireless spirit
pore eagerly over the parchment, until it has exhausted both fingers and
eyes by the long strain, yet it feels neither heat nor cold, but would seem to
be reclining upon the softest down. It is only fearful that it may be dragged
away, and holds fast the mutinous members. Only when sheer necessity
has compelled it to quit does it begin to flag. It takes a recess as a lazy ass

takes his pack when he is ordered up a sharp hill, and comes back again to its task as a tired ass to his well-filled manger. My mind finds itself refreshed by prolonged exercise, as the beast of burden by his food and rest. What then am I to do, since I cannot stop writing, or bear even the thought of rest? I write to you, not because what I have to say touches you nearly, but because there is no one so accessible just now who is at the same time so eager for news, especially about me, and so intelligently interested in strange and mysterious phenomena, and ready to investigate them.

I have just told you something of my condition and of my indefatigable brain, but I will tell you now an incident which may surprise you even more, and will at the same time prove the truth of what I have said. It happened at a time when, after a long period of neglect, I had just taken up my *Africa* again, and that with an ardor like that of the African sun itself. This is the task which, if anything will help me, I trust may some time moderate or assuage my insatiable thirst for work. One of my very dearest friends, seeing that I was almost done for with my immoderate toil, suddenly asked me to grant him a very simple favor. Although I was unaware of the nature of his request, I could not refuse one who I knew would ask nothing except in the friendliest spirit. He thereupon demanded the key of my cabinet. I gave it to him, wondering what he would do, when he proceeded to gather together and lock up carefully all my books and writing materials. Then, turning away, he prescribed ten days of rest, and ordered me, in view of my promise, neither to read nor write during that time. I saw his trick; to him I now seemed to be resting, although in reality I felt as if I were bound hand and foot. That day passed wearily, seeming as long as a year. The next day I had a headache from morning till night. The third day dawned and I began to feel the first signs of fever, when my friend returned, and seeing my plight gave me back the keys. I quickly recovered, and perceiving that I lived on work, as he expressed it, he never repeated his request.

Is it then true that this disease of writing, like other malignant disorders, is, as the Satirist claims, incurable, and, as I begin to fear, contagious as well? How many, do you reckon, have caught it from me? Within our memory, it was rare enough for people to write verses. But now there is no one who does not write them; few indeed write anything else. Some think that the fault, so far as our contemporaries are concerned, is largely mine. I have heard this from many, but I solemnly declare, as I hope some time to be granted immunity from the other ills of the soul – for I look for none from this – that I am now at last suddenly awakened for the first time by warning signs to a consciousness that this may perhaps be true; while intent only upon my own welfare, I may have been unwittingly injuring, at the same time, myself and others. I fear that the reproaches of an aged father, who unexpectedly came to me, with a long face and almost in tears, may not be without foundation. "While I," he said, "have always honored your name, see the return you make in compassing the ruin of my only son!"

I stood for a time in embarrassed silence, for the age of the man and the expression of his face, which told of great sorrow, went to my heart. Then, recovering myself, I replied, as was quite true, that I was unacquainted either with him or his son.

"What matters it," the old man answered, "whether you know him or not? He certainly knows you. I have spent a great deal in providing instruction for him in the civil law, but he declares that he wishes to follow in your footsteps. My fondest hopes have been disappointed, and I presume that he will never be either a lawyer or a poet."

At this neither I nor the others present could refrain from laughter, and he went off none the better humored. But now I recognize that this merriment was ill-timed, and that the poor old man deserved our consolation, for his complaints and his reproaches were not ungrounded. Our sons formerly employed themselves in preparing such papers as might be useful to themselves or their friends, relating to family affairs, business, or the wordy din of the courts. Now we are all engaged in the same occupation, and it is literally true, as Horace says, "learned or unlearned, we are all writing verses alike."

An Aztec Poet

(dates unknown)

The Aztecs, who flourished from the twelfth through the fifteenth centuries, were a collective group of people living in what is now central Mexico. They dominated Mexico until the Spanish conquered them in the mid-1500s, and elements of their language still survive in both Spanish and English. Much of our information about Aztec culture comes from Bernardino de Sahagún, a sixteenth-century missionary priest and ethnographer, who compiled his findings in La Historia General de las Cosas de Nueva Espana *(The General History of the Things of New Spain). Although he collected texts in the Aztec language, Nahuatl, they were later translated into Spanish, which is the language that poet Denise Levertov relied on when creating her own version of the Aztec original.*

Nahuatl literature had distinct prose and poetry traditions, and Aztec poetry tended to be thematically stylized and metaphorical. But Levertov's rendering of "The Artist" borrows a certain Whitmanesque expansiveness in its definition of the moral and imaginative responsibility of the artist. The word Toltec *in the first stanza refers to the people of an older Mesoamerican culture, whom the Aztecs saw as their intellectual forebears.*

The Artist

retold by Denise Levertov

The artist: disciple, abundant, multiple, restless.
The true artist: capable, practicing, skillful;
maintains dialogue with his heart, meets things with his mind.
The true artist: draws out all from his heart,
works with delight, makes things with calm, with sagacity,
works like a true Toltec, composes his objects, works dexterously, invents;
arranges materials, adorns them, makes them adjust.

The carrion artist: works at random, sneers at the people,
makes things opaque, brushes across the surface of the face of things,
works without care, defrauds people, is a thief.

Jan Kochanowski   (1530–1584)

Jan Kochanowski was a Polish scholar and translator. Although he also wrote in Latin, he is best known for the verse forms he introduced into Polish literature. In this way he parallels poets such as Dante and Milton, whose classical learning helped expand the imaginative and sonic possibilities of their vernacular poetry. Many of Kochanowski's poems centered on classical subjects, such as the Trojan War, or modeled themselves on Roman epigrams and elegies. But his most famous and most personal work was the Threnodies, *a set of nineteen laments on the death of his two-year-old daughter Urszula, which he published in 1580. In the following poem from that collection, Kochanowski argues for both a daughter's right to proclaim herself a poet and a father's right to cede his poetic power to her. Thus, he marks a quiet shift in the assumptions of a literary world dominated by men.*

Threnody 6

translated by Dorothy Prall

Dear little Slavic Sappho, we had thought,
Hearing thy songs so sweetly, deftly wrought,
That thou shouldst have an heritage one day
Beyond thy father's lands: his lute to play.
For not an hour of daylight's joyous round
But thou didst fill it full of lovely sound,
Just as the nightingale doth scatter pleasure
Upon the dark, in glad unstinted measure.
Then Death came stalking near thee, timid thing,
And thou in sudden terror tookest wing.
Ah, that delight, it was not overlong
And I pay dear with sorrow for brief song.
Thou still wert singing when thou cam'st to die;
Kissing thy mother, thus thou saidst good-bye:
       "My mother, I shall serve thee now no more
Nor sit about thy table's charming store;
I must lay down my keys to go from here,

To leave the mansion of my parents dear."
        This and what sorrow now will let me tell
No longer, were my darling's last farewell.
Ah, strong her mother's heart, to feel the pain
Of those last words and not to burst in twain.

Sir Philip Sidney (1554–1586)

Sir Philip Sidney was born into one of highest-ranking families in England. A member of Elizabeth I's court circle, he undertook several diplomatic missions and was eventually sent to the Netherlands as governor of Flushing. Meanwhile, he wrote poems, most famously the sonnet sequence Astrophel and Stella, *as well as the* Countess of Pembroke's Arcadia, *a prose romance dedicated to his sister. In 1586, Sidney took part in the Battle of Zutphen, where he was mortally wounded. He died at the age of thirty-two.*

Six years earlier, Sidney had written The Defence of Poesy, *also known as* An Apologie for Poetrie. *Sometimes called the first work of literary criticism in English, the* Defence *was a response to Plato's argument against the poets (see page 8). In his view, the fictions of poetry create a version of truth that reaches beyond a scholar's accumulation of facts – "for hee doth not onely shew the way, but giveth so sweete a prospect into the way, as will entice anie man to enter into it."*

In the following extract, Sidney mentions "Alloes" (aloe) and "Rhabarbarum" (rhubarb), which in his time were commonly used as medicines.

from *The Defence of Poesy*

Now therein of all Sciences . . . is our Poet the Monarch. For hee doth not onely shew the way, but giveth so sweete a prospect into the way, as will entice anie man to enter into it: Nay he doth as if your journey should lye through a faire vineyard, at the verie first, give you a cluster of grapes, that full of the taste, you may long to passe further. Hee beginneth not with obscure definitions, which must blurre the margent with interpretations, and loade the memorie with doubtfulnesse: but hee commeth to you with words set in delightfull proportion, either accompanied with, or prepared for the well enchanting skill of musicke, and with a tale forsooth he commeth unto you, with a tale, which holdeth children from play, and olde men from the Chimney corner; and pretending no more, doth intend the winning of the minde from wickednes to vertue; even as the child is often brought to take most wholesome things by hiding them in such other as have a pleasaunt taste: which if one should begin to tell them the nature of the Alloes or Rhabarbarum they should receive, wold sooner take their physic at their eares th[a]n at their mouth, so it is in men (most of which, are childish in the best things, til they be cradled in their graves) glad they will be to heare the tales of Hercules, Achilles, Cyrus, Aeneas, and hearing them, must needes heare the right description of wisdom, value, and justice; which if they had bene barely (that is to say Philosophically) set out, they would sweare they be brought to schoole againe; that imitation whereof Poetrie is, hath the most conveniencie to nature of al other: insomuch that as Aristotle saith, those things which in themselves are horrible, as cruel battailes, unnatural monsters, are made in poeticall imitation, delightfull.

William Shakespeare (1564–1616)

Without doubt, William Shakespeare is the greatest and most influential writer in the history of English literature, yet his working-class origins and lack of formal education continue to perplex his admirers. How could the son of a glover maker have constructed such subtle characters, such physically emotive metaphor, such complex dramatic movement? Whatever the answer, there is no doubt that the writer of Shakespeare's plays was a reader of poetry. In A Midsummer Night's Dream, *first produced in about 1596, he reveals not only classical influences such Ovid's* Metamorphoses *but also his familiarity with Chaucer's* The Canterbury Tales. *Far more than a lover's comedy spangled with literary references,* Midsummer *is a play about the power of the poetic imagination. A few scholars have even gone so far as to call it an* ars poetica. *In the following extract, spoken by Theseus, Duke of Athens, Shakespeare reminds us that, even though poets share the "seething brains" and "shaping fantasies" of "lovers and madmen," writing allows us to give "to aery nothing / A local habitation and a name" – a precise explanation of poetic creation that also evokes the physicality of the poetic imagination.*

from *A Midsummer Night's Dream*

Act 5, Scene 1, Lines 4–22
Lovers and madmen have such seething brains,
Such shaping fantasies, that apprehend
More than cool reason ever comprehends.
The lunatic, the lover, and the poet
Are of imagination all compact.
One sees more devils than vast hell can hold;
That is the madman. The lover, all as frantic,
Sees Helen's beauty in a brow of Egypt.
The poet's eye, in a fine frenzy rolling,
Doth glance from heaven to earth, from earth to heaven;
And as imagination bodies forth
The forms of things unknown, the poet's pen
Turns them to shapes, and gives to aery nothing

A local habitation and a name.
Such tricks hath strong imagination,
That if it would but apprehend some joy,
It comprehends some bringer of that joy;
Or in the night, imagining some fear,
How easy is a bush suppos'd a bear!

John Milton

(1608–1674)

John Milton is best known for his epic poem Paradise Lost, *but he also wrote numerous tracts, satires, and attacks, most of them lambasting the royalist party and the Church of England. In 1644, amid the turmoil of the English Civil War, he published* Areopagitica, *subtitled "A Speech of Mr. John Milton for the Liberty of Unlicenc'd Printing, to the Parlament of England." Licensing, or print censorship, was a governmental attempt to control dissent; and Milton's pamphlet passionately defended every author's right to freedom of expression.*

In the following extract, the poet refers to the Greek myth of the dragons' teeth, which, when sown in the ground, sprang up as fully armed warriors. His phrase fift essence, *synonymous with* quintessence, *implies the highest or purest essence.*

from *Areopagitica*

I deny not, but that it is of greatest concernment in the Church and Commonwealth, to have a vigilant eye how Bookes demeane themselves as well as men; and thereafter to confine, imprison, and do sharpest justice on them as malefactors: For Books are not absolutely dead things, but doe contain a potencie of life in them to be as active as that soule was whose progeny they are; nay they do preserve as in a violl the purest efficacie and extraction of that living intellect that bred them. I know they are as lively, and as vigorously productive, as those fabulous Dragons teeth; and being sown up and down, may chance to spring up armed men. And yet on the other hand, unlesse warinesse be us'd, as good almost kill a Man as kill a good Book; who kills a Man kills a reasonable creature, Gods Image; but hee who destroyes a good Booke, kills reason it selfe, kills the Image of God, as it were in the eye. Many a man lives a burden to the Earth; but a good Booke is the pretious life-blood of a master spirit, imbalm'd and treasur'd up on purpose to a life beyond life. 'Tis true, no age can restore a life, whereof perhaps there is no great losse; and revolutions of ages do not oft recover the losse of a rejected truth, for the want of which whole Nations fare the worse. We should be wary therefore what persecution we raise against the living labours of publick men, how we spill that season'd life of man preserv'd and stor'd up in Books; since we see a kinde of homicide may be thus committed, sometimes a martyrdome, and if it extend to the whole impression, a kinde of massacre, whereof the execution ends not in the slaying of an elementall life, but strikes at that ethereall and fift essence, the breath of reason it selfe, slaies an immortality rather th[a]n a life.

Anne Bradstreet

(1612–1672)

The daughter of English Puritans, Anne Bradstreet was eighteen years old when she emigrated to America with her husband and her father, both of whom eventually became governors of Massachusetts. Amid the rigors and tragedies of raising eight children and running a household on the colonial frontier, Bradstreet somehow managed to keep writing, although as her biographer, Charlotte Gordon, notes, "[colonial] debate over the limits that should be placed on female behavior was alarmingly linked to the problem of being a woman and setting pen to paper." Nonetheless, in 1647 Bradstreet's brother-in-law brought a collection of her poems back to London, and it was published there in 1650 as The Tenth Muse Lately Sprung Up in America – *the first book of poetry to emanate from the New World.*

In the following poem from that collection, Bradstreet shows how ambivalent a poet can be about her published work. She chooses to couch her anxieties in maternal terms; yet many poets, both men and women, have felt a similar ambivalence about publication. But she also offers a window into one poet's habits of revision – those erasures and additions that, even after publication, she can't help but inflict on her work.

The Author to Her Book

Thou ill-form'd offspring of my feeble brain,
Who after birth did'st by my side remain,
Till snatcht from thence by friends, less wise than true,
Who thee abroad expos'd to public view,
Made thee in rags, halting to th' press to trudge,
Where errors were not lessened (all may judge).
At thy return my blushing was not small,
My rambling brat (in print) should mother call.
I cast thee by as one unfit for light,
Thy Visage was so irksome in my sight,
Yet being mine own, at length affection would
Thy blemishes amend, if so I could.
I wash'd thy face, but more defects I saw,

And rubbing off a spot, still made a flaw.
I stretcht thy joints to make thee even feet,
Yet still thou run'st more hobbling than is meet.
In better dress to trim thee was my mind,
But nought save home-spun Cloth, i' th' house I find.
In this array, 'mongst Vulgars mayst thou roam.
In Critics' hands, beware thou dost not come,
And take thy way where yet thou art not known.
If for thy Father askt, say, thou hadst none;
And for thy Mother, she alas is poor,
Which caus'd her thus to send thee out of door.

Sor Juana Inés de la Cruz (1648–1695)

Sor Juana Inés de la Cruz was a colonial Mexican scholar and poet. Much of her written work focused on the need for intellectual and literary freedom, and she was often acid about the unfair treatment of women, whether they were scholars or prostitutes. But at the height of the Counter Reformation, when the reactionary Catholic establishment was targeting immorality in art and public behavior, her outspokenness was risky. Eventually she received a public reprimand from the Bishop of Puebla, written under the pseudonym "Sor Filotea de la Cruz." Respuesta de la Poetisa a la Muy Ilustre Sor Filotea de la Cruz *(The Poet's Answer to the Most Illustrious Sister Filotea de la Cruz) is Sor Juana's passionate defense of a woman's right to lead an intellectual and creative life; and as the following extract shows, she was not afraid to draw on domestic details as a way to defend the workings of brilliance.*

Lupercio Leonardo de Argensola, whom Sor Juana mentions in this extract, was a sixteenth-century Spanish poet and playwright.

from *Respuesta de la Poetisa a la Muy Ilustre Sor Filotea de la Cruz*

translated by Margaret Sayers Peden

And what shall I tell you, lady, of the natural secrets I have discovered while cooking? I see that an egg holds together and fries in butter or in oil, but, on the contrary, in syrup shrivels into shreds; observe that to keep sugar in a liquid state one need only add a drop or two of water in which a quince or other bitter fruit has been soaked; observe that the yolk and the white of one egg are so dissimilar that each with sugar produces a result not obtainable with both together. I do not wish to weary you with such inconsequential matters, and make mention of them only to give you full notice of my nature, for I believe they will be occasion for laughter. But, lady, as women, what wisdom may be ours if not the philosophies of the kitchen? Lupercio Leonardo spoke well when he said: how well one may philosophize when preparing dinner. And I often say, when observing these trivial details: had Aristotle prepared victuals, he would have written more. And pursuing the manner of my cogitations, I tell you that this process is so continuous in me that I have no need for books. And on one occasion, when because of a grave upset of the stomach the physicians forbade me to study, I passed thus some days, but then I proposed that it would be less harmful if they allowed me books, because so vigorous and vehement were my cogitations that my spirit was consumed more greatly in a quarter of an hour than in four days' studying books. And thus they were persuaded to allow me to read. And moreover, lady, not even have my dreams been excluded from this ceaseless agitation of my imagination; indeed, in dreams it is wont to work more freely and less encumbered, collating with greater clarity and calm the gleanings of the day, arguing and making verses, of which I could offer you an extended catalogue, as well as of some arguments and inventions that I have better achieved sleeping than awake.

Samuel Johnson

The son of a bookseller, Samuel Johnson was allowed to browse freely through his father's stock, and this early opportunity to read at will was a great influence on his lifelong habits of learning. Although his knowledge was vast, he always thought of reading as part of living, not as a separate scholarly pursuit. Nonetheless, in his struggles to stay out of debt, Johnson wrote constantly, often on assignment, churning out essays, reviews, and political articles. Among those assignments was Prefaces, Biographical and Critical, to the Works of the English Poets *(1779–81), better known today as* The Lives of the Poets. *In the opinion of Victorian poet and educational theorist Matthew Arnold, the most important of the* Lives *was the essay on John Milton, in which Johnson celebrates* Paradise Lost *yet admits that somehow he cannot love the poem. In the following extract, he demonstrates a similar ambivalence as he puzzles over Milton's diction and versification, which he wants to dislike but cannot dismiss, "for I cannot wish his work to be other than it is."*

from *John Milton*

Milton would not have excelled in dramatick writing; he knew human nature only in the gross, and had never studied the shades of character, nor the combinations of concurring, or the perplexity of contending passions. He had read much, and knew what books could teach; but had mingled little in the world, and was deficient in the knowledge which experience must confer.

Through all his greater works there prevails an uniform peculiarity of diction, a mode and cast of expression which bears little resemblance to that of any former writer; and which is so far removed from common use, that an unlearned reader, when he first opens his book, finds himself surprised by a new language.

This novelty has been, by those who can find nothing wrong in Milton, imputed to his laborious endeavours after words suitable to the grandeur of his ideas. "Our language," says Addison, "sunk under him." But the truth is, that, both in prose and verse, he had formed his style by a perverse and pedantick principle. He was desirous to use English words with a foreign idiom. This in all his prose is discovered and condemned; for there judgment operates freely, neither softened by the beauty, nor awed by the dignity of his thoughts; but such is the power of his poetry, that his call is obeyed without resistance, the reader feels himself in captivity to a higher and a nobler mind, and criticism sinks in admiration.

Milton's style was not modified by his subject; what is shown with greater extent in *Paradise Lost* may be found in *Comus*. One source of his peculiarity was his familiarity with the Tuscan poets; the disposition of his words is, I think, frequently Italian; perhaps, sometimes, combined with other tongues.

Of him, at last, may be said what Jonson says of Spenser, that "he wrote no language," but has formed what Butler calls a "Babylonish dialect," in itself harsh and barbarous, but made by exalted genius and extensive learning the vehicle of so much instruction, and so much pleasure, that, like other lovers, we find grace in its deformity.

Whatever be the faults of his diction, he cannot want the praise of copiousness and variety; he was master of his language in its full extent; and has selected the melodious words with such diligence, that from his book alone the art of English poetry might be learned.

After his diction, something must be said of his versification. The "measure," he says, "is the English heroick verse without rhyme." Of this mode he had many examples among the Italians, and some in his own country. The earl of Surrey is said to have translated one of Virgil's books without rhyme; and, beside our tragedies, a few short poems had appeared in blank verse, particularly one tending to reconcile the nation to Raleigh's wild attempt upon Guiana, and probably written by Raleigh himself. These petty performances cannot be supposed to have much influenced Milton, who, more probably took his hint from Trissino's *Italia Liberata*; and, finding blank verse easier than rhyme, was desirous of persuading himself that it is better.

"Rhyme," he says, and says truly, "is no necessary adjunct of true poetry." But, perhaps, of poetry, as a mental operation, metre or musick is no necessary adjunct: it is, however, by the musick of metre that poetry has been discriminated in all languages; and, in languages melodiously constructed with a due proportion of long and short syllables, metre is sufficient. But one language cannot communicate its rules to another; where metre is scanty and imperfect, some help is necessary. The musick of the English heroick lines strikes the ear so faintly, that it is easily lost, unless all the syllables of every line cooperate together; this cooperation can be only obtained by the preservation of every verse unmingled with another, as a distinct system of sounds; and this distinctness is obtained and preserved by the artifice of rhyme. The variety of pauses, so much boasted by the lovers of blank verse, changes the measures of an English poet to the periods of a declaimer; and there are only a few skilful and happy readers of Milton, who enable their audience to perceive where the lines end or begin. "Blank verse," said an ingenious critick, "seems to be verse only to the eye." Poetry may subsist without rhyme, but English poetry will not often please; nor can rhyme ever be safely spared, but where the subject is able to support itself. Blank verse makes some approach to that which is called the lapidary style; has neither the easiness of prose, nor the melody of numbers, and, therefore, tires by long continuance. Of the Italian writers without rhyme, whom Milton alleges as precedents, not one is popular; what reason could urge in its defence, has been confuted by the ear.

But, whatever be the advantage of rhyme, I cannot prevail on myself to wish that Milton had been a rhymer; for I cannot wish his work to be other than it is; yet, like other heroes, he is to be admired rather than imitated. He that thinks himself capable of astonishing may write blank verse; but those that hope only to please must condescend to rhyme.

The highest praise of genius is original invention. Milton cannot be said to have contrived the structure of an epick poem, and, therefore, owes reverence to that vigour and amplitude of mind to which all generations must be indebted, for the art of poetical narration, for the texture of the fable, the variation of incidents, the interposition of dialogue, and all the stratagems that surprise and enchain attention. But, of all the borrowers from Homer, Milton is, perhaps, the least indebted. He was naturally a thinker for himself, confident of his own abilities, and disdainful of help or hindrance: he did not refuse admission to the thoughts or images of his predecessors, but he did not seek them. From his contemporaries he neither courted nor received support; there is in his writings nothing by which the pride of other authors might be gratified, or favour gained; no exchange of praise, nor solicitation of support. His great works were performed under discountenance, and in blindness; but difficulties vanished at his touch; he was born for whatever is arduous; and his work is not the greatest of heroick poems, only because it is not the first.

David Crantz

(born 1723)

David Crantz was a German missionary, historian, and ethnographer. In 1759, the Moravian church sent him to Greenland to study the possibilities for missionary outreach and to bring back a description of the inhabitants. The result was a two-volume study of the Inuit people and their landscape. Although the 1765 work was originally published in German, it was released in England as A History of Greenland *(1767) and became very popular. Among its fascinated readers were Edmund Burke, who wrote a long synopsis for* The Annual Register, *and Samuel Taylor Coleridge, who pored over Crantz's descriptions of Arctic ice before writing the polar scenes in* The Rime of the Ancient Mariner.*

In the following extract, Crantz discusses the nith-song, *a public word duel that one Inuit participant has since described as "little, sharp word splinters, like the wooden splinters which I hack off with my axe." As late as the 1950s, anthropologists were still mentioning the* nith-song *as an extant method of solving disputes; and anyone who has watched a poetry slam may find elements of Crantz's description strangely familiar.*

from *A History of Greenland*

If a Greenlander thinks himself aggrieved by another, he discovers no symptom of revengeful designs, anger, or vexation, but he composes a satirical poem, which he recites with singing and dancing, in the presence of his domestics, and particularly the female part of his family, till they know it by rote. He then in the face of the whole country, challenges his antagonist to a satirical duel. The latter appears at the appointed place, and both parties enter the lists. The complainant begins to sing his satire dancing to the beat of the drum, and cheered by the echoing Amna ajah of his partisans, who join in every line, while he repeats so many ludicrous stories of which his adversary is the subject, that the auditors cannot forbear laughing. When he has finished, the respondent steps forth, and retorts the accusation, amidst the plaudits of his party, by a similar string of lampoons. The accuser renews the assault, and is again rebuffed; and this continues till one of the competitors is weary. He who has the last word wins the trial, and obtains thenceforward a reputable name. An opportunity is here offered of telling very plain and cutting truths, but there must be no mixture of rudeness or passion. The assembled spectators decide the victory, and the parties are in future the best of friends. This contest is seldom attended by any disorderly conduct, except that a man who is well seconded sometimes carries off a woman whom he wishes to marry. It serves a higher purpose than mere diversion. It is an excellent opportunity for putting immorality to the blush, and cherishing virtuous principles; for reminding debtors of the duty of repayment; for branding falsehood and detraction with infamy; for punishing fraud and injustice; and, most of all, for overwhelming adultery with its merited contempt. Nothing so effectually restrains a Greenlander from vice, as the dread of public disgrace. And this pleasant way of revenge even prevents many from wreaking their malice in acts of violence or bloodshed. Still it is easy to see that the whole affair depends upon volubility of tongue; and the most celebrated satirists and moral philosophers of the Greenlanders, are generally the most profligate in their lives.

The drum-dances of the Greenlanders are then their Olympic Games, their Areopagus, their rostrum, their theatre, their fair, and their Forum. Here they cite each other to appear and decide their differences without risking their lives in the duel, or wounding each other's honour by the envenomed pen.

Phillis Wheatley (c. 1753–1784)

*Phillis Wheatley was born in West Africa, where, as a child, she was kid-
napped and shipped to Boston as a slave. Educated by her owners, who even
went so far as to teach her Greek and Latin, she began writing poems as a
young teenager and at the age of twenty published* Poems on Various Sub-
jects, Religious and Moral *(1773). Wheatley has long been celebrated as
the first published African-American poet; and, after Anne Bradstreet, she was
the second woman in the North American colonies to publish her work. The
following poem from Wheatley's 1773 collection not only demonstrates her
familiarity with the style of Milton and Pope but even, in the fourth stanza,
seems to anticipate Keats's "On First Looking into Chapman's Homer."*

On Imagination

Thy various works, imperial queen, we see,
How bright their forms! how deck'd with pomp by thee!
Thy wond'rous acts in beauteous order stand,
And all attest how potent is thine hand.

  From *Helicon's* refulgent heights attend,
Ye sacred choir, and my attempts befriend:
To tell her glories with a faithful tongue,
Ye blooming graces, triumph in my song.

  Now here, now there, the roving *Fancy* flies,
Till some lov'd object strikes her wand'ring eyes,
Whose silken fetters all the senses bind,
And soft captivity involves the mind.

  Imagination! who can sing thy force?
Or who describe the swiftness of thy course?
Soaring through air to find the bright abode,
Th' empyreal palace of the thund'ring God,
We on thy pinions can surpass the wind,
And leave the rolling universe behind:

From star to star the mental optics rove,
Measure the skies, and range the realms above.
There in one view we grasp the mighty whole,
Or with new worlds amaze th' unbounded soul.

Though Winter frowns to *Fancy's* raptur'd eyes
The fields may flourish, and gay scenes arise;
The frozen deeps may break their iron bands,
And bid their waters murmur o'er the sands.
Fair Flora may resume her fragrant reign,
And with her flow'ry riches deck the plain;
Sylvanus may diffuse his honours round,
And all the forest may with leaves be crown'd:
Show'rs may descend, and dews their gems disclose,
And nectar sparkle on the blooming rose.

Such is thy pow'r, nor are thine orders vain,
O thou the leader of the mental train:
In full perfection all thy works are wrought,
And thine the sceptre o'er the realms of thought.
Before thy throne the subject-passions bow,
Of subject-passions sov'reign ruler Thou;
At thy command joy rushes on the heart,
And through the glowing veins the spirits dart.

Fancy might now her silken pinions try
To rise from earth, and sweep th' expanse on high:
From Tithon's bed now might Aurora rise,
Her cheeks all glowing with celestial dies,
While a pure stream of light o'erflows the skies.
The monarch of the day I might behold,
And all the mountains tipt with radiant gold,
But I reluctant leave the pleasing views,
Which *Fancy* dresses to delight the *Muse*;
Winter austere forbids me to aspire,
And northern tempests damp the rising fire;
They chill the tides of *Fancy's* flowing sea,
Cease then, my song, cease the unequal lay.

William Blake (1757–1827)

William Blake's talents and oddities appeared early. Even as a child, he claimed to see visions, and his drawings were striking and precocious. At age fourteen, he was apprenticed to an engraver; and although throughout his life he made various attempts to move into more prominent artistic circles, his livelihood always depended on his engraving skills. In addition to illustrating Dante's Inferno, *the Book of Job, and a version of Chaucer's* The Canterbury Tales, *he created paintings, prints, and drawings to accompany most of his own poetry.*

Blake has come to be seen as a central figure of English romanticism, but his writings were almost unknown during his lifetime; and even today most readers are familiar only with the poems in Songs of Innocence and Experience. *In the words of critic Northrop Frye, his work "is in proportion to its merits the least read body of poetry in the English language." Nonetheless, among certain devoted readers, he has achieved almost cult status. Beat poets such as Gregory Corso read him so intensely that their own poems began to borrow not only his fervor but also his grammatical idiosyncrasies. And as the following letter, written to his friend and patron Thomas Butts, makes clear, those idiosyncrasies were, in fact, vital to Blake's ability to reveal and explain the intersection between his visions and his workaday life.*

Letter to Thomas Butts

April 25, 1803

My Dear Sir

I write in haste having recieved a pressing Letter from my Brother. I intended to have sent the Picture of the Riposo which is nearly finishd much to my satisfaction but not quite you shall have it soon. I now send the 4 Numbers for Mr Birch with best Respects to him The Reason the Ballads have been suspended is the pressure of other business but they will go on again soon

Accept of my thanks for your kind & heartening Letter You have Faith in the Endeavors of Me your weak brother & fellow Disciple. how great must be your faith in our Divine Master. You are to me a Lesson of Humility while you Exalt me by such distinguishing commendations. I know that you see certain merits in me which by Gods Grace shall be made fully apparent & perfect in Eternity. in the mean time I must not bury the Talents in the Earth but do my endeavour to live to the Glory of our Lord & Saviour & I am also grateful to the kind hand that endeavours to lift me out of despondency even if it lifts me too high –

And now My Dear Sir Congratulate me on my return to London with the full approbation of Mr Hayley & with Promise – But Alas!

Now I may say to you what perhaps I should not dare to say to any one else. That I can alone carry on my visionary studies in London unannoyd & that I may converse with my friends in Eternity. See Visions, Dream Dreams, & prophecy & speak Parables unobserv'd & at liberty from the Doubts of other Mortals. perhaps Doubts proceeding from Kindness. but Doubts are always pernicious Especially when we Doubt our Friends Christ is very decided on this Point. "He who is Not With Me is Against Me" There is no Medium or Middle state & if a Man is the Enemy of my Spiritual Life while he pretends to be the Friend of my Corporeal. he is a Real Enemy – but the Man may be the friend of my Spiritual Life while he seems the Enemy of my Corporeal but Not Vice Versa

What is very pleasant. Every one who hears of my going to London again Applauds it as the only course for the interest of all concerned in My Works. Observing that I ought not to be away from the opportunities London affords of seeing fine Pictures and the various improvements in Works of Art going on in London

But none can know the Spiritual Acts of my three years Slumber on the banks of the Ocean unless he has seen them in the Spirit or unless he should read My long Poem descriptive of those Acts for I have in these three years composed an immense number of verses on One Grand Theme Similar to Homers Iliad or Miltons Paradise Lost the Persons & Machinery intirely new to the Inhabitants of Earth (some of the Persons Excepted) I have written lines at a time without Premeditation & even against my Will. the Time it has taken in writing was thus rendered Non Existent. & an immense Poem Exists which seems to be the Labour of a long Life all produced without Labour or Study. I mention this to shew you what I think the Grand Reason of my being brought down here

I have a thousand & ten thousand things to say to you. My heart is full of futurity. I percieve that the sore travel which has been given me these three years leads to Glory & Honour. I rejoice & I tremble "I am fearfully & wonderfully made". I had been reading the cxxxix Psalm a little before your Letter arrived. I take your advice. I see the face of my Heavenly Father he lays his Hand upon my Head & gives a blessing to all my works why should I be troubled why should my heart & flesh cry out. I will go on in the Strength of the Lord through Hell will I sing forth his Praises. that the Dragons of the Deep may praise him & that those who dwell in darkness & on the Sea coasts may be gatherd into his Kingdom. Excuse my perhaps too great Enthusiasm. Please to accept of & give our Loves to Mrs Butts & your amiable Family. & believe me to be be –

Ever Yours Affectionately

WILL. BLAKE.

William Wordsworth (1770 – 1850)

By the late 1700s, poet William Wordsworth and his sister, the naturalist Dorothy Wordsworth, had developed a close friendship with their poet-neighbor Samuel Taylor Coleridge. For the two men, one significant result was their collaborative volume, Lyrical Ballads, *first published in 1798 and introducing major poems such as Wordsworth's "Lines written above Tintern Abbey" and Coleridge's "The Rime of the Ancient Mariner."*

For a second expanded edition published in 1800, Wordsworth decided to write a preface explaining his theories about poetry – principally, that it should arise from everyday life and speech. Although it was intended to stand as an introduction to the poems in the volume, it became, in time, a sort of manifesto of romanticism, one that was both venerated and derided, most famously in Eliot's essay "Tradition and the Individual Talent" (see page 183). Nonetheless, many of Wordsworth's assertions, such as "poetry is the spontaneous overflow of powerful feelings: it takes its origin from emotion recollected in tranquillity," continue to resonate among poets who recognize creation as a complex synthesis of sudden overwhelming feeling and a careful, solitary reimagining of that experience.

Wordsworth tinkered with the Preface for years, adding and deleting large sections and eventually including an appendix in which he explained his thoughts about poetic diction. The following version includes his sizable addition of 1802 but does not reinsert sections that he subsequently removed.

Preface to the Second Edition of "Lyrical Ballads"

The First Volume of these Poems has already been submitted to general perusal. It was published, as an experiment, which, I hoped, might be of some use to ascertain, how far, by fitting to metrical arrangement a selection of the real language of men in a state of vivid sensation, that sort of pleasure and that quantity of pleasure may be imparted, which a Poet may rationally endeavour to impart.

I had formed no very inaccurate estimate of the probable effect of those Poems: I flattered myself that they who should be pleased with them would read them with more than common pleasure: and, on the other hand, I was well aware that by those who should dislike them, they would be read with more than common dislike. The result has differed from my expectation in this only, that I have pleased a greater number, than I ventured to hope I should please.

Several of my Friends are anxious for the success of these Poems, from a belief, that, if the views with which they were composed were indeed realised, a class of Poetry would be produced, well adapted to interest mankind permanently, and not unimportant in the quality, and in the multiplicity of its moral relations: and on this account they have advised me to prefix a systematic defence of the theory upon which the Poems were written. But I was unwilling to undertake the task, knowing that on this occasion the Reader would look coldly upon my arguments, since I might be suspected of having been principally influenced by the selfish and foolish hope of reasoning him into an approbation of these particular Poems: and I was still more unwilling to undertake the task, because, adequately to display the opinions, and fully to enforce the arguments, would require a space wholly disproportionate to a preface. For, to treat the subject with the clearness and coherence of which it is susceptible, it would be necessary to give a full account of the present state of the public taste in this country, and to determine how far this taste is healthy or depraved; which, again, could not be determined, without pointing out in what manner language and the human mind act and re-act on each other, and without retracing the revolutions, not of literature alone, but likewise of society itself. I have therefore altogether declined to enter regularly upon this defence; yet I am sensible, that there would be something like impropriety in abruptly obtruding upon the Public, without a few words of introduction, Poems so materially different from those upon which general approbation is at present bestowed.

It is supposed, that by the act of writing in verse an Author makes a formal engagement that he will gratify certain known habits of association; that he not only thus apprises the Reader that certain classes of ideas and expressions will be found in his book, but that others will be carefully excluded. This exponent or symbol held forth by metrical language must in different eras of literature have excited very different expectations: for example, in the age of Catullus, Terence, and Lucretius, and that of Statius or Claudian; and in our own country, in the age of Shakespeare and Beaumont and Fletcher, and that of Donne and Cowley, or Dryden, or Pope. I will not take upon me to determine the exact import of the promise which, by the act of writing in verse, an Author, in the present day makes to his reader: but it will undoubtedly appear to many persons that I have not fulfilled the terms of an engagement thus voluntarily contracted. They who have been accustomed to the gaudiness and inane phraseology of many modern writers, if they persist in reading this book to its conclusion, will, no doubt, frequently have to struggle with feelings of strangeness and awkwardness: they will look round for poetry, and will be induced to inquire by what species of courtesy these attempts can be permitted to assume that title. I hope therefore the reader will not censure me for attempting to state what I have proposed to myself to perform; and also (as far as the limits of a preface will permit) to explain some of the chief reasons which have determined me in the choice of my purpose: that at least he may be spared any unpleasant feeling of disappointment, and that I myself may be protected from one of the most dishonourable accusations which can be brought against an Author; namely, that of an indolence which prevents him from endeavouring to ascertain what is his duty, or, when his duty is ascertained, prevents him from performing it.

The principal object, then, proposed in these Poems was to choose incidents and situations from common life, and to relate or describe them, throughout, as far as was possible in a selection of language really used by men, and, at the same time, to throw over them a certain colouring of imagination, whereby ordinary things should be presented to the mind in an unusual aspect; and, further, and above all, to make these incidents and situations interesting by tracing in them, truly though not ostentatiously, the primary laws of our nature: chiefly, as far as regards the manner in which we associate ideas in a state of excitement. Humble and rustic life was generally chosen, because, in that condition, the essential passions of the heart find a better soil in which they can attain their maturity, are less under restraint, and speak a plainer and more emphatic language; because in that condition of life our elementary feelings co-exist in a state of greater simplicity, and, consequently, may be more accurately contemplated, and more forcibly communicated; because the manners of rural life germinate from those elementary feelings, and, from the necessary character of rural occupations, are more easily comprehended, and are more durable; and, lastly, because in that condition the passions of men are incorporated with the beautiful and permanent forms of nature. The language, too, of these men has been adopted (purified indeed from what appear to be its real defects, from all lasting and rational causes of dislike or disgust) because such men hourly communicate with the best objects from which the best part of language is originally derived; and because, from their rank in society and the sameness and narrow circle of their intercourse, being less under the influence of social vanity, they convey their feelings and notions in simple and unelaborated expressions. Accordingly, such a language,

arising out of repeated experience and regular feelings, is a more perma-
nent, and a far more philosophical language, than that which is frequently
substituted for it by Poets, who think that they are conferring honour upon
themselves and their art, in proportion as they separate themselves from
the sympathies of men, and indulge in arbitrary and capricious habits of
expression, in order to furnish food for fickle tastes and fickle appetites, of
their own creation.[1]

I cannot, however, be insensible to the present outcry against the triviality
and meanness, both of thought and language, which some of my contem-
poraries have occasionally introduced into their metrical compositions;
and I acknowledge that this defect, where it exists, is more dishonourable
to the Writer's own character than false refinement or arbitrary innovation,
though I should contend at the same time, that it is far less pernicious in
the sum of its consequences. From such verses the Poems in these volumes
will be found distinguished at least by one mark of difference, that each
of them has a worthy purpose. Not that I always began to write with a dis-
tinct purpose formally conceived; but habits of meditation have, I trust, so
prompted and regulated my feelings, that my descriptions of such objects
as strongly excite those feelings, will be found to carry along with them a
purpose. If this opinion be erroneous, I can have little right to the name of a
Poet. For all good poetry is the spontaneous overflow of powerful feelings:
and though this be true, Poems to which any value can be attached were
never produced on any variety of subjects but by a man who, being pos-
sessed of more than usual organic sensibility, had also thought long and
deeply. For our continued influxes of feeling are modified and directed by
our thoughts, which are indeed the representatives of all our past feelings;
and, as by contemplating the relation of these general representatives to
each other, we discover what is really important to men, so, by the rep-
etition and continuance of this act, our feelings will be connected with
important subjects, till at length, if we be originally possessed of much
sensibility, such habits of mind will be produced, that, by obeying blindly
and mechanically the impulses of those habits, we shall describe objects,
and utter sentiments, of such a nature, and in such connection with each
other, that the understanding of the Reader must necessarily be in some
degree enlightened, and his affections strengthened and purified.

It has been said that each of these poems has a purpose. Another circum-
stance must be mentioned which distinguishes these Poems from the

---

[1] It is worth while here to observe that the affecting parts of Chaucer are almost
always expressed in language pure and universally intelligible even to this day
[Wordsworth's note].

popular Poetry of the day; it is this, that the feeling therein developed gives importance to the action and situation, and not the action and situation to the feeling.

A sense of false modesty shall not prevent me from asserting, that the Reader's attention is pointed to this mark of distinction, far less for the sake of these particular Poems than from the general importance of the subject. The subject is indeed important! For the human mind is capable of being excited without the application of gross and violent stimulants; and he must have a very faint perception of its beauty and dignity who does not know this, and who does not further know, that one being is elevated above another, in proportion as he possesses this capability. It has therefore appeared to me, that to endeavour to produce or enlarge this capability is one of the best services in which, at any period, a Writer can be engaged; but this service, excellent at all times, is especially so at the present day. For a multitude of causes, unknown to former times, are now acting with a combined force to blunt the discriminating powers of the mind, and, unfitting it for all voluntary exertion, to reduce it to a state of almost savage torpor. The most effective of these causes are the great national events which are daily taking place, and the increasing accumulation of men in cities, where the uniformity of their occupations produces a craving for extraordinary incident, which the rapid communication of intelligence hourly gratifies. To this tendency of life and manners the literature and theatrical exhibitions of the country have conformed themselves. The invaluable works of our elder writers, I had almost said the works of Shak[e]speare and Milton, are driven into neglect by frantic novels, sickly and stupid German Tragedies, and deluges of idle and extravagant stories in verse. – When I think upon this degrading thirst after outrageous stimulation, I am almost ashamed to have spoken of the feeble endeavour made in these volumes to counteract it; and, reflecting upon the magnitude of the general evil, I should be oppressed with no dishonourable melancholy, had I not a deep impression of certain inherent and indestructible qualities of the human mind, and likewise of certain powers in the great and permanent objects that act upon it, which are equally inherent and indestructible; and were there not added to this impression a belief, that the time is approaching when the evil will be systematically opposed, by men of greater powers, and with far more distinguished success.

Having dwelt thus long on the subjects and aim of these Poems, I shall request the Reader's permission to apprise him of a few circumstances relating to their *style*, in order, among other reasons, that he may not censure me for not having performed what I never attempted. The Reader will find that personifications of abstract ideas rarely occur in these volumes; and are utterly rejected, as an ordinary device to elevate the style, and raise it above prose. My purpose was to imitate, and, as far as is possible, to adopt the very language of men; and assuredly such personifications do not make any natural or regular part of that language. They are, indeed, a figure of speech occasionally prompted by passion, and I have made use of them as such; but have endeavoured utterly to reject them as a mechanical device of style, or as a family language which Writers in metre seem to lay claim to by prescription. I have wished to keep the Reader in the company of flesh and blood, persuaded that by so doing I shall interest him. Others who pursue a different track will interest him likewise: I do not interfere with their claim, but wish to prefer a claim of my own. There will also be found in these volumes little of what is usually called poetic diction; as much pains [sic] has been taken to avoid it as is ordinarily taken to produce it; this has been done for the reason already alleged, to bring my language near to the language of men; and further, because the pleasure which I have proposed to myself to impart, is of a kind very different from that which is supposed by many persons to be the proper object of poetry. I do not know how to give my Reader a more exact notion of the style in which it was my wish and intention to write, than by informing him that I have at all times endeavoured to look steadily at my subject; consequently, there is I hope in these Poems little falsehood of description, and my ideas are expressed in language fitted to their respective importance. Something must have been gained by this practice, as it is friendly to one property of all good poetry, namely, good sense: but it has necessarily cut me off from a large portion of phrases and figures of speech which from father to son have long been regarded as the common inheritance of Poets. I have also thought it expedient to restrict myself still further, having abstained from the use of many expressions, in themselves proper and beautiful, but which have been foolishly repeated by bad Poets, till such feelings of disgust are connected with them as it is scarcely possible by any art of association to overpower.

If in a poem there should be found a series of lines, or even a single line, in which the language, though naturally arranged, and according to the strict laws of metre, does not differ from that of prose, there is a numerous class of critics who, when they stumble upon these prosaisms, as they call them, imagine that they have made a notable discovery, and exult over the Poet as over a man ignorant of his own profession. Now these men would establish a canon of criticism which the Reader will conclude he must utterly reject if he wishes to be pleased with these volumes. And it would be a most easy task to prove to him, that not only the language of a large portion of every good poem, even of the most elevated character, must necessarily, except with reference to the metre, in no respect differ from that of good prose, but likewise that some of the most interesting parts of the best poems will be found to be strictly the language of prose when prose is well written. The truth of this assertion might be demonstrated by innumerable passages from almost all the poetical writings, even of Milton himself. To illustrate the subject in a general manner, I will here adduce a short composition of [Thomas] Gray, who was at the head of those who, by their reasonings, have attempted to widen the space of separation betwixt Prose and Metrical composition, and was more than any other man curiously elaborate in the structure of his own poetic diction.

"In vain to me the smiling mornings shine,
And reddening Phoebus lifts his golden fire:
The birds in vain their amorous descant join,
Or cheerful fields resume their green attire.
These ears, alas! for other notes repine;
A different object do these eyes require;
My lonely anguish melts no heart but mine;
And in my breast the imperfect joys expire;
Yet morning smiles the busy race to cheer,
And new-born pleasure brings to happier men;
The fields to all their wonted tribute bear;
To warm their little loves the birds complain.
I fruitless mourn to him that cannot hear
And weep the more because I weep in vain."
["Sonnet on the Death of Richard West"]

It will easily be perceived that the only part of this Sonnet which is of any value is the lines printed in Italics: it is equally obvious, that, except in the rhyme, and in the use of the single word "fruitless" for fruitlessly, which is so far a defect, the language of these lines does in no respect differ from that of prose.

By the foregoing quotation it has been shown that the language of Prose may yet be well adapted to Poetry; and it was previously asserted, that a large portion of the language of every good poem can in no respect differ from that of good Prose. We will go further. It may be safely affirmed, that there neither is, nor can be, any essential difference between the language of prose and metrical composition. We are fond of tracing the resemblance between Poetry and Painting, and, accordingly, we call them Sisters: but where shall we find bonds of connection sufficiently strict to typify the affinity betwixt metrical and prose composition? They both speak by and to the same organs; the bodies in which both of them are clothed may be said to be of the same substance, their affections are kindred and almost identical, not necessarily differing even in degree; Poetry[2] sheds no tears "such as Angels weep" [a quotation from Milton's *Paradise Lost*], but natural and human tears; she can boast of no celestial ichor that distinguishes her vital juices from those of prose; the same human blood circulates through the veins of them both.

If it be affirmed that rhyme and metrical arrangement of themselves constitute a distinction which overturns what has just been said on the strict affinity of metrical language with that of prose, and paves the way for other artificial distinctions which the mind voluntarily admits, I answer that the language of such Poetry as is here recommended is, as far as is possible, a selection of the language really spoken by men; that this selection, wherever it is made with true taste and feeling, will of itself form a distinction far greater than would at first be imagined, and will entirely separate the composition from the vulgarity and meanness of ordinary life; and, if metre be superadded thereto, I believe that a dissimilitude will be altogether sufficient for the gratification of a rational mind. What other distinction would we have? Whence is it to come? And where is it to exist? Not, surely, where the Poet speaks through the mouths of his characters: it cannot be necessary here, either for elevation of style, or any of its supposed ornaments: for, if the Poet's subject be judiciously chosen, it will naturally, and upon fit occasion, lead him to passions the language of which, if selected truly and judiciously, must necessarily be dignified and variegated, and alive with metaphors and figures. I forbear to speak of an incongruity which would shock the intelligent Reader, should the Poet interweave any foreign splendour of his own with that which the passion naturally suggests: it is sufficient to say that such addition is unnecessary. And, surely, it is more probable that those passages, which with propriety abound with metaphors and figures, will have their due effect, if, upon other occasions where the passions are of a milder character, the style also be subdued and temperate.

But, as the pleasure which I hope to give by the Poems now presented to the Reader must depend entirely on just notions upon this subject, and, as it is in itself of high importance to our taste and moral feelings, I cannot content myself with these detached remarks. And if, in what I am about to

---

[2] I here use the word "Poetry" (though against my own judgment) as opposed to the word Prose, and synonymous with metrical composition. But much confusion has been introduced into criticism by this contradistinction of Poetry and Prose, instead of the more philosophical one of Poetry and Matter of Fact, of Science. The only strict antithesis to Prose is Metre; nor is this, in truth, a *strict* antithesis, because lines and passages of metre so naturally occur in writing prose, that it would be scarcely possible to avoid them, even were it desirable [Wordsworth's note].

say, it shall appear to some that my labour is unnecessary, and that I am like a man fighting a battle without enemies, such persons may be reminded, that, whatever be the language outwardly holden by men, a practical faith in the opinions which I am wishing to establish is almost unknown. If my conclusions are admitted, and carried as far as they must be carried if admitted at all, our judgments concerning the works of the greatest Poets both ancient and modern will be far different from what they are at present, both when we praise, and when we censure: and our moral feelings influencing and influenced by these judgments will, I believe, be corrected and purified.

Taking up the subject, then, upon general grounds, let me ask, what is meant by the word Poet? What is a Poet? To whom does he address himself? And what language is to be expected from him? – He is a man speaking to men: a man, it is true, endowed with more lively sensibility, more enthusiasm and tenderness, who has a greater knowledge of human nature, and a more comprehensive soul, than are supposed to be common among mankind; a man pleased with his own passions and volitions, and who rejoices more than other men in the spirit of life that is in him; delighting to contemplate similar volitions and passions as manifested in the goings-on of the Universe, and habitually impelled to create them where he does not find them. To these qualities he has added a disposition to be affected more than other men by absent things as if they were present; an ability of conjuring up in himself passions, which are indeed far from being the same as those produced by real events, yet (especially in those parts of the general sympathy which are pleasing and delightful) do more nearly resemble the passions produced by real events, than anything which, from the motions of their own minds merely, other men are accustomed to feel in themselves: – whence, and from practice, he has acquired a greater readiness and power in expressing what he thinks and feels, and especially those thoughts and feelings which, by his own choice, or from the external structure of his own mind, arise in him without immediate external excitement.

But whatever portion of this faculty we may suppose even the greatest Poet to possess, there cannot be a doubt that the language which it will suggest to him, must often, in liveliness and truth, fall short of that which is uttered by men in real life, under the actual pressure of those passions, certain shadows of which the Poet thus produces, or feels to be produced, in himself.

However exalted a notion we would wish to cherish of the character of a Poet, it is obvious, that while he describes and imitates passions, his employment is in some degree mechanical, compared with the freedom and power of real and substantial action and suffering. So that it will be the wish of the Poet to bring his feelings near to those of the persons whose feelings he describes, nay, for short spaces of time, perhaps, to let himself slip into an entire delusion, and even confound and identify his own feelings with theirs: modifying only the language which is thus suggested to him by a consideration that he describes for a particular purpose, that of giving pleasure. Here, then, he will apply the principle of selection which has been already insisted upon. He will depend upon this for removing what would otherwise be painful or disgusting in the passion; he will feel that there is no necessity to trick out or elevate nature: and, the more industriously he applies this principle, the deeper will be his faith that no words, which his fancy or imagination can suggest, will be to be [sic] compared with those which are the emanations of reality and truth.

But it may be said by those who do not object to the general spirit of these remarks, that, as it is impossible for the Poet to produce upon all occasions language as exquisitely fitted for the passion as that which the real passion itself suggests, it is proper that he should consider himself as in the situation of a translator, who does not scruple to substitute excellencies of another kind for those which are unattainable by him; and endeavours occasionally to surpass his original, in order to make some amends for the inferiority to which he feels that he must submit. But this would be to encourage idleness and unmanly despair. Further, it is the language of men who speak of what they do not understand; who talk of Poetry as of a matter of amusement and idle pleasure; who will converse with us as gravely about a *taste* for Poetry, as they express it, as if it were a thing as indifferent as a taste for rope-dancing, or Frontiniac [a French wine] or Sherry. Aristotle, as I have been told, has said, that Poetry is the most philosophic of all writing: it is so: its object is truth, not individual and local, but general, and operative; not standing upon external testimony, but carried alive into the heart by passion; truth which is its own testimony, which gives competence and confidence to the tribunal. Poetry is the image of man and nature. The obstacles which stand in the way of the fidelity of the Biographer and Historian, and of their consequent utility, are incalculably greater than those which are to be encountered by the Poet who comprehends the dignity of his art. The Poet writes under one restriction only, namely, the necessity of giving immediate pleasure to a human Being possessed of that information which may be expected from him, not as a lawyer, a physician, a mariner, an astronomer, or a natural philosopher, but as a Man. Except this one restriction, there is no object standing between the Poet and the image of things; between this, and the Biographer and Historian, there are a thousand.

Nor let this necessity of producing immediate pleasure be considered as a degradation of the Poet's art. It is far otherwise. It is an acknowledgment of the beauty of the universe, an acknowledgment the more sincere, because not formal, but indirect; it is a task light and easy to him who looks at the world in the spirit of love; further, it is a homage paid to the native and naked dignity of man, to the grand elementary principle of pleasure, by which he knows, and feels, and lives, and moves. We have no sympathy but what is propagated by pleasure: I would not be misunderstood; but wherever we sympathise with pain, it will be found that the sympathy is produced and carried on by subtle combinations with pleasure. We have no knowledge, that is, no general principles drawn from the contemplation of particular facts, but what has been built up by pleasure, and exists in us by pleasure alone. The Man of science, the Chemist and Mathematician, whatever difficulties and disgusts they may have had to struggle with, know and feel this. However painful may be the objects with which the Anatomist's knowledge is connected, he feels that his knowledge is pleasure; and where he has no pleasure he has no knowledge. What then does the Poet? He considers man and the objects that surround him as acting and re-acting upon each other, so as to produce an infinite complexity of pain and pleasure; he considers man in his own nature and in his ordinary life as contemplating this with a certain quantity of immediate knowledge, with certain convictions, intuitions, and deductions, which from habit acquire the quality of intuitions; he considers him as looking upon this complex scene of ideas and sensations, and finding every where objects that immediately excite in him sympathies which, from the necessities of his nature, are accompanied by an overbalance of enjoyment.

To this knowledge which all men carry about with them, and to these sympathies in which, without any other discipline than that of our daily life, we are fitted to take delight, the Poet principally directs his attention. He considers man and nature as essentially adapted to each other, and the mind of man as naturally the mirror of the fairest and most interesting properties of nature. And thus the Poet, prompted by this feeling of pleasure, which accompanies him through the whole course of his studies, converses with general nature, with affections akin to those, which, through labor and length of time, the Man of science has raised up in himself, by conversing with those particular parts of nature which are the objects of his studies. The knowledge both of the Poet and the Man of science is pleasure; but the knowledge of the one cleaves to us as a necessary part of our existence, our natural and unalienable inheritance; the other is a personal and individual acquisition, slow to come to us, and by no habitual and direct sympathy connecting us with our fellow-beings. The Man of science seeks truth as a remote and unknown benefactor; he cherishes and loves it in his solitude: the Poet, singing a song in which all human beings join with him, rejoices in the presence of truth as our visible friend and hourly companion. Poetry is the breath and finer spirit of all knowledge; it is the impassioned expression which is in the countenance of all Science. Emphatically may it be said of the Poet, as Shak[e]speare hath said of man, "that he looks before and after." He is the rock of defence for human nature; an upholder and preserver, carrying everywhere with him relationship and love. In spite of difference of soil and climate, of language and manners, of laws and customs: in spite of things silently gone out of mind, and things violently destroyed; the Poet binds together by passion and knowledge the vast empire of human society, as it is spread over the whole earth, and over all time. The objects of the Poet's thoughts are every where; though the eyes and senses of man are, it is true, his favourite guides, yet he will follow wheresoever he can find an atmosphere of sensation in which to move his wings. Poetry is the first and last of all knowledge – it is as immortal as the heart of man. If the labours of Men of science should ever create any material revolution, direct or indirect, in our condition, and in the impressions which we habitually receive, the Poet will sleep then no more than at present; he will be ready to follow the steps of the Man of science, not only in those general indirect effects, but he will be at his side, carrying sensation into the midst of the objects of the science itself. The remotest discoveries of the Chemist, the Botanist, or Mineralogist, will be as proper objects of the Poet's art as any upon which it can be employed, if the time should ever come when these things shall be familiar to us, and the relations under which they are contemplated by the followers of these respective sciences shall be manifestly and palpably material to us as enjoying and suffering beings. If the time should ever come when what is now called science, thus familiarised to men, shall be ready to put on, as it were, a form of flesh and blood, the Poet will lend his divine spirit to aid the transfiguration, and will welcome the Being thus produced, as a dear and genuine inmate of the household of man. – It is not, then, to be supposed that any one, who holds that sublime notion of Poetry which I have attempted to convey, will break in upon the sanctity and truth of his pictures by transitory and accidental ornaments, and endeavour to excite admiration of himself by arts, the necessity of which must manifestly depend upon the assumed meanness of his subject.

What has been thus far said applies to Poetry in general; but especially to those parts of composition where the Poet speaks through the mouths of his characters; and upon this point it appears to authorise the conclusion that there are few persons of good sense, who would not allow that the dramatic parts of composition are defective, in proportion as they deviate from the real language of nature, and are coloured by a diction of the Poet's own, either peculiar to him as an individual Poet or belonging simply to Poets in general; to a body of men who, from the circumstance of their compositions being in metre, it is expected will employ a particular language.

It is not, then, in the dramatic parts of composition that we look for this distinction of language; but still it may be proper and necessary where the Poet speaks to us in his own person and character. To this I answer by referring the Reader to the description before given of a Poet. Among the qualities there enumerated as principally conducing to form a Poet, is implied nothing differing in kind from other men, but only in degree. The sum of what was said is, that the Poet is chiefly distinguished from other men by a greater promptness to think and feel without immediate external excitement, and a greater power in expressing such thoughts and feelings as are produced in him in that manner. But these passions and thoughts and feelings are the general passions and thoughts and feelings of men. And with what are they connected? Undoubtedly with our moral sentiments and animal sensations, and with the causes which excite these; with the operations of the elements, and the appearances of the visible universe; with storm and sunshine, with the revolution of the seasons, with cold and heat, with loss of friends and kindred, with injuries and resentments, gratitude and hope, with fear and sorrow. These, and the like, are the sensations and objects which the Poet describes, as they are the sensations of other men, and objects which interest them. The Poet thinks and feels in the spirit of human passions. How, then, can his language differ in any material degree from that of all other men who feel vividly and see clearly? It might be proved that it is impossible. But supposing that this were not the case, the Poet might then be allowed to use a peculiar language when expressing his feelings for his own gratification, or that of men like himself. But Poets do not write for Poets alone, but for men. Unless therefore we are advocates for that admiration which subsists upon ignorance, and that pleasure which arises from hearing what we do not understand, the Poet must descend from this supposed height; and, in order to excite rational sympathy, he must express himself as other men express themselves. To this it may be added, that while he is only selecting from the language of real men, or, which amounts to the same thing, composing accurately in the spirit of such selection, he is treading upon safe ground, and we know what we are to expect from him. Our feelings are the same with respect to metre; for, as it may be proper to remind the Reader, the distinction of metre is regular and uniform, and not, like that which is produced by what is usually called POETIC DICTION, arbitrary, and subject to infinite caprices upon which no calculation whatever can be made. In the one case, the Reader is utterly at the mercy of the Poet, respecting what imagery or diction he may choose to connect with the passion; whereas, in the other, the metre obeys certain laws, to which the Poet and Reader both willingly submit because they are certain, and because no interference is made by them with the passion, but such as the concurring testimony of ages has shown to heighten and improve the pleasure which co-exists with it.

It will now be proper to answer an obvious question, namely, Why, professing these opinions, have I written in verse? To this, in addition to such answer as is included in what has already been said, I reply, in the first place, Because, however I may have restricted myself, there is still left open to me what confessedly constitutes the most valuable object of all writing, whether in prose or verse; the great and universal passions of men, the most general and interesting of their occupations, and the entire world of nature before me – to supply endless combinations of forms and imagery. Now, supposing for a moment that whatever is interesting in these objects may be as vividly described in prose, why should I be condemned for attempting to superadd to such description, the charm which, by the consent of all nations, is acknowledged to exist in metrical language? To this, by such as are yet unconvinced, it may be answered that a very small part of the pleasure given by Poetry depends upon the metre, and that it is injudicious to write in metre, unless it be accompanied with the other artificial distinctions of style with which metre is usually accompanied, and that, by such deviation, more will be lost from the shock which will thereby be given to the Reader's associations than will be counterbalanced by any pleasure which he can derive from the general power of numbers. In answer to those who still contend for the necessity of accompanying metre with certain appropriate colours of style in order to [sic] the accomplishment of its appropriate end, and who also, in my opinion, greatly under-rate the power of metre in itself, it might, perhaps, as far as relates to these Volumes, have been almost sufficient to observe, that poems are extant, written upon more humble subjects, and in a still more naked and simple style, which have continued to give pleasure from generation to generation. Now, if nakedness and simplicity be a defect, the fact here mentioned affords a strong presumption that poems somewhat less naked and simple are capable of affording pleasure at the present day; and, what I wished chiefly to attempt, at present, was to justify myself for having written under the impression of this belief.

But various causes might be pointed out why, when the style is manly, and the subject of some importance, words metrically arranged will long continue to impart such a pleasure to mankind as he who proves the extent of that pleasure will be desirous to impart. The end of Poetry is to produce excitement in co-existence with an overbalance of pleasure; but, by the supposition, excitement is an unusual and irregular state of the mind; ideas and feelings do not, in that state, succeed each other in accustomed order. If the words, however, by which this excitement is produced be in themselves powerful, or the images and feelings have an undue proportion of pain connected with them, there is some danger that the excitement may be carried beyond its proper bounds. Now the co-presence of something regular, something to which the mind has been accustomed in various moods and in a less excited state, cannot but have great efficacy in tempering and restraining the passion by an intertexture of ordinary feeling, and of feeling not strictly and necessarily connected with the passion. This is unquestionably true; and hence, though the opinion will at first appear paradoxical, from the tendency of metre to divest language, in a certain degree, of its reality, and thus to throw a sort of half-consciousness of unsubstantial existence over the whole composition, there can be little doubt but that more pathetic situations and sentiments, that is, those which have a greater proportion of pain connected with them, may be endured in metrical composition, especially in rhyme, than in prose. The metre of the old ballads is very artless; yet they contain many passages which would illustrate this opinion; and, I hope, if the following Poems be attentively perused, similar instances will be found in them. This opinion may be further illustrated by appealing to the Reader's own experience of the reluctance with which he comes to the re-perusal of the distressful parts of [Samuel Richardson's 1748 novel about] Clarissa Harlowe, or [Edward Moore's 1753 domestic tragedy] the Gamester; while Shak[e]speare's writings, in the most pathetic scenes, never act upon us, as pathetic, beyond the bounds of pleasure – an effect which, in a much greater degree than might first be imagined, is to be ascribed to small, but continual and regular impulses of pleasurable surprise from the metrical arrangement. – On the other hand (what it must be allowed will much more frequently happen) if the Poet's words should be incommensurate with the passion, and inadequate to raise the Reader to a height of desirable excitement, then, (unless the Poet's choice of his metre has been grossly injudicious) in the feelings of pleasure which the Reader has been accustomed to connect with metre in general, and in the feeling, whether cheerful or melancholy, which he has been accustomed to connect with that particular movement of metre, there will be found something which will greatly contribute to impart passion to the words, and to effect the complex end which the Poet proposes to himself.

If I had undertaken a SYSTEMATIC defence of the theory here maintained, it would have been my duty to develope the various causes upon which the pleasure received from metrical language depends. Among the chief of these causes is to be reckoned a principle which must be well known to those who have made any of the Arts the object of accurate reflection; namely, the pleasure which the mind derives from the perception of similitude in dissimilitude. This principle is the great spring of the activity of our minds, and their chief feeder. From this principle the direction of the sexual appetite, and all the passions connected with it, take their origin: it is the life of our ordinary conversation; and upon the accuracy with which similitude in dissimilitude, and dissimilitude in similitude are perceived, depend our taste and our moral feelings. It would not be a useless employment to apply this principle to the consideration of metre, and to show that metre is hence enabled to afford much pleasure, and to point out in what manner that pleasure is produced. But my limits will not permit me to enter upon this subject, and I must content myself with a general summary[.]

I have said that poetry is the spontaneous overflow of powerful feelings: it takes its origin from emotion recollected in tranquillity: the emotion is contemplated till, by a species of re-action, the tranquillity gradually disappears, and an emotion, kindred to that which was before the subject of contemplation, is gradually produced, and does itself actually exist in the mind. In this mood successful composition generally begins, and in a mood similar to this it is carried on; but the emotion, of whatever kind, and in whatever degree, from various causes, is qualified by various pleasures, so that in describing any passions whatsoever, which are voluntarily described, the mind will, upon the whole, be in a state of enjoyment. If Nature be thus cautious to preserve in a state of enjoyment a being so employed, the Poet ought to profit by the lesson held forth to him, and ought especially to take care, that, whatever passions he communicates to his Reader, those passions, if his Reader's mind be sound and vigorous, should always be accompanied with an overbalance of pleasure. Now the music of harmonious metrical language, the sense of difficulty overcome, and the blind association of pleasure which has been previously received from works of rhyme or metre of the same or similar construction, an indistinct perception perpetually renewed of language closely resembling that of real life, and yet, in the circumstance of metre, differing from it so widely – all these imperceptibly make up a complex feeling of delight, which is of the most important use in tempering the painful feeling always found intermingled with powerful descriptions of the deeper passions. This effect is always produced in pathetic and impassioned poetry; while, in lighter compositions, the ease and gracefulness with which the Poet manages his numbers are themselves confessedly a principal source of the gratification of the Reader. All that it is *necessary* to say, however, upon this subject, may be effected by affirming, what few persons will deny, that, of two descriptions, either of passions, manners, or characters, each of them equally well executed, the one in prose and the other in verse, the verse will be read a hundred times where the prose is read once.

Having thus explained a few of my reasons for writing in verse, and why I have chosen subjects from common life, and endeavoured to bring my language near to the real language of men, if I have been too minute in pleading my own cause, I have at the same time been treating a subject of general interest; and for this reason a few words shall be added with reference solely to these particular poems, and to some defects which will probably be found in them. I am sensible that my associations must have sometimes been particular instead of general, and that, consequently, giving to things a false importance, I may have sometimes written upon unworthy subjects; but I am less apprehensive on this account, than that my language may frequently have suffered from those arbitrary connections of feelings and ideas with particular words and phrases, from which no man can altogether protect himself. Hence I have no doubt, that, in some instances, feelings, even of the ludicrous, may be given to my Readers by expressions which appeared to me tender and pathetic. Such faulty expressions, were I convinced they were faulty at present, and that they must necessarily continue to be so, I would willingly take all reasonable pains to correct. But it is dangerous to make these alterations on the simple authority of a few individuals, or even of certain classes of men; for where the understanding of an Author is not convinced, or his feelings altered, this cannot be done without great injury to himself: for his own feelings are his stay and support; and, if he set them aside in one instance, he may be induced to repeat this act till his mind shall lose all confidence in itself, and become utterly debilitated. To this it may be added, that the critic ought never to forget that he is himself exposed to the same errors as the Poet, and, perhaps, in a much greater degree: for there can be no presumption in saying of most readers, that it is not probable they will be so well acquainted with the various stages of meaning through which words have passed, or with the fickleness or stability of the relations of particular ideas to each other; and, above all, since they are so much less interested in the subject, they may decide lightly and carelessly.

Long as the Reader has been detained, I hope he will permit me to caution him against a mode of false criticism which has been applied to Poetry, in which the language closely resembles that of life and nature. Such verses have been triumphed over in parodies, of which Dr. Johnson's stanza [parodying Thomas Perry's *The Hermit of Warkworth* (1771)] is a fair specimen:

> "I put my hat upon my head,
> And walk'd into the Strand,
> And there I met another man
> Whose hat was in his hand."

Immediately under these lines I will place one of the most justly-admired stanzas of [the anonymous ballad] the *"Babes in the Wood."*

> "These pretty Babes with hand in hand
> Went wandering up and down;
> But never more they saw the Man
> Approaching from the Town."

In both of these stanzas the words, and the order of the words, in no respect differ from the most unimpassioned conversation. There are words in both, for example, "the Strand," and "the Town," connected with none but the most familiar ideas; yet the one stanza we admit as admirable, and the other as a fair example of the superlatively contemptible. Whence arises this difference? Not from the metre, not from the language, not from the order of the words; but the matter expressed in Dr. Johnson's stanza is contemptible. The proper method of treating trivial and simple verses, to which Dr. Johnson's stanza would be a fair parallelism, is not to say, this is a bad kind of poetry, or, this is not poetry; but, this wants sense; it is neither interesting in itself, nor can lead to any thing interesting; the images neither originate in that sane state of feeling which arises out of thought, nor can excite thought or feeling in the Reader. This is the only sensible manner of dealing with such verses. Why trouble yourself about the species till you have previously decided upon the genus? Why take pains to prove that an ape is not a Newton, when it is self-evident that he is not a man?

One request I must to make of my reader, which is, that in judging these Poems he would decide by his own feelings genuinely, and not by reflection upon what will probably be the judgment of others. How common is it to hear a person say, I myself do not object to this style of composition, or this or that expression, but, to such and such classes of people it will appear mean or ludicrous! This mode of criticism, so destructive of all sound unadulterated judgment, is almost universal: let the Reader then abide, in-dependently, by his own feelings, and, if he finds himself affected, let him not suffer such conjectures to interfere with his pleasure.

If an Author, by any single composition, has impressed us with respect for his talents, it is useful to consider this as affording a presumption, that on other occasions where we have been displeased, he, nevertheless, may not have written ill or absurdly; and further, to give him so much credit for this one composition as may induce us to review what has displeased us, with more care than we should otherwise have bestowed upon it. This is not only an act of justice, but, in our decisions upon poetry especially, may conduce, in a high degree, to the improvement of our own taste; for an accurate taste in poetry, and in all the other arts, as [eighteenth-century painter] Sir Joshua Reynolds has observed, is an *acquired* talent, which can only be produced by thought and a long-continued intercourse with the best models of composition. This is mentioned, not with so ridiculous a purpose as to prevent the most inexperienced Reader from judging for himself, (I have already said that I wish him to judge for himself;) but merely to temper the rashness of decision, and to suggest, that, if Poetry be a subject on which much time has not been bestowed, the judgment may be erroneous; and that, in many cases, it necessarily will be so.

Nothing would, I know, have so effectually contributed to further the end which I have in view, as to have shown of what kind the pleasure is, and how that pleasure is produced, which is confessedly produced by metrical composition essentially different from that which I have here endeavoured to recommend: for the Reader will say that he has been pleased by such composition; and what more can be done for him? The power of any art is limited; and he will suspect, that, if it be proposed to furnish him with new friends, that can be only upon condition of his abandoning his old friends. Besides, as I have said, the Reader is himself conscious of the plea-sure which he has received from such composition, composition to which he has peculiarly attached the endearing name of Poetry; and all men feel an habitual gratitude, and something of an honourable bigotry, for the objects which have long continued to please them: we not only wish to be pleased, but to be pleased in that particular way in which we have been accustomed to be pleased. There is in these feelings enough to resist a host of arguments; and I should be the less able to combat them successfully, as I am willing to allow, that, in order entirely to enjoy the Poetry which I am recommending, it would be necessary to give up much of what is ordinar-ily enjoyed. But, would my limits have permitted me to point out how this pleasure is produced, many obstacles might have been removed, and the Reader assisted in perceiving that the powers of language are not so limited as he may suppose; and that it is possible for poetry to give other enjoyments, of a purer, more lasting, and more exquisite nature. This part of my subject has not been altogether neglected, but it has not so much my present aim to prove, that the interest excited by some other kinds of poetry is less vivid, and less worthy of the nobler powers of the mind, as to offer reasons for presuming, that if my purpose were fulfilled, a species of poetry would be produced, which is genuine poetry; in its nature well adapted to interest mankind permanently, and likewise important in the multiplicity and quality of its moral relations.

From what has been said, and from a perusal of the Poems, the Reader will be able clearly to perceive the object which I had in view: he will determine how far it has been attained; and, what is a much more important question, whether it be worth attaining: and upon the decision of these two questions will rest my claim to the approbation of the Public.

Dorothy Wordsworth (1771–1855)

The younger sister of poet William Wordsworth, naturalist Dorothy Words-
worth was his closest companion and lived with him for nearly all of her adult
life, even after his marriage to Mary Hutchinson. In August and September
of 1803, the two Wordsworths and Samuel Taylor Coleridge made a six-week
visit to Scotland, traveling more than six hundred miles over terrible roads
on what they partly envisioned as a pilgrimage to the homeland of Burns and
Scott. Dorothy Wordsworth kept a detailed journal of the trip and, in the fol-
lowing extract, describes their visit to Burns's house and grave in the town of
Dumfries in southwestern Scotland, which was relatively close to the Word-
sworths' home in the English Lake District. (As she notes, he would have been
able to see their own familiar mountains.) But like many literary tourists, she
find herself puzzled by the apparent disconnect between the poet and his land-
scape, a theme that Edward Thomas, writing in the years before World War I,
addresses more self-consciously in his essay on Herrick (see page 163).

---

from *Recollections of a Tour Made in Scotland*
A.D. *1803*

Thursday, August 18th. – Went to the churchyard where Burns is buried. A
bookseller accompanied us. He showed us the outside of Burns's house,
where he had lived the last three years of his life, and where he died. It has
a mean appearance, and is in a bye situation, whitewashed; dirty about the
doors, as almost all Scotch houses are; flowering plants in the windows.

Went on to visit his grave. He lies at a corner of the churchyard, and his
second son, Francis Wallace, beside him. There is no stone to mark the
spot; but a hundred guineas have been collected, to be expended on some
sort of monument. "There," said the bookseller, pointing to a pompous
monument, "there lies Mr. Such-a-one" – I have forgotten his name, – "a
remarkably clever man; he was an attorney, and hardly ever lost a cause he
undertook. Burns made many a lampoon upon him, and there they rest, as
you see." We looked at the grave with melancholy and painful reflections,
repeating to each other his own verses: –

"Is there a man whose judgment clear
Can others teach the course to steer,
Yet runs himself life's mad career
    Wild as the wave? –
Here let him pause, and through a tear
    Survey this grave.
The Poor Inhabitant below
Was quick to learn, and wise to know,
And keenly felt the friendly glow
    And softer flame;
But thoughtless follies laid him low,
    And stain'd his name."
[from Robert Burns, "A Bard's Epitaph," 1786]

The churchyard is full of grave-stones and expensive monuments in all sorts of fantastic shapes – obelisk-wise, pillar-wise, etc. . . . The church is like a huge house; indeed, so are all the churches, with a steeple, not a square tower or spire, – a sort of thing more like a glass-house chimney than a Church of England steeple; grave-stones in abundance, few verses, yet there were some – no texts. Over the graves of married women the maiden name instead of that of the husband, "spouse" instead of "wife," and the place of abode preceded by "in" instead of "of." When our guide had left us, we turned again to Burns's house. Mrs. Burns was gone to spend some time by the sea-shore with her children. We spoke to the servant-maid at the door, who invited us forward, and we sate down in the parlour. The walls were coloured with a blue wash; on one side of the fire was a mahogany desk, opposite to the window a clock, and over the desk a print from the "Cotter's Saturday Night," which Burns mentions in one of his letters having received as a present. The house was cleanly [sic] and neat in the inside, the stairs of stone, scoured white, the kitchen on the right side of the passage, the parlour on the left. In the room above the parlour the Poet died, and his son after him in the same room. The servant told us she had lived five years with Mrs. Burns, who was now in great sorrow for the death of "Wallace." She said that Mrs. Burns's youngest son was at Christ's Hospital.

We were glad to leave Dumfries, which is no agreeable place to them who do not love the bustle of a town that seems to be rising up to wealth. We could think of little else but poor Burns, and his moving about on that unpoetic ground. In our road to Brownhill, the next stage, we passed Ellisland at a little distance on our right, his farmhouse. We might there have had more pleasure in looking round, if we had been nearer to the spot; but there is no thought surviving in connexion with Burns's daily life that is not heart-depressing. Travelled through the vale of Nith, here little like a vale, it is so broad, with irregular hills rising up on each side, in outline resembling the old-fashioned valances of a bed. There is a great deal of arable land; the corn ripe; trees here and there – plantations, clumps, coppices, and a newness in everything. So much of the gorse and broom rooted out that you wonder why it is not all gone, and yet there seems to be almost as much gorse and broom as corn; and they grow one among another you know not how. Crossed the Nith; the vale becomes narrow, and very pleasant; cornfields, green hills, clay cottages; the river's bed rocky, with woody banks. Left the Nith about a mile and a half, and reached Brownhill, a lonely inn, where we slept. The view from the windows was pleasing, though some travellers might have been disposed to quarrel with it for its general nakedness; yet there was abundance of corn. It is an open country – open, yet all over hills. At a little distance were many cottages among trees, that looked very pretty. Brownhill is about seven or eight miles from Ellisland. I fancied to myself, while I was sitting in the parlour, that Burns might have caroused there, for most likely his rounds extended so far, and this thought gave a melancholy interest to the smoky walls. It was as pretty a room as a thoroughly dirty one could be – a square parlour painted green, but so covered over with smoke and dirt that it looked not unlike green seen through black gauze. There were three windows, looking three ways, a buffet ornamented with tea-cups, a superfine largeish looking-glass with gilt ornaments spreading far and wide, the glass spotted with dirt, some ordinary alehouse pictures, and above the chimney-piece a print in a much better style – as William guessed, taken from a painting by Sir Joshua Reynolds – of some lady of quality, in the character of Euphrosyne [in Greek mythology, one of the Three Graces]. "Ay," said the servant girl, seeing that we looked at it, "there's many travellers would give a deal for that, it's more admired than any in the house." We could not but smile; for the rest were such as may be found in the basket of any Italian image and picture hawker.

William and I walked out after dinner; Coleridge was not well, and slept upon the carriage cushions. We made our way to the cottages among the little hills and knots of wood, and then saw what a delightful country this part of Scotland might be made by planting forest trees. The ground all over heaves and swells like a sea; but for miles there are neither trees nor hedgerows, only "mound" fences and tracts; or slips of corn, potatoes, clover – with hay between, and barren land; but near the cottages many hills and hillocks covered with wood. We passed some fine trees, and paused under the shade of one close by an old mansion that seemed from its neglected state to be inhabited by farmers. But I must say that many of the "gentlemen's" houses which we have passed in Scotland have an air of neglect, and even of desolation. It was a beech, in the full glory of complete and perfect growth, very tall, with one thick stem mounting to a considerable height, which was split into four "thighs," as Coleridge afterwards called them, each in size a fine tree. Passed another mansion, now tenanted by a schoolmaster; many boys playing upon the lawn. I cannot take leave of the country which we passed through to-day, without mentioning that we saw the Cumberland mountains within half a mile of Ellisland, Burns's house, the last view we had of them. Drayton has prettily described the connexion which this neighbourhood has with ours when he makes [the Lake District mountain] Skiddaw say –

> "Scurfell from the sky,
> That Anadale doth crown, with a most amorous eye,
> Salutes me every day, or at my pride looks grim,
> Oft threatning me with clouds, as I oft threatning him."
> [from Michael Drayton's "Poly-Olbion," 1612]

These lines recurred to William's memory, and we talked of Burns, and of the prospect he must have had, perhaps from his own door, of Skiddaw and his companions, indulging ourselves in the fancy that we might have been personally known to each other, and he have looked upon those objects with more pleasure for our sakes. We talked of Coleridge's children and family, then at the foot of Skiddaw, and our own new-born John [William's eldest son] a few miles behind it; while the grave of Burns's son, which we had just seen by the side of his father, and some stories heard at Dumfries respecting the dangers his surviving children were exposed to, filled us with melancholy concern, which had a kind of connexion with ourselves. In recollection of this, William long afterwards wrote the following Address to the sons of the ill-fated poet: –

> "Ye now are panting up life's hill,
> 'Tis twilight time of good and ill,
> And more than common strength and skill
>   Must ye display,
> If ye would give the better will
>   Its lawful sway.
> Strong-bodied if ye be to bear
> Intemperance with less harm, beware,
> But if your Father's wit ye share,
>   Then, then indeed,
> Ye Sons of Burns, for watchful care
>   There will be need.

For honest men delight will take
To shew you favour for his sake,
Will flatter you, and Fool and Rake
    Your steps pursue,
And of your Father's name will make
    A snare for you.
Let no mean hope your souls enslave,
Be independent, generous, brave;
Your Father such example gave,
    And such revere,
But be admonished by his grave,
    And think and fear."

Samuel Taylor Coleridge (1772–1834)

A pattern of excitement, difficulty, and distraction dogged poet Samuel Taylor Coleridge all his life. Despite his brilliance, his production was erratic, and much of his work remained unfinished, thanks in large part to his opium addiction. But during the last eighteen years of his life, Coleridge did find a modicum of peace. He moved into the home of his doctor, James Gilman, where he was able to finish what became his greatest prose work, the Bio-graphia Literaria *(1817), part autobiography, part philosophical analysis, part literary criticism.*

In chapter 14 of the Biographia, *Coleridge considers the strengths and weaknesses of Wordsworth's* Preface to the Second Edition of the "Lyri-cal Ballads" *(page 59) and suggests his own definition of poetic power. The extract mentions the Roman poets Anacreon and Virgil, both of whom wrote poems in praise of ideally beautiful young men (Bathyllus and Alexis). Gaius Petronius Arbiter, a courtier during the reign of Nero, was probably the au-thor of the* Satyricon, *a Latin forerunner of the novel. Bishop Jeremy Taylor (1613–67) was an Anglican cleric famous for the poetic style of his devotional writings. Thomas Burnet (c. 1635–1715) was a theologian whose most fa-mous work, the* Telluris Theoria Sacra, *speculates on the origins of the earth.*

from *Biographia Literaria*

Chapter XIV: Occasion of the *Lyrical Ballads*, and the objects originally proposed – Preface to the second edition – The ensuing controversy, its causes and acrimony – Philosophic definitions of a poem and poetry with scholia.

During the first year that Mr. Wordsworth and I were neighbours, our conversations turned frequently on the two cardinal points of poetry, the power of exciting the sympathy of the reader by a faithful adherence to the truth of nature, and the power of giving the interest of novelty by the modifying colours of imagination. The sudden charm, which accidents of light and shade, which moon-light or sun-set diffused over a known and familiar landscape, appeared to represent the practicability of combining both. These are the poetry of nature. The thought suggested itself (to which of us I do not recollect) that a series of poems might be composed of two sorts. In the one, the incidents and agents were to be, in part at least, supernatural; and the excellence aimed at was to consist in the interesting of the affections by the dramatic truth of such emotions, as would naturally accompany such situations, supposing them real. And real in this sense they have been to every human being who, from whatever source of delusion, has at any time believed himself under supernatural agency. For the second class, subjects were to be chosen from ordinary life; the characters and incidents were to be such, as will be found in every village and its vicinity, where there is a meditative and feeling mind to seek after them, or to notice them, when they present themselves.

In this idea originated the plan of the *Lyrical Ballads*; in which it was agreed, that my endeavours should be directed to persons and characters supernatural, or at least romantic; yet so as to transfer from our inward nature a human interest and a semblance of truth sufficient to procure for these shadows of imagination that willing suspension of disbelief for the moment, which constitutes poetic faith. Mr. Wordsworth, on the other hand, was to propose to himself as his object, to give the charm of novelty to things of every day, and to excite a feeling analogous to the supernatural, by awakening the mind's attention from the lethargy of custom, and directing it to the loveliness and the wonders of the world before us; an inexhaustible treasure, but for which, in consequence of the film of familiarity and selfish solicitude we have eyes, yet see not, ears that hear not, and hearts that neither feel nor understand.

With this view I wrote the "Ancient Mariner," and was preparing among other poems, the "Dark Ladie," and the "Christabel," in which I should have more nearly realized my ideal, than I had done in my first attempt. But Mr. Wordsworth's industry had proved so much more successful, and the number of his poems so much greater, that my compositions, instead of forming a balance, appeared rather an interpolation of heterogeneous matter. Mr. Wordsworth added two or three poems written in his own character, in the impassioned, lofty, and sustained diction, which is characteristic of his genius. In this form the *Lyrical Ballads* were published; and were presented by him, as an experiment, whether subjects, which from their nature rejected the usual ornaments and extra-colloquial style of poems in general, might not be so managed in the language of ordinary life as to produce the pleasurable interest, which it is the peculiar business of poetry to impart. To the second edition he added a preface of considerable length; in which notwithstanding some passages of apparently a contrary import, he was understood to contend for the extension of this style to poetry of all kinds, and to reject as vicious and indefensible all phrases and forms of style that were not included in what he (unfortunately, I think, adopting an equivocal expression) called the language of real life. From this preface, prefixed to poems in which it was impossible to deny the presence of original genius, however mistaken its direction might be deemed, arose the whole long-continued controversy. For from the conjunction of perceived power with supposed heresy I explain the inveteracy and in some instances, I grieve to say, the acrimonious passions, with which the controversy has been conducted by the assailants.

Had Mr. Wordsworth's poems been the silly, the childish things, which they were for a long time described as being; had they been really distinguished from the compositions of other poets merely by meanness of language and inanity of thought; had they indeed contained nothing more than what is found in the parodies and pretended imitations of them; they must have sunk at once, a dead weight, into the slough of oblivion, and have dragged the preface along with them. But year after year increased the number of Mr. Wordsworth's admirers. They were found too not in the lower classes of the reading public, but chiefly among young men of strong sensibility and meditative minds; and their admiration (inflamed perhaps in some degree by opposition) was distinguished by its intensity, I might almost say, by its *religious* fervour. These facts, and the intellectual energy of the author, which was more or less consciously felt, where it was outwardly and even boisterously denied, meeting with sentiments of aversion to his opinions, and of alarm at their consequences, produced an eddy of criticism, which would of itself have borne up the poems by the violence, with which it whirled them round and round. With many parts of this preface in the sense attributed to them and which the words undoubtedly seem to authorize, I never concurred; but on the contrary objected to them as erroneous in principle, and as contradictory (in appearance at least) both to other parts of the same preface, and to the author's own practice in the greater number of the poems themselves. Mr. Wordsworth in his recent collection has, I find, degraded this prefatory disquisition to the end of his second volume, to be read or not at the reader's choice. But he has not, as far as I can discover, announced any change in his poetic creed. At all events, considering it as the source of a controversy, in which I have been honoured more than I deserve by the frequent conjunction of my name with his, I think it expedient to declare once for all, in what points I coincide with his opinions, and in what points I altogether differ. But in order to render myself intelligible I must previously, in as few words as possible, explain my ideas, first, of a Poem; and secondly, of Poetry itself, in kind, and in essence.

The office of philosophical disquisition consists in just distinction; while it is the privilege of the philosopher to preserve himself constantly aware, that distinction is not division. In order to obtain adequate notions of any truth, we must intellectually separate its distinguishable parts; and this is the technical process of philosophy. But having so done, we must then restore them in our conceptions to the unity, in which they actually co-exist; and this is the result of philosophy. A poem contains the same elements as a prose composition; the difference therefore must consist in a different combination of them, in consequence of a different object being proposed. According to the difference of the object will be the difference of the combination. It is possible, that the object may be merely to facilitate the recollection of any given facts or observations by artificial arrangement; and the composition will be a poem, merely because it is distinguished from prose by metre, or by rhyme, or by both conjointly. In this, the lowest sense, a man might attribute the name of a poem to the well-known enumeration of the days in the several months;

Thirty days hath September,
April, June, and November, &c.

and others of the same class and purpose. And as a particular pleasure is found in anticipating the recurrence of sounds and quantities, all compositions that have this charm super-added, whatever be their contents, *may* be entitled poems.

So much for the superficial *form*. A difference of object and contents supplies an additional ground of distinction. The immediate purpose may be the communication of truths; either of truth absolute and demonstrable, as in works of science; or of facts experienced and recorded, as in history. Pleasure, and that of the highest and most permanent kind, may *result* from the *attainment* of the end; but it is not itself the immediate end. In other works the communication of pleasure may be the immediate purpose; and though truth, either moral or intellectual, ought to be the *ultimate* end, yet this will distinguish the character of the author, not the class to which the work belongs. Blessed indeed is that state of society, in which the immediate purpose would be baffled by the perversion of the proper ultimate end; in which no charm of diction or imagery could exempt the Bathyllus even of an Anacreon, or the Alexis of Virgil, from disgust and aversion!

But the communication of pleasure may be the immediate object of a work not metrically composed; and that object may have been in a high degree attained, as in novels and romances. Would then the mere superaddition of metre, with or without rhyme, entitle *these* to the name of poems? The answer is, that nothing can permanently please, which does not contain in itself the reason why it is so, and not otherwise. If metre be superadded, all other parts must be made consonant with it. They must be such, as to justify the perpetual and distinct attention to each part, which an exact correspondent recurrence of accent and sound are calculated to excite. The final definition then so deduced, may be thus worded. A poem is that species of composition, which is opposed to works of science, by proposing for its *immediate* object pleasure, not truth; and from all other species (having *this* object in common with it) it is discriminated by proposing to itself such delight from the *whole*, as is compatible with a distinct ratification from each component part.

Controversy is not seldom excited in consequence of the disputants attaching each a different meaning to the same word; and in few instances has this been more striking, than in disputes concerning the present subject. If a man chooses to call every composition a poem, which is rhyme, or measure, or both, I must leave his opinion uncontroverted. The distinction is at least competent to characterize the writer's intention. If it were subjoined, that the whole is likewise entertaining or affecting, as a tale, or as a series of interesting reflections, I of course admit this as another fit ingredient of a poem, and an additional merit. But if the definition sought for be that of a *legitimate* poem, I answer, it must be one, the parts of which mutually support and explain each other; all in their proportion harmonizing with, and supporting the purpose and known influences of metrical arrangement. The philosophic critics of all ages coincide with the ultimate judgement of all countries, in equally denying the praises of a just poem, on the one hand, to a series of striking lines or distiches [couplets], each of which, absorbing the whole attention of the reader to itself, disjoins it from its context, and makes it a separate whole, instead of an harmonizing part; and on the other hand, to an unsustained composition, from which the reader collects rapidly the general result, unattracted by the component parts. The reader should be carried forward, not merely or chiefly by the mechanical impulse of curiosity, or by a restless desire to arrive at the final solution; but by the pleasurable activity of mind excited by the attractions of the journey itself. Like the motion of a serpent, which the Egyptians made the emblem of intellectual power; or like the path of sound through the air; at every step he pauses and half recedes, and from the retrogressive movement collects the force which again carries him onward. "Praecipitandus est *liber* spiritus" [The free spirit must be hurried onward], says Petronius Arbiter most happily. The epithet, liber, here balances the preceding verb; and it is not easy to conceive more meaning condensed in fewer words.

But if this should be admitted as a satisfactory character of a poem, we have still to seek for a definition of poetry. The writings of PLATO, and Bishop TAYLOR, and the *Theoria Sacra* of BURNET, furnish undeniable proofs that poetry of the highest kind may exist without metre, and even without the contra-distinguishing objects of a poem. The first chapter of [the Bible's book of] Isaiah (indeed a very large proportion of the whole book) is poetry in the most emphatic sense; yet it would be not less irrational than strange to assert, that pleasure, and not truth, was the immediate object of the prophet. In short, whatever *specific* import we attach to the word, poetry, there will be found involved in it, as a necessary consequence, that a poem of any length neither can be, or ought to be, all poetry. Yet if an harmonious whole is to be produced, the remaining parts must be preserved *in keeping* with the poetry; and this can be no otherwise effected than by such a studied selection and artificial arrangement, as will partake of *one*, though not *peculiar*, property of poetry. And this again can be no other than the property of exciting a more continuous and equal attention than the language of prose aims at, whether colloquial or written.

My own conclusions on the nature of poetry, in the strictest use of the word, have been in part anticipated in the preceding disquisition on the fancy and imagination. What is poetry? is so nearly the same question with, what is a poet? that the answer to the one is involved in the solution of the other. For it is a distinction resulting from the poetic genius itself, which sustains and modifies the images, thoughts, and emotions of the poet's own mind.

The poet, described in *ideal* perfection, brings the whole soul of man into activity, with the subordination of its faculties to each other, according to their relative worth and dignity. He diffuses a tone and spirit of unity, that blends, and (as it were) *fuses*, each into each, by that synthetic and magical power, to which we have exclusively appropriated the name of imagination. This power, first put in action by the will and understanding, and retained under their irremissive, though gentle and unnoticed, controul (*laxis effertur habenis* [it is carried onwards with loose reins]) reveals itself in the balance or reconciliation of opposite or discordant qualities: of sameness, with difference; of the general, with the concrete; the idea, with the image; the individual, with the representative; the sense of novelty and freshness, with old and familiar objects; a more than usual state of emotion, with more than usual order; judgement ever awake and steady self-possession, with enthusiasm and feeling profound or vehement; and while it blends and harmonizes the natural and the artificial, still subordinates art to nature; the manner to the matter; and our admiration of the poet to our sympathy with the poetry. "Doubtless," as Sir John Davies observes of the soul (and his words may with slight alteration be applied, and even more appropriately to the poetic IMAGINATION),

> Doubtless this could not be, but that she turns
>   Bodies to spirit by sublimation strange,
> As fire converts to fire the things it burns,
>   As we our food into our nature change.
>
> From their gross matter she abstracts their forms,
>   And draws a kind of quintessence from things;
> Which to her proper nature she transforms,
>   To bear them light, on her celestial wings.
>
> Thus does she, when from individual states
>   She doth abstract the universal kinds;
> Which then re-clothed in divers names and fates
>   Steal access through our senses to our minds.

[Coleridge's adaptation of Sir John Davies (1570–1626) "On the Soul of Man, and the Immortality thereof"]

Finally, GOOD SENSE is the BODY of poetic genius, FANCY its DRAPERY, MOTION its LIFE, and IMAGINATION the SOUL that is everywhere, and in each; and forms all into one graceful and intelligent whole.

George Gordon Byron (1788–1824)

George Gordon Byron, better known as Lord Byron, may have been the most famous Englishman of his day. Every element of his life became tabloid fodder: the sensuality of his poetry, the hot-tempered satires savaging his literary contemporaries, his complicated sex life, his revolutionary politics, his devotion to the cause of Greek liberation, and his sudden death en route to a military engagement against the Turks. Although today he is remembered most often for his close and checkered friendship with Percy Shelley, he was a great poet in his own right; and despite his romantic sensibilities, he had strong classical leanings. His poem Hints from Horace, *written in 1811 and published after his death in 1831, is a version of Horace's* Ars Poetica *(see page 17), reworked as a satire on the state of English poetry. In the following extract, he considers, somewhat ambivalently, the issues of praise and criticism.*

from *Hints from Horace*

Ye, who aspire to "build the lofty rhyme,"
Believe not all who laud your false "sublime";
But if some friend shall hear your work, and say,
"Expunge that stanza, lop that line away,"
And, after fruitless efforts, you return
Without amendment, and he answers, "Burn!"
That instant throw your paper in the fire,
Ask not his thoughts, or follow his desire;
But (if true Bard!) you scorn to condescend,
And will not alter what you can't defend,
If you will breed this Bastard of your Brains,
We'll have no words – I've only lost my pains.

Yet, if you only prize your favourite thought,
As critics kindly do, and authors ought;
If your cool friend annoy you now and then,
And cross whole pages with his plaguy pen;
No matter, throw your ornaments aside, –

Better let him than all the world deride.
Give light to passages too much in shade,
Nor let a doubt obscure one verse you've made;
Your friend's a "Johnson," not to leave one word,
However trifling, which may seem absurd;
Such erring trifles lead to serious ills,
And furnish food for critics, or their quills.

Percy Bysshe Shelley   (1792–1822)

Percy Bysshe Shelley wrote his long essay "A Defence of Poetry" in 1821 as a furious response to his friend Thomas Love Peacock's 1820 satirical essay "The Four Ages of Poetry," which declared that "a poet in our times is a semi-barbarian in a civilized community. He lives in the days that are past. His ideas, thoughts, feelings, associates, are all with barbarous manners, obsolete customs, and exploded superstitions. The march of his intellect is like that of a crab, backward." Shelley could not tolerate such cynicism, insisting instead that "a poem is the very image of life expressed in its eternal truth" and that poets are "the mirrors of the gigantic shadows which futurity casts upon the present."

A Defence of Poetry

According to one mode of regarding those two classes of mental action, which are called reason and imagination, the former may be considered as mind contemplating the relations borne by one thought to another, however produced; and the latter, as mind acting upon those thoughts so as to color them with its own light, and composing from them, as from elements, other thoughts, each containing within itself the principle of its own integrity. The one is the το ποιειν, or the principle of synthesis, and has for its objects those forms which are common to universal nature and existence itself; the other is the το λογιϛειν, or principle of analysis, and its action regards the relations of things simply as relations; considering thoughts, not in their integral unity, but as the algebraical representations which conduct to certain general results. Reason is the enumeration of qualities already known; imagination is the perception of the value of those qualities, both separately and as a whole. Reason respects the differences, and imagination the similitudes of things. Reason is to imagination as the instrument to the agent, as the body to the spirit, as the shadow to the substance.

Poetry, in a general sense, may be defined to be "the expression of the imagination": and poetry is connate with the origin of man. Man is an instrument over which a series of external and internal impressions are driven, like the alternations of an ever-changing wind over an Aeolian lyre, which move it by their motion to ever-changing melody. But there is a principle within the human being, and perhaps within all sentient beings, which acts otherwise than in a lyre, and produces not melody alone, but harmony, by an internal adjustment of the sounds or motions thus excited to the impressions which excite them. It is as if the lyre could accommodate its chords to the motions of that which strikes them, in a determined proportion of sound; even as the musician can accommodate his voice to the sound of the lyre. A child at play by itself will express its delight by its voice and motions; and every inflexion of tone and every gesture will bear exact relation to a corresponding antitype in the pleasurable impressions which awakened it; it will be the reflected image of that impression; and as the lyre trembles and sounds after the wind has died away; so the child seeks, by prolonging in its voice and motions the duration of the effect, to prolong also a consciousness of the cause. In relation to the objects which delight a child, these expressions are what poetry is to higher objects. The savage (for the savage is to ages what the child is to years) expresses the emotions produced in him by surrounding objects in a similar manner; and language and gesture, together with plastic or pictorial imitation, become the image of the combined effect of those objects, and of his apprehension of them. Man in society, with all his passions and his pleasures, next becomes the object of the passions and pleasures of man; an additional class of emotions produces an augmented treasure of expression; and language, gesture, and the imitative arts, become at once the representation and the medium, the pencil and the picture, the chisel and the statue, the chord and the harmony. The social sympathies, or those laws from which, as from its elements, society results, begin to develop themselves from the moment that two human beings coexist; the future is contained within the present as the plant within the seed; and equality, diversity, unity, contrast, mutual dependence, become the principles alone capable of affording the motives according to which the will of a social being is determined to action, inasmuch as he is social; and constitute pleasure in sensation, virtue in sentiment, beauty in art, truth in reasoning, and love in the intercourse of kind. Hence men, even in the infancy of society, observe a certain order in their words and actions, distinct from that of the objects and the impressions represented by them, all expression being subject to the laws of that from which it proceeds. But let us dismiss those more general considerations which might involve an inquiry into the principles of society itself, and restrict our view to the manner in which the imagination is expressed upon its forms.

In the youth of the world, men dance and sing and imitate natural objects, observing in these actions, as in all others, a certain rhythm or order. And, although all men observe a similar, they observe not the same order, in the motions of the dance, in the melody of the song, in the combinations of language, in the series of their imitations of natural objects. For there is a certain order or rhythm belonging to each of these classes of mimetic representation, from which the hearer and the spectator receive an intenser and purer pleasure than from any other: the sense of an approximation to this order has been called taste by modern writers. Every man in the infancy of art, observes an order which approximates more or less closely to that from which this highest delight results: but the diversity is not sufficiently marked, as that its gradations should be sensible, except in those instances where the predominance of this faculty of approximation to the beautiful (for so we may be permitted to name the relation between this highest pleasure and its cause) is very great. Those in whom it exists in excess are poets, in the most universal sense of the word; and the pleasure resulting from the manner in which they express the influence of society or nature upon their own minds, communicates itself to others, and gathers a sort of reduplication from that community. Their language is vitally metaphorical; that is, it marks the before unapprehended relations of things and perpetuates their apprehension, until words, which represent them, become, through time, signs for portions or classes of thought, instead of pictures of integral thoughts; and then, if no new poets should arise to create afresh the associations which have been thus disorganised, language will be dead to all the nobler purposes of human intercourse. These similitudes or relations are finely said by [seventeenth-century philosopher and scientist] Lord Bacon to be "the same footsteps of nature impressed upon the various subjects of the world"[1] – and he considers the faculty which perceives them as the storehouse of axioms common to all knowledge. In the infancy of society every author is necessarily a poet, because language itself is poetry; and to be a poet is to apprehend the true and the beautiful, in a word, the good which exists in the relation, subsisting, first between existence and perception, and secondly between perception and expression. Every original language near to its source is in itself the chaos of a cyclic poem: the copiousness of lexicography and the distinctions of grammar are the works of a later age, and are merely the catalogue and the form of the creations of poetry.

But poets, or those who imagine and express this indestructible order, are not only the authors of language and of music, of the dance, and architecture, and statuary, and painting; they are the institutors of laws and the founders of civil society, and the inventors of the arts of life, and the teachers, who draw into a certain propinquity with the beautiful and the true,

---

[1] "De Augment. Scient.," cap. i, lib. iii [Shelley's note].

that partial apprehension of the agencies of the invisible world which is called religion. Hence all original religions are allegorical or susceptible of allegory, and, like Janus, have a double face of false and true. Poets, according to the circumstances of the age and nation in which they appeared, were called, in the earlier epochs of the world, legislators or prophets: a poet essentially comprises and unites both these characters. For he not only beholds intensely the present as it is, and discovers those laws according to which present things ought to be ordered, but he beholds the future in the present, and his thoughts are the germs of the flower and the fruit of latest time. Not that I assert poets to be prophets in the gross sense of the word, or that they can foretell the form as surely as they foreknow the spirit of events: such is the pretence of superstition, which would make poetry an attribute of prophecy, rather than prophecy an attribute of poetry. A poet participates in the eternal, the infinite, and the one; as far as relates to his conceptions, time and place and number are not. The grammatical forms which express the moods of time, and the difference of persons, and the distinction of place, are convertible with respect to the highest poetry without injuring it as poetry; and the choruses of Aeschylus, and the book of Job, and Dante's Paradise, would afford, more than any other writings, examples of this fact, if the limits of this essay did not forbid citation. The creations of sculpture, painting, and music, are illustrations still more decisive.

Language, colour, form, and religious and civil habits of action, are all the instruments and materials of poetry; they may be called poetry by that figure of speech which considers the effect as a synonyme of the cause. But poetry in a more restricted sense expresses those arrangements of language, and especially metrical language, which are created by that imperial faculty, whose throne is curtained within the invisible nature of man. And this springs from the nature itself of language, which is a more direct representation of the actions and passions of our internal being, and is susceptible of more various and delicate combinations, than colour, form, or motion, and is more plastic and obedient to the control of that faculty of which it is the creation. For language is arbitrarily produced by the imagination, and has relation to thoughts alone; but all other materials, instruments, and conditions of art have relations among each other, which limit and interpose between conception and expression. The former is as a mirror which reflects, the latter as a cloud which enfeebles, the light of which both are mediums of communication. Hence the fame of sculptors, painters, and musicians, although the intrinsic powers of the great masters of these arts may yield in no degree to that of those who have employed language as the hieroglyphic of their thoughts, has never equalled that of poets in the restricted sense of the term; as two performers of equal skill will produce unequal effects from a guitar and a harp. The fame of legislators and founders of religions, so long as their institutions last, alone seems to exceed that of poets in the restricted sense; but it can scarcely be a question, whether, if we deduct the celebrity which their flattery of the gross opinions of the vulgar usually conciliates, together with that which belonged to them in their higher character of poets, any excess will remain.

We have thus circumscribed the word poetry within the limits of that art which is the most familiar and the most perfect expression of the faculty itself. It is necessary, however, to make the circle still narrower, and to determine the distinction between measured and unmeasured language; for the popular division into prose and verse is inadmissible in accurate philosophy.

Sounds as well as thoughts have relation both between each other and towards that which they represent, and a perception of the order of those relations has always been found connected with a perception of the order of the relations of thoughts. Hence the language of poets has ever affected a certain uniform and harmonious recurrence of sound, without which it were not poetry, and which is scarcely less indispensable to the communication of its influence, than the words themselves, without reference to that peculiar order. Hence the vanity of translation; it were as wise to cast a violet into a crucible that you might discover the formal principle of its colour and odour, as seek to transfuse from one language into another the creations of a poet. The plant must spring again from its seed, or it will bear no flower – and this is the burden of the curse of Babel.

An observation of the regular mode of the recurrence of harmony in the language of poetical minds, together with its relation to music, produced metre, or a certain system of traditional forms of harmony and language. Yet it is by no means essential that a poet should accommodate his language to this traditional form, so that the harmony, which is its spirit, be observed. The practice is indeed convenient and popular, and to be preferred, especially in such composition as includes much action: but every great poet must inevitably innovate upon the example of his predecessors in the exact structure of his peculiar versification. The distinction between poets and prose writers is a vulgar error. The distinction between philosophers and poets has been anticipated. Plato was essentially a poet – the truth and splendour of his imagery, and the melody of his language, are the most intense that it is possible to conceive. He rejected the measure of the epic, dramatic, and lyrical forms, because he sought to kindle a harmony in thoughts divested of shape and action, and he forbore to invent any regular plan of rhythm which would include, under determinate forms, the varied pauses of his style. Cicero sought to imitate the cadence of his periods, but with little success. Lord Bacon was a poet.[2] His language has a sweet and majestic rhythm, which satisfies the sense, no less than the almost superhuman wisdom of his philosophy satisfies the intellect; it is a strain which distends, and then bursts the circumference of the reader's mind, and pours itself forth together with it into the universal element with which it has perpetual sympathy. All the authors of revolutions in opinion are not only necessarily poets as they are inventors, nor even as their words unveil the permanent analogy of things by images which participate in the life of truth; but as their periods are harmonious and rhythmical, and contain in themselves the elements of verse; being the echo of the eternal music. Nor are those supreme poets, who have employed traditional forms of rhythm on account of the form and action of their subjects, less capable of perceiving and teaching the truth of things, than those who have omitted that form. Shak[e]speare, Dante, and Milton (to confine ourselves to modern writers) are philosophers of the very loftiest power.

A poem is the very image of life expressed in its eternal truth. There is this difference between a story and a poem, that a story is a catalogue of detached facts, which have no other connexion than time, place, circumstance, cause, and effect; the other is the creation of actions according to the unchangeable forms of human nature, as existing in the mind of the Creator, which is itself the image of all other minds. The one is partial, and applies only to a definite period of time, and a certain combination of events which can never again recur; the other is universal, and contains within itself the germ of a relation to whatever motives or actions have place in the possible varieties of human nature. Time, which destroys the beauty and the use of the story of particular facts, stripped of the poetry which should invest them, augments that of poetry, and for ever develops new and wonderful applications of the eternal truth which it contains. Hence epitomes have been called the moths of just history; they eat out the poetry of it. A story of particular facts is as a mirror which obscures and distorts that which should be beautiful; poetry is a mirror which makes beautiful that which is distorted.

The parts of a composition may be poetical, without the composition as a whole being a poem. A single sentence may be considered as a whole, though it may be found in the midst of a series of unassimilated portions; a single word even may be a spark of inextinguishable thought. And thus all the great historians, Herodotus, Plutarch, Livy, were poets; and although the plan of these writers, especially that of Livy, restrained them from developing this faculty in its highest degree, they made copious and ample

[2] See the Filium Labyrinthi, and the Essay on Death particularly [Shelley's note].

amends for their subjection, by filling all the interstices of their subjects with living images.

Having determined what is poetry, and who are poets, let us proceed to estimate its effects upon society.

Poetry is ever accompanied with pleasure: all spirits on which it falls open themselves to receive the wisdom which is mingled with its delight. In the infancy of the world, neither poets themselves nor their auditors are fully aware of the excellence of poetry: for it acts in a divine and unapprehended manner, beyond and above consciousness; and it is reserved for future generations to contemplate and measure the mighty cause and effect in all the strength and splendour of their union. Even in modern times, no living poet ever arrived at the fullness of his fame; the jury which sits in judgment upon a poet, belonging as he does to all time, must be composed of his peers: it must be empanelled by time from the selectest of the wise of many generations. A poet is a nightingale, who sits in darkness and sings to cheer its own solitude with sweet sounds; his auditors are as men entranced by the melody of an unseen musician, who feel that they are moved and softened, yet know not whence or why. The poems of Homer and his contemporaries were the delight of infant Greece; they were the elements of that social system which is the column upon which all succeeding civilisation has reposed. Homer embodied the ideal perfection of his age in human character; nor can we doubt that those who read his verses were awakened to an ambition of becoming like to Achilles, Hector, and Ulysses: the truth and beauty of friendship, patriotism, and persevering devotion to an object, were unveiled to the depths in these immortal creations: the sentiments of the auditors must have been refined and enlarged by a sympathy with such great and lovely impersonations, until from admiring they imitated, and from imitation they identified themselves with the objects of their admiration. Nor let it be objected, that these characters are remote from moral perfection, and that they are by no means to be considered as edifying patterns for general imitation. Every epoch, under names more or less specious, has deified its peculiar errors; Revenge is the naked idol of the worship of a semibarbarous age; and Self-deceit is the veiled image of unknown evil, before which luxury and satiety lie prostrate. But a poet considers the vices of his contemporaries as the temporary dress in which his creations must be arrayed, and which cover without concealing the eternal proportions of their beauty. An epic or dramatic personage is understood to wear them around his soul, as he may the ancient armour or modern uniform around his body; whilst it is easy to conceive a dress more graceful than either. The beauty of the internal nature cannot be so far concealed by its accidental vesture, but that the spirit of its form shall communicate itself to the very disguise, and indicate the shape it hides from the manner in which it is worn. A majestic form and graceful motions will express themselves through the most barbarous and tasteless costume. Few poets of the highest class have chosen to exhibit the beauty of their conceptions in its naked truth and splendour; and it is doubtful whether the alloy of costume, habit, &c., be not necessary to temper this planetary music for mortal ears.

The whole objection, however, of the immorality of poetry rests upon a misconception of the manner in which poetry acts to produce the moral improvement of man. Ethical science arranges the elements which poetry has created, and propounds schemes and proposes examples of civil and domestic life: nor is it for want of admirable doctrines that men hate, and despise, and censure, and deceive, and subjugate one another. But poetry acts in another and diviner manner. It awakens and enlarges the mind itself by rendering it the receptacle of a thousand unapprehended combinations of thought. Poetry lifts the veil from the hidden beauty of the world, and makes familiar objects be as if they were not familiar; it reproduces all that it represents, and the impersonations clothed in its Elysian light stand thenceforward in the minds of those who have once contemplated them, as memorials of that gentle and exalted content which extends itself over all thoughts and actions with which it coexists. The great secret of morals is love; or a going out of our own nature, and an identification of ourselves with the beautiful which exists in thought, action, or person, not our own. A man, to be greatly good, must imagine intensely and comprehensively; he must put himself in the place of another and of many others; the pains and pleasures of his species must become his own. The great instrument of moral good is the imagination; and poetry administers to the effect by acting upon the cause. Poetry enlarges the circumference of the imagination by replenishing it with thoughts of ever new delight, which have the power of attracting and assimilating to their own nature all other thoughts, and which form new intervals and interstices whose void for ever craves fresh food. Poetry strengthens the faculty which is the organ of the moral nature of man, in the same manner as exercise strengthens a limb. A poet therefore would do ill to embody his own conceptions of right and wrong, which are usually those of his place and time, in his poetical creations, which participate in neither. By this assumption of the inferior office of interpreting the effect, in which perhaps after all he might acquit himself but imperfectly, he would resign a glory in the participation of the cause. There was little danger that Homer, or any of the eternal poets, should have so far misunderstood themselves as to have abdicated this throne of their widest dominion. Those in whom the poetical faculty, though great, is less intense, as Euripides, [Roman poet] Lucan, [sixteenth-century Italian poet] Tasso, Spenser, have frequently affected a moral aim, and the effect of their poetry is diminished in exact proportion to the degree in which they compel us to advert to this purpose.

Homer and the cyclic poets were followed at a certain interval by the dramatic and lyrical poets of Athens, who flourished contemporaneously with all that is most perfect in the kindred expressions of the poetical faculty; architecture, painting, music, the dance, sculpture, philosophy, and we may add, the forms of civil life. For although the scheme of Athenian society was deformed by many imperfections which the poetry existing in chivalry and Christianity has erased from the habits and institutions of modern Europe; yet never at any other period has so much energy, beauty and virtue, been developed; never was blind strength and stubborn form so disciplined and rendered subject to the will of man, or that will less repugnant to the dictates of the beautiful and the true, as during the century which preceded the death of Socrates. Of no other epoch in the history of our species have we records and fragments stamped so visibly with the image of the divinity in man. But it is poetry alone, in form, in action, and in language, which has rendered this epoch memorable above all others, and the storehouse of examples to everlasting time. For written poetry existed at that epoch simultaneously with the other arts, and it is an idle inquiry to demand which gave and which received the light, which all, as from a common focus, have scattered over the darkest periods of succeeding time. We know no more of cause and effect than a constant conjunction of events: poetry is ever found to coexist with whatever other arts contribute to the happiness and perfection of man. I appeal to what has already been established to distinguish between the cause and the effect.

It was at the period here adverted to, that the drama had its birth; and however a succeeding writer may have equalled or surpassed those few great specimens of the Athenian drama which have been preserved to us, it is indisputable that the art itself never was understood or practised according to the true philosophy of it, as at Athens. For the Athenians employed language, action, music, painting, the dance, and religious institutions, to produce a common effect in the representation of the highest idealisms of passion and of power; each division in the art was made perfect in its kind by artists of the most consummate skill, and was disciplined into a beautiful proportion and unity one towards the other. On the modern stage a few only of the elements capable of expressing the image of the poet's conception are employed at once. We have tragedy without music and dancing; and music and dancing without the highest impersonations of which they are the fit accompaniment, and both without religion and solemnity. Re-

ligious institution has indeed been usually banished from the stage. Our
system of divesting the actor's face of a mask, on which the many expres-
sions appropriated to his dramatic character might be moulded into one
permanent and unchanging expression, is favourable only to a partial and
inharmonious effect; it is fit for nothing but a monologue, where all the
attention may be directed to some great master of ideal mimicry. The mod-
ern practice of blending comedy with tragedy, though liable to great abuse
in point of practice, is undoubtedly an extension of the dramatic circle; but
the comedy should be as in *King Lear*, universal, ideal, and sublime. It is
perhaps the intervention of this principle which determines the balance in
favor of *King Lear* against the *Oedipus Tyrannus* or the *Agamemnon*, or, if you
will, the trilogies with which they are connected; unless the intense power
of the choral poetry, especially that of the latter, should be considered as
restoring the equilibrium. *King Lear*, if it can sustain this comparison, may
be judged to be the most perfect specimen of the dramatic art existing in
the world; in spite of the narrow conditions to which the poet was subject-
ed by the ignorance of the philosophy of the drama which has prevailed in
modern Europe. [Seventeenth-century Spanish poet and dramatist Pedro]
Calderon, in his religious *Autos*, has attempted to fulfil some of the high
conditions of dramatic representation neglected by Shak[e]speare; such as
the establishing a relation between the drama and religion, and the ac-
commodating them to music and dancing; but he omits the observation of
conditions still more important, and more is lost than gained by the sub-
stitution of the rigidly-defined and ever-repeated idealisms of a distorted
superstition for the living impersonations of the truth of human passions.

But I digress. – The connection of scenic exhibitions with the improvement
or corruption of the manners of men, has been universally recognised: in
other words, the presence or absence of poetry in its most perfect and uni-
versal form, has been found to be connected with good and evil in conduct
or habit. The corruption which has been imputed to the drama as an effect,
begins, when the poetry employed in its constitution ends: I appeal to the
history of manners whether the periods of the growth of the one and the
decline of the other have not corresponded with an exactness equal to any
example of moral cause and effect.

The drama at Athens, or wheresoever else it may have approached to its
perfection, ever coexisted with the moral and intellectual greatness of the
age. The tragedies of the Athenian poets are as mirrors in which the specta-
tor beholds himself, under a thin disguise of circumstance, stript of all but
that ideal perfection and energy which everyone feels to be the internal
type of all that he loves, admires, and would become. The imagination is
enlarged by a sympathy with pains and passions so mighty, that they dis-

tend in their conception the capacity of that by which they are conceived, the good affections are strengthened by pity, indignation, terror and sorrow; and an exalted calm is prolonged from the satiety of this high exercise of them into the tumult of familiar life: even crime is disarmed of half its horror and all its contagion by being represented as the fatal consequence of the unfathomable agencies of nature; error is thus divested of its wilfulness; men can no longer cherish it as the creation of their choice. In the drama of the highest order there is little food for censure or hatred; it teaches rather self-knowledge and self-respect. Neither the eye nor the mind can see itself, unless reflected upon that which it resembles. The drama, so long as it continues to express poetry, is as a prismatic and many-sided mirror, which collects the brightest rays of human nature and divides and reproduces them from the simplicity of these elementary forms, and touches them with majesty and beauty, and multiplies all that it reflects, and endows it with the power of propagating its like wherever it may fall.

But in periods of the decay of social life, the drama sympathises with that decay. Tragedy becomes a cold imitation of the form of the great masterpieces of antiquity, divested of all harmonious accompaniment of the kindred arts; and often the very form misunderstood, or a weak attempt to teach certain doctrines, which the writer considers as moral truths; and which are usually no more than specious flatteries of some gross vice or weakness, with which the author, in common with his auditors, are infected. Hence what has been called the classical and domestic drama. [English dramatist Joseph] Addison's "Cato" [1713] is a specimen of the one; and would it were not superfluous to cite examples of the other! To such purposes poetry cannot be made subservient. Poetry is a sword of lightning, ever unsheathed, which consumes the scabbard that would contain it. And thus we observe that all dramatic writings of this nature are unimaginative in a singular degree; they affect sentiment and passion, which, divested of imagination, are other names for caprice and appetite. The period in our own history of the grossest degradation of the drama is the reign of Charles II, when all forms in which poetry had been accustomed to be expressed became hymns to the triumph of kingly power over liberty and virtue. Milton stood alone illuminating an age unworthy of him. At such periods the calculating principle pervades all the forms of dramatic exhibition, and poetry ceases to be expressed upon them. Comedy loses its ideal universality: wit succeeds to humour; we laugh from self-complacency and triumph, instead of pleasure; malignity, sarcasm, and contempt, succeed to sympathetic merriment; we hardly laugh, but we smile. Obscenity, which is ever blasphemy against the divine beauty in life, becomes, from the very veil which it assumes, more active if less disgusting: it is a monster for which the corruption of society for ever brings forth new food, which it devours in secret.

The drama being that form under which a greater number of modes of expression of poetry are susceptible of being combined than any other, the connexion of poetry and social good is more observable in the drama than in whatever other form. And it is indisputable that the highest perfection of human society has ever corresponded with the highest dramatic excellence; and that the corruption or the extinction of the drama in a nation where it has once flourished is a mark of a corruption of manners, and an extinction of the energies which sustain the soul of social life. But, as Machiavelli says of political institutions, that life may be preserved and renewed, if men should arise capable of bringing back the drama to its principles. And this is true with respect to poetry in its most extended sense: all language, institution, and form require not only to be produced but to be sustained: the office and character of a poet participates in the divine nature as regards providence, no less than as regards creation.

Civil war, the spoils of Asia, and the fatal predominance first of the Macedonian, and then of the Roman arms, were so many symbols of the extinction or suspension of the creative faculty in Greece. The bucolic writers, who found patronage under the lettered tyrants of Sicily and Egypt, were the latest representatives of its most glorious reign. Their poetry is intensely melodious; like the odour of the tuberose, it overcomes and sickens the spirit with excess of sweetness; whilst the poetry of the preceding age was as a meadow-gale of June, which mingles the fragrance of all the flowers of the field, and adds a quickening and harmonising spirit of its own which endows the sense with a power of sustaining its extreme delight. The bucolic and erotic delicacy in written poetry is correlative with that softness in statuary, music, and the kindred arts, and even in manners and institutions, which distinguished the epoch to which I now refer. Nor is it the poetical faculty itself, or any misapplication of it, to which this want of harmony is to be imputed. An equal sensibility to the influence of the senses and the affections is to be found in the writings of Homer and Sophocles: the former, especially, has clothed sensual and pathetic images with irresistible attractions. Their superiority in these to succeeding writers consists in the presence of those thoughts which belong to the inner faculties of our nature, not in the absence of those which are connected with the external: their incomparable perfection consists in a harmony of the union of all. It is not what the erotic poets have, but what they have not, in which their imperfection consists. It is not inasmuch as they were poets, but inasmuch as they were not poets, that they can be considered with any plausibility as connected with the corruption of their age. Had that corruption availed so as to extinguish in them the sensibility to pleasure, passion, and natural scenery, which is imputed to them as an imperfection, the last triumph of evil would have been achieved. For the end of social corruption is to destroy all sensibility to pleasure; and, therefore, it is corruption. It begins at the imagination and the intellect as at the core, and distributes itself thence as a paralysing venom, through the affections into the very appetites, until all become a torpid mass in which hardly sense survives. At the approach of such a period, poetry ever addresses itself to those faculties which are the last to be destroyed, and its voice is heard, like the footsteps of Astraea, departing from the world. Poetry ever communicates all the pleasure which men are capable of receiving: it is ever still the light of life; the source of whatever of beautiful or generous or true can have place in an evil time. It will readily be confessed that those among the luxurious citizens of Syracuse and Alexandria, who were delighted with the poems of Theocritus, were less cold, cruel, and sensual than the remnant of their tribe. But corruption must utterly have destroyed the fabric of human society before poetry can ever cease. The sacred links of that chain have never been entirely disjoined, which descending through the minds of many men is attached to those great minds, whence as from a magnet the invisible effluence is sent forth, which at once connects, animates, and sustains the life of all. It is the faculty which contains within itself the seeds at once of its own and of social renovation. And let us not circumscribe the effects of the bucolic and erotic poetry within the limits of the sensibility of those to whom it was addressed. They may have perceived the beauty of those immortal compositions, simply as fragments and isolated portions: those who are more finely organised, or born in a happier age, may recognise them as episodes to that great poem, which all poets, like the co-operating thoughts of one great mind, have built up since the beginning of the world.

The same revolutions within a narrower sphere had place in ancient Rome; but the actions and forms of its social life never seem to have been perfectly saturated with the poetical element. The Romans appear to have considered the Greeks as the selectest treasuries of the selectest forms of manners and of nature, and to have abstained from creating in measured language, sculpture, music, or architecture, any thing which might bear a particular relation to their own condition, whilst it should bear a general one to the universal constitution of the world. But we judge from partial evidence, and we judge perhaps partially. Ennius, Varro, Pacuvius, and Accius, all great poets, have been lost. Lucretius is in the highest, and Virgil in a very high sense, a creator. The chosen delicacy of expressions of the latter, are as a mist of light which conceal from us the intense and exceeding truth of his conceptions of nature. Livy is instinct with poetry. Yet Horace, Catullus, Ovid, and generally the other great writers of the Virgilian age, saw man and nature in the mirror of Greece. The institutions also, and the religion of Rome, were less poetical than those of Greece, as the shadow is less vivid than the substance. Hence poetry in Rome, seemed to follow, rather than accompany, the perfection of political and domestic society. The true poetry of Rome lived in its institutions; for whatever of beautiful, true, and majestic, they contained, could have sprung only from the faculty which creates the order in which they consist. The life of Camillus, the death of Regulus; the expectation of the senators, in their godlike state, of the victorious Gauls; the refusal of the republic to make peace with Hannibal, after the battle of Cannae, were not the consequences of a refined calculation of the probable personal advantage to result from such a rhythm and order in the shows of life, to those who were at once the poets and the actors of these immortal dramas. The imagination beholding the beauty of this order, created it out of itself according to its own idea; the consequence was empire, and the reward everlasting fame. These things are not the less poetry, *quia carent vate sacro* [because they lack the sacred bard]. They are the episodes of that cyclic poem written by Time upon the memories of men. The Past, like an inspired rhapsodist, fills the theatre of everlasting generations with their harmony.

At length the ancient system of religion and manners had fulfilled the circle of its evolutions. And the world would have fallen into utter anarchy and darkness, but that there were found poets among the authors of the Christian and chivalric systems of manners and religion, who created forms of opinion and action never before conceived; which, copied into the imaginations of men, became as generals to the bewildered armies of their thoughts. It is foreign to the present purpose to touch upon the evil produced by these systems: except that we protest, on the ground of the principles already established, that no portion of it can be attributed to the poetry they contain.

It is probable that the poetry of Moses, Job, David, Solomon, and Isaiah, had produced a great effect upon the mind of Jesus and his disciples. The scattered fragments preserved to us by the biographers of this extraordinary person, are all instinct with the most vivid poetry. But his doctrines seem to have been quickly distorted. At a certain period after the prevalence of a system of opinions founded upon those promulgated by him, the three forms into which Plato had distributed the faculties of mind underwent a sort of apotheosis, and became the object of the worship of the civilised world. Here it is to be confessed that "Light seems to thicken," and

> "The crow makes wing to the rooky wood,

Good things of day begin to droop and drowse,
And night's black agents to their preys do rouse."
[from Shakespeare's *Macbeth*]

But mark how beautiful an order has sprung from the dust and blood of this fierce chaos! how the world, as from a resurrection, balancing itself on the golden wings of knowledge and of hope, has reassumed its yet unwearied flight into the heaven of time. Listen to the music, unheard by outward ears, which is as a ceaseless and invisible wind, nourishing its everlasting course with strength and swiftness.

The poetry in the doctrines of Jesus Christ, and the mythology and institutions of the Celtic conquerors of the Roman Empire, outlived the darkness and the convulsions connected with their growth and victory, and blended themselves in a new fabric of manners and opinion. It is an error to impute the ignorance of the dark ages to the Christian doctrines or the predominance of the Celtic nations. Whatever of evil their agencies may have contained sprang from the extinction of the poetical principle, connected with the progress of despotism and superstition. Men, from causes too intricate to be here discussed, had become insensible and selfish: their own will had become feeble, and yet they were its slaves, and thence the slaves of the will of others: but fear, avarice, cruelty, and fraud, characterised a race amongst whom no one was to be found capable of creating in form, language, or institution. The moral anomalies of such a state of society are not justly to be charged upon any class of events immediately connected with them, and those events are most entitled to our approbation which could dissolve it most expeditiously. It is unfortunate for those who cannot distinguish words from thoughts, that many of these anomalies have been incorporated into our popular religion.

It was not until the eleventh century that the effects of the poetry of the Christian and chivalric systems began to manifest themselves. The principle of equality had been discovered and applied by Plato in his Republic, as the theoretical rule of the mode in which the materials of pleasure and of power produced by the common skill and labour of human beings ought to be distributed among them. The limitations of this rule were asserted by him to be determined only by the sensibility of each, or the utility to result to all. Plato, following the doctrines of Timaeus [a speaker in one of his dialogues] and Pythagoras, taught also a moral and intellectual system of doctrine, comprehending at once the past, the present, and the future condition of man. Jesus Christ divulged the sacred and eternal truths contained in these views to mankind, and Christianity, in its abstract purity, became the exoteric expression of the esoteric doctrines of the poetry and wisdom of antiquity. The incorporation of the Celtic nations with the exhausted population of the south, impressed upon it the figure of the poetry existing in their mythology and institutions. The result was a sum of the action and reaction of all the causes included in it; for it may be assumed as a maxim that no nation or religion can supersede any other without incorporating into itself a portion of that which it supersedes. The abolition of personal and domestic slavery, and the emancipation of women from a great part of the degrading restraints of antiquity, were among the consequences of these events.

The abolition of personal slavery is the basis of the highest political hope that it can enter into the mind of man to conceive. The freedom of women produced the poetry of sexual love. Love became a religion, the idols of whose worship were ever present. It was as if the statues of Apollo and the Muses had been endowed with life and motion, and had walked forth among their worshippers; so that earth became peopled with the inhabitants of a diviner world. The familiar appearance and proceedings of life became wonderful and heavenly, and a paradise was created as out of the wrecks of Eden. And as this creation itself is poetry, so its creators were poets; and language was the instrument of their art: "Galeotto fù il libro, e chi lo scrisse" [Galeotto was the book and he who wrote it]. The Provençal Trouveurs [troubadors], or inventors, preceded Petrarch, whose verses are as spells, which unseal the inmost enchanted fountains of the delight which is in the grief of love. It is impossible to feel them without becoming a portion of that beauty which we contemplate: it were superfluous to explain how the gentleness and the elevation of mind connected with these sacred emotions can render men more amiable, more generous and wise, and lift them out of the dull vapours of the little world of self. Dante understood the secret things of love even more than Petrarch. His *Vita Nuova* is an inexhaustible fountain of purity of sentiment and language: it is the idealized history of that period, and those intervals of his life which were dedicated to love. His apotheosis of Beatrice in Paradise, and the gradations of his own love and her loveliness, by which as by steps he feigns himself to have ascended to the throne of the Supreme Cause, is the most glorious imagination of modern poetry. The acutest critics have justly reversed the judgment of the vulgar, and the order of the great acts of the "Divine Drama," in the measure of the admiration which they accord to the Hell, Purgatory, and Paradise. The latter is a perpetual hymn of everlasting love. Love, which found a worthy poet in Plato alone of all the ancients, has been celebrated by a chorus of the greatest writers of the renovated world; and the music has penetrated the caverns of society, and its echoes still drown the dissonance of arms and superstition. At successive intervals, [fifteenth-century Italian poet] Ariosto, Tasso, Shak[e]speare, Spenser,

Calderon, Rousseau, and the great writers of our own age, have celebrated the dominion of love, planting as it were trophies in the human mind of that sublimest victory over sensuality and force. The true relation borne to each other by the sexes into which humankind is distributed has become less misunderstood; and if the error which confounded diversity with inequality of the powers of the two sexes has been partially recognised in the opinions and institutions of modern Europe, we owe this great benefit to the worship of which chivalry was the law, and poets the prophets.

The poetry of Dante may be considered as the bridge thrown over the stream of time, which unites the modern and ancient world. The distorted notions of invisible things which Dante and his rival Milton have idealised, are merely the mask and the mantle in which these great poets walk through eternity enveloped and disguised. It is a difficult question to determine how far they were conscious of the distinction which must have subsisted in their minds between their own creeds and that of the people. Dante at least appears to wish to mark the full extent of it by placing [the Trojan] Rhipaeus, whom Virgil calls *justissimus unus* [the one who is most just], in Paradise, and observing a most heretical caprice in his distribution of rewards and punishments. And Milton's poem contains within itself a philosophical refutation of that system of which, by a strange and natural antithesis, it has been a chief popular support. Nothing can exceed the energy and magnificence of the character of Satan as expressed in "Paradise Lost." It is a mistake to suppose that he could ever have been intended for the popular personification of evil. Implacable hate, patient cunning, and a sleepless refinement of device to inflict the extremest anguish on an enemy, these things are evil; and, although venial in a slave, are not to be forgiven in a tyrant; although redeemed by much that ennobles his defeat in one subdued, are marked by all that dishonours his conquest in the victor. Milton's Devil as a moral being is as far superior to his God, as one who perseveres in some purpose which he has conceived to be excellent in spite of adversity and torture, is to one who in the cold security of undoubted triumph inflicts the most horrible revenge upon his enemy, not from any mistaken notion of inducing him to repent of a perseverance in enmity, but with the alleged design of exasperating him to deserve new torments. Milton has so far violated the popular creed (if this shall be judged to be a violation) as to have alleged no superiority of moral virtue to his god over his devil. And this bold neglect of a direct moral purpose is the most decisive proof of the supremacy of Milton's genius. He mingled as it were the elements of human nature as colours upon a single pallet, and arranged them in the composition of his great picture according to the laws of epic truth, that is, according to the laws of that principle by which a series of actions of the external universe and of intelligent and ethical beings is calculated to excite the sympathy of succeeding generations of mankind. The *Divina Commedia* and *Paradise Lost* have conferred upon modern mythology a systematic form; and when change and time shall have added one more superstition to the mass of those which have arisen and decayed upon the earth, commentators will be learnedly employed in elucidating the religion of ancestral Europe, only not utterly forgotten because it will have been stamped with the eternity of genius.

Homer was the first and Dante the second epic poet: that is, the second poet, the series of whose creations bore a defined and intelligible relation to the knowledge and sentiment and religion of the age in which he lived, and of the ages which followed it: developing itself in correspondence with their development. For Lucretius had limed the wings of his swift spirit in the dregs of the sensible world; and Virgil, with a modesty that ill became his genius, had affected the fame of an imitator, even whilst he created anew all that he copied; and none among the flock of mock-birds, though their notes are sweet, Apollonius Rhodius, Quintus Calaber Smyrnaeus, Nonnus, Lucan, Statius, or Claudian [all poets of antiquity], have sought even to fulfil a single condition of epic truth. Milton was the third epic poet. For if the title of epic in its highest sense be refused to the *Aeneid*, still less can it be conceded to the *Orlando Furioso* [of Ariosto], the *Gerusalemme Liberata* [of Tasso], the *Lusiad* [by sixteenth-century Portuguese poet Luís Vaz de Camões], or the *Fairy Queen* [by Spenser].

Dante and Milton were both deeply penetrated with the ancient religion of the civilised world; and its spirit exists in their poetry probably in the same proportion as its forms survived in the unreformed worship of modern Europe. The one preceded and the other followed the Reformation at almost equal intervals. Dante was the first religious reformer, and Luther surpassed him rather in the rudeness and acrimony, than in the boldness of his censures, of papal usurpation. Dante was the first awakener of entranced Europe; he created a language, in itself music and persuasion, out of a chaos of inharmonious barbarisms. He was the congregator of those great spirits who presided over the resurrection of learning; the Lucifer of that starry flock which in the thirteenth century shone forth from republican Italy, as from a heaven, into the darkness of the benighted world. His very words are instinct with spirit; each is as a spark, a burning atom of inextinguishable thought; and many yet lie covered in the ashes of their birth, and pregnant with the lightning which has yet found no conductor. All high poetry is infinite; it is as the first acorn, which contained all oaks potentially. Veil after veil may be undrawn, and the inmost naked beauty of the meaning never exposed. A great poem is a fountain forever overflowing with the waters of wisdom and delight; and after one person and one age has exhausted all its divine effluence which their peculiar relations enable them to share, another and yet another succeeds, and new relations are ever developed, the source of an unforeseen and an unconceived delight.

The age immediately succeeding to that of Dante, Petrarch, and Boccaccio, was characterised by a revival of painting, sculpture, and architecture. Chaucer caught the sacred inspiration, and the superstructure of English literature is based upon the materials of Italian invention.

But let us not be betrayed from a defence into a critical history of poetry and its influence on society. Be it enough to have pointed out the effects of poets, in the large and true sense of the word, upon their own and all succeeding times.

But poets have been challenged to resign the civic crown to reasoners and mechanists, on another plea. It is admitted that the exercise of the imagination is most delightful, but it is alleged that that of reason is more useful. Let us examine, as the grounds of this distinction, what is here meant by utility. Pleasure or good, in a general sense, is that which the consciousness of a sensitive and intelligent being seeks, and in which, when found, it acquiesces. There are two kinds of pleasure, one durable, universal and permanent; the other transitory and particular. Utility may either express the means of producing the former or the latter. In the former sense, whatever strengthens and purifies the affections, enlarges the imagination, and adds spirit to sense, is useful. But a narrower meaning may be assigned to the word utility, confining it to express that which banishes the importunity of the wants of our animal nature, the surrounding men with security of life, the dispersing the grosser delusions of superstition, and the conciliating such a degree of mutual forbearance among men as may consist with the motives of personal advantage.

Undoubtedly the promoters of utility, in this limited sense, have their appointed office in society. They follow the footsteps of poets, and copy the sketches of their creations into the book of common life. They make space, and give time. Their exertions are of the highest value, so long as they confine their administration of the concerns of the inferior powers of our nature within the limits due to the superior ones. But whilst the sceptic destroys gross superstitions, let him spare to deface, as some of the French writers have defaced, the eternal truths charactered upon the imaginations of men. Whilst the mechanist abridges, and the political economist combines, labour, let them beware that their speculations, for want of correspondence with those first principles which belong to the imagination, do not tend, as they have in modern England, to exasperate at once the extremes of luxury and want. They have exemplified the saying, "To him that hath, more shall be given; and from him that hath not, the little that he hath shall be taken away." The rich have become richer, and the poor have become poorer; and the vessel of the state is driven between the Scylla and Charybdis of anarchy and despotism. Such are the effects which must ever flow from an unmitigated exercise of the calculating faculty.

It is difficult to define pleasure in its highest sense; the definition involving a number of apparent paradoxes. For, from an inexplicable defect of harmony in the constitution of human nature, the pain of the inferior is frequently connected with the pleasures of the superior portions of our being. Sorrow, terror, anguish, despair itself, are often the chosen expressions of an approximation to the highest good. Our sympathy in tragic fiction depends on this principle; tragedy delights by affording a shadow of that pleasure which exists in pain. This is the source also of the melancholy which is inseparable from the sweetest melody. The pleasure that is in sorrow is sweeter than the pleasure of pleasure itself. And hence the saying, "It is better to go to the house of mourning than to the house of mirth." Not that this highest species of pleasure is necessarily linked with pain. The delight of love and friendship, the ecstasy of the admiration of nature, the joy of the perception and still more of the creation of poetry, is often wholly unalloyed.

The production and assurance of pleasure in this highest sense is true utility. Those who produce and preserve this pleasure are poets or poetical philosophers.

The exertions of Locke, Hume, Gibbon, Voltaire, Rousseau and their disciples, in favour of oppressed and deluded humanity, are entitled to the gratitude of mankind.[3] Yet it is easy to calculate the degree of moral and intellectual improvement which the world would have exhibited, had they never lived. A little more nonsense would have been talked for a century or two; and perhaps a few more men, women, and children, burnt as heretics. We might not at this moment have been congratulating each other on the abolition of the Inquisition in Spain. But it exceeds all imagination to conceive what would have been the moral condition of the world if neither Dante, Petrarch, Boccaccio, Chaucer, Shakspeare, Calderon, Lord Bacon, nor Milton, had ever existed; if Raphael and Michael Angelo had never been born; if the Hebrew poetry had never been translated; if a revival of the study of Greek literature had never taken place; if no monuments of ancient sculpture had been handed down to us; and if the poetry of the religion of the ancient world had been extinguished together with its belief.

---

[3] Although Rousseau has been thus classed, he was essentially a poet. The others, even Voltaire, were mere reasoners [Shelley's note].

The human mind could never, except by the intervention of these excitements, have been awakened to the invention of the grosser sciences, and that application of analytical reasoning to the aberrations of society, which it is now attempted to exalt over the direct expression of the inventive and creative faculty itself.

We have more moral, political, and historical wisdom than we know how to reduce into practice; we have more scientific and economical knowledge than can be accommodated to the just distribution of the produce which it multiplies. The poetry, in these systems of thought, is concealed by the accumulation of facts and calculating processes. There is no want of knowledge respecting what is wisest and best in morals, government, and political economy, or at least what is wiser and better than what men now practise and endure. But we let *"I dare not wait upon I would, like the poor cat in the adage."* [The quotation is from *Macbeth*.] We want the creative faculty to imagine that which we know; we want the generous impulse to act that which we imagine; we want the poetry of life; our calculations have outrun conception; we have eaten more than we can digest. The cultivation of those sciences which have enlarged the limits of the empire of man over the external world, has, for want of the poetical faculty, proportionally circumscribed those of the internal world; and man, having enslaved the elements, remains himself a slave. To what but a cultivation of the mechanical arts in a degree disproportioned to the presence of the creative faculty, which is the basis of all knowledge, is to be attributed the abuse of all invention for abridging and combining labour, to the exasperation of the inequality of mankind? From what other cause has it arisen that the discoveries which should have lightened, have added a weight to the curse imposed on Adam? Poetry, and the principle of Self, of which money is the visible incarnation, are the God and Mammon of the world.

The functions of the poetical faculty are twofold; by one it creates new materials of knowledge, and power, and pleasure; by the other it engenders in the mind a desire to reproduce and arrange them according to a certain rhythm and order, which may be called the beautiful and the good. The cultivation of poetry is never more to be desired than at periods when, from an excess of the selfish and calculating principle, the accumulation of the materials of external life exceed the quantity of the power of assimilating them to the internal laws of human nature. The body has then become too unwieldy for that which animates it.

Poetry is indeed something divine. It is at once the centre and circumference of knowledge; it is that which comprehends all science, and that to which all science must be referred. It is at the same time the root and blossom of all other systems of thought; it is that from which all spring, and that which adorns all; and that which, if blighted, denies the fruit and the seed, and withholds from the barren world the nourishment and the succession of the scions of the tree of life. It is the perfect and consummate surface and bloom of all things; it is as the odour and the colour of the rose to the texture of the elements which compose it, as the form and splendour of unfaded beauty to the secrets of anatomy and corruption. What were virtue, love, patriotism, friendship, – what were the scenery of this beautiful universe which we inhabit; what were our consolations on this side of the grave – and what were our aspirations beyond it, if poetry did not ascend to bring light and fire from those eternal regions where the owl-winged faculty of calculation dare not ever soar? Poetry is not like reasoning, a power to be exerted according to the determination of the will. A man cannot say, "I will compose poetry." The greatest poet even cannot say it; for the mind in creation is as a fading coal, which some invisible influence, like an inconstant wind, awakens to transitory brightness; this power arises from within, like the colour of a flower which fades and changes as it is developed, and the conscious portions of our natures are unprophetic either of its approach or its departure. Could this influence be durable in its original purity and force, it is impossible to predict the greatness of the results; but when composition begins, inspiration is already on the decline, and the most glorious poetry that has ever been communicated to the world is probably a feeble shadow of the original conceptions of the poet. I appeal to the greatest poets of the present day, whether it is not an error to assert that the finest passages of poetry are produced by labour and study. The toil and the delay recommended by critics, can be justly interpreted to mean no more than a careful observation of the inspired moments, and an artificial connection of the spaces between their suggestions by the intertexture of conventional expressions; a necessity only imposed by the limitedness of the poetical faculty itself; for Milton conceived the *Paradise Lost* as a whole before he executed it in portions. We have his own authority also for the muse having "dictated" to him the "unpremeditated song." And let this be an answer to those who would allege the fifty-six various readings of the first line of the *Orlando Furioso*. Compositions so produced are to poetry what mosaic is to painting. The instinct and intuition of the poetical faculty is still more observable in the plastic and pictorial arts: a great statue or picture grows under the power of the artist as a child in a mother's womb; and the very mind which directs the hands in formation, is incapable of accounting to itself for the origin, the gradations, or the media of the process.

Poetry is the record of the best and happiest moments of the happiest and best minds. We are aware of evanescent visitations of thought and feeling, sometimes associated with place or person, sometimes regarding our own mind alone, and always arising unforeseen and departing unbidden, but elevating and delightful beyond all expression: so that even in the desire and the regret they leave, there cannot but be pleasure, participating as it does in the nature of its object. It is as it were the interpenetration of a diviner nature through our own; but its footsteps are like those of a wind over the sea, which the coming calm erases, and whose traces remain only, as on the wrinkled sand which paves it. These and corresponding conditions of being are experienced principally by those of the most delicate sensibility and the most enlarged imagination; and the state of mind produced by them is at war with every base desire. The enthusiasm of virtue, love, patriotism, and friendship, is essentially linked with such emotions; and whilst they last, self appears as what it is, an atom to a universe. Poets are not only subject to these experiences as spirits of the most refined organisation, but they can colour all that they combine with the evanescent hues of this ethereal world; a word, a trait in the representation of a scene or a passion, will touch the enchanted chord, and reanimate, in those who have ever experienced these emotions, the sleeping, the cold, the buried image of the past. Poetry thus makes immortal all that is best and most beautiful in the world; it arrests the vanishing apparitions which haunt the interlunations of life, and veiling them, or in language or in form, sends them forth among mankind, bearing sweet news of kindred joy to those with whom their sisters abide – abide, because there is no portal of expression from the caverns of the spirit which they inhabit into the universe of things. Poetry redeems from decay the visitations of the divinity in man.

Poetry turns all things to loveliness; it exalts the beauty of that which is most beautiful, and it adds beauty to that which is most deformed; it marries exultation and horror, grief and pleasure, eternity and change; it subdues to union, under its light yoke, all irreconcilable things. It transmutes all that it touches, and every form moving within the radiance of its presence is changed by wondrous sympathy to an incarnation of the spirit which it breathes: its secret alchemy turns to potable gold the poisonous waters which flow from death through life; it strips the veil of familiarity from the world, and lays bare the naked and sleeping beauty, which is the spirit of its forms.

All things exist as they are perceived; at least in relation to the percipient. "The mind is its own place, and of itself can make a heaven of hell, a hell of heaven." [Shelley is quoting Milton's *Paradise Lost*.] But poetry defeats the curse which binds us to be subjected to the accident of surrounding impressions. And whether it spreads its own figured curtain, or withdraws life's dark veil from before the scene of things, it equally creates for us a being within our being. It makes us the inhabitants of a world to which the familiar world is a chaos. It reproduces the common universe of which we are portions and percipients, and it purges from our inward sight the film of familiarity which obscures from us the wonder of our being. It compels us to feel that which we perceive, and to imagine that which we know. It creates anew the universe, after it has been annihilated in our minds by the recurrence of impressions blunted by reiteration. It justifies the bold and true words of Tasso: *Non merita nome di creatore, se non Iddio ed il Poeta* [no one merits the name of creator, no one but God and the poet].

A poet, as he is the author to others of the highest wisdom, pleasure, virtue, and glory, so he ought personally to be the happiest, the best, the wisest, and the most illustrious of men. As to his glory, let time be challenged to declare whether the fame of any other institutor of human life be comparable to that of a poet. That he is the wisest, the happiest, and the best, inasmuch as he is a poet, is equally incontrovertible: the greatest poets have been men of the most spotless virtue, of the most consummate prudence, and, if we would look into the interior of their lives, the most fortunate of men: and the exceptions, as they regard those who possessed the poetic faculty in a high yet inferior degree, will be found on consideration to confine rather than destroy the rule. Let us for a moment stoop to the arbitration of popular breath, and usurping and uniting in our own persons the incompatible characters of accuser, witness, judge, and executioner, let us decide without trial, testimony, or form, that certain motives of those who are "there sitting where we dare not soar," are reprehensible. [Shelley is paraphrasing a line from *Paradise Lost.*] Let us assume that Homer was a drunkard, that Virgil was a flatterer, that Horace was a coward, that Tasso was a madman, that Lord Bacon was a peculator, that Raphael was a libertine, that Spenser was a poet laureate. It is inconsistent with this division of our subject to cite living poets, but posterity has done ample justice to the great names now referred to. Their errors have been weighed and found to have been dust in the balance; if their sins "were as scarlet, they are now white as snow" [from the Bible's book of Isaiah]; they have been washed in the blood of the mediator and redeemer, time. Observe in what a ludicrous chaos the imputations of real or fictitious crime have been confused in the contemporary calumnies against poetry and poets; consider how little is, as it appears – or appears, as it is; look to your own motives, and judge not, lest ye be judged.

Poetry, as has been said, differs in this respect from logic, that it is not subject to the control of the active powers of the mind, and that its birth and recurrence have no necessary connexion with the consciousness or will. It is presumptuous to determine that these are the necessary conditions of all mental causation, when mental effects are experienced unsusceptible of being referred to them. The frequent recurrence of the poetical power, it is obvious to suppose, may produce in the mind a habit of order and harmony correlative with its own nature and with its effects upon other minds. But in the intervals of inspiration, and they may be frequent without being durable, a poet becomes a man, and is abandoned to the sudden reflux of the influences under which others habitually live. But as he is more delicately organised than other men, and sensible to pain and pleasure, both his own and that of others, in a degree unknown to them, he will avoid the one and pursue the other with an ardour proportioned to this difference. And he renders himself obnoxious to calumny, when he neglects to observe the circumstances under which these objects of universal pursuit and flight have disguised themselves in one another's garments.

But there is nothing necessarily evil in this error, and thus cruelty, envy, revenge, avarice, and the passions purely evil, have never formed any portion of the popular imputations on the lives of poets.

I have thought it most favourable to the cause of truth to set down these remarks according to the order in which they were suggested to my mind, by a consideration of the subject itself, instead of observing the formality of a polemical reply; but if the view which they contain be just, they will be found to involve a refutation of the arguers against poetry, so far at least as regards the first division of the subject. I can readily conjecture what should have moved the gall of some learned and intelligent writers who quarrel with certain versifiers; I, like them, confess myself unwilling to be stunned by the Theseids of the hoarse Codri of the day [in other words, grandiose poems written by popular but untalented poets]. Bavius and Maevius [a pair of famously cruel Roman critics] undoubtedly are, as they ever were, insufferable persons. But it belongs to a philosophical critic to distinguish rather than confound.

The first part of these remarks has related to poetry in its elements and principles; and it has been shown, as well as the narrow limits assigned them would permit, that what is called poetry in a restricted sense, has a common source with all other forms of order and of beauty, according to which the materials of human life are susceptible of being arranged, and which is poetry in an universal sense.

The second part will have for its object an application of these principles to the present state of the cultivation of poetry, and a defence of the attempt to idealise the modern forms of manners and opinions, and compel them into a subordination to the imaginative and creative faculty. For the literature of England, an energetic development of which has ever preceded or

accompanied a great and free development of the national will, has aris-
en as it were from a new birth. In spite of the low-thoughted envy which
would undervalue contemporary merit, our own will be a memorable age
in intellectual achievements, and we live among such philosophers and
poets as surpass beyond comparison any who have appeared since the last
national struggle for civil and religious liberty. The most unfailing herald,
companion, and follower of the awakening of a great people to work a
beneficial change in opinion or institution, is poetry. At such periods there
is an accumulation of the power of communicating and receiving intense
and impassioned conceptions respecting man and nature. The person in
whom this power resides, may often, as far as regards many portions of
their nature, have little apparent correspondence with that spirit of good
of which they are the ministers. But even whilst they deny and abjure, they
are yet compelled to serve, the power which is seated on the throne of their
own soul. It is impossible to read the compositions of the most celebrated
writers of the present day without being startled with the electric life which
burns within their words. They measure the circumference and sound the
depths of human nature with a comprehensive and all-penetrating spirit,
and they are themselves perhaps the most sincerely astonished at its mani-
festations; for it is less their spirit than the spirit of the age. Poets are the
hierophants of an unapprehended inspiration; the mirrors of the gigantic
shadows which futurity casts upon the present; the words which express
what they understand not; the trumpets which sing to battle, and feel not
what they inspire; the influence which is moved not, but moves. Poets are
the unacknowledged legislators of the world.

Johann Peter Eckermann (1792–1854)

In 1822 Johann Peter Eckermann met the eminent German poet Johann Wilhelm von Goethe (1749–1832) after sending him the manuscript of his Beiträge zur Poesie mit besonderer Hinweisung auf Goethe *(Contributions to Poetry, with Special Reference to Goethe). Eventually, Eckermann became Goethe's personal secretary, taking an active hand in helping the aging poet compile and edit his collected works. Today, however, he is most famous for* Gespräche mit Goethe *(Conversations with Goethe), first published in 1836 and often compared to Boswell's* Life of Johnson. *The book was widely admired: American journalist and critic Margaret Fuller was one of its first translators, and Nietzsche claimed that it was the best German book in existence.*

In the following extract, Eckermann records Goethe's opinions about the dangers of writing political poetry – not because the poet's life is at risk but because the very act of taking a political side may damage the writer's freedom. As an example, he mentions eighteenth-century Scottish poet James Thomson, who, in Goethe's opinion, tarnished his masterpiece, The Seasons, *by composing the lyrics to "Rule, Britannia." He also discusses his contemporary, Johann Ludwig Uhland, a well-known poet who became a regional legislator.*

from *Conversations with Goethe*

translated by John Oxenford

[March 1832.] We talked of the tragic idea of Destiny among the Greeks.

"It no longer suits our way of thinking," said Goethe; "it is obsolete, and is also in contradiction with our religious views. If a modern poet introduces such antique ideas into a drama, it always has an air of affectation. It is a costume which is long since out of fashion, and which, like the Roman toga, no longer suits us.

"It is better for us moderns to say with Napoleon, 'Politics are Destiny.' But let us beware of saying, with our latest literati, that politics are poetry, or a suitable subject for the poet. The English poet Thomson wrote a very good poem on the Seasons, but a very bad one on Liberty, and that not from want of poetry in the poet, but from want of poetry in the subject.

"If a poet would work politically, he must give himself up to a party; and so soon as he does that, he is lost as a poet; he must bid farewell to his free spirit, his unbiased view, and draw over his ears the cap of bigotry and blind hatred.

"The poet, as a man and citizen, will love his native land; but the native land of his poetic powers and poetic action is the good, noble, and beautiful, which is confined to no particular province or country, and which he seizes upon and forms wherever he finds it. Therein is he like the eagle, who hovers with free gaze over whole countries, and to whom it is of no consequence whether the hare on which he pounces is running in Prussia or in Saxony.

"And, then, what is meant by love of one's country? What is meant by patriotic deeds? If the poet has employed a life in battling with pernicious prejudices, in setting aside narrow views, in enlightening the minds, purifying the tastes, ennobling the feelings and thoughts of his countrymen, what better could he have done? How could he have acted more patriotically?

"To make such ungrateful and unsuitable demands upon a poet is just as if one required the captain of a regiment to show himself a patriot, by taking part in political innovations and thus neglecting his proper calling. The captain's country is his regiment, and he will show himself an excellent patriot by troubling himself about political matters only so far as they concern him, and bestowing all his mind and all his care on the battalions under him, trying so to train and discipline them that they may do their duty if ever their native land should be in peril.

"I hate all bungling like sin, but most of all bungling in state-affairs, which produces nothing but mischief to thousands and millions.

"You know that, on the whole, I care little what is written about me; but yet it comes to my ears, and I know well enough that, hard as I have toiled all my life, all my labors are as nothing in the eyes of certain people, just because I have disdained to mingle in political parties. To please such people I must have become a member of a Jacobin club, and preached bloodshed and murder. However, not a word more upon this wretched subject, lest I become unwise in railing against folly."

In the same manner he blamed the political course, so much praised by others, of Uhland.

"Mind," said he, "the politician will devour the poet. To be a member of the States, and to live amid daily jostlings and excitements, is not for the delicate nature of a poet. His song will cease, and that is in some sort to be lamented. Swabia [a cultural and linguistic region spanning parts of Bavaria and Württemberg] has plenty of men, sufficiently well educated, well meaning, able, and eloquent, to be members of the States, but only one poet of Uhland's class."

John Keats

(1795–1821)

Throughout his short life, John Keats was an eager and fluent correspondent, and many of his letters record his growing awareness of his poetic powers. In the following letter, written to his friend Richard Woodhouse, he describes the quality that, elsewhere, he labels negative capability *– a poet's ability to "continually [be] . . . filling some other Body." The first sentence quotes Horace's* Epistles, *which refer to "genus irritabile vatum" (the irritable tribe of poets).*

Letter to Richard Woodhouse

October 27, 1818

My dear Woodhouse,

Your Letter gave me a great satisfaction; more on account of its friendliness, than any relish of that matter in it which is accounted so acceptable in the "genus irritabile." The best answer I can give you is in a clerklike manner to make some observations on two principle points, which seem to point like indices into the midst of the whole pro and con, about genius, and views and atchievements and ambition and coetera. 1st As to the poetical Character itself, (I mean that sort of which, if I am any thing, I am a Member; that sort distinguished from the wordsworthian or egotistical sublime; which is a thing per se and stands alone) it is not itself – it has no self – it is every thing and nothing – It has no character – it enjoys light and shade; it lives in gusto, be it foul or fair, high or low, rich or poor, mean or elevated – It has as much delight in conceiving an Iago as an Imogen. What shocks the virtuous philosop[h]er, delights the camelion Poet. It does no harm from its relish of the dark side of things any more than from its taste for the bright one; because they both end in speculation. A Poet is the most unpoetical of any thing in existence; because he has no Identity – he is continually in for – and filling some other Body – The Sun, the Moon, the Sea and Men and Women who are creatures of impulse are poetical and have about them an unchangeable attribute – the poet has none; no identity – he is certainly the most unpoetical of all God's Creatures. If then he has no self, and if I am a Poet, where is the Wonder that I should say I would write no more? Might I not at that very instant [have] been cogitating on the Characters of saturn and Ops? It is a wretched thing to confess; but is a very fact that not one word I ever utter can be taken for granted as an opinion growing out of my identical nature – how can it, when I have no nature? When I am in a room with People if I ever am free from speculating on creations of my own brain, then not myself goes home to myself: but the identity of every one in the room begins [so] to press upon me that, I am in a very little time an[ni]hilated – not only among Men; it would be the same in a Nursery of children: I know not whether I make myself wholly understood: I hope enough so to let you see that no dependence is to be placed on what I said that day.

In the second place I will speak of my views, and of the life I purpose to myself – I am ambitious of doing the world some good: if I should be spared that may be the work of maturer years – in the interval I will assay to reach to as high a summit in Poetry as the nerve bestowed upon me will suffer. The faint conceptions I have of Poems to come brings the blood frequently into my forehead – All I hope is that I may not lose interest in human affairs – that the solitary indifference I feel for applause even from the finest Spirits, will not blunt any acuteness of vision I may have. I do not think it will – I feel assured I should write from the mere yearning and fondness I have for the Beautiful even if my night's labours should be burnt every morning and no eye ever shine upon them. But even now I am perhaps not speaking from myself; but from some character in whose soul I now live. I am sure however that this next sentence is from myself. I feel your anxiety, good opinion and friendliness in the highest degree, and am

Your's most sincerely

John Keats

Thomas Carlyle

(1795–1881)

Thomas Carlyle was a Scottish essayist and historian. Although he spent much of his professional life in London, he was still living on a farm in Scotland when he wrote "An Essay on Burns." First published in 1828, the piece became, by the early 1900s, a standard accompaniment to editions of Burns's poems and was used throughout the United States as a school text. It is likely, then, that Carlyle's defense of sincerity in poetry, his admonition not to "write from hearsay, but from sight and experience," influenced the ideas of a broad swath of twentieth-century American poets.

In the following extract from the essay, Carlyle quotes a phrase from Horace's Ars Poetica *(see page 17). It reads in full as "Si vis me flere, dolendum est primum ipsi tibi" (If you wish me to weep, you must mourn first yourself).*

from *An Essay on Burns*

The excellence of Burns is, indeed, among the rarest, whether in poetry or prose; but, at the same time, it is plain and easily recognized: his Sincerity, his indisputable air of Truth. Here are no fabulous woes or joys; no hollow fantastic sentimentalities; no wire-drawn refinings, either in thought or feeling: the passion that is traced before us has glowed in a living heart; the opinion he utters has risen in his own understanding, and been a light to his own steps. He does not write from hearsay, but from sight and experience; it is the scenes that he has lived and labored amidst, that he describes: those scenes, rude and humble as they are, have kindled beautiful emotions in his soul, noble thoughts, and definite resolves; and he speaks forth what is in him, not from any outward call of vanity or interest, but because his heart is too full to be silent. He speaks it with such melody and modulation as he can; "in homely rustic jingle"; but it is his own, and genuine. This is the grand secret for finding readers and retaining them: let him who would move and convince others, be first moved and convinced himself. Horace's rule, *Si vi me flere*, is applicable in a wider sense than the literal one. To every poet, to every writer, we might say, Be true, if you would be believed. Let a man but speak forth with genuine earnestness the thought, the emotion, the actual condition of his own heart; and other men, so strangely are we all knit together by the tie of sympathy, must and will give heed to him. In culture, in extent of view, we may stand above the speaker, or below him; but in either case, his words, if they are earnest and sincere, will find some response within us; for in spite of all casual varieties in outward rank or inward, as face answers to face, so does the heart of man to man.

Elizabeth Barrett Browning (1806–1861)

Elizabeth Barrett Browning was deeply interested in the social issues of her day, particularly the rights of women and the abolition of slavery, and many of those concerns emerge in her poetry. Aurora Leigh, first published in 1857, is a novel in blank verse about a young woman who wants to be a writer but is distracted and dismayed by Victorian assumptions about feminine roles and ambitions. In the following extract, Aurora muses over the difficulty of convincing both others and herself that a woman's subject matter has worth and that a female poet has as much right as a man does to strive for greatness.

Romney, mentioned in the second stanza, is the man Aurora loves.

from *Aurora Leigh*

from Fifth Book
Aurora Leigh, be humble. Shall I hope
To speak my poems in mysterious tune
With man and nature, – with the lava-lymph
That trickles from successive galaxies
Still drop by drop adown the finger of God,
In still new worlds? – with summer-days in this,
That scarce dare breathe, they are so beautiful? –
With spring's delicious trouble in the ground
Tormented by the quickened blood of roots,
And softly pricked by golden crocus-sheaves
In token of the harvest-time of flowers? –
With winters and with autumns, – and beyond,
With the human heart's large seasons, – when it hopes
And fears, joys, grieves, and loves? – with all that strain
Of sexual passion, which devours the flesh
In a sacrament of souls? with mother's breasts,
Which, round the new-made creatures hanging there,
Throb luminous and harmonious like pure spheres? –
With multitudinous life, and finally
With the great out-goings of ecstatic souls,

Who, in a rush of too long prisoned flame,
Their radiant faces upward, burn away
This dark of the body, issuing on a world
Beyond our mortal? – can I speak my verse
So plainly in tune to these things and the rest,
That men shall feel it catch them on the quick,
As having the same warrant over them
To hold and move them, if they will or no,
Alike imperious as the primal rhythm
Of that theurgic nature? I must fail,
Who fail at the beginning to hold and move
One man, – and he my cousin, and he my friend,
And he born tender, made intelligent,
Inclined to ponder the precipitous sides
Of difficult questions; yet, obtuse to me, –
Of me, incurious! likes me very well,
And wishes me a paradise of good,
Good looks, good means, and good digestion! – ay,
But otherwise evades me, puts me off
With kindness, with a tolerant gentleness, –
Too light a book for a grave man's reading! Go,
Aurora Leigh: be humble.
                                        There it is;
We women are too apt to look to one,
Which proves a certain impotence in art.
We strain our natures at doing something great,
Far less because it's something great to do,
Than, haply, that we, so, commend ourselves
As being not small, and more appreciable
To some one friend. We must have mediators
Betwixt our highest conscience and the judge;
Some sweet saint's blood must quicken in our palms,
Or all the life in heaven seems slow and cold:
Good only, being perceived as the end of good,
And God alone pleased, – that's too poor, we think,
And not enough for us, by any means.
Ay – Romney, I remember, told me once
We miss the abstract, when we comprehend!
We miss it most when we aspire, . . . and fail.

Yet, so, I will not. – This vile woman's way
Of trailing garments, shall not trip me up.

I'll have no traffic with the personal thought
In art's pure temple. Must I work in vain,
Without the approbation of a man?
It cannot be; it shall not. Fame itself,
That approbation of the general race,
Presents a poor end, (though the arrow speed,
Shot straight with vigorous finger to the white,)
And the highest fame was never reached except
By what was aimed above it. Art for art,
And good for God Himself, the essential Good!
We'll keep our aims sublime, our eyes erect,
Although our woman-hands should shake and fail;
And if we fail . . . But must we? –
                              Shall I fail?
The Greeks said grandly in their tragic phrase,
"Let no one be called happy till his death."
To which I add, – Let no one till his death
Be called unhappy. Measure not the work
Until the day's out and the labour done;
Then bring your gauges. If the day's work's scant,
Why, call it scant; affect no compromise;
And, in that we have nobly striven at least,
Deal with us nobly, women though we be,
And honour us with truth, if not with praise.

Edgar Allan Poe   (1809–1849)

In addition to writing both poetry and fiction, Edgar Allan Poe produced numerous book reviews and critical essays, many of which excoriated the work of his contemporaries. Although his sharp tongue inspired attacks and enmity, fellow poet and critic James Russell Lowell believed that, in reading Poe's criticism, "we are reading the thoughts of a man who thinks for himself and says what he thinks, and knows well what he is talking about. His analytic powers would furnish forth bravely some score of ordinary critics."

In 1848 Poe delivered a lecture on what he called "the poetic principle" before a large Rhode Island audience. After the text of the lecture was stolen from his suitcase, he rewrote it, first as a transcript for a Virginia lecture and eventually as an essay, "The Poetic Principle." But before it could be published, he was found wandering the streets of Baltimore, incoherent and delirious. He died a few days later, and the essay appeared posthumously in 1850. In the following extract from that piece, Poe argues that "'a long poem' is simply a flat contradiction in terms," despite nineteenth-century critics' preference for "sustained effort," and declares that a poem should be judged "by the effect it produces [rather] than by the time it took to impress the effect."

---

from *The Poetic Principle*

In speaking of the Poetic Principle, I have no design to be either thorough or profound. While discussing, very much at random, the essentiality of what we call Poetry, my principal purpose will be to cite for consideration, some few of those minor English or American poems which best suit my own taste, or which, upon my own fancy, have left the most definite impression. By "minor poems" I mean, of course, poems of little length. And here, in the beginning, permit me to say a few words in regard to a somewhat peculiar principle, which, whether rightfully or wrongfully, has always had its influence in my own critical estimate of the poem. I hold that a long poem does not exist. I maintain that the phrase, "a long poem," is simply a flat contradiction in terms.

I need scarcely observe that a poem deserves its title only inasmuch as it excites, by elevating the soul. The value of the poem is in the ratio of this elevating excitement. But all excitements are, through a psychal necessity, transient. That degree of excitement which would entitle a poem to be so called at all, cannot be sustained throughout a composition of any great length. After the lapse of half an hour, at the very utmost, it flags – fails – a revulsion ensues – and then the poem is, in effect, and in fact, no longer such.

There are, no doubt, many who have found difficulty in reconciling the critical dictum that the "Paradise Lost" is to be devoutly admired through-out, with the absolute impossibility of maintaining for it, during perusal, the amount of enthusiasm which that critical dictum would demand. This great work, in fact, is to be regarded as poetical, only when, losing sight of that vital requisite in all works of Art, Unity, we view it merely as a series of minor poems. If, to preserve its Unity – its totality of effect or impression – we read it (as would be necessary) at a single sitting, the result is but a constant alternation of excitement and depression. After a passage of what we feel to be true poetry, there follows, inevitably, a passage of platitude which no critical pre-judgment can force us to admire; but if, upon com-pleting the work, we read it again, omitting the first book – that is to say, commencing with the second – we shall be surprised at now finding that admirable which we before condemned – that damnable which we had previously so much admired. It follows from all this that the ultimate, ag-gregate, or absolute effect of even the best epic under the sun, is a nullity: – and this is precisely the fact.

In regard to the Iliad, we have, if not positive proof, at least very good reason for believing it intended as a series of lyrics; but, granting the epic intention, I can say only that the work is based in an imperfect sense of art. The modern epic is, of the supposititious ancient model, but an inconsid-erate and blindfold imitation. But the day of these artistic anomalies is over. If, at any time, any very long poem were popular in reality, which I doubt, it is at least clear that no very long poem will ever be popular again.

That the extent of a poetical work is, *ceteris paribus*, the measure of its merit, seems undoubtedly, when we thus state it, a proposition sufficiently ab-surd – yet we are indebted for it to the Quarterly Reviews. Surely there can be nothing in mere *size*, abstractly considered – there can be nothing in mere *bulk*, so far as a volume is concerned, which has so continuously elicited admiration from these saturnine pamphlets! A mountain, to be sure, by the mere sentiment of physical magnitude which it conveys, *does* impress us with a sense of the sublime – but no man is impressed after *this* fashion by the material grandeur of even [American poet Joel Barlow's 1807 epic] "The Columbiad." Even the Quarterlies have not instructed us to be so impressed by it. As *yet*, they have not *insisted* on our estimating

[French poet and politican Alphonse de] Lamartine by the cubic foot, or [Scottish poet Robert] Pollock by the pound – but what else are we to *infer* from their continual prating about "sustained effort"? If, by "sustained effort," any little gentleman has accomplished an epic, let us frankly commend him for the effort – if this indeed be a thing commendable – but let us forbear praising the epic on the effort's account. It is to be hoped that common sense, in the time to come, will prefer deciding upon a work of Art, rather by the impression it makes – by the effect it produces – than by the time it took to impress the effect, or by the amount of "sustained effort" which had been found necessary in effecting the impression. The fact is, that perseverance is one thing and genius quite another – nor can all the Quarterlies in Christendom confound them. By and by, this proposition, with many which I have been just urging, will be received as self-evident. In the meantime, by being generally condemned as falsities, they will not be essentially damaged as truths.

On the other hand, it is clear that a poem may be improperly brief. Undue brevity degenerates into mere epigrammatism. A very short poem, while now and then producing a brilliant or vivid, never produces a profound or enduring effect. There must be the steady pressing down of the stamp upon the wax. [French poet and songwriter Pierre] de Béranger has wrought innumerable things, pungent and spirit-stirring; but, in general, they have been too imponderous to stamp themselves deeply into the public attention; and thus, as so many feathers of fancy, have been blown aloft only to be whistled down the wind.

Mikhail Yurievich Lermontov

(1814–1841)

After Pushkin, Mikhail Yurievich Lermontov was Russia's most famous nine-teenth-century poet. His work is lush and sensuous, and even in his lifetime it was often equated with Byron's. Yet Lermontov was uncomfortable with that equation; and in the following brief poem (written in 1832), he struggles to balance his admiration for Byron with his own sense of voice and self. The translator, Martha Dickinson Bianchi, was Emily Dickinson's niece and a well-known editor of her aunt's poems.

I Am Not Byron

translated by Martha Dickinson Bianchi

I am not Byron – yet I am
One fore-elected, yet one more
Unknown, world-hunted wanderer,
A Russian in my mood and mind.

Scant from my seed the corn was ripe,
My mouth spoke young, was early hushed;
In depths of my own soul, the wreck
Of hope lies as in deep-sea sunk.

Who shall the counsels of the sea,
Its awe sublime unloose? Who shall
Read clear my spirit and my soul?
Unless it be a Poet – no man!

Henry David Thoreau (1817–1862)

The poet William Ellery Channing described his friend Henry David Thoreau as a "poet-naturalist"; and as the following journal entry demonstrates, Thoreau did have a remarkable ability to focus poetic language precisely on his physical observations of the natural world, a manner of concentration that greatly influenced twentieth-century poet-naturalists such as John Haines and W. S. Merwin. Yet in the midst of his fierce concentration on the world, Thoreau also reminds us that patience and empty time are essential to poetry. "The art of life, of a poet's life, is, not having anything to do, to do something."

Journal Entry

April 29, 1852

Observed a fire yesterday on the railroad, – Emerson's Island that was. The leaves are dry enough to burn; and I see a smoke this afternoon in the west horizon. There is a slight haziness on the woods as I go to Mayflower Road at 2.30 P.M., which advances me further into summer. Is that the arrowhead, so forward with its buds, in the Nut Meadow ditch? The ground is dry. I smell the dryness of the woods. Their shadows look more inviting, and I am reminded of the hum of bees. The pines have an appearance which they have not worn before, yet not easy to describe. The mottled light (sunlight) and shade, seen looking into the woods, is more like summer. But the season is most forward at the Second Division Brook, where the cowslip is in blossom, – and nothing yet planted at home, – these bright-yellow *suns* of the meadow, in rich clusters, their flowers contrasting with the green leaves, from amidst the all-producing, dark-bottomed water. A flower-fire bursting up, as if through crevices in the meadow. They are very rich, seen in the meadow where they grow, and the most conspicuous flower at present, but held in the hand they are rather coarse. But their yellow and green are really rich, and in the meadow they are the most delicate objects. Their bright yellow is something incredible when first beheld. There is still considerable snow in the woods, where it has not melted since winter. Here is a small reddish-topped rush (is it the *Juncus effusus*, common or soft rush?), now a foot high, in the meadow with the cowslips. It is the greatest growth of the grass form I have seen. The butterflies are now more numerous, red and blue-black or dark velvety. The art of life, of a poet's life, is, not having anything to do, to do something. People are going to see [Hungarian freedom fighter Lajos] Kossuth, but the same man does not attract me and [Concord businessman] George Loring. If he could come openly to Boston without the knowledge of Boston, it might be worth my while to go and see him.

The mayflower on the point of blossoming. I think I may say that it will blossom to-morrow. The blossoms of this plant are remarkably concealed beneath the leaves, perhaps for protection. It is singularly unpretending, not seeking to exhibit or display its simple beauty. It is the most delicate flower, both to eye and to scent, as yet. Its weather-worn leaves do not adorn it. If it had fresh spring leaves it would be more famous and sought after. Observed two thrushes arrived which I do not know. I discover a hawk over my head by his shadow on the ground; also small birds. The acorns among the leaves have been sprouted for a week past, the shells open and the blushing (red) meat exposed at the sprout end, where the sprout is already turning toward the bowels of the earth, already thinking of the tempests which it is destined as an oak to withstand, if it escapes worm and squirrel. Pick these up and plant them, if you would make a forest.

Old Mrs. Francis Wheeler thinks the river has not risen so high as recently for sixty-three years; that was in June!! that it was then higher. Noah Wheeler never saw it so high as lately. I think it doubtful if it was higher in 1817.

F. Wheeler, Jr., saw dandelions in bloom the 20th of April. Garfield's folks used them for greens. They grew in a springy place behind Brigham's in the Corner.

The *Fringilla hyemalis* [dark-eyed junco, a small bird] is still here, though apparently not so numerous as before. The *Populus grandidentata* [white poplar] in blossom, the sterile (?) flowers, though I cannot count, at most, more than five or six stamens. I observe the light-green leaves of a pyrola (?) [wintergreen] standing high on the stem in the woods, with the last year's fruit; the "one-sided" or else the "oval-leaved," I think.

As I come home over the Corner road, the sun, now getting low, is reflected very bright and silvery from the water on the meadows, seen through the pines of Hubbard's Grove. The causeway will be passable on foot to-morrow.

Frederick Douglass (1818–1895)

While Frederick Douglass was not himself a poet, his influence on later generations of readers and writers has been incalculable. As Paul Laurence Dunbar (1872–1906) wrote in his poem "Frederick Douglass,"

> And he was no soft-tongued apologist;
> He spoke straightforward, fearlessly uncowed;
> The sunlight of his truth dispelled the mist,
> And set in bold relief each dark hued cloud;
> To sin and crime he gave their proper hue,
> And hurled at evil what was evil's due.

In the following extract from Narrative of the Life of Frederick Douglass *(1845), a recollection of his years in slavery, Douglass describes his sudden realization that reading and writing "were the pathway from slavery to freedom."*

from *Narrative of the Life of Frederick Douglass*

from Chapter 6

Very soon after I went to live with Mr. and Mrs. Auld, she very kindly commenced to teach me the A, B, C. After I had learned this, she assisted me in learning to spell words of three or four letters. Just at this point of my progress, Mr. Auld found out what was going on, and at once forbade Mrs. Auld to instruct me further, telling her, among other things, that it was unlawful, as well as unsafe, to teach a slave to read. To use his own words, further, he said, "If you give a nigger an inch, he will take an ell. A nigger should know nothing but to obey his master – to do as he is told to do. Learning would *spoil* the best nigger in the world. Now," said he, "if you teach that nigger (speaking of myself) how to read, there would be no keeping him. It would forever unfit him to be a slave. He would at once become unmanageable, and of no value to his master. As to himself, it could do him no good, but a great deal of harm. It would make him discontented and unhappy." These words sank deep into my heart, stirred up sentiments within that lay slumbering, and called into existence an entirely new train of thought. It was a new and special revelation, explaining dark and mysterious things, with which my youthful understanding had struggled, but struggled in vain. I now understood what had been to me a most perplexing difficulty – to wit, the white man's power to enslave the black man. It was a grand achievement, and I prized it highly. From that moment, I understood the pathway from slavery to freedom. It was just what I wanted, and I got it at a time when I the least expected it. Whilst I was saddened by the thought of losing the aid of my kind mistress, I was gladdened by the invaluable instruction which, by the merest accident, I had gained from my master. Though conscious of the difficulty of learning without a teacher, I set out with high hope, and a fixed purpose, at whatever cost of trouble, to learn how to read. The very decided manner with which he spoke, and strove to impress his wife with the evil consequences of giving me instruction, served to convince me that he was deeply sensible of the truths he was uttering. It gave me the best assurance that I might rely with the utmost confidence on the results which, he said, would flow from teaching me to read. What he most dreaded, that I most desired. What he most loved, that I most hated. That which to him was a great evil, to be carefully shunned, was to me a great good, to be diligently sought; and the argument which he so warmly urged, against my learning to read, only served to inspire me with a desire and determination to learn. In learning to read, I owe almost as much to the bitter opposition of my master, as to the kindly aid of my mistress. I acknowledge the benefit of both.

Emily Brontë

(1818–1848)

Although the Brontë sisters are most often remembered as novelists, all began their adult writing careers as poets. Only after 1846, when Charlotte decided to publish a selection of their poems under the pseudonyms Currer, Ellis, and Acton Bell, did each woman decide to undertake a novel. Until she began writing Wuthering Heights, *much of Emily's writing energy was consumed by tales of the imaginary land of Gondal. But one day in 1834, she decided, uncharacteristically, to write in her own voice about her own daily life. Although she signed this diary paper "Emily and Anne," scholars believe that it was clearly Emily's work, jumbling together, as her biographer Katherine Frank notes, "the real and the mundane, and the imaginary and sublime." Emily wrote several more diary papers over the course of her brief life, and all open a window into her writing practice, not only her distractions and obsessions but also her vivid curiosity and comic eye.*

Two Diary Papers

November 24, 1834

I fed Rainbow, Diamond, Snowflake, Jasper pheasant (alias). This morning Branwell went down to Mr Driver's and brought news that Sir Robert Peel was going to be invited to stand for Leeds. Anne and I have been peeling potatoes for Charlotte to make us an apple pudding and for Aunt nuts and apples. Charlotte said she made puddings perfectly and she was of a quick but limited intellect. Tab[b]y said just now "Come, Anne pilloputate" (i.e. pill a potato). Aunt has come into the kitchen just now and said "where are your feet Anne?" Anne answered, "on the floor, Aunt." Papa opened the parlour door and gave Branwell a letter saying, "here, Branwell, read this and show it to your Aunt and Charlotte" – the Gondals are discovering the interior of Gaaldine. Sally Mosely is washing in the back kitchen.

It is past Twelve o'clock. Anne and I have not tidied ourselves, done our bedwork or done our lessons and we want to go out to play. We are going to have for Dinner Boiled Beef, Turnips, potatoes and applepudding. The kitchin is in a very untidy state. Anne and I have not done our music exercise which consists of b major. Tab[b]y said on my putting a pen in her face, "Ya pitter pottering there instead of pilling a potate." I answered, "O Dear, O Dear, O dear I will directly." With that I get up, take a knife and begin pilling. Finished pilling the potatoes. Papa going to walk. Mr Sunderland expected.

Anne and I say I wonder what we shall be like and what we shall be and where we shall be if all goes on well in the year 1874 – in which year I shall be in my 57th year. Anne will be in her 55th year Branwell will be going in his 58th year and Charlotte in her 59th year. Hoping we shall all be well at that time we close our paper.

Emily and Anne

June 26, 1837

Monday evening June 26 1837 A bit past 4 o'clock. Charlotte working in Aunt's room, Branwell reading Eugene Aram to her – Anne and I writing in the drawing room – Anne a poem beginning "Fair was the evening and brightly the sun" – I Agustus-Almeda's life, 1st v. 1 – 4th page from the last – fine rather coolish thin grey cloudy but sunny day. Aunt working in the little room the old nursery Papa – gone out. Tabby in the kitchin – the Emperors and Empresses of Gondal and Gaaldine preparing to depart from Gaaldine to Gondal to prepare for the coronation which will be on the 12th of July. Queen Vittoria ascended the throne this month. Northangerland in Moncey's Isle – Zamorna at Eversham. All tight and right in which condition it is to be hoped we shall all be on this day 4 years at which time Charlotte will be 25 and 2 months – Branwell just 24, it being his birthday – myself 22 and 10 months and a peice Anne 21 and nearly a half. I wonder where we shall be and how we shall be and what kind of day it will be then – let us hope for the best.

Emily Jane Brontë – Anne Brontë

I guess that this day 4 years we shall all be in this drawing-room comfortable I hope it may be so. Anne guesses we shall all be gone somewhere comfortable We hope it may be so indeed. Aunt: Come Emily it's past 4 o'clock

Emily: Yes, Aunt Exit Aunt

Ann[e]: Well, do you intend to write in the evening Emily: Well, what think you (We agreed to go out 1st to make sure if we got into the humour. We may stay in –)

Walt Whitman (1819–1892)

In 1848 poet Walt Whitman and his brother traveled to New Orleans, planning to work for a newspaper there. That trip down the Mississippi changed his life: now he began to comprehend the largeness of his country, the variety of its places and people. Once he returned to New York, he found that the style and substance of his poems were reflecting his new perceptions. Eventually, in 1855, he borrowed a printing press and set up a handful of these poems, along with a preface, and published the collection as the first edition of Leaves of Grass.

In the following extract from the 1855 preface, Whitman quantifies the poet's task; for "folks expect of the poet to indicate more than the beauty and dignity which always attach to dumb real objects . . . they expect him to indicate the path between reality and their souls." All of the ellipses in the passage are Whitman's own.

from *Preface to the 1855 Edition of "Leaves of Grass"*

The greatest poet hardly knows pettiness or triviality. If he breathes into any thing that was before thought small it dilates with the grandeur and life of the universe. He is a seer . . . he is individual . . . he is complete in himself . . . the others are as good as he, only he sees it and they do not. He is not one of the chorus . . . he does not stop for any regulations . . . he is the president of regulation. What the eyesight does to the rest he does to the rest. Who knows the curious mystery of the eyesight? The other senses corroborate themselves, but this is removed from any proof but its own and foreruns the identities of the spiritual world. A single glance of it mocks all the investigations of man and all the instruments and books of the earth and all reasoning. What is marvelous? what is unlikely? what is impossible or baseless or vague? after you have once just opened the space of a peachpit and given audience to far and near and to the sunset and had all things enter with electric swiftness softly and duly without confusion or jostling or jam.

The land and sea, the animals fishes and birds, the sky of heaven and the orbs, the forests mountains and rivers, are not small themes . . . but folks expect of the poet to indicate more than the beauty and dignity which always attach to dumb real objects . . . they expect him to indicate the path between reality and their souls. Men and women perceive the beauty well enough . . . probably as well as he. The passionate tenacity of hunters, woodmen, early risers, cultivators of gardens and orchards and fields, the love of healthy women for the manly form, seafaring persons, drivers of horses, the passion for light and the open air, all is an old varied sign of the unfailing perception of beauty and of a residence of the poetic in outdoor people. They can never be assisted by poets to perceive . . . some may but they never can. The poetic quality is not marshalled in rhyme or uniformity or abstract addresses to things nor in melancholy complaints or good precepts, but is the life of these and much else and is in the soul. The profit of rhyme is that it drops seeds of a sweeter and more luxuriant rhyme, and of uniformity that it conveys itself into its own roots in the ground out of sight. The rhyme and uniformity of perfect poems show the free growth of metrical laws and bud from them as unerringly and loosely as lilacs or roses on a bush, and take shapes as compact as the shapes of chestnuts and oranges and melons and pears, and shed the perfume impalpable to form. The fluency and ornaments of the finest poems or music or orations or recitations are not independent but dependent. All beauty comes from beautiful blood and a beautiful brain. If the greatnesses are in conjunction in a man or woman it is enough . . . the fact will prevail through the universe . . . but the gaggery and gilt of a million years will not prevail. Who troubles himself about his ornaments or fluency is lost. This is what you shall do: Love the earth and sun and the animals, despise riches, give alms to every one that asks, stand up for the stupid and crazy, devote your income and labor to others, hate tyrants, argue not concerning God, have patience and indulgence toward the people, take off your hat to nothing known or unknown or to any man or number of men, go freely with powerful uneducated persons and with the young and with the mothers of families, read these leaves in the open air every season of every year of your life, re-examine all you have been told at school or church or in any book, dismiss whatever insults your own soul, and your very flesh shall be a great poem and have the richest fluency not only in its words but in the silent lines of its lips and face and between the lashes of your eyes and in every motion and joint of your body. . . . The poet shall not spend his time in unneeded work. He shall know that the ground is always ready plowed and manured . . . others may not know it but he shall. He shall go directly to the creation. His trust shall master the trust of everything he touches . . . and shall master all attachment.

Charles Sangster (1822–1893)

Charles Sangster was born at the navy yard in Kingston, Ontario, where his father worked as a shipbuilder. Although he began his career as a cartridge maker at Fort Henry, he eventually turned to journalism and also began writing poetry. By the 1850s his poems were appearing in national journals; and in 1856 he published his first collection, The St. Lawrence and the Saguenay, and Other Poems, *which was well received both in Canada and abroad. His second book was equally acclaimed, and Sangster seemed to be on the road to literary fame. But he was increasingly dogged by depression, which was exacerbated by family deaths and the drudgery of his day job. The situation worsened in 1868, when he accepted a post-office position in Ottawa. He remained there for eighteen miserable years, writing and revising almost nothing until his retirement. Finally, during the last five years of his life, he recovered enough poetic energy to complete two more collections, but neither was published during his lifetime.*

The sequence titled Sonnets Written in the Orillia Woods *is dated August 1859 and appeared in Sangster's second collection,* Hesperus, and Other Poems and Lyrics *(1860). In the following sonnet from that sequence, he considers the persistent human yearning to create, our need "to bring forth fruits and flowers" despite – or because of – our [rotting] sins."*

from *Sonnets Written in the Orillia Woods*

VII

Our life is like a forest, where the sun
Glints down upon us through the throbbing leaves;
The full light rarely finds us. One by one,
Deep rooted in our souls, there springeth up
Dark groves of human passion, rich in gloom,
At first no bigger than an acorn-cup.
Hope threads the tangled labyrinth, but grieves
Till all our sins have rotted in their tomb,
And made the rich loam of each yearning heart
To bring forth fruits and flowers to a new life.

We feel the dew from heaven, and there start
From some deep fountain little rills whose strife
Is drowned in music. Thus in light and shade
We live, and move, and die, through all this earthly glade.

Matthew Arnold   (1822–1888)

Matthew Arnold was an English poet, essayist, literary critic, and educational reformer and, along with Tennyson, Browning, and Barrett Browning, one of the best-known poets in Victorian England. In 1865 he published the first of a series called Essays in Criticism, *which included a piece about the life and writings of French poet Maurice de Guérin (1810–39). In the following extract from that essay, Arnold considers poetry's power "to awaken in us a wonderfully full, new, and intimate sense of [things], and of our relations with them."*

---

from *Essay on the Life and Genius of Maurice de Guérin*

The grand power of poetry is its interpretative power; by which I mean, not a power of drawing out in black and white an explanation of the mystery of the universe, but the power of so dealing with things as to awaken in us a wonderfully full, new, and intimate sense of them, and of our relations with them. When this sense is awakened in us, as to objects without us, we feel ourselves to be in contact with the essential nature of those objects, to be no longer bewildered and oppressed by them, but to have their secret, and to be in harmony with them; and this feeling calms and satisfies us as no other can. Poetry, indeed, interprets in another way besides this; but one of its two ways of interpreting, of exercising its highest power, is by awakening this sense in us. I will not now inquire whether this sense is illusive, whether it can be proved not to be illusive, whether it does absolutely make us possess the real nature of things; all I say is, that poetry can awaken it in us, and that to awaken it is one of the highest powers of poetry. The interpretations of science do not give us this intimate sense of objects as the interpretations of poetry give it; they appeal to a limited faculty, and not to the whole man. It is not [botanist Carl] Linnaeus, or [chemist Henry] Cavendish, or [naturalist Georges] Cuvier who gives us the true sense of animals, or water, or plants, who seizes their secret for us, who makes us participate in their life; it is Shakespeare, with his

     "daffodils
That come before the swallow dares, and take
The winds of March with beauty"
[from *The Winter's Tale*];

it is Wordsworth, with his

         "voice . . . heard
In spring-time from the cuckoo-bird,
Breaking the silence of the seas
Among the farthest Hebrides"
[from "The Solitary Reaper"];

it is Keats, with his

     "moving waters at their priestlike task
Of cold ablution round Earth's human shores"
[from "Bright Star"].

Thomas Wentworth Higginson

(1823–1911)

Thomas Wentworth Higginson was an American poet, essayist, editor, minister, and prominent abolitionist. Although he wrote numerous books and articles over the course of his long life, including biographies of Margaret Fuller and Henry Wadsworth Longfellow, he is most often remembered today as Emily Dickinson's correspondent and an early editor of her work.

During the Civil War, Higginson served as colonel of the First South Carolina Volunteers, the army's first official regiment of freedmen, an experience he describes in Army Life in a Black Regiment, *published in 1870. He was intensely interested in the expressive lives of the soldiers under his command and became one of the first white students of African-American music. In 1867 the* Atlantic Monthly *published his article "Negro Spirituals," which transcribed and discussed many of the songs he had heard during the war. Most readers had never before seen these lyrics in print or heard them discussed as an art form comparable to the European ballad tradition.*

from *Negro Spirituals*

The war brought to some of us, besides its direct experiences, many a strange fulfilment of dreams of other days. For instance, the present writer has been a faithful student of the Scottish ballads, and had always envied Sir Walter [Scott] the delight of tracing them out amid their own heather, and of writing them down piecemeal from the lips of aged crones. It was a strange enjoyment, therefore, to be suddenly brought into the midst of a kindred world of unwritten songs, as simple and indigenous as the Border Minstrelsy, more uniformly plaintive, almost always more quaint, and often as essentially poetic.

This interest was rather increased by the fact that I had for many years heard of this class of songs under the name of "Negro Spirituals," and had even heard some of them sung by friends from South Carolina. I could now gather on their own soil these strange plants, which I had before seen as in museums alone. True, the individual songs rarely coincided; there was a line here, a chorus there, – just enough to fix the class, but this was unmistakable. It was not strange that they differed, for the range seemed almost endless, and South Carolina, Georgia, and Florida seemed to have nothing but the generic character in common, until all were mingled in the united stock of camp-melodies.

. . . Writing down in the darkness, as I best could – perhaps with my hand in the safe covert of my pocket, – the words of the song, I have afterwards carried it to my tent, like some captured bird or insect, and then, after examination, put it by. Or, summoning one of the men at some period of leisure, – Corporal Robert Sutton, for instance, whose iron memory held all the details of a song as if it were a ford or a forest, – I have completed the new specimen by supplying the absent parts. The music I could only retain by ear, and though the more common strains were repeated often enough to fix their impression, there were others that occurred only once or twice.

The words will be here given, as nearly as possible, in the original dialect; and if the spelling seems sometimes inconsistent, or the misspelling insufficient, it is because I could get no nearer. I wished to avoid what seems to me the only error of [James Russell] Lowell's "Biglow Papers" in respect to dialect, – the occasional use of an extreme misspelling, which merely confuses the eye, without taking us any closer to the peculiarity of sound.

. . . Almost all their songs were thoroughly religious in their tone, however quaint their expression, and were in a minor key, both as to words and music. The attitude is always the same, and, as a commentary on the life of the race, is infinitely pathetic. Nothing but patience for this life, – nothing but triumph in the next. Sometimes the present predominates, sometimes the future; but the combination is always implied.

. . . [Here] is one of the wildest and most striking of the whole series: there is a mystical effect and a passionate striving throughout the whole. The Scriptural struggle between Jacob and the angel, which is only dimly expressed in the words, seems all uttered in the music. I think it impressed my imagination more powerfully than any other of these songs.

WRESTLING JACOB

"O wrestlin' Jacob, Jacob, day's a-breakin';
I will not let thee go!
O wrestlin' Jacob, Jacob, day's a-breakin';
He will not let me go!
O, I hold my brudder wid a tremblin' hand;
I would not let him go!
I hold my sister wid a tremblin' hand;
I would not let her go!

"O, Jacob do hang from a tremblin' limb,
He would not let him go!
O, Jacob do hang from a tremblin' limb;
De Lord will bless my soul.
O wrestlin' Jacob, Jacob," &c.

. . . These quaint religious songs were to the men more than a source of relaxation; they were a stimulus to courage and a tie to heaven. I never overheard in camp a profane or vulgar song. With the trifling exceptions given, all had a religious motive, while the most secular melody could not have been more exciting. A few youths from Savannah, who were comparatively men of the world, had learned some of the "Ethiopian Minstrel" ditties, imported from the North. These took no hold upon the mass; and, on the other hand, they sang reluctantly, even on Sunday, the long and short metres of the hymnbooks, always gladly yielding to the more potent excitement of their own "spirituals." By these they could sing themselves, as had their fathers before them, out of the contemplation of their own low estate, into the sublime scenery of the Apocalypse. I remember that this minor-keyed pathos used to seem to me almost too sad to dwell upon, while slavery seemed destined to last for generations; but now that their patience has had its perfect work, history cannot afford to lose this portion of its record. There is no parallel instance of an oppressed race thus sustained by the religious sentiment alone. These songs are but the vocal expression of the simplicity of their faith and the sublimity of their long resignation.

Walter Pater

Walter Pater was an English fiction writer, essayist, and art and literary critic whose ideas about style and aesthetics influenced early modernists such as Joyce, Proust, and Yeats. In 1889, Pater published Appreciations, with an Essay on Style, *a collection of articles about English writers, including Shakespeare, Wordsworth, and Coleridge. It opens with an essay, "Style," in which he lays out his ideas about the aesthetics of prose and poetry. In the following extract from that essay, Pater considers a literary artist's obligations to "the abundant and often recondite laws" of the language.*

from *Style*

The literary artist is of necessity a scholar, and in what he proposes to do will have in mind, first of all, the scholar and the scholarly conscience – the male conscience in this matter, as we must think it, under a system of education which still to so large an extent limits real scholarship to men. In his self-criticism, he supposes always that sort of reader who will go (full of eyes) warily, considerately, though without consideration for him, over the ground which the female conscience traverses so lightly, so amiably. For the material in which he works is no more a creation of his own than the sculptor's marble. Product of a myriad various minds and contending tongues, compact of obscure and minute association, a language has its own abundant and often recondite laws, in the habitual and summary recognition of which scholarship consists. A writer, full of a matter he is before all things anxious to express, may think of those laws, the limitations of vocabulary, structure, and the like, as a restriction, but if a real artist will find in them an opportunity. His punctilious observance of the proprieties of his medium will diffuse through all he writes a general air of sensibility, of refined usage. *Exclusiones debitae naturae* – the exclusions, or rejections, which nature demands – we know how large a part these play, according to [philosopher and scientist Francis] Bacon, in the science of nature. In a somewhat changed sense, we might say that the art of the scholar is summed up in the observance of those rejections demanded by the nature of his medium, the material he must use. Alive to the value of an atmosphere in which every term finds its utmost degree of expression, and with all the jealousy of a lover of words, he will resist a constant tendency on the part of the majority of those who use them to efface the distinctions of language, the facility of writers often reinforcing in this respect the work of the vulgar. He will feel the obligation not of the laws only, but of those affinities, avoidances, those mere preferences, of his language, which through the associations of literary history have become a part of its nature, prescribing the rejection of many a neology, many a license, many a gipsy phrase which might present itself as actually expressive. His appeal, again, is to the scholar, who has great experience in literature, and will show no favour to short-cuts, or hackneyed illustration, or an affectation of learning designed for the unlearned. Hence a contention, a sense of self-restraint and renunciation, having for the susceptible reader the effect of a challenge for minute consideration; the attention of the writer, in every minutest detail, being a pledge that it is worth the reader's while to be attentive too, that the writer is dealing scrupulously with his instrument, and therefore, indirectly, with the reader himself also, that he has the science of the instrument he plays on, perhaps, after all, with a freedom which in such case will be the freedom of a master.

For meanwhile, braced only by those restraints, he is really vindicating his liberty in the making of a vocabulary, an entire system of composition, for himself, his own true manner; and when we speak of the manner of a true master we mean what is essential in his art. Pedantry being only the scholarship of *le cuistre* (we have no English equivalent [but "prig" is close]) he is no pedant, and does but show his intelligence of the rules of language in his freedoms with it, addition or expansion, which like the spontaneities of manner in a well-bred person will still further illustrate good taste. – The right vocabulary! Translators have not invariably seen how all-important that is in the work of translation, driving for the most part at idiom or construction; whereas, if the original be first-rate, one's first care should be with its elementary particles, Plato, for instance, being often reproducible by an exact following, with no variation in structure, of word after word, as the pencil follows a drawing under tracing-paper, so only each word or syllable be not of false colour, to change my illustration a little.

Well! that is because any writer worth translating at all has winnowed and searched through his vocabulary, is conscious of the words he would select in systematic reading of a dictionary, and still more of the words he would reject were the dictionary other than Johnson's; and doing this with his peculiar sense of the world ever in view, in search of an instrument for the adequate expression of that, he begets a vocabulary faithful to the colouring of his own spirit, and in the strictest sense original. That living authority which language needs lies, in truth, in its scholars, who recognising always that every language possesses a genius, a very fastidious genius, of its own, expand at once and purify its very elements, which must needs change along with the changing thoughts of living people. Ninety years ago, for instance, great mental force, certainly, was needed by Wordsworth, to break through the consecrated poetic associations of a century, and speak the language that was his, that was to become in a measure the language of the next generation. But he did it with the tact of a scholar also. English, for a quarter of a century past, has been assimilating the phraseology of pictorial art; for half a century, the phraseology of the great German metaphysical movement of eighty years ago; in part also the language of mystical theology: and none but pedants will regret a great consequent increase of its resources. For many years to come its enterprise may well lie in the naturalisation of the vocabulary of science, so only it be under the eye of a sensitive scholarship – in a liberal naturalisation of the ideas of science too, for after all the chief stimulus of good style is to possess a full, rich, complex matter to grapple with. The literary artist, therefore, will be well aware of physical science; science also attaining, in its turn, its true literary ideal. And then, as the scholar is nothing without the historic sense, he will be apt to restore not really obsolete or really worn-out words, but the finer edge of words still in use: *ascertain, communicate, discover* – words like these it has been part of our "business" to misuse. And still, as language was made for man, he will be no authority for correctnesses which, limiting freedom of utterance, were yet but accidents in their origin; as if one vowed not to say "*its*," which ought to have been in Shakespeare; "*his*" and "*hers*," for inanimate objects, being but a barbarous and really inexpressive survival. Yet we have known many things like this. Racy Saxon monosyllables, close to us as touch and sight, he will intermix readily with those long, savoursome, Latin words, rich in "second intention." In this late day certainly, no critical process can be conducted reasonably without eclecticism. Of such eclecticism we have a justifying example in one of the first poets of our time. How illustrative of monosyllabic effect, of sonorous Latin, of the phraseology of science, of metaphysic, of colloquialism even, are the writings of Tennyson; yet with what a fine, fastidious scholarship throughout!

A scholar writing for the scholarly, he will of course leave something to the willing intelligence of his reader. "To go preach to the first passer-by," says Montaigne, "to become tutor to the ignorance of the first I meet, is a thing I abhor"; a thing, in fact, naturally distressing to the scholar, who will therefore ever be shy of offering uncomplimentary assistance to the reader's wit. To really strenuous minds there is a pleasurable stimulus in the challenge for a continuous effort on their part, to be rewarded by securer and more intimate grasp of the author's sense. Self-restraint, a skilful economy of means, *ascêsis*, that too has a beauty of its own; and for the reader supposed there will be an aesthetic satisfaction in that frugal closeness of style which makes the most of a word, in the exaction from every sentence of a precise relief, in the just spacing out of word to thought, in the logically filled space connected always with the delightful sense of difficulty overcome.

Different classes of persons, at different times, make, of course, very various demands upon literature. Still, scholars, I suppose, and not only scholars, but all disinterested lovers of books, will always look to it, as to all other fine art, for a refuge, a sort of cloistral refuge, from a certain vulgarity in the actual world. A perfect poem like [Milton's] *Lycidas*, a perfect fiction like [Thackeray's *Henry*] *Esmond*, the perfect handling of a theory like Newman's *Idea of a University*, has for them something of the uses of a religious "retreat." Here, then, with a view to the central need of a select few, those "men of a finer thread" who have formed and maintain the literary ideal, everything, every component element, will have undergone exact trial, and, above all, there will be no uncharacteristic or tarnished or vulgar decoration, permissible ornament being for the most part structural, or necessary. As the painter in his picture, so the artist in his book, aims at the production by honourable artifice of a peculiar atmosphere. "The artist," says [philosopher Johann von] Schiller, "may be known rather by what he *omits*"; and in literature, too, the true artist may be best recognised by his tact of omission. For to the grave reader words too are grave; and the ornamental word, the figure, the accessory form or colour or reference, is rarely content to die to thought precisely at the right moment, but will inevitably linger awhile, stirring a long "brain-wave" behind it of perhaps quite alien associations.

Just there, it may be, is the detrimental tendency of the sort of scholarly attentiveness of mind I am recommending. But the true artist allows for it. He will remember that, as the very word ornament indicates what is in itself non-essential, so the "one beauty" of all literary style is of its very essence, and independent, in prose and verse alike, of all removable decoration; that it may exist in its fullest lustre, as in Flaubert's *Madame Bovary*, for instance, or in Stendhal's *Le Rouge et Le Noir*, in a composition utterly unadorned, with hardly a single suggestion of visibly beautiful things. Parallel, allusion, the allusive way generally, the flowers in the garden: – he knows the narcotic force of these upon the negligent intelligence to which any diversion, literally, is welcome, any vagrant intruder, because one can go wandering away with it from the immediate subject. Jealous, if he have a really quickening motive within, of all that does not hold directly to that, of the facile, the otiose, he will never depart from the strictly pedestrian process, unless he gains a ponderable something thereby. Even assured of its congruity, he will still question its serviceableness. Is it worth while, can we afford, to attend to just that, to just that figure or literary reference, just then? – Surplusage! he will dread that, as the runner on his muscles. For in truth all art does but consist in the removal of surplusage, from the last finish of the gem-engraver blowing away the last particle of invisible dust, back to the earliest divination of the finished work to be, lying somewhere, according to Michelangelo's fancy, in the rough-hewn block of stone.

Emily Dickinson

(1830–1886)

In 1862 Emily Dickinson sent a letter to Thomas Wentworth Higginson, a Massachusetts minister and regular contributor to the Atlantic Monthly. In his 1891 article "Emily Dickinson's Letters," Higginson recalled:

> The letter was postmarked "Amherst," and it was in a handwriting so peculiar that it seemed as if the writer might have taken her first lessons by studying the famous fossil bird-tracks in the museum of that college town. Yet it was not in the slightest degree illiterate, but cultivated, quaint, and wholly unique. Of punctuation there was little; she used chiefly dashes, and it has been thought better, in printing these letters, as with her poems, to give them the benefit in this respect of the ordinary usages; and so with her habit as to capitalization, as the printers call it, in which she followed the Old English and present German method of thus distinguishing every noun substantive. But the most curious thing about the letter was the total absence of a signature. It proved, however, that she had written her name on a card, and put it under the shelter of a smaller envelope inclosed in the larger; and even this name was written – as if the shy writer wished to recede as far as possible from view – in pencil, not in ink."

Yet despite Higginson's discomfort with her style and Dickinson's discomfort with what she called his "surgery," their epistolary friendship continued until her death.

Because complex copyright issues surround the manuscript transcriptions of Dickinson's poems, I have excerpted the following letters from Higginson's article. They include the anxious punctuation and capitalization "corrections" that also appear in the first published collection of Dickinson's poems, which he edited with Mabel Loomis Todd. Higginson's remarks in his introduction to that collection reveal the grip of nineteenth-century notions of propriety, even at the grammatical level: "The main quality of these poems is that of extraordinary grasp and insight, uttered with an uneven vigor sometimes exasperating, seemingly wayward, but really unsought and inevitable. After all, when a thought takes one's breath away, a lesson on grammar seems an impertinence."

Two Letters to Thomas Wentworth Higginson

edited by Thomas Wentworth Higginson

received on April 16, 1862

Mr. Higginson, – Are you too deeply occupied to say if my verse is alive?

The mind is so near itself, it cannot see distinctly, and I have none to ask.

Should you think it breathed, and had you the leisure to tell me, I should feel quick gratitude.

If I make the mistake, that you dared to tell me would give me sincerer honor toward you.

I inclose my name, asking you, if you please, sir, to tell me what is true?

That you will not betray me it is needless to ask, since honor is it's [*sic*] own pawn.

received on April 26, 1862

Mr. Higginson, – Your kindness claimed earlier gratitude, but I was ill, and write to-day from my pillow.

Thank you for the surgery; it was not so painful as I supposed. I bring you others, as you ask, though they might not differ. While my thought is un-dressed, I can make the distinction; but when I put them in the gown, they look alike and numb.

You asked how old I was? I made no verse, but one or two, until this winter, sir.

I had a terror since September, I could tell to none; and so I sing, as the boy does of the burying ground, because I am afraid.

You inquire my books. For poets, I have Keats, and Mr. and Mrs. Browning. For prose, Mr. Ruskin, Sir Thomas Browne, and the Revelations. I went to school, but in your manner of the phrase had no education. When a little girl, I had a friend who taught me Immortality; but venturing too near, himself, he never returned. Soon after my tutor died, and for several years my lexicon was my only companion. Then I found one more, but he was not contented I be his scholar, so he left the land.

You ask my companions, Hills, sir, and the sundown, and a dog large as myself that my father bought me. They are better than beings because they know but do not tell; and the noise in the pool at noon excels my piano.

I have a brother and sister; my mother does not care for thought, and father, too busy with his briefs to notice what we do. He buys me many books, but begs me not to read them, because he fears they joggle the mind. They are religious, except me, and address an eclipse, every morning, whom they call their "Father."

But I fear my story fatigues you. I would like to learn. Could you tell me how to grow, or is it unconveyed, like melody or witchcraft?

You speak of Mr. Whitman, I never read his book, but was told that it was disgraceful.

I read Miss Prescott's Circumstance, but it followed me in the dark, so I avoided her.

Two editors of journals came to my father's house this winter, and asked me for my mind, and when I asked them "why" they said I was penurious, and they would use it for the world.

I could not weigh myself, myself. My size felt small to me. I read your chapters in the "Atlantic," and experienced honor for you. I was sure you would not reject a confiding question.

Is this, sir, what you asked me to tell you? Your friend,

E. Dickinson.

Paul Verlaine

Paul Verlaine was a French poet and one of the major voices of the Symbolist movement. Influenced early by the work of Charles Baudelaire, Verlaine published three collections of poetry by the time he was in his mid-twenties. But in 1871, married for only a year, he left his wife and embarked on a fraught and tumultuous affair with the poet Arthur Rimbaud, which ended in 1873, when a drunken Verlaine shot Rimbaud in the wrist. Jailed for a year and a half, Verlaine concentrated on reading and writing and produced some of his best-known poems during his incarceration. One of those poems was "Art Poétique" (The Art of Poetry), written in 1874 but not published until 1882. Verlaine dedicated it to poet Charles Morice, who later published the complete edition of Verlaine's poems. The ellipses in the final stanza appear in the original.

The Art of Poetry

translated by Paul Driver

à Charles Morice

The tune is everything –
        so prefer the irregular
                line that dissolves in the air,
to the stodginess of "meaning."

Don't let your choice of words
        fight shy of error –
                adore the flushed grey area
where precise and imprecise are blurred –

like eyes behind a veil,
        or the noonday shimmer,
                or the sky at the end of summer
with the stars a lucid muddle.

For what we need's a subtler tone –
  less colour, more of the shade
    that alone can let the dream invade
the dream, the flute the horn.

Avoid, above all, the killer retort,
  the "rapier" thrust of wit,
    the salty, the satiric –
seasonings cheaply bought.

Take eloquence and wring its neck!,
  and, while you're at it, confine
    that egregious chancer, rhyme:
untethered, it asks for a wreck.

Yes, who will deplore this crime? –
  invention of some wild
    jewel-faker or deaf child,
a hollowness behind the gleam.

The tune, the music, is what counts,
  to lift your verse to the air
    to speak of new worlds there.
On a scale of blue it mounts

in its brave adventure,
  a piece with the crispy morning-time,
    with the fragrance of mint of or thyme . . .
And all the rest is "literature."

Gerard Manley Hopkins (1844–1889)

Gerard Manley Hopkins was both a poet and a Jesuit priest, a rhythmic in-novator who applied a scientist's concentration to the details of the natural world. In the following extract from his notebooks, he considers the sensation he called instress *– when "what you look at hard seems to look at you" – which he saw as a necessary step in recognizing* inscape, *an object or identity's dis-tinct, individual design.*

from *Notebook Entry*

Spring 1871

What you look hard at seems to look hard at you, hence the true and the false instress of nature. One day early in March when long streamers [of clouds] were rising from over Kemble End one large flake loop-shaped, not a streamer but belonging to the string, moving too slowly to be seen, seemed to cap and fill the zenith with a white shire of cloud. I looked long up at it till the tall height and the beauty of the scaping – regularly curled knots springing if I remember from fine stems, like foliation in wood or stone – had strongly grown on me. It changed beautiful changes, growing more into ribs and one stretch of running into branching like corals. Un-less you refresh the mind from time to time you cannot always remember or believe how deep the inscape in things is.

William Butler Yeats (1865–1939)

The following extract is from Four Years *(1921), which poet William Butler Yeats first published in the* London Mercury. *An autobiographical sketch of his youth in the years between 1887 and 1891, the piece chronicles his vain struggle to fit his actual self into his preconception of what a poet should be. At the time of the sketch's appearance, Yeats had long been a world-renowned literary figure, yet the piece is a vivid portrait of the fumbling artistic apprenticeship that nearly all poets must endure.*

from *Four Years*

Chapter 19

I generalized a great deal and was ashamed of it. I thought that it was my business in life to be an artist and a poet, and that there could be no business comparable to that. I refused to read books, and even to meet people who excited me to generalization, but all to no purpose. I said my prayers much as in childhood, though without the old regularity of hour and place, and I began to pray that my imagination might somehow be rescued from abstraction, and become as pre-occupied with life as had been the imagination of Chaucer. For ten or twelve years more I suffered continual remorse, and only became content when my abstractions had composed themselves into picture and dramatization. My very remorse helped to spoil my early poetry, giving it an element of sentimentality through my refusal to permit it any share of an intellect which I considered impure. Even in practical life I only very gradually began to use generalizations, that have since become the foundation of all I have done, or shall do, in Ireland. For all I know, all men may have been as timid; for I am persuaded that our intellects at twenty contain all the truths we shall ever find, but as yet we do not know truths that belong to us from opinions caught up in casual irritation or momentary phantasy. As life goes on we discover that certain thoughts sustain us in defeat, or give us victory, whether over ourselves or others, & it is these thoughts, tested by passion, that we call convictions. Among subjective men (in all those, that is, who must spin a web out of their own bowels) the victory is an intellectual daily recreation of all that exterior fate snatches away, and so that fate's antithesis; while what I have called "the mask" is an emotional antithesis to all that comes out of their internal nature. We begin to live when we have conceived life as a tragedy.

Robert Frost (1874–1963)

In 1912, during a stay in England, Robert Frost met Edward Thomas, an Anglo-Welsh essayist and literary critic. The two men developed a close friendship, which they maintained even after Frost returned to the United States. It was Frost who convinced Thomas to begin writing poems. But with the outbreak of World War I, Thomas joined the British army, and he was killed in action in France, just before the publication of his second collection, much of which he wrote during his war service. The following poem, which appeared in New Hampshire *(1923), is Frost's elegy to their friendship.*

To E. T.

I slumbered with your poems on my breast,
Spread open as I dropped them half-read through
Like dove wings on a figure on a tomb,
To see if in a dream they brought of you

I might not have the chance I missed in life
Through some delay, and call you to your face
First soldier, and then poet, and then both,
Who died a soldier-poet of your race.

I meant, you meant, that nothing should remain
Unsaid between us, brother, and this remained –
And one thing more that was not then to say:
The Victory for what it lost and gained.

You went to meet the shell's embrace of fire
On Vimy Ridge; and when you fell that day
The war seemed over more for you than me,
But now for me than you – the other way.

How over, though, for even me who knew
The foe thrust back unsafe beyond the Rhine,
If I was not to speak of it to you
And see you pleased once more with words of mine?

Rainer Maria Rilke

Letters to a Young Poet *is a series of ten letters that German poet Rainer Maria Rilke wrote to nineteen-year-old Franz Kappus, who was trying to choose between a military and a literary career. Kappus initiated the correspondence in 1902, and it continued for six years. Following is the second letter in the series, written when Rilke was visiting Viareggio, Italy. Describing that solitary sojourn to his wife Clara, he said, "Everyone must find in his work the center of his life and be able to grow out radially as far as may be. And no one else may watch him in the process . . . for not even he himself may do that."*

from *Letters to a Young Poet*

translated by M. D. Herter Norton

from Letter 2: April 5, 1903

Irony: Do not let yourself be governed by it, especially not in uncreative moments. In creative moments try to make use of it as one more means of grasping life. Cleanly used, it too is clean, and one need not be ashamed of it; and if you feel you are getting too familiar with it, if you fear this growing intimacy with it, then turn to great and serious objects, before which it becomes small and helpless. Seek the depth of things: thither irony never descends – and when you come thus close to the edge of greatness, test out at the same time whether this ironic attitude springs from a necessity of your nature. For under the influence of serious things either it will fall from you (if it is something fortuitous), or else it will (if it really innately belongs to you) strengthen into a stern instrument and take its place in the series of tools with which you will have to shape your art.

Edward Thomas (1878–1917)

*Edward Thomas was an Anglo-Welsh poet, novelist, and essayist. After gradu-
ating from Oxford, he became a regular contributor to the* Daily Chronicle
*and wrote extensively about poets and poetry, although he did not begin writ-
ing poems himself until after 1912, when he met Robert Frost, who was then
living in England. Thomas was killed in action in World War I, and today he
is remembered as one of England's best soldier poets.*

*The following essay about English poet Robert Herrick (1591–1674) is from
Thomas's* A Literary Pilgrim in England *(1917), a compilation of his essays
about poets and place. In his somewhat tongue-in-cheek consideration of the
link between art and the countryside, Thomas quotes widely from Herrick's*
Hesperides, or the Works, both Humane and Divine of Robert Herrick,
Esq., *first published in 1648. All ellipses are Thomas's.*

Herrick

When we think of Herrick, we think of Dean Prior in Devonshire, where
he was Vicar from 1629 to 1647, and from 1662 until his death in 1674,
when he was eighty-three. Yet the greater part of his life was passed in Lon-
don. The family was from Leicester. Nicholas Herrick, the poet's father, was
a goldsmith, with a house in Goldsmiths' Row. There Robert was born.
When his father died from a fall out of an upper window of this house,
he went to live in Wood Street with an uncle, also a goldsmith, and with
him served an apprenticeship till 1614. Then he went to St. John's Col-
lege, Cambridge. He ceased to be a goldsmith. On leaving Cambridge he
entered literary society, and in particular "the tribe of Ben" – that is to say,
the company of poets and gentlemen who acknowledged Ben Jonson's su-
premacy, and met

> "At those lyric feasts
>   Made at the Sun,
> The Dog, the Triple Tun,
>   Where we such clusters had
> As made us nobly wild, not mad;

> And yet each verse of thine
> Outdid the meat, outdid the frolic wine."

Jonson lived on until 1637, but Herrick could not stay in London so long. How he lived is not known. He had well-to-do relatives, but in 1627 he accompanied the expedition to the Isle of Rhe as chaplain, and in 1629 went into his Devonshire exile. He was then thirty-eight, and must have had some good reason for dropping himself into so remote and small a place.

To all appearances he must by that time have been a complete Londoner, one who was well used to the variety and convenience of the city, and to the safe civilized beauty of the suburban country. [In this paragraph and the following extract, Thomas quotes from Thomas Randolph's "Ode to Master Anthony Stafford to Hasten Him into the Country."] There is no indication that he preferred "old simplicity, though hid in grey," to "foppery in plush and scarlet clad." If he went to "see the wholesome country girls make hay," it was not from any disdain of

> "The beauties of the Cheap, and wives of Lombard Street."

A "sweet disorder" and "wild civility" in park and meadow was probably as pleasant to him as in woman's dress, and he could have all that he desired by a short journey on foot or in a barge. When he was away at Dean Prior, he sent his tears and "supremest kiss"

> "To thee, my silver-footed Thamesis.
> No more shall I reiterate thy, Strand,
> Whereon so many stately structures stand:
> Nor in the summer's sweeter evenings go
> To bathe in thee as thousand others do;
> No more shall I along thy crystal glide
> In barge with boughs and rushes beautified,
> With soft, smooth virgins for our chaste disport,
> To Richmond, Kingston, and to Hampton Court.
> Never again shall I with finny oar
> Put from, or draw unto the faithful shore:
> And landing here, or safely landing there,
> Make way to my beloved Westminster,
> Or to the Golden Cheapside, where the earth
> Of Julia Herrick gave to me my birth. . . ."

M. Delattre thinks it probable that "Corinna's Maying" describes May Day as it was celebrated in London in those days, when the young men fetched boughs of hawthorn and brier to ornament the doors of Cheapside, Cornhill, Gracechurch Street, and "every man would walk into the sweet meadows and green woods, there to rejoice their spirits with the beauty and savour of sweet flowers, and with the harmony of birds, praising God in their kind." The fourth verse, for example, shows a perfectly suburban scene:

"Come, my Corinna, come; and coming, mark
How each field turns a street, each street a park,
    Made green and trimm'd with trees! See how
    Devotion gives each house a bough
    Or branch! Each porch, each door, ere this,
    An ark, a tabernacle is,
Made up of whitethorn, neatly interwove,
As if here were those cooler shades of love.
    Can such delights be in the street
    And open fields, and we not see't?
    Come, we'll abroad : and let's obey
    The proclamation made for May,
And sin no more, as we have done, by staying.
But, my Corinna, come, let's go a-Maying."

It is not easy to imagine what more Herrick wanted than this combination or alternation of street and park, with good company.

But already in 1610 Herrick had begun to write in praise of pure country life. His brother Thomas had left London with a bride, and Herrick congratulated him on exchanging the city for

"The country's sweet simplicity:
And it to know and practise, with intent
    To grow the sooner innocent
By studying to know virtue, and to aim
    More at her nature than her name."

Possibly at nineteen Herrick really believed that in the country all was "purling springs, groves, birds, and well-weav'd bowers, with fields enamelled with flowers"; that there were none of those "desperate cares th' industrious merchant has"; that men there ate only "to cool, not cocker appetite," and "content makes all ambrosia" – "boiled nettles" and all. But it is more likely that Herrick got it all from books. He accepted the view that the golden age was not yet over in the country, though he must have been pretending when he called his Muse a "mad maiden" who might

"sit and piping please
The poor and private cottages. . . .
There, there, perhaps, such lines as these
May take the simple villages."

He said,

> "Contempt in courts and cities dwell,
> No critic haunts the poor man's cell,"

but gives us no real reason to believe him when he goes on to say, as if he liked it, that in the poor man's cell you can hear your own lines read "by no one tongue censured." To make neat verses was one of his recreations, and so he wrote:

> "To bread and water none is poor;
> And having these, what need of more?
> Though much from out the cess be spent,
> Nature with little is content."

Sometimes he was practically translating, as when he bade his worthy friend Thomas Falconbridge

> "Lastly, be mindful, when thou art grown great,
> That towers high rear'd dread most the lightning's threat:
> Whereas the humble cottages not fear
> The cleaving bolt of Jove the Thunderer."

On the other hand, he wrote in the same strain after he had been some time in Devonshire; and since it is obvious that Dean Prior was in many ways rude and inconvenient, it is equally obvious that without compensations he did not sit down in his Vicarage and write about "His Content in the Country," with Prudence Baldwin, his maidservant:

> "Here, here I live with what my board
> Can with the smallest cost afford.
> Though ne'er so mean the viands be,
> They well content my Prew and me.
> Or pea, or bean, or wort, or beet,
> Whatever comes, content makes sweet.
> Here we rejoice, because no rent
> We pay for our poor tenement
> Wherein we rest, and never fear
> The landlord or the usurer.
> The quarter-day does ne'er affright
> Our peaceful slumbers in the night.
> We eat our own and batten more,
> Because we feed on no man's score;
> But pity those whose flanks grow great,
> Swell'd with the lard of others' meat.
> We bless our fortunes when we see
> Our own beloved privacy;

And like our living, where we're known
To very few, or else to none."

The compensation probably was a contented mind, and his later praise of country life is by this much better than his early, that it does tell us something about the country as well as exclaiming:

"O happy life! if that their good
The husbandmen but understood!"

He put in the game of "fox i' th' hole," or distinguished between the "cock-rood" for snaring woodcocks and the "glade" for catching pheasants, not for local colour in an otherwise conventional praise of country life, but because these things had become familiar to him; he had really in some measure become a countryman.

If he had not, need he ever have gone back in 1662 when the King enjoyed his own again? He had found the wherewithal to live in London from the year of his ejection, 1647, and he would not have gone back at the age of sixty-nine without a strong preference. Dean Prior was a very remote village lying close under the high south-eastern edge of Dartmoor. The road from Exeter to Plymouth passes Herrick's church on the left a little more than a mile out of Buckfastleigh. Anciently, I believe, the road left Dean Prior Church somewhat to the left, but not so far as to be said to leave it in the mud even in days of villainous roads. To-day the railway misses it and the hill beyond it by making a sharp detour down the valley of the Dart from Buckfastleigh.

No trace of Herrick is left in the hamlet except an epitaph, not his own, but one written by him for his neighbours, Sir Edward and Lady Giles, of Dean Court. Their effigies kneel facing one another in the costume of Charles I.'s reign, and underneath have been cut these words:

"No trust to metals nor to marbles, when
Those have their fate and wear away as men;
Times, titles, trophies may be lost and spent,
But virtue rears the eternal monument.
What more than these can tombs or tombstones pay?
But here's the sunset of a tedious day:
These two asleep are: I'll but be undress'd,
And so to bed: pray wish us all good rest."

Herrick was truly himself only on the subject of flowers, domestic things, and women. For his own epitaph he had addressed the Robin Redbreast, asking it to cover him with leaves and moss-work, and sing his dirge, and write in foliage these words:

"Here, here the tomb of Robin Herrick is."

Had the task been left to the birds, the result could not have been less to-day. Neither stone nor epitaph marks the grave of Herrick. But the church remains among beeches, and Dean Court, now a farm, and the Vicarage. Here he wrote and thanked God for it, and for his bread, his firing,

"The worts, the purslain, and the mess
Of watercress,"

and his "beloved beet," the spiced drink, the corn from the glebe, the hen that laid an egg a day, the ewes that bore twins every year, the kine that "run cream for wine." This was "His Grange, or Private Wealth":

"Though clock,
To tell how night draws hence, I've none,
    A cock
I have to sing how day draws on.
    I have
A maid, my Prew, by good luck sent
    To save
That little Fates me gave or lent.
    A hen
I keep, which, creeking day by day,
    Tells when
She goes her long white egg to lay.
    A goose
I have, which with a jealous ear
    Lets loose
Her tongue to tell that danger's near.
    A lamb
I keep (tame) with my morsels fed,
    Whose dam
An orphan left him (lately dead).
    A cat
I keep that plays about my house,
    Grown fat
With eating many a miching mouse.
    To these
A Tracy I do keep whereby
    I please
The more my rural privacy;
    Which are
But toys to give my heart some ease;

Where care
None is, slight things do lightly please."

Tracy was his spaniel. That hen must have been such a wonder that it can be understood how he came to compare Julia's leg to that daily "long white egg." The cat, too, is very real. He must have been a lover of cats, for in his earliest poem, that to his brother on country life, he speaks of the roof that maintains a fireside cricket choir,

"And the brisk mouse may feast herself with crumbs
Till that the green-eyed kitten comes."

Outside the Vicarage he does not stray far. If he "traced the hare i' th' treacherous snow," he gives us no idea of the sport or of the country. Perhaps he was short-sighted, for he seems to see very clearly little things which he could not have seen at all without special attention. His daffodils have not Wordsworth's wild moorland air. They are just flowers isolated, but they are as real as Wordsworth's. Real, too, is that "savour like unto a blessed field,"

"when the bedabbled morn
Washes the golden ears of corn."

No poet ever loved perfumes more, indoors and out of doors, the breaths of flowers, of spices, of women, of bees, of amber, of burning wood, of wine, of milk and cream, of baked pear.

He confessed or professed that his eye and heart doted "less on Nature than on Art," and declared – in writing to an old London friend, Sir Clipseby Crew – that since coming to the country he had lost his "former flame." But, then, on the other hand, he wrote:

"More discontents I never had
Since I was born than here,
Where I have been, and still am sad,
In this dull Devonshire;
Yet, justly too, I must confess
I ne'er invented such
Ennobled numbers for the press
Than where I loathed so much."

Did he show this to Sir Clipseby? Probably not. What he said to the knight was very different:

"Cold and hunger never yet
Could a noble verse beget;
But your bowls with sack replete,
Give me these, my knight, and try

In a minute's space how I
Can run mad and prophesy."

Too much has been made of his insulting farewell "to Dean Bourn, a rude river in Devon, by which sometimes he lived." Perhaps he got splashed in crossing it on his way to London, and wrote these verses against the savage Devonians just to amuse the Londoners. Or he might have been badly treated at the ejection in 1647. In any case, a great measure of eagerness in looking forward to London might have been expected, and a proportionate disgust with whatever thwarted or delayed him "in loathed Devonshire." When he set foot in London "from the dull confines of the drooping West," he exclaimed:

"O fruitful Genius! that bestowest here
An everlasting plenty year by year.
O place ! O people ! manners ! framed to please
All nations, customs, kindreds, languages!
I am a free-born Roman ; suffer, then,
That I amongst you live a citizen.
London my home is, though by hard fate sent
Into a long and irksome banishment. . . ."

This, I think, was mainly an exercise for London eyes. It is rather less than more sincere sounding than his praises of a country life.

How much he wrote at Dean Prior will never be known certainly. But the poem "To the Little Spinners" must have been; and the one on "Oberon's Palace," where Oberon and Mab are "led by the shine of snails"; and "Oberon's Feast," with its "papery butterflies" and "the unctuous dewlaps of a snail." The rural poems were obviously written there, poems like "The Hock-Cart, or Harvest Home," with its picture of labourers devoutly following the waggon, while others,

"less attent
To prayers than to merriment.
Run after with their breeches rent . . ."

and then the great feast, the

"large and chief
Foundation of your feast, fat beef:
With upper stories, mutton, veal. And bacon. . . ."

The conclusion seems to prove him a thorough countryman of the land-owning or employing class; for he bids the labourers work after their holiday, because

"Feed him ye must, whose food fills you;
And that this pleasure is like grain,
Not sent ye for to drown your pain,
But for to make it spring again."

He was not without company. Among his friends was John Weekes, Dean
of St. Burian in Cornwall. He visited this man's house, and either there or
at Dean Prior would sit with him regretting past times, but drinking until
they were

"Plump as the cherry,
Though not so fresh, yet full as merry
As the cricket,"

until they saw

"the fire less shine
From th' embers than the kitling's eyne."

Prue Baldwin, his maidservant, never forsook him; others, mere "summer
birds" of passage, soon flew away, but not she. He did her the honour to
waste his scholarship in these lines on her sickness:

"Prue, my dearest maid, is sick
Almost to be lunatic:
Aesculapius! come and bring
Means for her recovering;
And a gallant cock shall be
Offered up by her to thee."

It seems impossible to guess whether Julia or Anthea ever lived in the same
house with him. Or could Prue supply suggestions for those ladies as well
as light the fires and cook the dinners? For a time Elizabeth Herrick, widow
of his brother Thomas, kept house for him. Julia, at least, was a substantial
and not a transitory person, and when he bids her make the wedding cake
for a bride, it looks as if she were an inmate, whether subordinate or not, at
the Vicarage. And there is a quite exceptional touch of reality in the protes-
tation to Julia, where he says:

"As if we should for ever part. . . .
After a day or two or three,
I would come back and live with thee."

At Dean Court the Gileses had no children, but they had nieces living with
them, and doubtless other visitors coming and going. He wrote "The En-
tertainment: or Porch-Verse" for the marriage of one niece, Lettice Yarde;
and a "Meadow-Verse: or Anniversary" for another, Bridget Lowman. Many

times in the manor-house at Dean Court, now a farmhouse, Herrick must have seen the holly up. He paints the holly and the rosemary and bay, but not the hall or the house; as he paints the flowers and a typical meadow, but not Dartmoor. In fact, there seems no connexion between Herrick and Dean Prior, except that he lived there over thirty years. It does not remind us of him, nor does his work remind us of it. But the association is growing up, and already it is a piquant, pleasant thing to fancy, or to try to establish, the connexion between the southern foot of Dartmoor and the author of those daintiest poems to flowers and ladies.

Wallace Stevens (1879–1955)

Wallace Stevens's poetry had a tremendous influence on younger readers, and one of those young admirers was José Rodríguez Feo, who published a literary review in Cuba and who, in 1944, wrote to Stevens asking for permission to publish some translations of his poems. Their epistolary friendship quickly blossomed – Stevens told a friend that Feo was "his most exciting correspondent" – and it continued until the poet's death. In the following letter, Stevens refers to criticisms of T. S. Eliot's recent lecture on Milton, which Feo had attended in New York City, and the necessity of "hold[ing] fast" to one's "own gods" in the face of complaint and unpopularity.

Letter to José Rodríguez Feo

May 23, 1947

Dear José:

Hartford was never lovelier than it is right now, notwithstanding all the rain, most of which comes from Quebec and back of Quebec. I shall bear in mind that you will be at the Berkshire, but I am not at all sure it will be possible for me to be in New York during your stay. I hope so.

I was in New York last week and had dinner with the editors of the *Partisan Review*. One of them told me that Eliot's brother had just died. He had come over to this country, I believe, for the purpose of being with his brother. I know nothing about his family, but, since he is said to have several sisters, the death of his brother with whom the sisters lived probably makes it necessary for him to take over to some extent. I did not see *Time* magazine, but from what you say gather that someone has taken a crack at Eliot. Someone takes a crack at everybody sooner or later: not only at everybody but at everything. In the long run, as Poe said in one of his essays which nobody reads, the generous man comes to be regarded as the stingy man; the beautiful woman comes to be regarded as an old witch; the scholar becomes the ignoramus. The hell with all this. For my own part I like to live in a classic atmosphere, full of my own gods and to be true to them until I have some better authority than a merely contrary opinion for not being true to them. We have all to learn to hold fast.

Yours very truly,

Wallace Stevens

Lytton Strachey (1880–1932)

---

*In the following extract from his 1907 essay "The Last Elizabethan," historian
and critic Lytton Strachey considers the poet Thomas Lovell Beddoes (1803–
49), best known for his verse play* Death's Jest-Book: or The Fool's Tragedy.
*Death was Beddoes's primary literary subject as well his own personal preoc-
cupation; and he was only in his mid-forties when, after several attempts, he
finally managed to commit suicide. Yet Strachey sees him as "the least morbid
of human beings," a poet for whom death was, in the end, equivalent to love.
The ellipses in the excerpt are Strachey's.*

---

from *The Last Elizabethan*

To find Beddoes in his most characteristic mood, one must watch him
weaving his mysterious imagination upon the woof of mortality. One must
wander with him through the pages of *Death's Jest Book*, one must grow ac-
customed to the dissolution of reality, and the opening of the nettled lips
of graves; one must learn that "the dead are most and merriest," one must
ask – "Are the ghosts eavesdropping?" – one must realise that "murder is
full of holes." Among the ruins of his Gothic cathedral, on whose cloister
walls the Dance of Death is painted, one may speculate at ease over the
fragility of existence, and, within sound of that dark ocean,

> Whose tumultuous waves
> Are heaped, contending ghosts,

one may understand how it is that

> Death is mightier, stronger, and more faithful
> To man than Life.

Lingering there, one may watch the Deaths come down from their cloister,
and dance and sing amid the moonlight; one may laugh over the grotesque
contortions of skeletons; one may crack jokes upon corruption; one may
sit down with phantoms, and drink to the health of Death.

In private intercourse Beddoes was the least morbid of human beings. His
mind was like one of those Gothic cathedrals of which he was so fond –

mysterious within, and filled with a light at once richer and less real than the light of day; on the outside, firm, and towering, and immediately impressive; and embellished, both inside and out, with grinning gargoyles. His conversation, Kelsall tells us, was full of humour and vitality, and untouched by any trace of egoism or affectation. He loved discussion, plunging into it with fire, and carrying it onward with high dexterity and good-humoured force. His letters are excellent; simple, spirited, spicy, and as original as his verse; flavoured with that vein of rattling open-air humour which had produced his school-boy novel in the style of [Henry] Fielding. He was a man whom it would have been a rare delight to know. His character, so eminently English, compact of courage, of originality, of imagination, and with something coarse in it as well, puts one in mind of Hamlet: not the melodramatic sentimentalist of the stage; but the real Hamlet, Horatio's Hamlet, who called his father's ghost old truepenny, who forged his uncle's signature, who fought Laertes, and ranted in a grave, and lugged the guts into the neighbour room. His tragedy, like Hamlet's, was the tragedy of an overpowerful will – a will so strong as to recoil upon itself, and fall into indecision. It is easy for a weak man to be decided – there is so much to make him so; but a strong man, who can do anything, sometimes leaves everything undone. Fortunately Beddoes, though he did far less than he might have done, possessed so rich a genius that what he did, though small in quantity, is in quality beyond price. "I might have been, among other things, a good poet," were his last words. "Among other things!" aye, there's the rub. But, in spite of his own "might have been," a good poet he was. Perhaps for him, after all, there was very little to regret; his life was full of high nobility; and what other way of death would have befitted the poet of death? There is a thought constantly recurring throughout his writings – in his childish as in his most mature work – the thought of the beauty and the supernal happiness of soft and quiet death. He had visions of "rosily dying," of turning to daisies gently in the grave," of a "pink reclining death," of death coming like a summer cloud over the soul. "Let her deathly life pass into death," says one of his earliest characters, "like music on the night wind." And in *Death's Jest Book*, Sybilla has the same thoughts:

> O Death! I am thy friend,
> I struggle not with thee, I love thy state;
> Thou canst be sweet and gentle, be so now;
> And let me pass praying away into thee,
> As twilight still does into starry night.

Did his mind, obsessed and overwhelmed by images of death, crave at last for the one thing stranger than all these – the experience of it? It is easy to believe so, and that, ill, wretched, and abandoned by [his lover Konrad] Degen at the miserable Cigogne Hotel, he should seek relief in the gradual dissolution which attends upon loss of blood. And then, when he had recovered, when he was almost happy once again, the old thoughts, perhaps, came crowding back upon him – thoughts of the futility of life, and the supremacy of death and the mystical whirlpool of the unknown, and the long quietude of the grave. In the end, Death had grown to be something more than Death to him – it was, mysteriously and transcendentally, Love as well.

> Death's darts are sometimes Love's. So Nature tells,
> When laughing waters close o'er drowning man;
> When in flowers' honied corners poison dwells;
> When Beauty dies: and the unweared ken
> Of those who seek a cure for long despair
> Will learn . . .

What learning was it that rewarded him? What ghostly knowledge of eternal love?

> If there are ghosts to raise
>   What shall I call
> Out of hell's murky haze,
>   Heaven's blue pall?
> – Raise my loved long-lost boy
> To lead me to his joy. –
>   There are no ghosts to raise;
>   Out of death lead no ways;
>   Vain is the call.
>
>   – Know'st thou not ghosts to sue?
>   No love thou hast.
> Else lie, as I will do,
>   And breathe thy last.
> So out of Life's fresh crown
> Fall like a rose-leaf down.
>   Thus are the ghosts to woo;
>   Thus are all dreams made true,
>   Ever to last!

Virginia Woolf

(1882–1941)

Virginia Woolf was unmatched in her ability to write cogently about the sensation of being an engaged reader. The following extract is from her novel Jacob's Room, *first published in 1922. In it she describes the intoxications of talking about literature – that heady, emotional, hallucinatory belief that "we are the only people in the world" who know what our favorite writers are really saying.*

from *Jacob's Room*

The Greeks – yes, that was what they talked about – how when all's said and done, when one's rinsed one's mouth with every literature in the world, including Chinese and Russian (but these Slavs aren't civilized), it's the flavour of Greek that remains. Durrant quoted Aeschylus – Jacob Sophocles. It is true that no Greek could have understood or professor refrained from pointing out – Never mind; what is Greek for if not to be shouted on Haverstock Hill in the dawn? Moreover, Durrant never listened to Sophocles, nor Jacob to Aeschylus. They were boastful, triumphant; it seemed to both that they had read every book in the world; known every sin, passion, and joy. Civilizations stood round them like flowers ready for picking. Ages lapped at their feet like waves fit for sailing. And surveying all this, looming through the fog, the lamplight, the shades of London, the two young men decided in favour of Greece.

"Probably," said Jacob, "we are the only people in the world who know what the Greeks meant."

They drank coffee at a stall where the urns were burnished and little lamps burnt along the counter.

Taking Jacob for a military gentleman, the stall-keeper told him about his boy at Gibraltar, and Jacob cursed the British army and praised the Duke of Wellington. So on again they went down the hill talking about the Greeks.

Ezra Pound (1885–1972)

By 1911 Ezra Pound had published several collections of poetry as well as a book of essays, and his influence increased after he released an anthology of Imagist poetry, which included his own work as well as poems by H.D., William Carlos Williams, Amy Lowell, and many others. In 1913 the experimental journal The New Freewoman *published Pound's "Emotion and Poesy" as the final part of a longer essay titled "The Serious Artist." In the following extract from that essay, Pound explains his definition of "Good writing" and expounds on the differences between prose and poetry.*

from *Emotion and Poesy*

Obviously, it is not easy to be a great poet. If it were, many more people would have done so. At no period in history has the world been free of people who have mildly desired to be great poets and not a few have endeavoured conscientiously to be such.

I am aware that adjectives of magnitude are held to savour of barbarism. Still there is no shame in desiring to give great gifts and an enlightened criticism does not draw ignominious comparisons between Villon and Dante. The so-called major poets have most of them given their own gift but the peculiar term "major" is rather a gift to them from Chronos. I mean that they have been born upon the stroke of their hour and that it has been given to them to heap together and arrange and harmonize the results of many men's labour. This very faculty for amalgamation is a part of their genius and it is, in a way, a sort of modesty, a sort of unselfishness. They have not wished for property.

The men from whom Dante borrowed are remembered as much for the fact that he did borrow as for their own compositions. At the same time he gave of his own, and no mere compiler and classifier of other men's discoveries is given the name of "major poet" for more than a season.

If Dante had not done a deal more than borrow rhymes from Arnaut Daniel and theology from Aquinas he would not be published by Dent in the year of grace 1913.

We might come to believe that the thing that matters in art is a sort of energy, something more or less like electricity or radioactivity, a force transfusing, welding, and unifying. A force rather like water when it spurts up through very bright sand and sets it in swift motion. You may make what image you like.

I do not know that there is much use in composing an answer to the often asked question: What is the difference between poetry and prose?

I believe that poetry is the more highly energized. But these things are relative. Just as we say that a certain temperature is hot and another cold. In the same way we say that a certain prose passage "is poetry" meaning to praise it, and that a certain passage of verse is "only prose" meaning dispraise. And at the same time "Poetry!!!" is used as a synonym for "Bosh! Rot!! Rubbish!!!" The thing that counts is "Good writing."

And "Good writing" is perfect control. And it is quite easy to control a thing that has in it no energy – provided that it be not too heavy and that you do not wish to make it move.

And, as all the words that one would use in writing about these things are the vague words of daily speech, it is nearly impossible to write with scientific preciseness about "prose and verse" unless one writes a complete treatise on the "art of writing," defining each word as one would define the terms in a treatise on chemistry. And on this account all essays about "poetry" are usually not only dull but inaccurate and wholly useless. And on like account if you ask a good painter to tell you what he is trying to do to a canvas he will very probably wave his hands helplessly and murmur that "He – eh – eh – he can't talk about it." And that if you "see anything at all, he is quite – eh – more or less – eh – satisfied."

Nevertheless it has been held for a shameful thing that a man should not be able to give a reason for his acts and words. And if one does not care about being taken for a mystificateur one may as well try to give approximate answers to questions asked in good faith. It might be better to do the thing thoroughly, in a properly accurate treatise, but one has not always two or three spare years at one's disposal, and one is dealing with very subtle and complicated matter, and even so, the very algebra of logic is itself open to debate.

Roughly then, Good writing is writing that is perfectly controlled, the writer says just what he means. He says it with complete clarity and simplicity. He uses the smallest possible number of words. I do not mean that he skimps paper, or that he screws about like Tacitus to get his thought crowded into the least possible space. But, granting that two sentences are at times easier to understand than one sentence containing the double meaning, the author tries to communicate with the reader with the greatest possible dispatch, save where for any one of forty reasons he does not wish to do so.

Also there are various kinds of clarity. There is the clarity of the request: Send me four pounds of ten-penny nails. And there is the syntactical simplicity of the request: Buy me the kind of Rembrandt I like. This last is an utter cryptogram. It presupposes a more complex and intimate understanding of the speaker than most of us ever acquire of anyone. It has as many meanings, almost, as there are persons who might speak it. To a stranger it conveys nothing at all.

It is the almost constant labour of the prose artist to translate this latter kind of clarity into the former; to say "Send me the kind of Rembrandt I like" in the terms of "Send me four pounds of ten-penny nails."

The whole thing is an evolution. In the beginning simple words were enough: Food; water; fire. Both prose and poetry are but an extension of language. Man desires to communicate with his fellows. He desires an ever increasingly complicated communication. Gesture serves up to a point. Symbols may serve. When you desire something not present to the eye or when you desire to communicate ideas, you must have recourse to speech. Gradually you wish to communicate something less bare and ambiguous than ideas. You wish to communicate an idea and its modifications, an idea and a crowd of its effects, atmospheres, contradictions. You wish to question whether a certain formula works in every case, or in what per cent. of cases, etc., etc., etc., you get the Henry James novel.

You wish to communicate an idea and its concomitant emotions, or an emotion and its concomitant ideas, or a sensation and its derivative emotions, or an impression that is emotive, etc., etc., etc. You begin with the yeowl and the bark, and you develop into the dance and into music, and into music with words, and finally into words with music, and finally into words with a vague adumbration of music, words suggestive of music, words measured, or words in rhythm that preserves some accurate trait of the emotive impression or of the sheer character of the fostering or parental emotion.

When this rhythm, or when the vowel and consonantal melody or sequence seems truly to bear the trace of emotion which the poem (for we have come at last to the poem) is intended to communicate, we say that this part of the work is good. And "this part of the work" is by now "technique." That "dry, dull, pedantic" technique, that all bad artists rail against.

It is only a part of technique, it is rhythm, cadence, and the arrangement of sounds.

Also the "prose," the words and their sense must be such as fit the emotion. Or, from the other side, ideas, or fragments of ideas, the emotion and concomitant emotions of this "Intellectual and Emotional Complex" (for we have come to the intellectual and emotional complex) must be in harmony, they must form an organism, they must be an oak sprung from an acorn.

When you have words of a lament set to the rhythm and tempo of *There'll be a Hot Time in the Old Town To-night* you have either an intentional burlesque or you have rotten art. Shelley's *Sensitive Plant* is one of the rottenest poems ever written, at least one of the worst ascribable to a recognized author. It jiggles to the same tune as *A little peach in the orchard grew*. Yet Shelley recovered and wrote the fifth act of the Cenci.

T. S. Eliot (1888–1965)

T. S. Eliot's essay "Tradition and the Individual Talent" first appeared in the
Egoist *in 1919 and was reprinted in his first essay collection,* The Sacred
Wood. *In it he considers the definition of literary tradition and insists "that
the poet must develop or procure the consciousness of the past and that he
should continue to develop this consciousness throughout his career." The
Greek quotation that opens section 3 of the essay is from Aristotle's* De Anima;
*classicist J. A. Smith translates it as "The mind is, no doubt, something more
divine and impassible."*

Tradition and the Individual Talent

I

In English writing we seldom speak of tradition, though we occasionally
apply its name in deploring its absence. We cannot refer to "the tradi-
tion" or to "a tradition"; at most, we employ the adjective in saying that
the poetry of So-and-so is "traditional" or even "too traditional." Seldom,
perhaps, does the word appear except in a phrase of censure. If otherwise,
it is vaguely approbative, with the implication, as to the work approved,
of some pleasing archaeological reconstruction. You can hardly make the
word agreeable to English ears without this comfortable reference to the
reassuring science of archaeology.

Certainly the word is not likely to appear in our appreciations of living or
dead writers. Every nation, every race, has not only its own creative, but its
own critical turn of mind; and is even more oblivious of the shortcomings
and limitations of its critical habits than of those of its creative genius.
We know, or think we know, from the enormous mass of critical writing
that has appeared in the French language the critical method or habit of
the French; we only conclude (we are such unconscious people) that the
French are "more critical" than we, and sometimes even plume ourselves a
little with the fact, as if the French were the less spontaneous. Perhaps they
are; but we might remind ourselves that criticism is as inevitable as breath-
ing, and that we should be none the worse for articulating what passes in
our minds when we read a book and feel an emotion about it, for criticiz-

ing our own minds in their work of criticism. One of the facts that might come to light in this process is our tendency to insist, when we praise a poet, upon those aspects of his work in which he least resembles any one else. In these aspects or parts of his work we pretend to find what is individual, what is the peculiar essence of the man. We dwell with satisfaction upon the poet's difference from his predecessors, especially his immediate predecessors; we endeavour to find something that can be isolated in order to be enjoyed. Whereas if we approach a poet without this prejudice we shall often find that not only the best, but the most individual parts of his work may be those in which the dead poets, his ancestors, assert their immortality most vigorously. And I do not mean the impressionable period of adolescence, but the period of full maturity.

Yet if the only form of tradition, of handing down, consisted in following the ways of the immediate generation before us in a blind or timid adherence to its successes, "tradition" should positively be discouraged. We have seen many such simple currents soon lost in the sand; and novelty is better than repetition. Tradition is a matter of much wider significance. It cannot be inherited, and if you want it you must obtain it by great labour. It involves, in the first place, the historical sense, which we may call nearly indispensable to anyone who would continue to be a poet beyond his twenty-fifth year; and the historical sense involves a perception, not only of the pastness of the past, but of its presence; the historical sense compels a man to write not merely with his own generation in his bones, but with a feeling that the whole of the literature of Europe from Homer and within it the whole of the literature of his own country has a simultaneous existence and composes a simultaneous order. This historical sense, which is a sense of the timeless as well as of the temporal and of the timeless and of the temporal together, is what makes a writer traditional. And it is at the same time what makes a writer most acutely conscious of his place in time, of his own contemporaneity.

No poet, no artist of any art, has his complete meaning alone. His significance, his appreciation is the appreciation of his relation to the dead poets and artists. You cannot value him alone; you must set him, for contrast and comparison, among the dead. I mean this as a principle of aesthetic, not merely historical, criticism. The necessity that he shall conform, that he shall cohere, is not one-sided; what happens when a new work of art is created is something that happens simultaneously to all the works of art which preceded it. The existing monuments form an ideal order among themselves, which is modified by the introduction of the new (the really new) work of art among them. The existing order is complete before the new work arrives; for order to persist after the supervention of novelty, the whole existing order must be, if ever so slightly, altered; and so the relations, proportions, values of each work of art toward the whole are readjusted; and this is conformity between the old and the new. Whoever has approved this idea of order, of the form of European, of English literature will not find it preposterous that the past should be altered by the present as much as the present is directed by the past. And the poet who is aware of this will be aware of great difficulties and responsibilities.

In a peculiar sense he will be aware also that he must inevitably be judged by the standards of the past. I say judged, not amputated, by them; not judged to be as good as, or worse or better than, the dead; and certainly not judged by the canons of dead critics. It is a judgment, a comparison, in which two things are measured by each other. To conform merely would be for the new work not really to conform at all; it would not be new, and would therefore not be a work of art. And we do not quite say that the new is more valuable because it fits in; but its fitting in is a test of its value – a test, it is true, which can only be slowly and cautiously applied, for we are none of us infallible judges of conformity. We say: it appears to conform, and is perhaps individual, or it appears individual, and may conform; but we are hardly likely to find that it is one and not the other.

To proceed to a more intelligible exposition of the relation of the poet to the past: he can neither take the past as a lump, an indiscriminate bolus, nor can he form himself wholly on one or two private admirations, nor can he form himself wholly upon one preferred period. The first course is inadmissible, the second is an important experience of youth, and the third is a pleasant and highly desirable supplement. The poet must be very conscious of the main current, which does not at all flow invariably through the most distinguished reputations. He must be quite aware of the obvious fact that art never improves, but that the material of art is never quite the same. He must be aware that the mind of Europe – the mind of his own country – a mind which he learns in time to be much more important than his own private mind – is a mind which changes, and that this change is a development which abandons nothing en route, which does not superannuate either Shakespeare, or Homer, or the rock drawing of the Magdalenian draughtsmen. That this development, refinement perhaps, complication certainly, is not, from the point of view of the artist, any improvement. Perhaps not even an improvement from the point of view of the psychologist or not to the extent which we imagine; perhaps only in the end based upon a complication in economics and machinery. But the difference between the present and the past is that the conscious present is an awareness of the past in a way and to an extent which the past's awareness of itself cannot show.

Some one said: "The dead writers are remote from us because we know so much more than they did." Precisely, and they are that which we know.

I am alive to a usual objection to what is clearly part of my programme for the *métier* of poetry. The objection is that the doctrine requires a ridiculous amount of erudition (pedantry), a claim which can be rejected by appeal to the lives of poets in any pantheon. It will even be affirmed that much learning deadens or perverts poetic sensibility. While, however, we persist in believing that a poet ought to know as much as will not encroach upon his necessary receptivity and necessary laziness, it is not desirable to confine knowledge to whatever can be put into a useful shape for examinations, drawing-rooms, or the still more pretentious modes of publicity. Some can absorb knowledge, the more tardy must sweat for it. Shakespeare acquired more essential history from Plutarch than most men could from the whole British Museum. What is to be insisted upon is that the poet must develop or procure the consciousness of the past and that he should continue to develop this consciousness throughout his career.

What happens is a continual surrender of himself as he is at the moment to something which is more valuable. The progress of an artist is a continual self-sacrifice, a continual extinction of personality.

There remains to define this process of depersonalization and its relation to the sense of tradition. It is in this depersonalization that art may be said to approach the condition of science. I shall, therefore, invite you to consider, as a suggestive analogy, the action which takes place when a bit of finely filiated platinum is introduced into a chamber containing oxygen and sulphur dioxide.

II

Honest criticism and sensitive appreciation are directed not upon the poet but upon the poetry. If we attend to the confused cries of the newspaper critics and the susurrus of popular repetition that follows, we shall hear the names of poets in great numbers; if we seek not Blue-book knowledge but the enjoyment of poetry, and ask for a poem, we shall seldom find it. I have tried to point out the importance of the relation of the poem to other poems by other authors, and suggested the conception of poetry as a living whole of all the poetry that has ever been written. The other aspect of this Impersonal theory of poetry is the relation of the poem to its author. And I hinted, by an analogy, that the mind of the mature poet differs from that of the immature one not precisely in any valuation of "personality," not being necessarily more interesting, or having "more to say," but rather by being a more finely perfected medium in which special, or very varied, feelings are at liberty to enter into new combinations.

The analogy was that of the catalyst. When the two gases previously mentioned are mixed in the presence of a filament of platinum, they form sulphurous acid. This combination takes place only if the platinum is present; nevertheless the newly formed acid contains no trace of platinum, and the platinum itself is apparently unaffected; has remained inert, neutral, and unchanged. The mind of the poet is the shred of platinum. It may partly or exclusively operate upon the experience of the man himself; but, the more perfect the artist, the more completely separate in him will be the man who suffers and the mind which creates; the more perfectly will the mind digest and transmute the passions which are its material.

The experience, you will notice, the elements which enter the presence of the transforming catalyst, are of two kinds: emotions and feelings. The effect of a work of art upon the person who enjoys it is an experience different in kind from any experience not of art. It may be formed out of one emotion, or may be a combination of several; and various feelings, inhering for the writer in particular words or phrases or images, may be added to compose the final result. Or great poetry may be made without the direct use of any emotion whatever: composed out of feelings solely. Canto XV of the *Inferno* (Brunetto Latini) is a working up of the emotion evident in the situation; but the effect, though single as that of any work of art, is obtained by considerable complexity of detail. The last quatrain gives an image, a feeling attaching to an image, which "came," which did not develop simply out of what precedes, but which was probably in suspension in the poet's mind until the proper combination arrived for it to add itself to. The poet's mind is in fact a receptacle for seizing and storing up numberless feelings, phrases, images, which remain there until all the particles which can unite to form a new compound are present together.

If you compare several representative passages of the greatest poetry you see how great is the variety of types of combination, and also how completely any semi-ethical criterion of "sublimity" misses the mark. For it is not the "greatness," the intensity, of the emotions, the components, but the intensity of the artistic process, the pressure, so to speak, under which the fusion takes place, that counts. The episode of Paolo and Francesca employs a definite emotion, but the intensity of the poetry is something quite different from whatever intensity in the supposed experience it may give the impression of. It is no more intense, furthermore, than Canto XXVI, the voyage of Ulysses, which has not the direct dependence upon an emotion. Great variety is possible in the process of transmutation of emotion:

the murder of Agamemnon, or the agony of Othello, gives an artistic effect apparently closer to a possible original than the scenes from Dante. In the *Agamemnon*, the artistic emotion approximates to the emotion of an actual spectator; in *Othello* to the emotion of the protagonist himself. But the difference between art and the event is always absolute; the combination which is the murder of Agamemnon is probably as complex as that which is the voyage of Ulysses. In either case there has been a fusion of elements. The ode of Keats contains a number of feelings which have nothing particular to do with the nightingale, but which the nightingale, partly, perhaps, because of its attractive name, and partly because of its reputation, served to bring together.

The point of view which I am struggling to attack is perhaps related to the metaphysical theory of the substantial unity of the soul: for my meaning is, that the poet has, not a "personality" to express, but a particular medium, which is only a medium and not a personality, in which impressions and experiences combine in peculiar and unexpected ways. Impressions and experiences which are important for the man may take no place in the poetry, and those which become important in the poetry may play quite a negligible part in the man, the personality.

I will quote a passage [from *The Revenger's Tragedy*, first performed in 1606 and written by either Cyril Tourneur or Thomas Middleton] which is unfamiliar enough to be regarded with fresh attention in the light – or darkness – of these observations:

> And now methinks I could e'en chide myself
> For doating on her beauty, though her death
> Shall be revenged after no common action.
> Does the silkworm expend her yellow labours
> For thee? For thee does she undo herself?
> Are lordships sold to maintain ladyships
> For the poor benefit of a bewildering minute?
> Why does yon fellow falsify highways,
> And put his life between the judge's lips,
> To refine such a thing – keeps horse and men
> To beat their valours for her? . . .

In this passage (as is evident if it is taken in its context) there is a combination of positive and negative emotions: an intensely strong attraction toward beauty and an equally intense fascination by the ugliness which is contrasted with it and which destroys it. This balance of contrasted emotion is in the dramatic situation to which the speech is pertinent, but that situation alone is inadequate to it. This is, so to speak, the structural emotion, provided by the drama. But the whole effect, the dominant tone, is due to the fact that a number of floating feelings, having an affinity to this emotion by no means superficially evident, have combined with it to give us a new art emotion.

It is not in his personal emotions, the emotions provoked by particular events in his life, that the poet is in any way remarkable or interesting. His particular emotions may be simple, or crude, or flat. The emotion in his poetry will be a very complex thing, but not with the complexity of the emotions of people who have very complex or unusual emotions in life. One error, in fact, of eccentricity in poetry is to seek for new human emotions to express; and in this search for novelty in the wrong place it discovers the perverse. The business of the poet is not to find new emotions, but to use the ordinary ones and, in working them up into poetry, to express feelings which are not in actual emotions at all. And emotions which he has never experienced will serve his turn as well as those familiar to him. Consequently, we must believe [Wordsworth's remark] that "emotion recollected in tranquillity" is an inexact formula. For it is neither emotion, nor recollection, nor, without distortion of meaning, tranquillity. It is a concentration, and a new thing resulting from the concentration, of a very great number of experiences which to the practical and active person would not seem to be experiences at all; it is a concentration which does not happen consciously or of deliberation. These experiences are not "recollected," and they finally unite in an atmosphere which is "tranquil" only in that it is a passive attending upon the event. Of course this is not quite the whole story. There is a great deal, in the writing of poetry, which must be conscious and deliberate. In fact, the bad poet is usually unconscious where he ought to be conscious, and conscious where he ought to be unconscious. Both errors tend to make him "personal." Poetry is not a turning loose of emotion, but an escape from emotion; it is not the expression of personality, but an escape from personality. But, of course, only those who have personality and emotions know what it means to want to escape from these things.

III

ο δε νους ισως Θειοτερον τι και απαθες εστιν.

This essay proposes to halt at the frontier of metaphysics or mysticism, and confine itself to such practical conclusions as can be applied by the responsible person interested in poetry. To divert interest from the poet to the poetry is a laudable aim: for it would conduce to a juster estimation of actual poetry, good and bad. There are many people who appreciate the expression of sincere emotion in verse, and there is a smaller number of people who can appreciate technical excellence. But very few know when there is an expression of *significant* emotion, emotion which has its life in the poem and not in the history of the poet. The emotion of art is impersonal. And the poet cannot reach this impersonality without surrendering himself wholly to the work to be done. And he is not likely to know what is to be done unless he lives in what is not merely the present, but the present moment of the past, unless he is conscious, not of what is dead, but of what is already living.

Vladimir Nabokov (1899–1977)

Speak, Memory *is novelist Vladimir Nabokov's memoir of his childhood in* Russia before the revolution. *It appeared in installments between 1936 and 1951 and was first published in book form in 1951. In the following excerpt, Nabokov recalls his early attempts to write poems and his discovery "that a person hoping to become a poet must have the capacity of thinking of several things at a time."*

from *Speak, Memory*

from Chapter 11

In the avid heat of the early afternoon, benches, bridges, and boles (all things, in fact, save the tennis court) were drying with incredible rapidity, and soon little remained of my initial inspiration. Although the bright fissure had closed, I doggedly went on composing. My medium happened to be Russian but could have been just as well Ukrainian, or Basic English, or Volapük. The kind of poem I produced in those days was hardly anything more than a sign I made of being alive, of passing or having passed, or hoping to pass, through certain intense human emotions. It was a phenomenon of orientation rather than of art, thus comparable to stripes of paint on a roadside rock or to a pillared heap of stones marking a mountain trail.

But then, in a sense, all poetry is positional: to try to express one's position in regard to the universe embraced by consciousness, is an immemorial urge. The arms of consciousness reach out and grope, and the longer they are the better. Tentacles, not wings, are Apollo's natural members. Vivian Bloodmark, a philosophical friend of mine, in later years, used to say that while the scientist sees everything that happens in one point of space, the poet feels everything that happens in one point of time. Lost in thought, he taps his knee with his wandlike pencil, and at the same instant a car (New York license plate) passes along the road, a child bangs the screen door of a neighboring porch, an old man yawns in a misty Turkestan orchard, a granule of cinder-gray sand is rolled by the wind on Venus, a Docteur

Jacques Hirsch in Grenoble puts on his reading glasses, and trillions of other such trifles occur – all forming an instantaneous and transparent organism of events, of which the poet (sitting in a lawn chair, at Ithaca, N.Y.) is the nucleus.

That summer I was still far too young to evolve any wealth of "cosmic synchronization" (to quote my philosopher again). But I did discover, at least, that a person hoping to become a poet must have the capacity of thinking of several things at a time. In the course of the languid rambles that accompanied the making of my first poem, I ran into the village schoolmaster, an ardent Socialist, a good man, intensely devoted to my father (I welcome this image again), always with a tight posy of wild flowers, always smiling, always perspiring. While politely discussing with him my father's sudden journey to town, I registered simultaneously and with equal clarity not only his wilting flowers, his flowing tie and the blackheads on the fleshy volutes of his nostrils, but also the dull little voice of a cuckoo coming from afar, and the flash of a Queen of Spain settling on the road, and the remembered impression of the pictures (enlarged agricultural pests and bearded Russian writers) in the well-aerated classrooms of the village school which I had once or twice visited; and – to continue a tabulation that hardly does justice to the ethereal simplicity of the whole process – the throb of some utterly irrelevant recollection (a pedometer I had lost) was released from a neighboring brain cell, and the savor of the grass stalk I was chewing mingled with the cuckoo's note and the fritillary's takeoff, and all the while I was richly, serenely aware of my own manifold awareness.

He beamed and bowed (in the effusive manner of a Russian radical), and took a couple of steps backward, and turned, and jauntily went on his way, and I picked up the thread of my poem. During the short time I had been otherwise engaged, something seemed to have happened to such words as I had already strung together: they did not look quite as lustrous as they had before the interruption. Some suspicion crossed my mind that I might be dealing in dummies. Fortunately, this cold twinkle of critical perception did not last. The fervor I had been trying to render took over again and brought its medium back to an illusory life. The rank of words I reviewed were again so glowing, with their puffed out little chests and trim uniforms, that I put down to mere fancy the sagging I had noticed out of the corner of my eye.

Theodore Roethke (1908–1963)

Poet Theodore Roethke taught at a number of institutions, including Benning-ton College, Michigan State University, and the University of Washington; and his students included Carolyn Kizer, James Wright, Richard Hugo, and many others. "A Psychic Janitor" is a selection of entries that one of those former students, poet David Wagoner, compiled from notebooks that Roethke had kept between 1959 and 1963. It was first published in Straw for the Fire: From the Notebooks of Theodore Roethke, 1943–63 *(1972).*

In the following entry, Roethke considers Robert Frost's famous dislike of free verse and stakes a claim for "some of us out in the provinces [who have] oper-ated under difficulties, [who have] had to use free verse, on occasion." The ellipses in the excerpt are Wagoner's.

from *A Psychic Janitor*

I've always found Robert Frost's remark about free verse – he'd rather play tennis with the net down – I've always found this wonderfully suggestive, as an old coach, in a great number of ways. For one thing I coached at Penn State. We played in clothing cast off – laundered of course – by the football team. Of course, my derriere being what it is, I frequently found not only the net at least semi-down, but also my pants. . . . You know how things get from too much laundering: the rubber in the various intimate equipment disintegrates, the string would bust in my sweat pants: there'd be a hole in my racket. Well, do you get the analogy: that's me and free verse. Frost, he had a racket and balls all his life; but some of us out in the provinces oper-ated under difficulties: we've had our disorganized lives and consequently our intractable material: we've had to use free verse, on occasion.

Czesław Miłosz (1911–2004)

In 1980 Polish poet and essayist Czesław Miłosz was awarded the Nobel Prize for Literature. In the lecture that follows, which he delivered in Stockholm after receiving the prize, he dwells on the connections between poets and history – in particular, the horrors of the Holocaust in Eastern Europe – "for we all who are here, both the speaker and you who listen, are no more than links between the past and the future."

Nobel Lecture

December 8, 1980

I

My presence here, on this tribune, should be an argument for all those who praise life's God-given, marvelously complex unpredictability. In my school years I used to read volumes of a series then published in Poland – "The Library of the Nobel Laureates." I remember the shape of the letters and the color of the paper. I imagined then that the Nobel laureates were writers, namely persons who write thick works in prose, and even when I learned that there were also poets among them, for a long time I could not get rid of that notion. And certainly, when, in 1930, I published my first poems in our university review, *Alma Mater Vilnensis*, I did not aspire to the title of a writer. Also much later, by choosing solitude and giving myself to a strange occupation, that is, to writing poems in Polish while living in France or America, I tried to maintain a certain ideal image of a poet, who, if he wants fame, he wants to be famous only in the village or the town of his birth.

One of the Nobel laureates whom I read in childhood influenced to a large extent, I believe, my notions of poetry. That was Selma Lagerlöf. Her *Wonderful Adventures of Nils*, a book I loved, places the hero in a double role. He is the one who flies above the Earth and looks at it from above but at the same time sees it in every detail. This double vision may be a metaphor of the poet's vocation. I found a similar metaphor in a Latin ode of a seventeenth-century poet, Maciej Sarbiewski, who was once known all over Europe under the pen-name of Casimire. He taught poetics at my university. In that ode he describes his voyage – on the back of Pegasus – from Vilno to Antwerp, where he is going to visit his poet-friends. Like Nils Holgersson he beholds under him rivers, lakes, forests, that is, a map, both distant and yet concrete. Hence, two attributes of the poet: avidity of the eye and the desire to describe that which he sees. Yet, whoever considers poetry as "to see and to describe" should be aware that he engages in a quarrel with modernity, fascinated as it is with innumerable theories of a specific poetic language.

Every poet depends upon generations who wrote in his native tongue; he inherits styles and forms elaborated by those who lived before him. At the same time, though, he feels that those old means of expression are not adequate to his own experience. When adapting himself, he hears an internal voice that warns him against mask and disguise. But when rebelling, he falls in turn into dependence upon his contemporaries, various movements of the avant-garde. Alas, it is enough for him to publish his first volume of poems to find himself entrapped. For hardly has the print dried, when that work, which seemed to him the most personal, appears to be enmeshed in the style of another. The only way to counter an obscure remorse is to continue searching and to publish a new book, but then everything repeats itself, so there is no end to that chase. And it may happen that leaving books behind as if they were dry snake skins, in a constant escape forward from what has been done in the past, he receives the Nobel Prize.

What is this enigmatic impulse that does not allow one to settle down in the achieved, the finished? I think it is a quest for reality. I give to this word its naive and solemn meaning, a meaning having nothing to do with philosophical debates of the last few centuries. It is the Earth as seen by Nils from the back of the gander and by the author of the Latin ode from the back of Pegasus. Undoubtedly, that Earth is and her riches cannot be exhausted by any description. To make such an assertion means to reject in advance a question we often hear today: "What is reality?," for it is the same as the question of Pontius Pilate: "What is truth?" If among pairs of opposites which we use every day, the opposition of life and death has such an importance, no less importance should be ascribed to the oppositions of truth and falsehood, of reality and illusion.

II

Simone Weil, to whose writings I am profoundly indebted, says: "Distance is the soul of beauty." Yet sometimes keeping distance is nearly impossible.

I am *A Child of Europe*, as the title of one of my poems admits, but that is a bitter, sarcastic admission. I am also the author of an autobiographical book which in the French translation bears the title *Une autre Europe*. Undoubtedly, there exist two Europes and it happens that we, inhabitants of the second one, were destined to descend into "the heart of darkness of the twentieth century." I wouldn't know how to speak about poetry in general. I must speak of poetry in its encounter with peculiar circumstances of time and place. Today, from a perspective, we are able to distinguish outlines of the events which by their death-bearing range surpassed all natural disasters known to us, but poetry, mine and my contemporaries', whether of inherited or avant-garde style, was not prepared to cope with those catastrophes. Like blind men we groped our way and were exposed to all the temptations the mind deluded itself with in our time.

It is not easy to distinguish reality from illusion, especially when one lives in a period of the great upheaval that begun a couple of centuries ago on a small western peninsula of the Euro-Asiatic continent, only to encompass the whole planet during one man's lifetime with the uniform worship of science and technology. And it was particularly difficult to oppose multiple intellectual temptations in those areas of Europe where degenerate ideas of dominion over men, akin to the ideas of dominion over Nature, led to paroxysms of revolution and war at the expense of millions of human beings destroyed physically or spiritually. And yet perhaps our most precious acquisition is not an understanding of those ideas, which we touched in their most tangible shape, but respect and gratitude for certain things which protect people from internal disintegration and from yielding to tyranny. Precisely for that reason some ways of life, some institutions became a target for the fury of evil forces, above all, the bonds between people that exist organically, as if by themselves, sustained by family, religion, neighborhood, common heritage. In other words, all that disorderly, illogical humanity, so often branded as ridiculous because of its parochial attachments and loyalties. In many countries traditional bonds of *civitas* have been subject to a gradual erosion and their inhabitants become disinherited without realizing it. It is not the same, however, in those areas where suddenly, in a situation of utter peril, a protective, life-giving value of such bonds reveals itself. That is the case of my native land. And I feel this is a proper place to mention gifts received by myself and by my friends in our part of Europe and to pronounce words of blessing.

It is good to be born in a small country where Nature was on a human scale, where various languages and religions cohabited for centuries. I have in mind Lithuania, a country of myths and of poetry. My family already in the sixteenth century spoke Polish, just as many families in Finland spoke Swedish and in Ireland, English; so I am a Polish, not a Lithuanian, poet. But the landscapes and perhaps the spirits of Lithuania have never abandoned me. It is good in childhood to hear words of Latin liturgy, to translate Ovid in high school, to receive a good training in Roman Catholic dogmatics and apologetics. It is a blessing if one receives from fate school and university studies in such a city as Vilno. A bizarre city of baroque architecture transplanted to northern forests and of history fixed in every stone, a city of forty Roman Catholic churches and of numerous synagogues. In those days the Jews called it a Jerusalem of the North. Only when teaching in America did I fully realize how much I had absorbed from the thick walls of our ancient university, from formulas of Roman law learned by heart, from history and literature of old Poland, both of which surprise young Americans by their specific features: an indulgent anarchy, a humor disarming fierce quarrels, a sense of organic community, a mistrust of any centralized authority.

A poet who grew up in such a world should have been a seeker for reality through contemplation. A patriarchal order should have been dear to him, a sound of bells, an isolation from pressures and the persistent demands of his fellow men, silence of a cloister cell. If books were to linger on a table, then they should be those which deal with the most incomprehensible quality of God-created things, namely being, the *esse*. But suddenly all this is negated by demoniac doings of History which acquires the traits of a bloodthirsty Deity. The Earth which the poet viewed in his flight calls with a cry, indeed, out of the abyss and doesn't allow itself to be viewed from above. An insoluble contradiction appears, a terribly real one, giving no peace of mind either day or night, whatever we call it, it is the contradiction between being and action, or, on another level, a contradiction between art and solidarity with one's fellow men. Reality calls for a name, for words, but it is unbearable and if it is touched, if it draws very close, the poet's mouth cannot even utter a complaint of Job: all art proves to be nothing compared with action. Yet, to embrace reality in such a manner that it is preserved in all its old tangle of good and evil, of despair and hope, is possible only thanks to a distance, only by soaring above it – but this in turn seems then a moral treason.

Such was the contradiction at the very core of conflicts engendered by the twentieth century and discovered by poets of an Earth polluted by the crime of genocide. What are the thoughts of one of them, who wrote a certain number of poems which remain as a memorial, as a testimony? He thinks that they were born out of a painful contradiction and that he would prefer to have been able to resolve it while leaving them unwritten.

III

A patron saint of all poets in exile, who visit their towns and provinces only in remembrance, is always Dante. But how has the number of Florences increased! The exile of a poet is today a simple function of a relatively recent discovery: that whoever wields power is also able to control language and not only with the prohibitions of censorship, but also by changing the meaning of words. A peculiar phenomenon makes its appearance: the language of a captive community acquires certain durable habits; whole zones of reality cease to exist simply because they have no name. There is, it seems, a hidden link between theories of literature as *Écriture*, of speech feeding on itself, and the growth of the totalitarian state. In any case, there is no reason why the state should not tolerate an activity that consists of creating "experimental" poems and prose, if these are conceived as autonomous systems of reference, enclosed within their own boundaries. Only if we assume that a poet constantly strives to liberate himself from borrowed styles in search for reality is he dangerous. In a room where people unanimously maintain a conspiracy of silence, one word of truth sounds like a pistol shot. And, alas, a temptation to pronounce it, similar to an acute itching, becomes an obsession which doesn't allow one to think of anything else. That is why a poet chooses internal or external exile. It is not certain, however, that he is motivated exclusively by his concern with actuality. He may also desire to free himself from it and elsewhere, in other countries, on other shores, to recover, at least for short moments, his true vocation – which is to contemplate Being.

That hope is illusory, for those who come from the "other Europe," wherever they find themselves, notice to what extent their experiences isolate them from their new milieu – and this may become the source of a new obsession. Our planet that gets smaller every year, with its fantastic proliferation of mass media, is witnessing a process that escapes definition, characterized by a refusal to remember. Certainly, the illiterates of past centuries, then an enormous majority of mankind, knew little of the history of their respective countries and of their civilization. In the minds of modern illiterates, however, who know how to read and write and even teach in schools and at universities, history is present but blurred, in a state of strange confusion; Molière becomes a contemporary of Napoleon, Voltaire, a contemporary of Lenin. Also, events of the last decades, of such primary importance that knowledge or ignorance of them will be decisive for the future of mankind, move away, grow pale, lose all consistency as if Frederic Nietzsche's prediction of European nihilism found a literal fulfillment. "The eye of a nihilist" – he wrote in 1887 – "is unfaithful to his memories: it allows them to drop, to lose their leaves; . . . And what he does not do for himself, he also does not do for the whole past of mankind: he lets it drop." We are surrounded today by fictions about the past, contrary to common sense and to an elementary perception of good and evil. As *The Los Angeles Times* recently stated, the number of books in various languages which deny that the Holocaust ever took place, that it was invented by Jewish propaganda, has exceeded one hundred. If such an insanity is possible, is a complete loss of memory as a permanent state of mind improbable? And would it not present a danger more grave than genetic engineering or poisoning of the natural environment?

For the poet of the "other Europe" the events embraced by the name of the Holocaust are a reality, so close in time that he cannot hope to liberate himself from their remembrance unless, perhaps, by translating the Psalms of David. He feels anxiety, though, when the meaning of the word *Holocaust* undergoes gradual modifications, so that the word begins to belong to the history of the Jews exclusively, as if among the victims there were not also millions of Poles, Russians, Ukrainians and prisoners of other nationalities. He feels anxiety, for he senses in this a foreboding of a not distant future when history will be reduced to what appears on television, while the truth, as it is too complicated, will be buried in the archives, if not totally annihilated. Other facts as well, facts for him quite close but distant for the West, add in his mind to the credibility of H. G. Wells's vision in *The Time Machine*: the Earth inhabited by a tribe of children of the day, carefree, deprived of memory and, by the same token, of history, without defense when confronted with dwellers of subterranean caves, cannibalistic children of the night.

Carried forward, as we are, by the movement of technological change, we realize that the unification of our planet is in the making and we attach importance to the notion of international community. The days when the League of Nations and the United Nations were founded deserve to be remembered. Unfortunately, those dates lose their significance in comparison with another date which should be invoked every year as a day of mourning, while it is hardly known to younger generations. It is the date of 23 August 1939. Two dictators then concluded an agreement provided with a secret clause by the virtue of which they divided between themselves neighboring countries possessing their own capitals, governments and parliaments. That pact not only unleashed a terrible war; it re-established a colonial principle, according to which nations are not more than cattle, bought, sold, completely dependent upon the will of their instant masters. Their borders, their right to self-determination, their passports ceased to exist. And it should be a source of wonder that today people speak in a whisper, with a finger to their lips, about how that principle was applied by the dictators forty years ago.

Crimes against human rights, never confessed and never publicly denounced, are a poison which destroys the possibility of a friendship between nations. Anthologies of Polish poetry publish poems of my late friends – Wladyslaw Sebyla and Lech Piwowar, and give the date of their deaths: 1940. It is absurd not to be able to write how they perished, though everybody in Poland knows the truth: they shared the fate of several thousand Polish officers disarmed and interned by the then accomplices of Hitler, and they repose in a mass grave. And should not the young generations of the West, if they study history at all, hear about the 200,000 people killed in 1944 in Warsaw, a city sentenced to annihilation by those two accomplices?

The two genocidal dictators are no more and yet, who knows whether they did not gain a victory more durable than those of their armies. In spite of the Atlantic Charter, the principle that nations are objects of trade, if not chips in games of cards or dice, has been confirmed by the division of Europe into two zones. The absence of the three Baltic states from the United Nations is a permanent reminder of the two dictators' legacy. Before the war those states belonged to the League of Nations but they disappeared from the map of Europe as a result of the secret clause in the agreement of 1939.

I hope you forgive my laying bare a memory like a wound. This subject is not unconnected with my meditation on the word "reality," so often misused but always deserving esteem. Complaints of peoples, pacts more treacherous than those we read about in Thucydides, the shape of a maple leaf, sunrises and sunsets over the ocean, the whole fabric of causes and effects, whether we call it Nature or History, points towards, I believe, another hidden reality, impenetrable, though exerting a powerful attraction that is the central driving force of all art and science. There are moments when it seems to me that I decipher the meaning of afflictions which befell the nations of the "other Europe" and that meaning is to make them the bearers of memory – at the time when Europe, without an adjective, and America possess it less and less with every generation.

It is possible that there is no other memory than the memory of wounds. At least we are so taught by the Bible, a book of the tribulations of Israel. That book for a long time enabled European nations to preserve a sense of continuity – a word not to be mistaken for the fashionable term, historicity.

During the thirty years I have spent abroad I have felt I was more privileged than my Western colleagues, whether writers or teachers of literature, for events both recent and long past took in my mind a sharply delineated, precise form. Western audiences confronted with poems or novels written in Poland, Czechoslovakia or Hungary, or with films produced there, possibly intuit a similarly sharpened consciousness, in a constant struggle against limitations imposed by censorship. Memory thus is our force, it protects us against a speech entwining upon itself like the ivy when it does not find a support on a tree or a wall.

A few minutes ago I expressed my longing for the end of a contradiction which opposes the poet's need of distance to his feeling of solidarity with his fellow men. And yet, if we take a flight above the Earth as a metaphor of the poet's vocation, it is not difficult to notice that a kind of contradiction is implied, even in those epochs when the poet is relatively free from the snares of History. For how to be above and simultaneously to see the Earth in every detail? And yet, in a precarious balance of opposites, a certain equilibrium can be achieved thanks to a distance introduced by the flow of time. "To see" means not only to have before one's eyes. It may mean also to preserve in memory. "To see and to describe" may also mean to reconstruct in imagination. A distance achieved, thanks to the mystery of time, must not change events, landscapes, human figures into a tangle of shadows growing paler and paler. On the contrary, it can show them in full light, so that every event, every date becomes expressive and persists as an eternal reminder of human depravity and human greatness. Those who are alive receive a mandate from those who are silent forever. They can fulfill their duties only by trying to reconstruct precisely things as they were, and by wresting the past from fictions and legends.

Thus both – the Earth seen from above in an eternal now and the Earth that endures in a recovered time – may serve as material for poetry.

IV

I would not like to create the impression that my mind is turned toward the past, for that would not be true. Like all my contemporaries I have felt the pull of despair, of impending doom, and reproached myself for succumbing to a nihilistic temptation. Yet on a deeper level, I believe, my poetry remained sane and, in a dark age, expressed a longing for the Kingdom of Peace and Justice. The name of a man who taught me not to despair should be invoked here. We receive gifts not only from our native land, its lakes and rivers, its traditions, but also from people, especially if we meet a powerful personality in our early youth. It was my good fortune to be treated nearly as a son by my relative Oscar Miłosz, a Parisian recluse and a visionary. Why he was a French poet could be elucidated by the intricate story of a family as well as of a country once called the Grand Duchy of Lithuania. Be that as it may, it was possible to read recently in the Parisian press words of regret that the highest international distinction had not been awarded half a century earlier to a poet bearing the same family name as my own.

I learned much from him. He gave me a deeper insight into the religion of the Old and New Testament and inculcated a need for a strict, ascetic hierarchy in all matters of mind, including everything that pertains to art, where as a major sin he considered putting the second-rate on the same level with the first-rate. Primarily, though, I listened to him as a prophet who loved people, as he says, "with old love worn out by pity, loneliness and anger" and for that reason tried to address a warning to a crazy world rushing towards a catastrophe. That a catastrophe was imminent, I heard from him, but also I heard from him that the great conflagration he predicted would be merely a part of a larger drama to be played to the end.

He saw deeper causes in an erroneous direction taken by science in the eighteenth century, a direction which provoked landslide effects. Not unlike William Blake before him, he announced a New Age, a second renaissance of imagination now polluted by a certain type of scientific knowledge, but, as he believed, not by all scientific knowledge, least of all by science that would be discovered by men of the future. And it does not matter to what extent I took his predictions literally: a general orientation was enough.

Oscar Miłosz, like William Blake, drew inspirations from the writings of Emanuel Swedenborg, a scientist who, earlier than anyone else, foresaw the defeat of man, hidden in the Newtonian model of the Universe. When, thanks to my relative, I became an attentive reader of Swedenborg, interpreting him not, it is true, as was common in the Romantic era, I did not imagine I would visit his country for the first time on such an occasion as the present one.

Our century draws to its close, and largely thanks to those influences I would not dare to curse it, for it has also been a century of faith and hope. A profound transformation, of which we are hardly aware, because we are a part of it, has been taking place, coming to the surface from time to time in phenomena that provoke general astonishment. That transformation has to do, and I use here words of Oscar Miłosz, with "the deepest secret of toiling masses, more than ever alive, vibrant and tormented." Their secret, an unavowed need of true values, finds no language to express itself and here not only the mass media but also intellectuals bear a heavy responsibility. But transformation has been going on, defying short term predictions, and it is probable that in spite of all horrors and perils, our time will be judged as a necessary phase of travail before mankind ascends to a new awareness. Then a new hierarchy of merits will emerge, and I am convinced that Simone Weil and Oscar Miłosz, writers in whose school I obediently studied, will receive their due. I feel we should publicly confess our attachment to certain names because in that way we define our position more forcefully than by pronouncing the names of those to whom we would like to address a violent "no." My hope is that in this lecture, in spite of my meandering thought, which is a professional bad habit of poets, my "yes" and "no" are clearly stated, at least as to the choice of succession. For we all who are here, both the speaker and you who listen, are no more than links between the past and the future.

A Keresan Poet

Keresan is a language spoken by certain groups of the Pueblo people, most of whom live in New Mexico. In 1919 and 1920 anthropologist Franz Boas (1858–1942) collected a set of songs and stories he had learned from several Keresan speakers, which he compiled as Keresan Texts *(1928). Among those texts was one he titled "Grinding Song of the Water Clan." Boas immediately noted, "It was impossible to obtain a translation of this song." But his informant nonetheless did make a few comments, and poet Armand Schwerner (1927–99) reworked Boas's transcription into the following poem – one that serves as a reminder of poetry's power to withhold as well as reveal.*

what the informant said to Franz Boas in 1920

translated by Armand Schwerner

long ago her mother
had to sing this song and so
she had to grind along with it
the corn people have a song too
it is very good
I refuse to tell it

Hayden Carruth (1921–2008)

In the following essay, first published in The Nation *in 1963, poet Hayden Carruth considers poetry's political responsibility and the way in which he and his contemporaries have managed to evade it. In his eyes "American poetry [in the early 1960s] . . . is stupefied by a massive neurosis – terror, suppression, spasmodic hysteria – and I cannot conceive of a therapy ingenious enough to cure it."*

Poets Without Prophecy

Beginning with whom? – not Eliot – with Arnold perhaps? – well, beginning rather a long time ago the meaning of the words *poem* and *poet* shifted finally from a matter of substance to matter of technique. Today we can find vestiges of that older way of speaking. In the country where I live people still say, when you tell them a lie, "Oh, that's poetry," and I suppose somewhere people may still exclaim, "How poetic!" upon seeing a sunset. We do not say these things. We consider them offensive. For us a poem is a work of art, a composition of verbal materials, a thing, and the poet is the maker who makes it.

I don't want to suggest that we are wrong; certainly I don't want to excuse the sentimentality and unctuousness which were the end products of the old view. But I would like to point out that these end products were a long time in coming – centuries, in fact – and that there distinctly was something grand and ennobling, something essential. And we have lost it.

I don't know what to call it precisely. It's hard to move back into that area of old custom without falling prey to the soft, foolish terms it spawned so readily toward its close. But let's extend to one another the charity of understanding and agree on an acknowledged orotundity: "the larger vision of humanity." Once the poet was our spokesman and not our oracle, our advocate and not our secret agent, or at least he was as much the one as the other; and if he did not speak for us, all of us, fully and warmly, if his poems lacked the larger vision of humanity, we said he was deficient in one of the qualities that, virtually by definition, make a poet.

This attitude survived among the older poets of our time, though their own theories about poetry tended to suppress it; the larger vision of humanity was still a part of their poetic instinct. *The Cantos, The Waste Land*, and *Paterson* are alive with it; Frost's poems reveal an unmistakably general feeling; so do the poems of Cummings, Aiken, Ransom; Stevens veiled his concern under his marvelous verbal textures and his epistemological preoccupations, but it was there, especially in the later poems where a sense of brooding pity underlies almost every word. Even Marianne Moore, whose writing has never appealed to me, conveys a kind of coy consciousness of sodality in her least timid poems. The point is that all these poets came into the world at a time when the poet's direct responsibility to mankind at large still hadn't been quite laughed out of existence. They themselves were the ones who set off the final burst of laughter when, in order to discredit the impressionistic views of the previous age, they directed attention away from the representative role of the poet and toward his work as experimentalist, hierophant, artifex, oneirocritic, or what have you.

It should be clear that my topic is poetry and politics, though I have chosen to work my way into it by means of concepts which show political feeling as what it really is, rather than as mere partisanship.

Next came the thirties, the time when poetry was avowedly political, the time of Archibald MacLeish, Muriel Rukeyser, Alfred Hayes, and the British socialists, the time equally of the Southern Agrarians. I myself find this poetry refreshing to read today, especially the radical poetry; its motives and objectives were so forceful that often a kind of vividness was the result, against which our own verse, striving for greater richness, seems only muddy. I wonder if we aren't ready for a revival of interest in proletarian writing, similar to the Jazz Age revival which occurred a few years back. Serious attention is being given again to John Steinbeck, thanks to his Nobel Prize, and that is to the good. Others also deserve reconsideration. I nominate Malcolm Cowley and Kenneth Fearing. Nowadays they are scarcely thought of as poets, yet they each wrote a few first-rate poems.

At the same time one cannot avoid seeing that the larger vision of humanity became more specialized in the poetry of the thirties, narrowed and reduced, and that this constriction grew even tighter in our poetry of the war. We had some fine war poems, things like Eberhart's "Fury of Aerial Bombardment" and Jarrell's "Death of a Ball Turret Gunner"; they have become standard anthology pieces. Yet if we compare them with the poems of the First World War we see a great difference. In the poems of Wilfred Owen, for instance, or even in such a highly wrought work as David Jones's *In Parenthesis*, the larger vision is instinct in every word and very profoundly expressed in some; but Jarrell's gunner, whose remains are washed out of his turret with a hose, is a far more specialized figure. He does not live in our minds as a fully realizable exponent of our own suffering. The figures created by Bill Mauldin and Ernie Pyle, though shallow, come closer to this and closer to the Tommies of Owen's poetry. This isn't Jarrell's fault. He is a fine poet, and the reason for his narrowed sensibility (which I don't think he desired at all) lies in the cultural evolution of the century. There had been an attrition of poetic consciousness. Far too complicated a matter to be easily explained; yet I think we can all see the difference between Owen and Jarrell, and I think most of us can concede that it is connected with the increasing refinement of the poet as a self-appointed agent of sensibility in an insensible and ever more hostile society.

Since then this erosion of the larger view has reached a point at which poetry has become almost totally apolitical. The supreme political fact of our lives is the atomic bomb. Am I wrong? It is enormous; it occupies the whole world. It is not only what it is but also the concentrated symbol of all hatred and injustice in every social and economic sphere. Speaking for myself, I have lived in fear of it for fifteen years, fear that it will go off, one way or another, and kill me and my family, or render our lives so intolerable that we won't wish to go on. Maybe I am more timorous than most people; I believe there are actually some Americans who never think about the bomb. But poets? That would be incredible. No matter how hard they try they cannot escape being included among society's most percipient members. Yet if one were to judge by their output one would have to believe that poets are the least concerned people in the world, not only on their own account but on everyone's.

Poetry, under the editorship of Henry Rago, is as representative of the various groups among American poets as any single magazine could probably be. I have just gone through all the issues for 1961, the only recent year for which I could find a complete set on my shelves. The year produced 335 poems by 139 poets, and although I skimmed through them rapidly, it has still taken me several hours to make up a count; I didn't go so quickly that my figures are likely to be off by more than a little. In the whole year I found two explicit references to the bomb, one a passing seriocomic remark, and ten poems on the general theme of suffering in war, two of which were translations from foreign poets of an earlier time. There were a great many poems on sex in its various aspects, religion, growing old, being young, thought and feeling, the uses of knowledge, themes unintelligible to me, and painting, music, and poetry.

That's it, of course, that last – poetry. The only topic poets will admit. Time after time they say so. Robert Creeley, one of the best alive, asserts his allegiance to "the poem supreme addressed to / emptiness. . . . " At the other end of the country, Howard Nemerov, a good academic poet, speaks of himself as

> Dreaming preposterous mergers and divisions
> Of vowels like water, consonants like rock
> (While everyone kept discussing values
> And the need for values), for words that would
> Enter the silence and be there as light.

Could anything be plainer? And I believe you could find statements of this precise credo – belief in the poem as an isolated act of absolutely and solely intrinsic goodness – in 90 percent of the books published by American poets in the past ten or fifteen years. There are a couple in my own.

Not spokesmen then. But hermits, lone wolves, acolytes – building poems in the wilderness for their own salvation.

The poets will retort in two ways. First they will say that art has always been lonely work, that the artist must use his own experience, and that ultimately he must put together his vision of reality – or, as some would say, discover it – within himself. This is self-evident; but it does not require the poet to withdraw himself so far from the general experience of his time that he becomes merely a specialist pursuing specialized ends. In fact it ought to mean just the opposite: that the poet, within himself, identifies and augments the general experience in such a way that it will excite a renewed susceptibility in everyone else.

Second, the poets will say that their isolated poems are acts of an implied political significance. They will say that in evil times the individual person exerts a force for good by carrying on his private endeavor with exemplary honesty. They will say that by refining their own purity as artists and by rejecting the false values of the world they are expressing a political attitude of considerable importance and firmness, and are doing so in terms more durable than could be used in direct statements about immediate political objectives. In the past I have said this myself, and I do not think it is sophistry. But it comes close to it. Politics is practicality, and a political act is by nature an act committed in the context of immediate objectives. And isn't the "context of immediate objectives" simply a jargonistic equivalent of the "larger vision of humanity"? This context still exists, I grant you, in the very remote background of today's estranged poetry. But when the correlation between the output of *Poetry* magazine and the leading headlines of, for example, the *New York Times* is as disparate as my little tabulation for 1961 indicates, then the context has receded so far that it no longer furnishes a useful field of reference to most of the people who read the poetry.

This is the point. The larger vision has been turned over to the newspapers, to the so-called industry of so-called mass communications. I imagine there's not a single reporter covering the discussions at Geneva for whom the larger vision isn't so fully, consistently present that he must drink himself or weep himself to sleep every night. But poetry is not his job; and if he is a good reporter he knows this and steers clear of it.

The Beats are the exception to what I have been saying. At least so they seemed at first, though I wonder if they aren't simply the other side of the coin. I mean the hard core of poets who still flourish on their Beat credentials. Among them we find explicitly political poems in great numbers, poems designed to incite impeachments, riots, revolutions, etc. To my mind they fail. The best of these poets is Gregory Corso, an exceedingly talented poet who has written perhaps two dozen really good poems; and that is enough to make anyone envious. But all these good poems are non-political, most are apolitical, and the best are not particularly Beat. His most popular poem is a diatribe called "The Bomb," but for me it seems only a long composition made up partly of rant and shapeless anger and partly of attempts to exorcise the bomb in the name of some numinous human essence; it turns politics into a sort of gang war supervised by the old ladies from the settlement house. In short it contains no poetry, no imagined transmutation of experience, no single realized image to which our thought and feeling can cling. In this respect, that is, the reintroduction of poetry to politics, it seems to me that the Beats, whom we all hoped (some of us secretly) would succeed, have failed almost completely, and what success they have had has been on the wrong level.

Poets are never liberals or conservatives, they are always radicals or reactionaries; and today, of course, public life rejects these indecorous extremes. True, the far right has worked up something resembling a movement in recent years, but it remains intellectually disreputable. On the left, in spite of sporadic efforts in New York and California, those of us who are born anarchists have to agree there isn't much doing. In other words the political attitudes usually endorsed by poets are now amorphous, disintegrated, anachronistic, without programs. Yet this ought to be exactly the political condition in which poets can flourish and in which politically directed poems – and I mean poems in the completest sense – can be written without becoming debased by doctrinaire points of view. I cannot speak for reaction; but it is hard for me to believe that any radical poet in the country today lacks a point on which he can stand firm, a point from which, as the spokesman of us all, he can attack known injustices and stupidities. Isn't the bomb, our monstrous, inescapable, political absurdity, the place to begin? And why then isn't it happening?

[Nineteenth-century French poet] Théophile Gautier, while discussing his fellow writers, said: "To be of one's own time – nothing seems easier and nothing is more difficult. One can go straight through one's age without seeing it, and this is what has happened to many eminent minds."

Yes, of our time too. We poets have gone straight through fifteen years without seeing them. One can think of a hundred reasons: the extraordinary burden of the poetry of our immediate past, the long evolution of formal preoccupations, the sociology of the culture hero; but none of these, or even all together, can suffice against the bomb, none can explain two poems out of 335. I think American poetry, to speak of only that element of our civilization, is stupefied by a massive neurosis – terror, suppression, spasmodic hysteria – and I cannot conceive of a therapy ingenious enough to cure it.

Philip Larkin (1922–1985)

In 1955 D. J. Enright invited fellow poet Philip Larkin to contribute work to an anthology, Poets of the 1950s, *slated for publication in 1956. Along with the poems, Enright asked him to include a brief essay about poetry. According to Larkin, "I assumed he would use [it] as raw material for an introduction; I was rather dashed to find [it] printed* verbatim.*" Following is the essay that Larkin wrote for Enright, and on page 343 you will find poet Rory Waterman's response to it.*

Statement

I find it hard to give any abstract views on poetry and its present condition as I find theorizing on the subject no help to me as a writer. In fact it would be true to say that I make a point of not knowing what poetry is or how to read a page or about the function of myth. It is fatal to decide, intellectually, what good poetry is because you are then in honour bound to try to write it, instead of the poems that only you can write.

I write poems to preserve things I have seen / thought / felt (if I may so indicate a composite and complex experience) both for myself and for others, though I feel that my prime responsibility is to the experience itself, which I am trying to keep from oblivion for its own sake. Why I should do this I have no idea, but I think the impulse to preserve lies at the bottom of all art. Generally my poems are related, therefore, to my own personal life, but by no means always, since I can imagine horses I have never seen or the emotions of a bride without ever having been a woman or married.

As a guiding principle I believe that every poem must be its own sole freshly created universe, and therefore have no belief in "tradition" or a common myth-kitty or casual allusions in poems to other poems or poets, which last I find unpleasantly like the talk of literary understrappers letting you see they know the right people. A poet's only guide is his own judgement; if that is defective his poetry will be defective, but he had still better judge for himself than listen to anyone else. Of the contemporary scene I can say only that there are not enough poems written according to my ideas, but then if there were I should have less incentive to write myself.

Denise Levertov

(1923–1997)

In Tesserae: Memories & Suppositions *(1995), poet Denise Levertov compiled a set of chronological yet fragmentary memoir-essays, which she called* tesserae – *the separate pieces of stone or glass that together form a mosaic. Here, in the book's final essay, she recalls a dream that became a poem that became the memory of a poem.*

A Lost Poem

I had seen cathedrals, and I had lived a while in Florence, where the trams ground clanging past the grandeur of the Duomo in January's icy mists. I had read somewhere of a king's ransom in jewels decorating the carved saints in Peru or Brazil, where Indios shuffled on their knees toward them, like those I had seen in Mexico, in the shadows and golden candlelight of enormous colonial churches. And in a dream these things danced together and reassembled: I saw a vast cathedral advance its majestic prow into a small piazza or zocalo that was the very heart of its city. Round it, all day, and far into the night, the noisy tramcars labored, drudging busily as tugboats, tiny and puerile below that solemn height, ringing their urgent bells. Within them the crowds – and the cars were always crowded – all gazed up at the façade, and leaned out of the open sides towards it, stretching out their hands. The tramline passed so close that they could actually touch it – touch that famous and extraordinary wall of riches. For this was the fabled Cathedral of Pearls: the entire façade was a cliff encrusted with pearls – its smallest interstices filled with seed pearls, its planes and cornices and whole height studded with pearls of every size; pearls the size of bantam eggs gracing the crowns and breastplates of the virgin martyrs, the archangels, black pearls and pink among the white, the whole dress of the madonna a soft luminescence of pearls. And all day – through years, through centuries – the brown hands of the poor reached out to touch them, caressively, with awe and affection. Never was one pearl missing.

That was the dream, and I remember writing it as a poem – "Cathedral of Pearls." Though the poem was published, I believe in some fugitive magazine, it is more than thirty years ago and I have lost all trace of it. If it ever turns up, like another poem I thought lost, a poem about Swiss peasants, men, women, and children, returning to their valley after a harvest day in the mountain pastures – will it tell me anything more, anything I have forgotten? What remains with me is not the idea – though that cannot fail to occur – that the poor would be less poor if the cathedral were stripped bare and the pearls sold, but the sense of the murky darkness of the city even in daylight, the darkness of the stone in which the pearls were embedded, the glimmering beauty of the pearls – magical barnacles upon a great vessel risen from the sea – and the deep pleasure that beauty was to those who passed and repassed.

John Berger (born 1926)

Poet, essayist, and art critic John Berger has long been concerned with interrelationships among history, cruelty, art, and the human spirit. In his essay "The Hour of Poetry," written in 1982, he opens with a consideration of torture and then moves into a discussion of language, which "even allows space for the unspeakable." In his view, "poetry opposes more absolutely than any other force in the world the monstrous cruelties by which the rich today defend their ill-gotten riches. This is why the hour of the furnaces is also the hour of poetry."

The Hour of Poetry

We all know the number of steps
compañero, from the cell
to that room.

If it's twenty
they're not taking you to the bathroom.
If it's forty-five
they can't be taking you out
for exercise.

If you get past eighty
and begin
to stumble blindly
up a staircase
oh if you get past eighty
there's only one place
they can take you
there's only one place
there's only one place
now there's only one place left
they can take you.

There's a hotel by a lake, near where I live. During the last war it was the local headquarters of the Gestapo. Many people were interrogated and tortured there. Today it is a hotel again. From the bar you look out across the water to the mountains on the far side; you look out on a scene that would have appealed to hundreds of romantic painters in the nineteenth century as sublime. And it was on to this scene that, before and after their interrogations, the tortured looked out. It was before this scene that loved ones and friends of the tortured stopped, powerless, to stare at the building, in which their own was being subjected to unspeakable pain or a lingering and agonizing death. Between the sublime and their present reality, what did they see in those mountains and that lake?

Of all experiences, systematic human torture is probably the most indescribable. Not simply because of the intensity of the suffering involved, but also because the initiative of such torture is opposed to the assumption on which all languages are based: the assumption of mutual understanding across what differentiates. Torture smashes language: its purpose is to tear language from the voice and words from the truth. The one being tortured knows: they are breaking me. His or her resistance consists in trying to limit the *me* being broken. Torture tears apart.

> Don't believe them when they show you
> the photo of my body,
> don't believe them.
> Don't believe them when they tell you
> the moon is the moon,
> if they tell you the moon is the moon,
> that this is my voice on tape,
> that this is my signature on a confession,
> if they say a tree is a tree,
> don't believe them,
> don't believe
> anything they tell you
> anything they swear to
> anything they show you,
> don't believe them.

Torture has a very long and widespread history. If people today are surprised by the scale of its reappearance (did it ever disappear?), it is perhaps because they have ceased believing in evil. Torture is not shocking because it is rare or because it belongs to the past: it is shocking because of what it does. The opposite of torture is not *progress* but *charity*. (The subject is so close to the New Testament that its terms are usable.)

The majority of torturers are neither sadists – in the clinical sense of the word – nor incarnations of pure evil. They are men and women who have been conditioned to accept and then use a certain practice. There are formal and informal schools for torturers, mostly state-financed. But the first conditioning begins, before the school, with ideological propositions that a certain category of people are fundamentally different and that their difference constitutes a supreme threat. The tearing apart of the third person, *them*, from *us* and *you*. The next lesson, now in the schools for torture, is that *their* bodies are lies because, as bodies, they claim not to be so different: torture is a punishment for this lie. When and if the torturers begin to question what they have learnt, they still continue, out of fear of what they have already done; they torture now to save their own untortured skins.

The fascist regimes of Latin America – Pinochet's Chile, for example – have recently and systematically extended the logic of torture. Not only do they tear apart the bodies of their victims, but they also try to tear up – so that they cannot be read – their very names. It would be wrong to suppose that these regimes do this out of shame or embarrassment: they do it in the hope of eliminating martyrs and heroes, and in order to produce the maximum intimidation among the population.

A woman or man is openly arrested, taken away in a car from his home at night, or from his workplace during the day. The arresters, the abductors, wear plain clothes. After this it is impossible to have any news of the one who has disappeared. Police, ministers, courts, deny all knowledge of the missing person. Yet the missing persons are in the hands of the military intelligence services. Months, years, pass. To believe that the missing are dead is to betray those who have thus been torn away; yet to believe that they are alive is to dream of them being tortured and then, often later, to be forced to admit their death. No letter, no sign, no whereabouts, no one responsible, no one to appear to, no imaginable end to the sentence, because no sentence. Normally silence means a lack of sound. Here silence is active and has been turned, once again systematically, into an instrument, this time for torturing the heart. Occasionally corpses are washed up on the beaches and identified as belonging to the list of the missing. Occasionally one or two return with some news of the others who are still missing: released intentionally perhaps, so as to sow again hopes which will torture thousands of hearts.

> My son has been
> missing
> since May 8
> of last year.

> > They took him
> > just for a few hours
> > they said
> > just for some routine
> > questioning.

After the car left,
the car with no licence plate,
we couldn't

    find out

anything else
about him.

But now things have changed.
We heard from a compañero
who just got out
that five months later
they were torturing him
in Villa Grimaldi,
at the end of September
they were questioning him
in the red house
that belonged to the Grimaldis.

    They say they recognized
    his voice his screams
    they say.

Somebody tell me frankly
what times are these
what kind of world
what country?
What I'm asking is
how can it be
that a father's
joy
a mother's
joy
is knowing
that they
that they are still
torturing
their son?
Which means
that he was alive
five months later

and our greatest
hope
will be to find out
next year
    that they're still torturing him
eight months later

and he may   might   could
still be alive.

Physical torture often concentrates upon the genitalia because of their sensitivity, because of the humiliation involved, and because thus the victim is threatened with sterility. In the emotional torture of the women and men who love those who have been made to disappear, their hopes are chosen as the point of application for pain, so as to produce – at another level – a comparable threat of sterility.

If he were dead
I'd know it.
Don't ask me how.
I'd know.

I have no proof,
no clues, no answer,
nothing that proves
or disproves.

    There's the sky,
    the same blue
    it always was.

But that's no proof.
Atrocities go on
and the sky never changes.

    There are the children.
    They've finished playing.
    Now they'll start to drink
    like a herd of wild
    horses.
    Tonight they'll be asleep
    as soon as their heads
    touch the pillow.

But who would accept that
as proof
that their father
is not dead?

In the face of such practices and their increasing frequency and the in-
volvement of US agencies in their preparation, if not their daily routine,
every sort of active protest and resistance needs to be mounted. (Amnesty
International is coordinating some of them.) In addition, poets – such as
the Chilean Ariel Dorfman – will write poems (all of the above quotations
are from Dorfman's *Missing*, published by Amnesty International). In face
of the monstrous machinery of modern totalitarian power, so often now
compared to that of the Inferno, poems will increasingly be written.

During the eighteenth and nineteenth centuries many protests against so-
cial injustice were written in prose. They were reasoned arguments written
in the belief that, given time, people would come to see reason; and that,
finally, history was on the side of reason. Today this is by no means so clear.
The outcome is by no means guaranteed. The suffering of the present and
the past is unlikely to be redeemed by a future era of universal happiness.
And evil is an ineradicable reality. All this means that the resolution – the
coming to terms with the sense to be given to life – cannot be deferred. The
future cannot be trusted. The moment of truth is now. And more and more
it will be poetry, rather than prose, that receives this truth. Prose is far more
trusting than poetry: poetry speaks to the immediate wound.

The boon of language is not tenderness. All that it holds, it holds with
exactitude and without pity. Even a term of endearment: the term is impar-
tial; the context is all. The boon of language is that *potentially* it is complete,
it has the potentiality of holding with words the totality of human experi-
ence. Everything that has occurred and everything that may occur. It even
allows space for the unspeakable. In this sense one can say of language that
it is potentially the only human home, the only dwelling place that cannot
be hostile to man. For prose this home is a vast territory, a country which it
crosses through a network of tracks, paths, highways; for poetry this home
is concentrated on a single centre, a single voice.

One can say anything to language. This is why it is a listener, closer to us
than any silence or any god. Yet its very openness often signified indiffer-
ence. (The indifference of language is continually solicited and employed
in bulletins, legal records, communiqués, files.) Poetry addresses language
in such a way as to close this indifference and to incite a caring. How does
poetry incite this caring? What is the labour of poetry?

By this I do not mean the work involved in writing a poem, but the work of the written poem itself. Every authentic poem contributes to the labour of poetry. And the task of this unceasing labour is to bring together what life has separated or violence has torn apart. Physical pain can usually be lessened or stopped by action. All other human pain, however, is caused by one form or another of separation. And here the act of assuagement is less direct. Poetry can repair no loss, but it defies the space which separates. And it does this by its continual labour of reassembling what has been scattered.

> O my beloved
> how sweet it is
> to go down
> and bathe in the pool
> before your eyes
> letting you see how
> my drenched linen dress
> marries
> the beauty of my body.
> Come, look at me
> *Poem inscribed on an Egyptian statue, 1500 BC*

Poetry's impulse to use metaphor, to discover resemblance, is not for the sake of making comparisons (all comparisons as such are hierarchical), nor is it to diminish the particularity of any event; it is to discover those correspondences of which the sum total would be proof of the indivisible totality of existence. To this totality poetry appeals, and its appeal is the opposite of a sentimental one; sentimentality always pleads for an exemption, for something which is divisible.

Apart from reassembling by metaphor, poetry reunites by its *reach*. It equates the reach of a feeling with the reach of the universe; after a certain point the type of extremity involved becomes unimportant and all that matters is its degree; by their degree alone extremities are joined.

> I bear equally with you
> the black permanent separation.
> Why are you crying? Rather give me your hand,
> promise to come again in a dream.
> You and I are a mountain of grief.
> You and I will never meet on this earth.
> If only you could send me at midnight
> a greeting through the stars.
> *– Anna Akhmatova*

To argue here that the subjective and objective are confused is to return to an empirical view which the extent of present suffering challenges; strangely enough it is to claim an unjustified privilege.

Poetry makes language care because it renders everything intimate. This intimacy is the result of the poem's labour, the result of the bringing-to-gether-into-intimacy of every act and noun and event and perspective to which the poem refers. There is often nothing more substantial to place against the cruelty and indifference of the world than this caring.

> From where does Pain come to us?
> From where does he come?
> He has been the brother of our visions from time immemorial
> And the guide of our rhymes

writes the Iraqi poet Nazik al-Mil'-ika.

To break the silence of events, to speak of experience however bitter or lacerating, to put into words, is to discover the hope that these words may be heard, and that when heard, the events will be judged. This hope is, of course, at the origin of prayer, and prayer – as well as labour – was probably at the origin of speech itself. Of all uses of language, it is poetry that preserves most purely the memory of this origin.

Every poem that works as a poem is original. And *original* has two meanings: it means a return to the origin, the first which engendered everything that followed; and it means that which has never occurred before. In poetry, and in poetry alone, the two senses are united in such a way that they are no longer contradictory.

Nevertheless poems are not simple prayers. Even a religious poem is not exclusively and uniquely addressed to God. Poetry is addressed to language itself. If that sounds obscure, think of a lamentation – there words lament loss to their language. Poetry is addressed to language in a comparable but wider way.

To put into words is to find the hope that the words will be heard and the events they described judged. Judged by God or judged by history. Either way the judgment is distant. Yet the language – which is immediate, and which is sometimes wrongly thought of as being only a means – offers, obstinately and mysteriously, its own judgment when it is addressed by poetry. This judgment is distinct from that of any moral code, yet it promises, within its acknowledgment of what it has heard, a distinction between good and evil – as though language itself had been created to preserve just that distinction!

This is why poetry opposes more *absolutely* than any other force in the world the monstrous cruelties by which the rich today defend their ill-gotten riches. This is why the hour of the furnaces is also the hour of poetry.

Philip Levine

(born 1928)

"[His] poems are personal, love poems, poems of horror, poems about the ex-periencing of America," wrote English poet Stephen Spender in an essay about Philip Levine's work, which is rooted in the characters and landscape of the industrial midwest. Yet as Levine explains in this essay from The Bread of Time: Toward an Autobiography *(1994), poets find their influences in un-expected places. "By one of those magical strokes of luck that come to the poet in need," a twenty-five-year-old factory worker opened Federico García Lorca's* Poet in New York, *written in the 1930s, and discovered a writer who had somehow "come to understand my life [and] . . . the details of my rage."*

The Poet in New York in Detroit

In the winter of 1953 I was working at Chevrolet Gear and Axle, a fac-tory in Detroit long ago dismantled and gone to dust. I worked the night shift, from midnight to eight in the morning, then returned by bus to my apartment, slept for a time, and rose to try to write poetry, for I believed even then that if I could transform my experience into poetry I would give it the value and dignity it did not begin to possess on its own. I thought too that if I could write about it I could come to understand it; I believed that if I could understand my life – or at least the part my work played in it – I could embrace it with some degree of joy, an element conspicuously missing from my life. No, I was not a young Werther seeking some outlet for my romantic longings for the world. I was a humiliated wage slave em-ployed by a vast corporation I loathed. The job I worked at each night was difficult, boring, and stupefying, for there in the forge room the noise was oceanic and the heat in our faces ferocious. And the work was dangerous; one older man I worked with lost both hands to a defective drop forge, and within a few hours – after a cursory inspection – the machine was back in operation being tended by another man equally liable to give his body for General Motors. A friend had given me a copy of Goethe's saga. I'd read it and merely laughed. If you had the time to survey the mountains and the sky, what was the problem? Oh, yes, you had to embrace the world in all its splendor, you had to reach with aching arms to hold the ungraspable, the sublime. I nicknamed the book *Stormy Werther* and threw it away. I too had aching arms, a thickened back, swollen wrists, and a heart full of emotions I couldn't deal with, fury and rage at a world that seemed already to have defeated me.

Since I worked only eight hours a day and slept only five or six each morning, I had plenty of time to attack my poems. My inspiration at that time was Keats, but though he knew a world at least as difficult as mine it scarcely entered his poetry clothed in the terms in which he encountered it. It was there barely disguised in the third stanza of the "Ode to a Nightingale," which I would recite over and over to myself:

> Fade far away, dissolve, and quite forget
>> What thou among the leaves hast never known,
> The weariness, the fever, and the fret
>> Here, where men sit and hear each other groan;
> Where palsy shakes a few, sad, last grey hairs,
>> Where youth grows pale, and spectre-thin, and dies;
>>> Where but to think is to be full of sorrow
>>>> And leaden-eyed despairs.
> Where Beauty cannot keep her lustrous eyes,
>> Or new Love pine at them beyond to-morrow.

Unquestionably his life had been far harder than mine, and yet he had made immortal poetry out of it. He had struggled against poverty, trying his best to support two younger brothers and a sister; I had only myself and my impossible first wife. He – as a student surgeon – had walked among the sick and dying, at twenty-three he had nursed an eighteen-year-old brother to his death, and even with the first unmistakable signs of TB in his own body – the disease that had killed his brother – he had gone on transforming his life into poetry. I had my health, my strength, and a whole undiscovered continent to write about, and yet I sat at the kitchen table each afternoon failing to complete a single poem that satisfied me, one that could capture the rage I felt at a world that reduced men to what I had become. Of course he had the advantage of being a genius, and another advantage too: he had inherited a tradition that by age twenty-three he knew intimately, one that showed him how to achieve Beauty. He also knew something that I wouldn't learn for years: that Beauty mattered, that it could transform our experience into something worthy, that like love it could redeem our lives. I wanted fire and I wanted gunfire, I wanted to burn down Chevrolet and waste the government of the United States of America.

On weekends I would often go to the Detroit Institute of Arts to try to enter another world, if only for an afternoon. There I found what at first I thought might be the model for the poetry I hoped to write, Diego Rivera's famous frescoes, especially those panels which depict the making of an automobile at Ford's River Rouge empire. I knew no other great art that dealt with my working life. Dos Passos's *U.S.A.* contained a mediocre chapter concerned with assembly-line workers in Detroit as well as a brilliant portrait of Henry Ford, one a worker could love. I thought Céline, in his fury, might show me the way in *Journey to the End of the Night*, but, reading the book, I discovered he clearly was not familiar with industrial labor. It was Rivera, the sworn enemy of my enemies, or no one.

From a distance the frescoes were a miracle of design that left me breathless. As the weeks passed I began to discover why his images were not helping me with my poetry. As I drew closer I found the bodies beautiful, their gestures like those of dancers as they moved in concert, and although their faces were often averted, turned away from the eye of the beholder as though shamed by peonage, those I could see were calm, dignified, and concentrated upon their tasks. The bodies tended to be elongated, the limbs long and slender, turning on their narrow waists as they lifted in unison. And the tones, dominated by warm earth colors, were wrong, far brighter and more vivid than those of the actual world I knew. When I closed my eyes I saw it all in black and white, black men and white men and white fire. And the actual bodies I knew were otherwise, so heavily muscled they seemed earthbound like Blake's Newton, perhaps made of earth, certainly thickened with earth and the metals of the earth. The habitual gaze of those of us who worked at Chevy was downward too, as though whatever stood above us was stunning and victorious and not to be gazed at for fear it could kill, this strange God of the underworld, for surely we were in the underworld. I wondered seriously if Rivera had seen a different world, if the Ford plant at River Rouge, then the world's largest industrial complex, could be that different from Chevy.

Some months later, employed as a driver for a company that repaired electric motors, I entered Ford Rouge – because of Ford's notorious anti-Semitism I refused to seek a job there – to pick up a burned-out motor on the assembly line, and found the same world I knew at Chevy, black and white and gray. I heard the same deafening roar, and saw the same men, stunted and isolated by their labors. Rivera's great design, his beautiful dance, was nonsense; automobiles were produced by a colossal accident that shattered men and women. It was what I'd known it was: a world that must be raged against with all the eloquence and fury a poet could muster. And then, by one of those magical strokes of luck that come to the poet in need, I read,

> I denounce everyone
> who ignores the other half,

the half that can't be redeemed,
who lift their mountains of cement
where the hearts beat
inside forgotten little animals
and where all of us will fall
in the last feast of pneumatic drills.
I spit in all your faces.

I had known García Lorca only as the author of the "gypsy poems," a writer of lovely, exotic poems that meant little to me. But now one Saturday afternoon became a miracle as I stood in the stacks of the Wayne University library, my hands trembling, and read my life in his words. How had this strange young Andalusian, later murdered by his countrymen, come to understand my life, how had he mastered the language of my rage? This poet of grace and "deep song" had somehow caught my emotions in a way I never had, and suddenly he opened a door for me to a way of speaking about my life. I accepted his gift. That's what they give us, the humble workers in the field of poetry, these amazingly inspired geniuses, gifts that change our lives. I later read that upon first entering New York he had cried, "I don't understand, I don't understand," as I had cried in the face of Detroit. Months later, taken by a friend to view Wall Street at midnight in moonlight, he had cried, "I do understand." What I knew even on the first afternoon in the library was that, before understanding had come, poetry had come.

I dove into the *Poet in New York* and everything I could find about its author. "Gongorism," "surrealism," "obscurity": the critics' terms were useless to me. What I was reading made perfect sense to me and at the same time no sense at all. I had discovered the poet could live in the tiny eye at the center of chaos and write. I had at last discovered the true meaning of what my earlier hero, Keats, had called Negative Capability, "when man is capable of being in uncertainties, Mysteries, doubts without any irritable reaching after fact and reason."

What an extraordinary gift to receive in my twenty-fifth year. I would like to be able to say that immediately my own poems flowed from his model and his inspiration, but that was not so. He was a genius, I was a humble and dedicated worker. My own great mentor, John Berryman, had already taught me that certain poets were too much themselves to allow you to imitate them with impunity; he had said that when warning me away from that other great poet of New York, Hart Crane, and toward the influence of Hardy and Frost. What Lorca gave me as no other poet had was a validation of my own emotions, which meant a validation of what I was trying and failing to write. As Wilfred Owen's poetry eight years before had taught me that I was a worthy human being even though I hated and feared the possibility of killing or being killed in war, García Lorca's *Poet in New York* taught me I was a worthy human being although I was filled with hatred for the life I was living, for what capitalist, industrialized America had reduced me to. I saw also in this great book that, if I were able to remain true to my own personal vision of this America, sooner or later my poetry would come – certainly not a poetry as amazing as his, but nonetheless a poetry no one else could write.

Never in poetry written in English had I found such a direct confrontation of one image with another or heard such violence held in abeyance and enclosed in so perfect a musical form. What in my work had been chaotic rant was in his a stately threnody circling around a center of riot. Here was the first clue to what my poetry would have to become if I were to capture my experience. Had I not read

> A wooden wind from the south, slanting through the black mire,
> spits on the broken boats and drives tacks into shoulders.
> A south wind that carries
> tusks, sunflowers, alphabets,
> and a battery with drowned wasps

I could not have written

> Out of burlap sacks, out of bearing butter,
> Out of black bean and wet slate bread,
> Out of the acids of rage, the candor of tar,
> Out of creosote, gasoline, drive shafts, wooden dollies,
> They Lion grow.

I had to work another thirteen years before I was able to begin to realize his gift to me, which is not really very long when you consider the life of a poem that means something. This is not to suggest that my poems mean anything to anyone else or will outlive me. I do know my poems are themselves, and tributes both to the people I shared my life with way back then and to this amazing visitor to our shores, whose voice rings as truly today as it did that Saturday almost forty years ago when I first read

> No, no: I denounce it all.
> I denounce the conspiracy
> of these deserted offices
> that radiate no agony,
> that erase the forest's plans,
> and I offer myself as food for the cows wrung dry
> when their bellowing fills the valley
> where the Hudson gets drunk on oil.

Adrienne Rich (1929–2012)

Speaking of Adrienne Rich's poems, writer Erica Jong once said, "They are about loneliness and the various forms it takes." In the following poem, from Rich's 1971 collection The Will to Change, *the poet borrows the title of seventeenth-century poet John Donne's famous metaphysical celebration of marriage to consider, among other things, how the exactions of language and art contribute to loneliness.*

A Valediction Forbidding Mourning

My swirling wants. Your frozen lips.
The grammar turned and attacked me.
Themes, written under duress.
Emptiness of the notations.

They gave me a drug that slowed the healing of wounds.

I want you to see this before I leave:
the experience of repetition as death
the failure of criticism to locate the pain
the poster in the bus that said:
my bleeding is under control.

A red plant in a cemetery of plastic wreaths.

A last attempt: the language is a dialect called metaphor.
These images go unglossed: hair, glacier, flashlight.
When I think of a landscape I am thinking of a time.
When I talk of taking a trip I mean forever.
I could say: these mountains have a meaning
but further than that I could not say.

To do something very common, in my own way.

Gregory Corso (1930–2001)

Gregory Corso's 1958 collection Gasoline *(1958) opened with an epigraph he had written himself: "[Poetry] comes, I tell you, immense with gasolined rags and bits of wire and old bent nails, a dark arriviste, from a dark river within." Yet Corso constantly had second thoughts about those arrivistes. In the following letter to his publisher, Lawrence Ferlinghetti of City Lights Books – written in Paris on Christmas Day – he frets about almost every element of the proofs, from the poems themselves to the type size and the color of the cover. The ellipses in the last paragraph also appear in Bill Morgan's edition of Corso's letters.*

Letter to Lawrence Ferlinghetti

December 25, 1957

Dear Larry,

When I got the proofs I felt both good and sad, good because there are some very good poems in book, and sad because there aren't any poems that bespeak my dream my idea my lyric, God knows what, but I definitely feel the book lacks the dessert of my poetry. I had it in *H. G. Wells* in *How Happy I Used To Be* and in *Power*, all that I had in those poems are in those poems and not in book. All right, I can easily solve that, I send you three definitely good poems, I send you news also that I am very unhappy about *Poem On Death Again* and *H* and *Dream* and *Written Sept 18 1956*, that makes four bad poems. They are no good Larry, and matching them against the poems I now send you I'm sure you'll agree. Yes, it will cost money to boot them out, all right, I send you twenty dollars, it's all I have, I'd give you a hundred dollars just to have *Gasoline* perfect; being that it took so long, let it take a little longer, but let's have a great book. All my short poems say almost the same thing. I love the poems, but where's my real poetry, my mad great poetry? I am at fault, I've always had it, but I had it in bad form or incomplete form, well these poems I send you, now that you have two pages free, and that those bad for meaningless poems will be taken out, will find room I'm sure. Also, instead of putting poems in chronological order, put them in any order you see fit, try to get as much room as possible, many of the short poems can go two on a page, also, the *Downfallen Rose* poem should not precede the *Sun* poem because they seem repetitious together. I honestly feel *Gasoline* will be a better book if you follow these pleas of mine. Today's Xmas, it's breaking my heart to send you the twenty bucks, I sure could use it, but I want to show good faith, and concern not only for book but for you, and for myself, for surely they are going to pan me badly. I know, these poems I send you and the poems in book can withstand any putdown. I wrote to *Esquire* and *Partisan* [*Review*] for permission to use, so give credit to them *Esquire* for *Ode To Coit Tower*, *Partisan* for *In Fleeting Hand Of Time*, and also *Evergreen* for *Amnesia In Memphis* and *This Was My Meal*, I guess you can put credits on library catalogue page.

As for titles, don't you prefer the smaller print better? I do. But that's not so important. I don't wish to bug you with such detail. Got William Carlos Williams' *Kora* [*in Hell*], his cover is the cover I thought I'd have, what color will I have? How's about purple? I hope my corrections on proofs don't screw things up too much. If it cost more to do all changes I ask let me know and I will comply. *Vestal Lady* fucked up. I'd hate to see this go the same way. I send you typed script for *Italian Extravaganza* linotype sure screwed up on that. Boy what with Ginsburg's last line in intro and Kerouac's praise I feel I got a lot to stand up to and prove somehow, anyway, even if they are right, I'm still my old same modest self. Of course smaller titles make bigger room to put two small poems on same page. Yes today Xmas I go to Notre Dame and maybe hear jingle bells, let me know as soon as you get this, don't keep me waiting, please, and when do you think book will finally get out? I mean this is the most I have to do with book, it's all up to you now, *Ode To Coit Tower* as you can see is very inspired poem. God, but I always hated *Dream* and *Poem On Death Again* and *H* and *Written 1956*, they are such bad writings. I didn't realize I sent them to you, you asked for everything, and remember I was bugged when I sent them to you, I didn't care then, but I do care now, I live my life for poetry, and I'm willing to die for it, therefore I deserve only to have good poems published. Them fucking traditionalists ain't gonna die for poetry so let them publish bad poems.

Anyway had a nice Xmas party at George Whitman's, he made Scotch and ice cream and doughnuts and had songs, very nice guy.

Let me know your real personal feelings about *Coit Tower*, I feel it to be one of the best poems I ever wrote, really inspired lines like: "sparks issued from a wild sharper's wheel / in that infinitive solitude where illusion

spoke Truth's divine dialect / like the dim lights of some hallucinating fa-
çade" etc. and what enlightenment when I ended it with "Swindleresque
Ink," I wrote swindleresque ink in Frisco depicting some of the phony verse
abounding there, ala, Harmon, Stock and clique, but never [k]new where
to put it, well it's found it's [sic] bed . . . therefore I had Allen cut out quote
from intro, also I took out send money to publisher because it doesn't
dignify book in that it lessens seriousness of both publisher and poet (?)
anyway I'd like it out. Well, Larry, that's it, I send you back everything. I am
alone. I leave it all to you, I am happy now, I send you my heart's joy and
love, if you can't find room for all poems I send you, then leave out *Rotter-
dam*, although I'm sure you'll have sufficient room now that those four bad
poems go out, and some of the shorter ones go together on same page. Yes,
now book will have truth. Thank you Larry, and my love for you and wife
for New Year that will bring both illumination and grand visions.

Ever faithful and obedient I am, Gregory Corso

Write right away, I'm anxious.

Gary Snyder

(born 1930)

In this essay, poet and environmental activist Gary Snyder argues that artists have a responsibility to stand up for the rights of the natural world, to be "caretakers of the lore of the culture" and "open themselves to representation from other life-forms." Originally a speech delivered at the Center for the Study of Democratic Institutions in Santa Barbara, California, it was later published in Snyder's collection Turtle Island, *which won the 1975 Pulitzer Prize for Poetry.*

The Wilderness

I am a poet. My teachers are other poets, American Indians, and a few Buddhist priests in Japan. The reason I am here is because I wish to bring a voice from the wilderness, my constituency. I wish to be a spokesman for a realm that is not usually represented either in intellectual chambers or in the chambers of government.

I was climbing Glacier Peak in the Cascades of Washington several years ago, on one of the clearest days I had ever seen. When we reached the summit of Glacier Peak we could see almost to the Selkirks in Canada. We could see south far beyond the Columbia River to Mount Hood and Mount Jefferson. And, of course, we could see Mount Adams and Mount Rainier. We could see across Puget Sound to the ranges of the Olympic Mountains. My companion, who is a poet, said: "You mean there is a senator for all this?"

Unfortunately, there isn't a senator for all that. And I would like to think of a new definition of humanism and a new definition of democracy that would include the nonhuman, that would have representation from those spheres. This is what I think we mean by an ecological conscience.

I don't like Western culture because I think it has much in it that is inherently wrong and that is at the root of the environmental crisis that is not recent; it is very ancient; it has been building up for a millennium. There are many things in Western culture that are admirable. But a culture that alienates itself from the very ground of its own being – from the wilderness outside (that is to say, wild nature, the wild, self-contained, self-informing ecosystems) and from that other wilderness, the wilderness within – is doomed to a very destructive behavior, ultimately perhaps self-destructive behavior.

The West is not the only culture that carries these destructive seeds. China had effectively deforested itself by 1000 A.D. India had effectively deforested itself by 800 A.D. The soils of the Middle East were ruined even earlier. The forests that once covered the mountains of Yugoslavia were stripped to build the Roman fleet, and these mountains have looked like Utah ever since. The soils of southern Italy and Sicily were ruined by latifundia slave-labor farming in the Roman Empire. The soils of the Atlantic seaboard in the United States were effectively ruined before the American Revolution because of the one-crop (tobacco) farming. So the same forces have been at work in East and West.

You would not think a poet would get involved in these things. But the voice that speaks to me as a poet, what Westerners have called the Muse, is the voice of nature herself, whom the ancient poets called the great goddess, the Magna Mater. I regard that voice as a very real entity. At the root of the problem where our civilization goes wrong is the mistaken belief that nature is something less than authentic, that nature is not as alive as man is, or as intelligent, that in a sense it is dead, and that animals are of so low an order of intelligence and feeling, we need not take their feelings into account.

A line is drawn between primitive peoples and civilized peoples. I think there is wisdom in the worldview of primitive peoples that we have to refer ourselves to, and learn from. If we are on the verge of postcivilization, then our next step must take account of the primitive worldview which has traditionally and intelligently tried to open and keep open lines of communication with the forces of nature. You cannot communicate with the forces of nature in a laboratory. One of the problems is that we simply do not know much about primitive people and primitive cultures. If we can tentatively accommodate the possibility that nature has a degree of authenticity and intelligence that requires that we look at it more sensitively, then we can move to the next step. "Intelligence" is not really the right word. The ecologist Eugene Odum uses the term "biomass."

Life-biomass, he says, is stored information; living matter is stored information in the cells and in the genes. He believes there is more information of a higher order of sophistication and complexity stored in a few square yards of forest than there is in all the libraries of mankind. Obviously, that is a different order of information. It is the information that has been flowing for millions of years. In this total information context, man may not necessarily be the highest or most interesting product.

Perhaps one of its most interesting experiments at the point of evolution, if we can talk about evolution in this way, is not man but a high degree of biological diversity and sophistication opening to more and more possibilities. Plants are at the bottom of the food chain; they do the primary energy transformation that makes all the life-forms possible. So perhaps plant-life is what the ancients meant by the great goddess. Since plants support the other life-forms, they became the "people" of the land. And the land – a country – is a region within which the interactions of water, air, and soil and the underlying geology and the overlying (maybe stratospheric) wind conditions all go to create both the microclimates and the large climactic patterns that make a whole sphere or realm of life possible. The people in that realm include animals, humans, and a variety of wild life.

What we must find a way to do, then, is incorporate the other people – what the Sioux Indians called the creeping people, and the standing people, and the flying people, and the swimming people – into the councils of government. This isn't as difficult as you might think. If we don't do it, they will revolt against us. They will submit non-negotiable demands about our stay on the earth. We are beginning to get non-negotiable demands right now from the air, the water, the soil.

I would like to expand on what I mean by representation here at the Center from these other fields, these other societies, these other communities. Ecologists talk about the ecology of oak communities, or pine communities. They *are* communities. This institute – this Center – is of the order of a kiva of elders. Its function is to maintain and transmit the lore of the tribe on the highest levels. If it were doing its job completely, it would have a cycle of ceremonies geared to the seasons, geared perhaps to the migrations of the fish and to the phases of the moon. It would be able to instruct in what rituals you follow when a child is born, when someone reaches puberty, when someone gets married, when someone dies. But, as you know, in these fragmented times, one council cannot perform all these functions at one time. Still it would be understood that a council of elders, the caretakers of the lore of the culture, would open themselves to representation from other life-forms. Historically this has been done through art. The paintings of bison and bears in the caves of southern France were of that order. The animals were speaking through the people and making their point. And when, in the dances of the Pueblo Indians and other peoples, certain individuals became seized, as it were, by the spirit of the deer, and danced as a deer would dance, or danced the dance of the corn maidens, or impersonated the squash blossoms, they were no longer speaking for humanity, they were taking it on themselves to interpret, through their humanity, what these other life-forms were. That is about all we know so far concerning the possibilities of incorporating spokesmanship for the rest of life in our democratic society.

Let me describe how a friend of mine from a Rio Grande pueblo hunts. He is twenty-seven years old. The Pueblo Indians, and I think probably most of the other Indians of the Southwest, begin their hunt, first, by purifying themselves. They take emetics, a sweat bath, and perhaps avoid their wife for a few days. They also try not to think certain thoughts. They go out hunting in an attitude of humility. They make sure that they need to hunt, that they are not hunting without necessity. Then they improvise a song while they are in the mountains. They sing aloud or hum to themselves while they are walking along. It is a song to the deer, asking the deer to be willing to die for them. They usually still-hunt, taking a place alongside a trail. The feeling is that you are not hunting the deer, the deer is coming to you; you make yourself available for the deer that will present itself to you, that has given itself to you. Then you shoot it. After you shoot it, you cut the head off and place the head facing east. You sprinkle corn meal in front of the mouth of the deer, and you pray to the deer, asking it to forgive you for having killed it, to understand that we all need to eat, and to please make a good report to the other deer spirits that he has been treated well. One finds this way of handling things and animals in all primitive cultures.

Audre Lorde (1934–1992)

Poet Audre Lorde always spoke out forcefully on issues of race, class, and sex. She delivered the following speech in 1978 at Mount Holyoke College in Hadley, Massachusetts, and later included it in Sister Outsider: Essays and Speeches *(1984).*

Uses of the Erotic: The Erotic As Power

There are many kinds of power, used and unused, acknowledged or otherwise. The erotic is a resource within each of us that lies in a deeply female and spiritual plane, firmly rooted in the power of our unexpressed or unrecognized feeling. In order to perpetuate itself, every oppression must corrupt or distort those various sources of power within the culture of the oppressed that can provide energy for change. For women, this has meant a suppression of the erotic as a considered source of power and information within our lives.

We have been taught to suspect this resource, vilified, abused, and devalued within western society. On the one hand, the superficially erotic has been encouraged as a sign of female inferiority; on the other hand, women have been made to suffer and to feel both contemptible and suspect by virtue of its existence.

It is a short step from there to the false belief that only by the suppression of the erotic within our lives and consciousness can women be truly strong. But that strength is illusory, for it is fashioned within the context of male models of power.

As women, we have come to distrust that power which rises from our deepest and nonrational knowledge. We have been warned against it all our lives by the male world, which values this depth of feeling enough to keep women around in order to exercise it in the service of men, but which fears this same depth too much to examine the possibilities of it within themselves. So women are maintained at a distant/inferior position to be psychically milked, much the same way ants maintain colonies of aphids to provide a life-giving substance for their masters.

But the erotic offers a well of replenishing and provocative force to the woman who does not fear its revelation, nor succumb to the belief that sensation is enough.

The erotic has often been misnamed by men and used against women. It has been made into the confused, the trivial, the psychotic, the plasticized sensation. For this reason, we have often turned away from the exploration and consideration of the erotic as a source of power and information, confusing it with its opposite, the pornographic. But pornography is a direct denial of the power of the erotic, for it represents the suppression of true feeling. Pornography emphasizes sensation without feeling.

The erotic is a measure between the beginnings of our sense of self and the chaos of our strongest feelings. It is an internal sense of satisfaction to which, once we have experienced it, we know we can aspire. For having experienced the fullness of this depth of feeling and recognizing its power, in honor and self-respect we can require no less of ourselves.

It is never easy to demand the most from ourselves, from our lives, from our work. To encourage excellence is to go beyond the encouraged mediocrity of our society. But giving in to the fear of feeling and working to capacity is a luxury only the unintentional can afford, and the unintentional are those who do not wish to guide their own destinies.

This internal requirement toward excellence which we learn from the erotic must not be misconstrued as demanding the impossible from ourselves nor from others. Such a demand incapacitates everyone in the process. For the erotic is not a question only of what we do; it is a question of how acutely and fully we can feel in the doing. Once we know the extent to which we are capable of feeling that sense of satisfaction and completion, we can then observe which of our various life endeavors bring us closest to that fullness.

The aim of each thing which we do is to make our lives and the lives of our children richer and more possible. Within the celebration of the erotic in all our endeavors, my work becomes a conscious decision – a longed-for bed which I enter gratefully and from which I rise up empowered.

Of course, women so empowered are dangerous. So we are taught to separate the erotic demand from most vital areas of our lives other than sex. And the lack of concern for the erotic root and satisfactions of our work is felt in our disaffection from so much of what we do. For instance, how often do we truly love our work even at its most difficult?

The principal horror of any system which defines the good in terms of profit rather than in terms of human need, or which defines human need to the exclusion of the psychic and emotional components of that need – the principal horror of such a system is that it robs our work of its erotic value, its erotic power and life appeal and fulfillment. Such a system reduces work to a travesty of necessities, a duty by which we earn bread or oblivion for ourselves and those we love. But this is tantamount to blinding a painter and then telling her to improve her work, and to enjoy the act of painting. It is not only next to impossible, it is also profoundly cruel.

As women, we need to examine the ways in which our world can be truly different. I am speaking here of the necessity for reassessing the quality of all the aspects of our lives and of our work, and of how we move toward and through them.

The very word *erotic* comes from the Greek word *eros*, the personification of love in all its aspects – born of Chaos, and personifying creative power and harmony. When I speak of the erotic, then, I speak of it as an assertion of the lifeforce of women; of that creative energy empowered, the knowledge and use of which we are now reclaiming in our language, our history, our dancing, our work, our lives.

There are frequent attempts to equate pornography and eroticism, two diametrically opposed uses of the sexual. Because of these attempts, it has become fashionable to separate the spiritual (psychic and emotional) from the political, to see them as contradictory or antithetical. "What do you mean, a poetic revolutionary, a meditating gun-runner?" The same way, we have attempted to separate the spiritual and the erotic, thereby reducing the spiritual to a world of flattened affect, a world of the ascetic who aspires to feel nothing. But nothing is farther from the truth. For the ascetic position is one of the highest fear, the gravest immobility. The severe abstinence of the ascetic becomes the ruling obsession. And it is one not of self-discipline but of self-abnegation.

The dichotomy between the spiritual and the political is also false, resulting from an incomplete attention to our erotic knowledge. For the bridge which connects them is formed by the erotic – the sensual – those physical, emotional, and psychic expressions of what is deepest and strongest and richest within each of us, being shared: the passions of love, in its deepest meanings.

Beyond the superficial, the considered phrase, "It feels right to me," acknowledges the strength of the erotic into a true knowledge, for what that means is the first and most powerful guiding light toward any understanding. And understanding is a handmaiden which can only wait upon, or clarify, that knowledge, deeply born. The erotic is the nurturer or nurse-maid of all our deepest knowledge.

The erotic functions for me in several ways, and the first is in providing the power which comes from sharing deeply any pursuit with another person. The sharing of joy, whether physical, emotional, psychic, or intellectual, forms a bridge between the sharers which can be the basis for understanding much of what is not shared between them, and lessens the threat of their difference.

Another important way in which the erotic connection functions is the open and fearless underlining of my capacity for joy. In the way my body stretches to music and opens into response, hearkening to its deepest rhythms, so every level upon which I sense also opens to the erotically satisfying experience, whether it is dancing, building a bookcase, writing a poem, examining an idea.

That self-connection shared is a measure of the joy which I know myself to be capable of feeling, a reminder of my capacity for feeling. And that deep and irreplaceable knowledge of my capacity for joy comes to demand from all of my life that it be lived within the knowledge that such satisfaction is possible, and does not have to be called marriage, nor god, nor an afterlife.

This is one reason why the erotic is so feared, and so often relegated to the bedroom alone, when it is recognized at all. For once we begin to feel deeply all the aspects of our lives, we begin to demand from ourselves and from our life-pursuits that they feel in accordance with that joy which we know ourselves to be capable of. Our erotic knowledge empowers us, becomes a lens through which we scrutinize all aspects of our existence, forcing us to evaluate those aspects honestly in terms of their relative meaning within our lives. And this is a grave responsibility, projected from within each of us, not to settle for the convenient, the shoddy, the conventionally expect-ed, nor the merely safe.

During World War II, we bought sealed plastic packets of white, uncolored margarine, with a tiny, intense pellet of yellow coloring perched like a to-paz just inside the clear skin of the bag. We would leave the margarine out for a while to soften, and then we would pinch the little pellet to break it inside the bag, releasing the rich yellowness into the soft pale mass of margarine. Then taking it carefully between our fingers, we would knead it gently back and forth, over and over, until the color had spread throughout the whole pound bag of margarine, thoroughly coloring it.

I find the erotic such a kernel within myself. When released from its intense and constrained pellet, it flows through and colors my life with a kind of energy that heightens and sensitizes and strengthens all my experience.

We have been raised to fear the yes within ourselves, our deepest cravings. But, once recognized, those which do not enhance our future lose their power and can be altered. The fear of our desires keeps them suspect and indiscriminately powerful, for to suppress any truth is to give it strength beyond endurance. The fear that we cannot grow beyond whatever distortions we may find within ourselves keeps us docile and loyal and obedient, externally defined, and leads us to accept many facets of our oppression as women.

When we live outside ourselves, and by that I mean on external directives only rather than from our internal knowledge and needs, when we live away from those erotic guides from within ourselves, then our lives are limited by external and alien forms, and we conform to the needs of a structure that is not based on human need, let alone an individual's. But when we begin to live from within outward, in touch with the power of the erotic within ourselves, and allowing that power to inform and illuminate our actions upon the world around us, then we begin to be responsible to ourselves in the deepest sense. For as we begin to recognize our deepest feelings, we begin to give up, of necessity, being satisfied with suffering and self-negation, and with the numbness which so often seems like their only alternative in our society. Our acts against oppression become integral with self, motivated and empowered from within.

In touch with the erotic, I become less willing to accept powerlessness, or those other supplied states of being which are not native to me, such as resignation, despair, self-effacement, depression, self-denial.

And yes, there is a hierarchy. There is a difference between painting a back fence and writing a poem, but only one of quantity. And there is, for me, no difference between writing a good poem and moving into sunlight against the body of a woman I love.

This brings me to the last consideration of the erotic. To share the power of each other's feelings is different from using another's feelings as we would use a kleenex. When we look the other way from our experience, erotic or otherwise, we use rather than share the feelings of those others who participate in the experience with us. And use without the consent of the used is abuse.

In order to be utilized, our erotic feelings must be recognized. The need for sharing deep feeling is a human need. But within the european-american tradition, this need is satisfied by certain proscribed erotic comings-together. These occasions are almost always characterized by a simultaneous looking away, a pretense of calling them something else, whether a religion, a fit, mob violence, or even playing doctor. And this misnaming of the need and the deed give rise to that distortion which results in pornography and obscenity – the abuse of feeling.

When we look away from the importance of the erotic in the development and sustenance of our power, or when we look away from ourselves as we satisfy our erotic needs in concert with others, we use each other as objects of satisfaction rather than share our joy in the satisfying, rather than make connection with our similarities and our differences. To refuse to be conscious of what we are feeling at any time, however comfortable that might seem, is to deny a large part of the experience, and to allow ourselves to be reduced to the pornographic, the abused, and the absurd.

The erotic cannot be felt secondhand. As a Black lesbian feminist, I have a particular feeling, knowledge, and understanding for those sisters with whom I have danced hard, played, or even fought. This deep participation has often been the forerunner for joint concerted actions not possible before.

But this erotic charge is not easily shared by women who continue to operate under an exclusively european-american male tradition. I know it was not available to me when I was trying to adapt my consciousness to this mode of living and sensation.

Only now, I find more and more women-identified women brave enough to risk sharing the erotic's electrical charge without having to look away, and without distorting the enormously powerful and creative nature of that exchange. Recognizing the power of the erotic within our lives can give us the energy to pursue genuine change within our world, rather than merely settling for a shift of characters in the same weary drama.

For not only do we touch our most profoundly creative source, but we do that which is female and self-affirming in the face of a racist, patriarchal, and anti-erotic society.

Toi Derricotte

In 2004, two eighth-grade students, Joseph Hudson and Desmond Seegars, interviewed poet Toi Derricotte for hArtworks, *the literary magazine of Charles Hart Middle School in Washington, D.C. Their conversation reveals both the necessary difficulty of communicating the influence of a particular time and its circumstances as well as our ongoing human commitment to poetry's power and allure.*

Interview with Toi Derricotte

by Joseph Hudson and Desmond Seegars

Joseph Hudson: What inspired you to start writing?

Toi Derricotte: Well, let's see. I think probably now that I look back, I think you don't know it when you're a kid, but something in me was thinking like a poet when I was very, very young. My father and grandfather were undertakers, and had I turned out to be an undertaker, I'd probably be telling you, you know, I was thinking like an undertaker when I was two years old. Because it depends on how you read your history. Whatever you become, you read it backwards in a biased kind of way. But I remember when I was about two years old, I started drawing things. I'd draw a car and I would think it was a real car. Or I'd draw a house and I'd think it was a real house, and I couldn't understand why people felt they didn't have things. Like they wanted a house, they wanted cars. And I thought, well, you could just draw it and have it. And I thought it was magic, and I thought only I knew. Because people seemed to be unhappy, and I could just draw whatever I wanted. So what I'm saying to you is, things written on paper were very real to me.

Desmond Seegars: What inspired you to write the book, "Tender"?

Ms. Derricotte: Trying to figure out what makes people mean, what makes people hurt me. And I've been trying to figure out that for a long, long time.

Joseph: How was your childhood?

Ms. Derricotte: Well, you know, it had lots of good stuff and lots of bad stuff. Some of the good stuff was that my family wasn't poor, my mother and father had jobs. We lived in a neighborhood where I felt pretty safe. I felt safer when I was out of my house than when I was in my house, if you know what I mean. I'd stay out from 8 in the morning until 11 at night. Because there was a lot of unhappiness inside my house. My neighborhood was really fun and we played together. There were lots of kids and we had ball games, and we hid and ran, and there were no cars. You could hang out, you could make fun of the neighbors, you could have mystery trips climbing up in some attic. You'd find keys and try to find out where the keys belonged to. I always had lots of friends and I had a cousin. I didn't have any brothers or sisters, but I had two girl cousins and one was my age, and we were "like that." *(holds two fingers together)* So I was very lucky in all those ways. Some of the things I was not lucky about, I didn't seem to be able to get it right for my mother and father. They were both very unhappy people. I think they had gone through a lot themselves. I think that maybe they suffered from depression, and maybe my father was an alcoholic. So it was pretty hairy when I was with my mother and father. There was a lot of violence, my father beat me a lot. And my mother wanted me to be a certain kind of person. Did you ever hear of the "Paper Bag Test" for black people?

Joseph: Put a paper bag over your head?

Ms. Derricotte: *(laughter)* Well, in the thirties and the twenties, color was a really big issue for black people, and it may still be. And my mother and father both looked white. They were both black, but they looked white. And when my mother came from Louisiana, when she came up north, she was very beautiful, she looked white. And in black society at that time, people who had money, there was something they called the "Paper Bag Test." Can you imagine what it is?

Joseph: You walk around and see how many people think you're black or white?

Ms. Derricotte: You're real close. There were certain clubs that black people belonged to, and in order to get in you had to be lighter than a paper bag.

Joseph: Ohhhh!

Desmond: Okay.

Joseph: Not a plastic bag, a paper bag. They have it in the grocery store. It's like a brown bag.

Desmond: It's like a box bag.

Joseph: And you have to be lighter than that to get into the club? Or if you're darker than that, you can't? So were these clubs wealthy?

Ms. Derricotte: Yes.

Desmond: How old were you when you wrote your first book?

Ms. Derricotte: Well, let me finish telling you this story. So then, my father could have belonged to clubs like that because his grandparents grew up in Detroit. And sometimes, you probably know nothing like this, but in old times it mattered if you were new to a place. If your parents had lived there, or your grandparents had lived there, it gave you more status.

Joseph: Like representing?

Ms. Derricotte: Yeah, like representing a group of people. My mother was new to Detroit, but my father's family had lived there for generations. So what my mother wanted, she wanted us to be a family that hung out with these really wealthy people, because she thought they had power. And they did have power. They had wealth; they had power. And we could have done it because my father was an undertaker, he was a professional man. And she wanted me to hang out with these kids who were in these clubs called "Jack and Jill" and "Links," and they were all these kids of well-to-do professionals, and they were all light skinned. And she used to take me to all these things and I just didn't get along with the kids. I felt uncomfortable with these kids and I didn't know why, and my mother was mad at me because she wanted me to become friends with these kids. I liked the kids in my neighborhood. My neighborhood kids were everybody: poor kids, middle-class kids. I got along with kids in my neighborhood, but all through my childhood, my mother wanted me to join these well-to-do kids, and I never did. And then as I got older, I used to hang out with groups of people who were what they called "beatniks." And beatniks were like people in the fifties, who were really intellectuals. They liked to read, they liked to talk about ideas, play chess, they liked jazz. People like that. What are people like that called now?

Joseph: Old-timers?

Ms. Derricotte: Old-timers, yeah. Maybe old-timers. They were the first people who grew beards and grew their hair long, too, so they would look different. They would dress in black. And then after that, I moved to New York and started hanging out with poets. But I didn't ever think of myself as a poet when I was young, because black people at that time, you never thought about becoming a poet or writer. You'd think about going to school and becoming a teacher. Can you think you'll become a playwright one day?

Joseph: No.

Ms. Derricotte: Yeah, you've got to think of something practical, right?

Joseph: Yeah.

Ms. Derricotte: That's how we were. We had to think about, okay, we are going to teach school, become a doctor, whatever. And that's how I thought. And I did become a teacher, and I did teach school, but I kept writing poetry at night. And then I started studying poetry when I was in college. And I started meeting lots of poets who were publishing. And then I got into a community where people were writing and publishing, and pretty soon I was publishing. But not until I was in my thirties. By then I had a kid thirteen years old.

Joseph: At thirteen, or he was thirteen?

Ms. Derricotte: He was thirteen by that time.

Desmond: How old were you when you wrote your first book?

Ms. Derricotte: How old was I? About thirty-three.

Desmond: What was the name of it?

Ms. Derricotte: "The Empress of the Death House."

Joseph: So what kind of influence did you think the poets had on you?

Ms. Derricotte: It was after I moved to New York. The thing is that when I was in Detroit I would write but I would sort of hide it. It would be my private writing, nobody would know about it. And it was kind of my way of having a friend. It was sort of my therapist. You know what a therapist is, how you can talk to a therapist? Well, my book was my therapist, my notebook. So I'd keep it hidden and I didn't want people to see it. And then when I got to New York I started sharing what I was writing in my journals, and I used to be thinking about, "How do you make poems out of what you feel in your deep, deep heart and you don't tell anybody?" How to make poems out of the deepest parts of you, the secrets inside you. I wanted to do that, because I thought: Maybe I'm not the only one. I used to feel so lonely, and then I'd think maybe I'm not the only one who has feelings like that. Maybe other people feel that way too. And if I say it, maybe other people will say, "Oh, I've felt that way too." And maybe they'll like me; maybe they won't hate me if I have feelings like that. And then I started writing feelings like that and people did say, "Oh my goodness, I feel that way too." And then I felt like I had a community. A real community, not a phony community. Like if I had joined those people who were the "Paper Bag Test" people, that would have been a community, but I wouldn't have felt good about myself. I found a community that I felt comfortable with, my kind of community, like you guys.

Joseph: What made you become a poet, instead of becoming a doctor or a teacher?

Ms. Derricotte: I did become a teacher, I taught. But I became a poet because I really loved, loved, loved poetry, and I love the people who write it. I love it, love it, love it, love it. It's very, very hard to be a poet. A lot of times you don't publish anything; a lot of times people don't like your work. To be a really good poet, you have to work hours, and hours, and hours. Every day. For years and years. It's harder than being a doctor. To really be an important poet – I mean anybody can sit down and write a poem. But to study poetry, to have control over what you're doing, and to write with a deep, unique voice that nobody else has so that somebody would recognize your poem if 4,000 poems were read; they'd say, "Oh, that's the poem by Joseph Hudson."

So I would have had to really want to do this. And every day, something keeps me wanting to do it. Sometimes I feel like I'm not a writer. Sometimes I don't write. Sometimes I feel what I write is horrible. I feel scared I'll never write again. All those things. But something keeps making me write.

Desmond: So what is one thing you really love?

Ms. Derricotte: You young writers! That's one thing I really love. Deeply. Because I know you're going to be great. I know you're going to change the world. I know you've got to work really hard, and not everybody can do it. But some people will, and I want you guys to keep trying.

Desmond: Did you have one poem that really came from deep down in your heart?

Joseph: Something that you'll never forget? A poem that says everything you have to say?

Ms. Derricotte: Maybe this poem. It sounds like it's about a bird, but it's not really a bird. When I was three years old, I buried a bird that I had found dead. And then thirty years later I wrote about a bird that was buried, but I didn't know I was writing about this bird.

> buried birds
> are usually dead.
> fallen from the sky
> because of too much
> something.
>> too much high.

    too much steep.
    too much long.
    too much deep.
but sometimes
one has been known
to go underground.
you do not hear a peep
for years.
then one day
you go back to the spot
thinking you will not find
a feather   or a few
scattered bones
& you hear something
pecking   trying
to get out of there.
you are afraid to believe
it is still alive.
afraid that even if it is
in being freed, it will die.
still,
slowly,
you go about freeing the bird.
you scrape away the grave
which in some mysterious way
has not suffocated her.
you free her scrawny head.
her dangling wing.
you keep thinking her body
must be broken beyond healing.
you keep thinking the delicate
instruments of flight
will never pull again.
still,
you free her.
feed her from the tip of your finger.
teach her the cup of your hand.
you breathe on her.
one day,
you open up your hand
& show her sky.

Galsan Tschinag (born 1944)

Tuvan poet, actor, and shaman Galsan Tschinag grew up in a Mongolian sub-culture that does not have its own written language. In the following speech, translated from the German, he talks about a life spent defending the essence of traditional poetry, even though he must use a foreign language to do so. For "defence of poetry," he declares, "means: defence of humanity, defence of authenticity, it means defence of the stone against plaster, defence of wood against plastic, defence of the word of the mother tongue against the foreign word, the technical jargon, defence of feeling against hypocrisy and finally defence of everything real and true against the fashion of the day and intentional lies." The ellipses are the author's.

Defence of Poetry 1999

translated by Kathrin Lang

Who am I, standing here in this place of honour, in front of so many select minds of our time from all over the world, and who is being expected to make some useful statements? It is true, though, that I, standing here with my Asian face, my nomadic national costume and shamanic way of thinking must be something special. Thirteen books of mine are available in the German-speaking countries at the moment; if you add the translations into other languages it would make two good herds of stallions according to the nomadic concept of quantity. The books could be my justification.

I come from a back pocket of the nomadic world of Central Asia, many of you present here might even consider it an ancient time, a different culture. The mountains of the High Altai in Mongolia are my home, and up to the present day they have kept the members of my tribe together with our history and with the traces of my childhood hidden away. The Turkic-speaking Mongol Tuva to which I belong are considered by some to be behind the times. And indeed there are a couple of things they do not have, such as their own script. Everything is handed on orally, history as well as stories, first of all the epics, which are considered sacred and powerful, so powerful that they can only be recited when the time of the thunderstorms is over.

From the beginning I knew that I would use a foreign language if destiny chose me to become the first writing poet of my people. In a roundabout way, via foreign languages and scripts, I had to get there. First it was Mongolian, recordable in a version of the Cyrillic alphabet which had been extended by two more letters; later two more languages and scripts were added.

We escaped time, as it were; what others consider behind the times is close to the roots, and, therefore, vital to us. For the primeval times in which we still live match with the concept of the world that we inherit from our grown-ups and which we, once grown-ups ourselves, will hand on to our children. This is a simple image: man is part of a complete whole fully pervaded by life, and as such he is kindred with all creatures; that is why he is equal in status with the smallest as well as the greatest before Father Heaven and Mother Earth.

Since my early childhood my Self has been shaped by shamanism. My first verses were shamanic chants, praises and pleas to the spirits of the rocks and trees and water that surrounded me. To create verses on the spot and to fit them into a suitable melody was the daily exercise I had to attend to as an apprentice of shamanism. Later when I became modern and learned how to write, this was very helpful. I was trained in making up verses, my senses were sharpened for the melodious sound of words and the proper order of things.

It is particular for the Tuva shamans that every one of them is a poet, a singer; hence everything is expressed in songs based on verse. To the shaman, a song is like tinder, he is enraptured by his own creation, he gets in top form, in trance, which is necessary for the dialogue with the spirits. Essential is the state in which the shaman as well as the poet needs to be: they are inspired, enthusiastic. For this state of mind of both, our language has got one and the same word.

Shaman and poet are not particularly unassuming beings. They do not want to accept moderation, nor do they want to be tamed. Both suffer from megalomania, they compare themselves to great things, to the mountain, the sea, the sky, its thunder and lightning. They get dangerously close to madness when they start working.

And this illness is given, it has been enclosed in the bag of fortune that according to our belief every human being has been endowed with by the Creator. It has been given to them, and it is a gift indeed. It is highly vulnerable, it can be healed in the sense that it gets lost, blunted. But because in the world where I come from both shaman and poet still have a high reputation, everything is done so that this illness will not wane, that it becomes chronic and more persistent with every break-out, and gets refined.

Human relationships, which live on closeness and sharing and are thus based on the manifoldness of things, are most valuable to us Tuvans. We always tolerate the one who is different by regarding the different quality as extra-ordinary and by leaving the burden to the one to whom it belongs. This tolerance is based on the knowledge: only the shaman, the poet, who competes with infinity, can achieve what is denied to others, but which will eventually be beneficial to everyone. It is above all and particularly these extra-ordinary people who give advice and live, because they have experienced the extra-ordinary and even rapturous side of life; this enables them to put things that have fallen apart or into disorder back into their proper place.

It seems that with the advancement of civilization, people with an innate and active sensitivity are treated with less tolerance. Suddenly other measures are in force. As if the modern man with his second hand sensory devices now despises his human senses and also the innate feelers that he had been equipped with by Mother Nature, and does not trust them any more. He considers the malady of creativity futile and irritating. Hence he tends to ignore nature within himself and in everyone beside him, to suppress it, and does not allow for man's authenticity. Therefore it is one of the main problems of an artist today that sooner or later he has to hide his nature and adjust himself to society.

Defence of poetry thus means: defence of humanity, defence of authenticity, it means defence of the stone against plaster, defence of wood against plastic, defence of the word of the mother tongue against the foreign word, the technical jargon, defence of feeling against hypocrisy and finally defence of everything real and true against the fashion of the day and intentional lies.

When it comes to poetry, it is necessary to ask the essential questions of life. Which are these? They concern the beginning and the end: birth and death. And therefore I want to know: where do I come from? Where do I go? In nomadic terms: it is about the roots, and eventually the fruits. Roots can be geographical-spacial, historical-temporal and cultural-religious, but for us they are above all fateful, meant to be our destiny. Fruits can be children, deeds, words.

Which mountain's stone am I, which well's water, which steppe's grass? The sooner and more definitely I find an answer to that, the clearer will be the poetry that flows from within me.

In my life, too, there have been aberrations, here and there I stumbled on roundabout ways, wandered astray. It seems to me as if I once thought that I had to be like the Saxons and the Prussians, because the world to which I suddenly awoke was inhabited and formed by them, especially since these people fed me physically as well as intellectually in those times. Another time I probably believed that I could give my soul to Italy, which was so foreign to me, because on the search for everything beautiful I met some of its spirits, and I felt particularly strongly attracted to one of them, Robertino Loretti was his name, a young singer like me. And again another time I felt obliged to the last of the Indians who lived beyond the worlds I knew and I thought that in a niche of the fronts of the official cold war I could open a personal hot war against the pale-faced and soulless U.S. demon. The results of my crazy ideas lie half digested inside me, they press heavily on my conscience, and the files that keep away these futile wasted emotions and times will remain tragic proof of my unusual life.

But this life has always been accompanied by good spirits. And they have always quickly pushed me from the side paths back to the main street of creation. The shaman enjoys the company of innumerable spirits. And each of them is known to him by a particular name. It has been like that on my ways and paths in the realm of poetry. And the spirits that I met and who often interfered with my life in a painful way, did not hide their names from me. Once they were called Erwin and Eva, came from two tribes, formed a single unit and then were called Strittmatter. Another one was named Yasunari Kawabata, another one Haldor Laxness, and again another one Chingiz Aitmatov – they became my permanent spirits and merged into inseparable triplets in the yurt of my heart. Then there were spirits who lost one of their halves on their way to me, and they reached me only with their first names.

I owe it to these and all the other ten thousand good spirits which a shaman addresses in his incantations night after night, that I have not lost the way that was given to me and which I have therefore always had the right of. And it is this way that every poet has to defend, because it leads him to his very own Self, as well as it leads the poet within him back to his poetry.

Poetry is an enormous counter-force against the oppressing weight of the material world. It is a spice in everyday life, a sting against habit, it changes life, which is more and more outweighed by consumption. Poetry, after all, belongs to the side of the heart in opposition to the stomach.

One of the most serious weaknesses of our time is the priority that is ascribed to the stomach. Gluttony is rephrased and praised as prosperity, and it has already got hold of other parts of the human being, most of all the body; that too has to carry a heavy weight, has to be over-decorated and overloaded. The spirit, too, is overfed – with an enormous amount of information waste, which it does not need, simply because it will never be able to digest it. The result is: body and spirit are stuffed and overburdened, the full stomach presses like a stone on the neighbouring vessels and debilitates circulation.

And all this happens while the heart is reduced to a mere pump that is dying of thirst.

With those people who have an overfed stomach and an oppressed heart, poetry has a hard time. Like our inner parts, so are our thoughts. From disturbed, dulled thoughts springs disturbed, weakened poetry. The reduction of poetry to decoration, as part of consumption, chopped-up prose, the unimaginative, pathetic play with form, the shameless, shallow pomposity about truism, the stringing-together of sentences that are grammatically correct but cold and death in their structure – a pseudo poetry, produced on a massive scale almost like shoes, hamburgers and non-returnable bottles, but with one decisive consequence: it annoys the readers and kills their feeling for poetry.

Barrenness prevails in the nomadic world, and life is still highly dependent on the times of day and year, it is subject to the laws of nature. Yet it seems as if the outer modesty necessarily provokes a counterbalance: inner abundance. The member of a kinship group is confined by tradition; he has to draw his intellectual and spiritual nourishment from the stony slopes of the barren, bleak mountains.

Yes, especially the mountains – they personify the very essence of nature. They are also grandfathers to us whom we address in verse several times a day and to whom we give offerings as well. This way the nomad has a strong bond with the earth, through and beyond the mountains he is rooted in the water, the woods and the dimensions of space. And likewise with his own human roots and fruits, with his ancestors and future companions. With all of them, as well as with every single element of creation he feels akin, feels responsible for them, thus it is part of his daily life to deal with them like he deals with his fellow creatures. And the particularity about this is that one has to address the cult objects with a refined, clear and powerful poetic language in order to be heard.

In this world of nomadism and its shamanic spirits, essential elements could keep their integrity up to the present day. And the same is true for literature. Therefore poetry and prose are not clearly distinguishable, they merge into each other. Prose is the smooth, fertile ground from which poetry grows to the sublime. Here follows an example to illustrate what I mean, an excerpt from the short story "A Tuvan Story":

Around noon the whole sky was overcast, and suddenly a storm arose from the Northwest. Sand filled the air, and the gravel that was whirled up by the hooves of the horses was caught by the wind and hurled at horse and rider. Cranes tottered in the air, trying in vain to fly against the storm, until finally they surrendered to its force and glided off, abandoned to their fate. . . . The snowy mountains were out of sight, as were the steppe and the sky, and one saw nothing but the furious white roar. We turned to the left and let the horses run as fast as they could. Now the wind caught us from the side, crushed into us like a solid mass, hit our faces and took our breath away. The storm did not wane, the thunder broke. Because of the howling of the wind and the tapping of the hooves we first perceived the rain as a kind of humming, then as a stronger roaring, until it drummed down on us like a devastating wet blaze. We rode slowly again. Large bright drops coming from the side hit the gravel, bounced back, and it looked as if a sea of glistening round beetles skipped along over the steppe. The fire that flared up from all directions illuminated them brightly and the thunderclaps that followed the lightning made them quiver and shake. Crackling, blue flames flashed over the horses' manes, it smelled of singed hair. The animals snorted and shook their manes, we men pulled on the reins to bring them under control, but the smell of burning had scared them and they reared. So we let them run free.

When I set foot in written literature with this story, I consciously clung to the broad and lively poetic narrative tradition of our heroic epics, which meant that I kept away from the style of socialist realism current in the East at that time, but also from the reserved, dissecting-mending writing technique of the modern time.

Poetry as the highest-developed organ in the body of human life had to protect its traditional position in nomadic literature up to today, and had succeeded in doing so. It is the interrelation between nature and man. It is the images that are passed on from the mother, nature, directly to us, one of her children. It is the elements that attract each other, rush towards each other and immediately form a unity, in whatsoever form.

Which are the elements that surround the shaman poet? It is the water, it is the wind, it is the fire, it is the earth. He is at their mercy, they blow and go through him. He accepts their challenge with devotion and wants to live on and with and in them. Nature herself provides his heroes. And because he is so devoted to her, goes to her, she is well-disposed towards him. So they, nature and the shamanic poet, are interwoven with each other. And in this fusion, in the mutual penetration, there lies the birthplace of poetry. Part of it is a quest that grows into an obsession and only ceases when a find is made; both are full with longing, it burns in the one and the other, sparks fly, flames flash, words are uttered. This is shamanic, this is the primeval force at work.

Where nature and poet meet, a unity is formed. Something becomes whole, is healed. And what is healed and whole is holy, is powerful.

I know that words like sky, earth, holy, cause fear in the conquering man who turned his back on nature and placed himself above her. But in the nomadic world where the child has not yet conquered and enslaved his mother, they are still fresh and charged, sparkling vigorously. Probably because the things underlying these names are still elements of everyday life. Our sky does not only dome above us, it also lives within us. And one day when we transform into the condition that others call death and consider the end, we will turn into the sky entirely. Dying has many meanings in our language, to turn into the sky is probably one of the most beautiful ones.

Another one, two examples, which will blow some wind at what has been said so far, and will smooth the way for the things to come. Following the customs of the local culture, I have to ask you now, Ladies and Gentlemen, and the spirits that are with you, to forgive me quoting myself again. Further explanations will follow later on.

What is it like, then, when the poet wants to make known his love, for our sake? He does not need to plead, he does not need to use polite words. Like the wind brings the rain without asking the plain if it might rush down on it, so a poet is no supplicant, either. He himself is the wind who can grow into a storm, a fireblaze, or a snowstorm:

> Now I stood behind you within range
> a load of storm your new hunter
> with the first snow I came to you
> and in your presence I swore to heaven
> to blow away all the traces of foreign winds on you.

As part of a whole, the poet is never alone; even his most personal matters he likes to share with the other forces around him:

> Clouds foam,
> forests blow in the wind
> primeval forces
> are working
>
> Indigestible
> you lie
> crossways within me

Never will I be able
to tame you.

In my point of view, the poetic *I* is nowadays more endangered than ever. It is quite possible that the inner parts of man shrink more and more, and that they become more impervious to the influences of great heat and hot flushes with the extension of the outer cover. Expressions in poetry collections become increasingly duller and more pathetic. Either the former wild and unpredictable nature of the poet has been infected by social norms and has taken cover in a warm, comfortable place in the house of order, and lets us know that we can rely on it. Or it is opposing every order, rejects everything conventional but also everything that proved to be worthwhile, and finally, unable to produce anything better, it makes a lot of fuss about nothing. Both have in common that they lack fire and impact. And the one like the other is afraid of pathos and incapable of passion. History tells us: lack of pathos and passion have always led to decline.

The poetic *I* needs, as every one of us knows, more than our flat images. But also the experiences that oneself, the people and the past era, this holy trinity, have had, are not sufficient to enable it to cope with life, in my point of view. It can and must absorb all the knowledge that mankind acquired throughout the ages, everything that is embraced by outer space and all the single elements that it offers. The form within us, which always, when it comes to poetry, has to rise up and above itself, has become more modest, tame, meager. It must be nourished, like the shaman nourishes his spirits. It is not only permitted but also necessary that in the house of etiquette, fear and the tyranny of order, into which the world has turned, some must break the ice of habit, eradicate the fat of self-satisfaction and slay the chains of cowardice. Nevertheless in view of what happened so far and what comes over us in even thicker, lower and darker clouds; we would, in shamanic terms, liberate this planet from the burden of a multiple dubiousness and heal mankind from a number of afflictions.

The life of the poet can or at least should be a poem itself. Only when he lives like that will he be a real one. Having the choice between the life of an unsuccessful, idealistic knight or that of a successful, materialist banker, again and again he should prefer quixotism to Rothschildism.

Now is the moment that I should come out with a thought that was touched upon earlier and which is essential for every poet who wants to be identified with his background and his time. It concerns the poet as person.

As far as I am concerned I treat my person in a quite relaxed way. I have a good reason for that. Because I am neither Galsan nor Tschinag. I do not consider the literature that I present far away from home to be my very own creation, but rather the collective work of a people that has never ever had the possibility to find its own language, or even its voice. In this sense I consider myself a necessity of our time, the swansong of a culture that has been overpowered by a predominator and forced to give way. I am not a poet in the sense that I have extraordinary talent, but that I am the messenger of an epoch that has been late. I was cast far away from my world and my people, I have been picked up as a find, was refined and handed back – to where I came from. From the European point of view I have in me a bit of Asian, a hint of nomadism and shamanism, a shadow of ancient times, and also a scrap of Europe, a trace of civilization and a fluff of present time, seen from the other, our point of view. As much as I was born and sent by the archaic East, the modern Western world formed me and sent me back. I became a bridge between worlds and times, so to speak. Besides, I was granted the privilege to be witness to radical historical changes: I was born into primeval times, into a primitive society, I grew up in socialism and now I stand face to face with capitalism. Each system has formed me, I profited from all of them. I was lucky, therefore, in the Goethean sense of the word.

Ladies and Gentlemen, the last key word came to me by itself, as it were; by all means I wanted to include it at this honourable gathering of minds who belong, despite all, to one epoch and world: Goethe.

Indeed, all over the world the year 1999 stands in the light of the spirit of the highest-ranking German poet. As a student of German half a generation ago, I can admit today that I had quite some troubles with him. He wrote and achieved too much, lived too long, life had meant too well with him while others around him either had to leave early or had to suffer, but in any case had to leave behind their work unfinished. Probably I was also bothered, and I am still today, that he is quoted too often. Goethe and God are not only very similar to each other in the spelling of their names.

But I was not able, however, to hate or even despise him, as many of my fellow students did. Something united me and this man. Now I know what that is: it is the shamanic aspect in his work. It is also the human mountain into which the son of a patrician from Frankfurt on the Main knew how to grow. According to our sense of profundity, which is the word for philosophy in language, every man is on the way to the mountain.

If he makes full use of his possibilities, if he has reached his own peak, he has turned into a mountain.

Johann Wolfgang von Goethe succeeded in climbing up and beyond his own peak as well as the peak of his people and to grow into the formula and measurement of the noble German mind which is willing and able to absorb the worlds and times and cultures and at the same time to pervade them.

The great spirit of Goethe be our guiding star.

And also all the other good spirits with and beside him may shine at the sky above and within us, free themselves from quotation boxes, decorated shields and protective padding and be our companions in life and fate!

I thank your for your patience that carried me a short half an hour of life.

And I want to assure every one of you: my world of spirits has been enriched by you!

Yusef Komunyakaa (born 1947)

In Andalusia, the term duende *traditionally applied to bullfighters and flamenco artists, but poet Federico García Lorca (1898–1936) expanded it to include all the arts, defining it, according to scholar and translator Christopher Maurer, as artists' "ability, on rare occasions, to send waves of emotion through those watching and listening to them." In the following brief essay, first published in 1995, poet Yusef Komunyakaa applies García Lorca's concept of duende to blues singers such as Willie Dixon and Bessie Smith and to his own poetic ambitions – "the sounds of the soil, of the earth turning around in its monumental mystery – conception and birth sounds that stumble out of the night, the violent serenity that Jean Toomer attempted to capture in* Cane, *and the fact that for one to embrace such moments is antithetical to the European psyche and its classic fear of the unknown."*

Forces That Move the Spirit: Duende and Blues

When Federico García Lorca talks about duende, the influence of Andalusian Gypsies on his poetry, how they shaped the concept of *cante jondo* [deep song], I feel that he's talking about a similar, if not the same, emotional soil from which has sprung the blues. I think of Son House, Leadbelly, Charley Patton, Ma Rainey, Blind Lemon Jefferson, etc., with the Mississippi as a slow-motion backdrop. I think of the delta's rich bottomland, the sweat and blood that have gone into endless rituals of survival, the brute force and almost obscene beauty of its peasantry, and how the music and songs are closer to prayers than anything else – and earthy atticism. If one can squeeze love out of these songs, he can taste distilled mercy. Or terror. Here's a class of people refusing to lie down and be counted as victims.

Willie Dixon says that "The whole of life itself expresses the blues. That's why I always says the blues are the true facts of life expressed in words and song, inspiration, feeling and understanding." Indeed, the blues are existential. They are also black and basic. And it is this down-to-earthness that I hope informs the main tenor of my poetry – a language that deals with the atrabilious nature of our existence as well as the emotional weight of its beauty. This is what Lorca saw in the *cante jondo*. Apparently, the Gypsy singer Manuel Torre said in 1922, as Manuel de Falla played *Nights in the Gardens of Spain*, that "Whatever has black sounds has *duende*." The sounds of the soil, of the earth turning around in its monumental mystery – conception and birth sounds that stumble out of the night, the violent serenity that Jean Toomer attempted to capture in *Cane*, and the fact that for one to embrace such moments is antithetical to the European psyche and its classic fear of the unknown.

I love the raw lyricism of the blues. Its mystery and conciseness. I admire and cherish how the blues singer attempts to avoid abstraction; he makes me remember that balance and rhythm also keep our lives almost whole. The essence of mood is also important here. Mood becomes directive; it becomes the bridge that connects us to who we are philosophically and poetically. Emotional texture is drawn from the aesthetics of insinuation and nuance. But to do this well the poet has to have a sense of history. Of course, this often means that one has to reeducate oneself. James Baldwin talks about having taken recordings of Bessie Smith to Switzerland to begin to recreate where he came from before he could write *Another Country* – the natural tongue of his beginnings. Perhaps he desired only a certain mood. I agree with analysis of Janheinz Jahn: "The blues do not arise from a mood, but produce one. Like every art in African culture, song too is an attitude which affects something. The spiritual produces God, the secularized blues produce a mood."

The mood I desire in my poetry is one in which the truth can survive. I love satire. How the Fool operates in *King Lear* is brilliant: he is the wise man in the midst of a cultivated system of evasions and self-deception. Likewise, often the blues singer can get us closer to truth than the philosopher. This is the function of my poetry.

Baron Wormser (born 1948)

In the following essay, first published in the Manhattan Review *in 2009, poet Baron Wormser compares what, on the surface, might seem to be two entirely dissimilar works of art:* The Wire, *an HBO television series broadcast between 2002 and 2008, and T. S. Eliot's "weirdly magisterial" poem* The Waste Land *(1922). But as Wormser notes, "the nightmare that Eliot portrays is the one that underlies* The Wire – *the extinguishing of compassion. . . . [Both works] exemplify the vise of fate but as art they refute it. Without such art we are little more than our dubious achievements."*

The Wire *and* The Waste Land

Without monsters and gods, art cannot enact our drama. . . .
– Mark Rothko

If T. S. Eliot's weirdly magisterial poem *The Waste Land* were cast into the form of a television show, what would it look like? Yes, this is an absurd question because *The Waste Land* is a frightfully verbal entity – the stuff of evocations, shouts, whispers, drones, quotations, laments and exclamations. To say that the poem lacks a plot would be an understatement. Yet if its spirit were to be translated into a foreign medium such as television, surely a major part of that translation would lie in addressing the poem's forthright title. The challenge would be to actualize that daunting metaphor.

It's a fair surmise that the creators of the HBO series *The Wire* – a title at once literal as it refers to wiretapping and metaphorical as it refers to the thin thread that binds both sides of the law – did not set out to do what they did with T. S. Eliot in mind. Saturated as it is in street smarts, the television show is anything but allusive. Whatever footnotes one might need would have to do with the argot of drug dealers. Yet *The Wire* brings Eliot's metaphor to life in a way nothing in television ever has done. Indeed, it brings the metaphor to life in a way that few other works of art have done in any format. I will return in this essay to that metaphor but first I want to dwell on *The Wire*.

When HBO ran Tony Kushner's glowing assessment of *The Wire* as an ad in *The New Yorker*, it was a rare moment when intelligent criticism and commercialism came together. The series, which ran for five years, deserved all the kudos it received. Encompassing as it does dozens of characters from very different strata of American society, *The Wire* was what television has been waiting to do. It created a show that could take advantage of successive episodes (much like the installments of a Victorian novel) to forge a world that was as rich in incident, humor and grief as life itself. It also focused on the nightmare of hard drugs and violence that has plagued the nation for decades and has gone largely unabated despite the enormous amounts of money poured into the "war on drugs." There is no winning in the world of *The Wire*. As one of the characters reflects when asked who is winning a football game that he is watching on TV, "No one wins. One side loses more slowly."

To say that this viewpoint does not sit well with the Protestant optimism of pursuing-happiness America would be an understatement. Only because it deals with the largely African-American underclass involved in the movement of drugs on the streets of Baltimore can *The Wire* go to places that in terms of suffering and fate smack of nothing so much as Greek tragedy. The hard knocks are not the handiwork of Olympian gods but reflect the hazards of birth that are played out under the aegis of racism, poverty, the breakdown of the two-parent family, the tangible financial opportunity drug dealing represents, gun-stoked violence, an overwhelmed educational system and the oblivion of addiction. When one watches the show, one marvels that anyone climbs out from under this weight. Some do and in that regard the show is a testament to human resilience. Many don't.

The show presents an artistic vision of what life is like at the dawn of a new millennium in an American city. It does not purport to be a documentary. It is a drama and thrives on the conflicts that characterize drama. Characters are at cross-purposes with each other in more ways than one can begin to count: drug dealers don't get along; politicians don't get along; cops don't get along. Each professional group (and the drug dealers are ferocious about their professionalism) exists in its own world that has its formal rules and informal codes. Criminality is a fact of life and that includes white-collar crime of which there is plenty in *The Wire*. The degree to which anyone understands anyone else is limited though there are moments of powerful insight. The degree to which the good intentions of the police and the politicians misfire is appalling and profoundly upsetting. All groups make gestures of good will (drug dealers sponsor basketball teams, for instance), however different those gestures are. How much of this is genuine good will and how much of it is arrant cynicism is up to the viewer to decide. Everyone is trapped inside his or her own symbolic actions. When a character tries to flee what he (for typically it is a male) has been taught about manhood or success, he is punished. Everyone needs everyone else in ways that are ghastly and sometimes moving. The strange mix of bare-bones individualism, commercialism and disrespect for any inclusive comity that might characterize the United States has rarely been better expressed. *The Wire* displays the war on the home front, a war that has become so much a fact we barely notice it.

The complaints I have heard about the series focus on two issues. One is that people don't speak like the characters on the show. The imagination and pithiness of the language used by police officers, politicians and drug dealers offend some people's sense of verisimilitude. To this I would answer that anyone who underestimates the terrible pungency of the American vernacular – be it black or white – is ignoring a crucial part of this nation's genius. To say that people don't speak this way is to condescend to the pre-scient shrewdness that has nowhere to go but into figurative language. To say that people don't speak this way is to dismiss poetry as something that is reserved for the pages of books.

The other complaint is that the show is too bleak. Character after character is ground down. Many are killed. Mayhem is a way of life. So is frustration – bureaucracy thrives but people don't. The answer to this is to pick up a copy of the beleaguered daily newspaper of Baltimore and see what is hap-pening. The count for the current year – a year in which the murder-rate is down – is twenty-four juvenile homicides. Each one is a very young life snuffed out. And then there is the number of heroin addicts – an issue the show addresses forthrightly in its third season where a weary police official cordons off a section of the city and declares it a drug trafficking zone. The question that *The Wire* implicitly asks about the murders and the drugs is "What kind of society countenances this?"

Of course the society doesn't publicly countenance this. On the contrary, there are endless attempts ("initiatives") to undo this misery. The success of these is demonstrated by statistics, which are the target of much un-happy mirth on the part of the police in *The Wire*. The larger issues – why, for instance, our American energies go to things rather than spirit or why art plays such a tiny role in the life of the average citizen – go unexam-ined. Larger issues tend to be like that, however. Beneath practicality lies the swamp of myth. Only poets have time for those legends that motivate each blessed and unblessed day.

T. S. Eliot's *The Waste Land* is a poem that is based on a book about a legend – "Jessie L. Weston's book on the Grail legend: *From Ritual to Romance*" (to quote from Eliot's notes). The theme of *The Wire* is the same as the theme of *The Waste Land* – death in life, that rote that turns us all into zombies. "A crowd flowed over London Bridge, so many, / I had not thought death had undone so many," wrote Eliot. (In one episode of *The Wire* a group of boys considers whether the corpses being stashed in abandoned houses are indeed zombies. It is a commentary at once mordant and fanciful.) One of the reasons for the extraordinary resonance of Eliot's poem is that it identified the crucial theme of the twentieth century, a theme that is not leaving us anytime in the near future. It is the theme that underlies modern life, the great cities humanity has created, the fabled progress of technology and of the art – *Guernica, Survival at Auschwitz, One Day in the Life of Ivan Denisovich* – that has sought to elucidate the massive scale of modern violence, to say nothing of the smaller murders. It is the theme that speaks the unspeakable – that we are undone by our brilliant, futile doing.

In his later poetry Eliot grants us the margin of prayer. Though it is relentlessly profane, *The Wire* acknowledges the presence of religion. The strength of the African-American church can not be gainsaid. Yet spirit must play itself out in the context of deal making. The disabused ministers of black Baltimore try to get from the politicians what they can get for their congregations. The ministers know first-hand what Christ knew, money trumps spirit. How much it trumps spirit is the crucial question. The various captains of drug dealing in *The Wire* do not have any use for what they cannot buy and sell. Though they make a show of solidarity, they are more than willing to sell one another out. They aren't the only ones who live according to a brutal bottom line, hence the feeling for drama – spirit's struggle – and the cry of tragedy. Though the ministers believe in the active presence of God, they know that prayers are as much for someone about to be murdered as for church.

The Waste Land is a vision as much as what is presented in *The Wire* is a vision. Baltimore has many other dimensions than what is purveyed on the TV series (see Barry Levinson's movies, for instance) but that doesn't matter. What matters is the coherence of the vision that is presented. What matters is how genuine that vision feels, since coherence can be manufactured as readily as any entity. (Every four years, the two American political parties manufacture a national coherence whose genuineness is dubious.) One of the initial charges against *The Waste Land* was that it made no sense; it was incoherent. It was a jumble of voices and fragments. Even the author admitted as much at the end of the poem when he wrote "These fragments I have shored against my ruins." One can argue that the aesthetic of modern times is incoherence. The rejection by many of modern art's difficulty ("the difficulties of the poem" in Eliot's own note) is the rejection of incoherence. "What is this?" more than one student has said to me after trying to read *The Waste Land*. And more pointedly, they have asked, "What is this to me? Why should I care about this?"

What *this* is is a lyric drama of the soul. It is one poet's soul at one juncture in that poet's life but it is the souls of many. What is at stake is whether we are alive in this world in any meaningful sense or whether we are amiable or not-so-amiable automatons flowing across London Bridge or doing our various jobs in Baltimore. Characters in *The Wire* speak of "the game" often. It is the code by which they live. They take it very seriously in certain ways (snitches are punished ruthlessly, for instance) and yet in other ways they dismiss it as the price of doing business. Souls are at stake in *The Wire* but not in the sense of salvation. They are at stake in regards to their humanity, how much they let themselves feel about what is occurring around them and to them. When a frustrated street level drug dealer kicks out the windows of a car in angry response to the endless murders perpetrated by a drug gang, it is his humanity that is surfacing. The irony is brutal because eventually he is seen talking with a police officer and for that reason murdered by that drug gang. His show of feeling earns him his death.

The word "humanity" is not a word anyone in the show would use. It is a precious word – the great voice that dwells in our being human – but it has no place amid the routine inhumanity of crime. In that context it can only be a learned word, a pointless word, a well-meaning word. It is what everyone would seem to have forfeited. Even the police, who are the putative good guys, would be the first to say that they are not very good. That is not their job. And it is a word that for all its meaningfulness Eliot would have dismissed as being so much secular palaver. The aridity – at once matter of fact and terrible – that afflicts the inhabitants of *The Waste Land* is not going to be fixed by any sort of progress or program or uplift. The "unreal" cities evoked in section V of the poem are the destroyers of souls. No one in east Baltimore would argue with that.

The drama in *The Wire* is the standard issue drama of different human beings who want very different things and who, for all their fidelity to Baltimore, come from very different places. It is the drama of democracy and there are numerous parodies of cooperation on both sides of the law-and-order fence. (The drug dealers organize a co-op; the police argue about whether a body floating in the harbor is the responsibility of the city or the county.) There are numerous machinations, also, as members jockey for position in the drug hierarchy and in the police hierarchy. These are office politics of a sort but the stakes can be life and death.

In *The Waste Land* the drama is inferred. There exists a sort of pressure throughout the poem that lends even its lyric moments a foreboding chill. Because we never know where exactly we are in the poem's constantly shuttling, evocative geography, we are forced to orient ourselves according to a series of mere voices. They possess authority as they make various assertions but we don't know whose authority. These points of view mesh with one another as they are presented within the inclusive context of a poem but they don't mesh with one another in regards to their attitudes. It is a long way from the suppliant voice in section V of the poem ("Here is no water but only rock") to the voice bidding "Goonight. Goonight" at the end of section II. The tonal range is startling. It is part of what has made my students throw up their exasperated hands.

As it shifts from one character and scene to another, the poem is a series of soft collisions. It keeps moving and has no compunctions about shifting viewpoints. On the contrary, it revels in such shifts. Eliot, the lyric dramatist, has no interest in resolution. People go on doing what they do, whether dire or mild. He may invoke an Upanishad but "Hieronymo's mad againe." The enormous power of the first-person lyric, that belief in the powers of the subsuming, creative "I" – a power that fuels most of the poems one reads these days – is not the power Eliot employs. He purposefully eschews it. The power of drama resides in the power of conflict not in the power of an identified narrator.

The conflicts in *The Wire* range from simple – certain drugs are against the law – to devious – raising money to support a certified union by illegal means. The numerous shifts of scenes and characters that occur within an hour's viewing display the scope of the conflicts and how they play out. It is the language of the cinema (a scene may last less than a minute) but one that can use successive episodes to build a stunning tableau. Imagine a play that takes sixty hours with a thousand scenes and you have one sense of what *The Wire* accomplishes.

Eliot was aiming for something similar in *The Waste Land*. The pages constitute the stage. Space is created by the poem's voices. This space is, as the poem's title indicates, actual and metaphorical. Duration is the time that lapses as one reads the poem. The drama is spiritual, at once pointed and subdued. The sprawl of characters seems off-hand, the various stuff of the modern city – merchants, typists, clerks, fortune tellers, people in pubs. How much anyone influences anyone else is part of the evocative mystery of the whole. The vision is of a broken choir but a choir nonetheless. The voices are themselves; they do not represent anything more than themselves. Yet they are the voices of the city and of other moments and texts that the poet sees fit to access. The whole poem is a very careful dissolution but what certitude was there in the first place to dissolve? The Grail with which the poem concerns itself doesn't exist. The search for it is noble and absurd.

This arcane agony is far away from the police sirens and automatic weapons of *The Wire* – and yet what animates the television show is a vision of suffering that is not far removed from *The Waste Land*. The stature of the poem, above and beyond its remarkable language, rests in the passionate engagement on the part of the poet with a world of suffering. The poem is close up as it presents characters and scenes – "I said, / What you get married for if you don't want children?" – yet oracular – "O Lord Thou pluckest me out." The tenor varies radically; Eliot was steeped in Jacobean drama with its quick changes of mood. The quiet agonies – "I can connect / Nothing with nothing" – remain. The poem embraces the impossibility of how much we may feel as human beings and puts that impossibility into one poem. Those who don't consider Eliot to be a truly American poet might ponder the scope of *The Waste Land*. Its spaciousness echoes Whitman but it is a dark spaciousness. The misgivings that Whitman increasingly felt in the decades after the Civil War have come home to roost in ways that the "adhesive" Whitman barely could have imagined. The imaginative breadth of Eliot's poem is intoxicating and close to unbearable.

It is precisely this dark spaciousness that distinguishes *The Wire* from anything ever done on television. We are given the sense of a whole experience that is panoramic yet gritty in the extreme. The major irony at work is that virtually everyone suffers from a sense of being caught in scripts that are not of their device: this includes those in charge, be it a drug lord or a mayor. When characters seek to make the scripts their own – taking an investigation personally or deciding they can be straight businessmen rather than gangsters – they cause more grief, not less. Yet the elemental drama of free will never ceases to play itself out. A man can admit he has been a "dope fiend" his whole life. An incarcerated father can admit that his son has opportunities that never came his way and that his son deserves those opportunities. These are, however, rare moments. As in Greek tragedy, the forces that grind up people are relentless. The characters in *The Wire* (*pace* Rothko's remark) are being mocked by gods who do not exist.

Societies that cannot admit suffering are doomed to shallowness at best and vengefulness at worst. In the former case, they must pretend that suffering is a passing fact, not a permanent one. They must put a good face on what does not want a good face. In *The Wire* what the policemen see in their line of work is what often messes up their home lives. They cannot dismiss what they know too well. In the case of vengefulness – and here one can choose from a panoply of nations and wars – the suffering is transfigured into a myth that demands blood. One of the most quietly harrowing moments in *The Wire* occurs when a prison inmate in a literature discussion group talks at some length about that crucible of suffering, *The Great Gatsby*, and what an individual in the United States is up against. It is a moment of real insight and empathy and one that is clearly insupportable in the world in which the prisoner lives. As he starts to separate himself from his criminal cohorts in jail, he marks himself as unreliable. For that he is murdered.

The violence that *The Waste Land* engages is spiritual. It is the violence of denial and lack of sustenance. It is the violence of tawdriness and thoughtlessness – what one might call the underlying violence of human life, the texture of our days on earth with one another. Eliot renders this texture brilliantly as he invents the mindless likes of Madame Sosostris and the "young man carbuncular." The drama he is pursuing is much quieter than that of *The Wire* yet in its way even more devastating. There is the joy of the chase that both the cops and criminals in the television show relish. For better and mostly for worse it makes them feel alive. It banishes the death in life. Omar, the character who robs drug dealers, is many things but he is not dreary. In Eliot, however, the death in life has an awful primacy and cannot be dislodged. What seems disconnected is terribly concatenated. There is not so much a field of force as a field of anomie. It is very strong: "each in his prison / Thinking of his key." In *The Wire* the prison is actual; in *The Waste Land* the prison is metaphorical but no less actual.

Our dramas, as they give voice to our conflicts, compromises, decisions and hopes, are our dignity as human beings. They demonstrate what can't be talked away. One of the delusions of modern times, brought about by the model of progressive market capitalism and the psychological, therapeutic outlook that goes with it – goods and people both getting newer and better – is that we somehow are beyond the ministrations of drama. The talking self – be it on a radio show, in a therapist's office or on the page – replaces the dramatic sense. Although the situation the talking self engages is typically mundane – a memory, an anecdote, a joke, an opinion – it is vivifying since it indulges the self's viewpoint. It is comforting in that it seems to free us from the arbitrary, interfering hands of the gods. In this regard, the genius of democracy is sincerity. Yet, because it puts great weight on the mere individual, the talking self is burdensome. The individual is ever explaining – not for the purposes of salvation but definition. For some that explanatory weight is borne up by the advantages – wealth and skin color, to name two – their society bequeaths them. For others the weight is insupportable. The need for those drugs being sold in Baltimore is genuine.

This situation would seem to banish the tragic sense of life that both *The Wire* and *The Waste Land* pursue. The tragic is the cold and unavoidable (Eliot's eye is a famously austere one) yet it is fraught with enormous human feeling. We can point to a chain of causes in *Oedipus Rex* or *Lear* but tragedy remains. The facticity of the chain defies the rational mind and savages our sense of self-importance. For his part, Eliot had to look no further than World War I for that savaging. The shadow of the "Great War" stalks his poem – "He's been in the army four years, he wants a good time." How true. "A good time" is the equivalent of our American "fun" – that all-purpose enjoyment that banishes suffering, to say nothing of the tragic.

Neither work argues with our need to cheer ourselves up; both feature scenes in pubs. The issue is whether we are trading one oblivion for another. That may be our fate – to use an uncomfortable, non-modern word. Neither work has any belief in progress as anything more than a notion that motivates many of us to get up in the morning. Having been emancipated from the malicious caprices of the monsters and gods, we enact our cheerful duty. We play at gods and we play at monsters and we succeed in ways that are appalling and occasionally beautiful – "Looking into the heart of light, the silence," as Eliot so aptly put it.

No one quotes poetry in *The Wire* but why would they? It would be an affectation on the part of the creators and the created. In a world that has disavowed the primacy of imagination, poetry continues to believe in the primacy of imagination. As someone who consciously abjured romanticism, Eliot smiled at this poetic faith. He was scrupulously careful to distinguish where poetry ended and religion began. Poetry was not a ticket to heaven or a creed. It trafficked in the mysteries but never rose up above its medium – mere language. In the wastelands of Baltimore the words of Eliot are just that – words. That is as it should be. The connection that poetry seeks – to fuse imagination and life in ways that make both more supportable, to create a context for the inherent magic of language – is quixotic by any standards.

The nightmare of violence that *The Wire* portrays has gone on for decades. It didn't have to play out the way it played out but the attitudes – making drug taking a crime – and the economics – enormous sums of money – have been paramount. Like an unwanted visitor, history, as every African-American well knows, lingers and lingers with all its prejudices, confusions and animosities. As it influences the medium of our moments – whether we go to town by foot, on a mule or in a car – history is where we live yet it is where we cannot live because it is the huge fumbling past, not the narrow concise present. Its powerful voice is ever muted.

The nightmare that Eliot portrays is the one that underlies *The Wire* – the extinguishing of compassion. Not the least of this is lack of compassion for ourselves that turns us into instruments of wrath and folly. *The Wire* brims with these instruments; *The Waste Land* alludes to them. Still, the characters in the poem or in the TV series are not immune to compassion. However the police in *The Wire* may scoff at it, they acknowledge, as they seek to help the citizens of Baltimore, its importance. Compassion is, however, endangered – to put it mildly. Compassion commands little respect; society wants results, not good intentions. Even the schools are in thrall to test results rather than aiding some very beleaguered young people. To put compassion at the head of the list, ahead of wealth, knowledge, power and pleasure, is a high and impractical aim.

Perhaps what moves me the most about the two works is that aspiration. They exemplify the vise of fate but as art they refute it. Without such art we are little more than our dubious achievements. The image of ourselves that we find in the television series and in the poem is a dark one but a true one. Amid the home boy banter and the voices raised in the pub, amid Lanvale Street and King William Street, amid the bedrooms and classrooms, we are "burning burning burning."

Bei Dao (born 1949)

Bei Dao is the pseudonym of Zhenkai Zhao, a Chinese poet, journal editor, and political activist. In this poem, from his 1994 collection Forms of Distance, *he considers how the creative mind seeks its own freedom, becoming "an alien voice sneaking into the dictionary / a dissident / perhaps a form of distance from the world."*

Corridor

translated by David Hinton

all those beer-bottle caps
where were they taken down busy streets
that year I cut class, in movie houses
inside the endless corridor of screens
I suddenly found myself enlarged
that moment was a wheelchair
and the days to come pushed me through distant travels –

the world's agents of freedom
entered me into their giant computer:
an alien voice sneaking into the dictionary
a dissident
perhaps a form of distance from the world

where the corridor ends, various words smolder
and a window robbed of its glass
looks out on the bureaucratic winter

Elizabeth McElrea (born 1951)

In the early 1970s, Swarthmore College sophomore Elizabeth McElrea won the college's poetry reading contest, judged by W. S. Merwin. The poem she chose to read was W. H. Auden's "In Memory of W. B. Yeats." To honor her victory, the staff of the Phoenix, *the college's newspaper, invited her to interview Auden, who had taught at Swarthmore during the 1940s and continued to maintain a relationship with the college. Following is McElrea's article, published in the November 19, 1971, issue.*

Famed Poet Auden Urges Authenticity, Plays Game of Life Seeking "Good Art"

"I don't ever remember having been bored, ever." W. H. Auden's declaration about himself is an observable truth. If talking with Auden reveals anything, it is simply an awareness of his unflagging interest in life. Writing poetry is the result of this preoccupation and his attempt to communicate it.

Of course, Auden's attempts are of a different magnitude than ours. His fame and literary reputation have been growing since he published his first volume of verse at age 23. Nevertheless, Auden communicates life to people through his writing, "a dialogue between the poet and reader, but with the poet out of the picture."

Since he cannot be part of the picture, Auden stresses the need for the poet to be authentic, to write in his own hand. Authenticity, he said, should not be confused with self-expression, the mistake of the Romantics.

Knowing the Rules

He continued, "I want a reader to be able to say 'I always knew that, but didn't realize it until I read this.'" Self-expression and sincerity are not enough. "Good art," Auden maintained, "is a source of joy." As such it can help us "to enjoy life or . . . to endure it a little better."

For all of his willingness to be philosophical and general about poetry, however, Auden is rather reluctant to speak of life and his experiences in the same way. His poetry speaks for itself – and does so in a particularly compelling manner when he reads it.

Auden's fascination with crossword puzzles, detective novels, and with "sticking to the rules of the game" when writing poetry is symptomatic of the nature of his life. Auden knows exactly what time it is; he knows the rules and the game.

Both poems and life "are never finished," he says, "but only abandoned." Auden has been too interested to want to abandon either, and is constantly tidying up, yet at the same time he is most interested "in what you're going to do next."

Auden's views on politics and pot are footnotes to his ideas about poetry. He asserts that one cannot write good political poetry. Politics is a self-conscious, necessary evil.

The business of governing should be dealt with as quickly as possible, so as to get on with the real business of life. "But there's always somebody on a committee who just loves it and draws out meetings unbearably."

Although Auden believes that art cannot change the course of history, he does not consider this a failure. '"Poets are not the legislators of the world." [This paraphrases the conclusion of Shelley's "A Defence of Poetry" (p. 93).] Auden is not giving us laws, but words to be "modified in the guts of the living."

On the subject of drugs Auden speaks from experience. His criticisms of marijuana use are that it reduces coherence, inflates egos, and for the young especially, prevents one from discovering his own identity. Artistically, he found the experience uncommunicatable and hence useless. With LSD, "nothing happened."

Other interesting trivia gleaned from the poet in his private talks include: "every girl and boy of sixteen should be given a cookbook; I hate cameras, they turn all fact into fiction; I wouldn't know what to do in a contemporary literature course"; and that, in regard to being a poet, "I had no regrets once I started."

Auden, at sixty-four, is still striving, still playing the game for mortal stakes. He writes as he lives; to see him and to hear him is to have an unexpected chance to feel his authenticity and witness his communication.

Charles Bernstein (born 1950)

Founder of the influential journal L=A=N=G=U=A=G=E *(1978–82), Charles Bernstein has long been active in the loose, diverse movement known as language poetry. In this excerpt from a 2010 interview in the* Chicago Weekly, *Bernstein shares what might be called a poetic credo.*

from *Interview with Charles Bernstein*

by Daniel Benjamin

Charles Bernstein: I am interested in poetry as a medium for exploring the possibilities, and resistances, to expression, not as a vehicle to express a message I have already formulated. My poetry doesn't convey what I know, it explores the conditions of how I know it. A lot of the kicking-up-dust aspects of 1970s discussions about poetry were, not surprisingly, centered around the problems of language and description. The word "poem" doesn't delimit all that much. It used to drive me crazy when people whose work I thought was terrific would say "poetry does this" and "poetry does that." I remember writing a letter to Jerome McGann saying I love this essay but I don't understand why you say poetry in this way; isn't it some poetry or this particular poem? And then I found myself doing exactly what I was complaining to McGann about, and for the same reason that McGann sometimes does it, as an expression of desire.

Poetry itself is a porous term; it means a lot of different things to different people. It's not an honorific. A work doesn't become a poem because it's good and cease to be a poem if it is bad. If somebody chooses to publish the TV listing from this hotel as a poem – and why not? – the problem would not be whether the work is a poem. Veronica Forrest-Thomson, in "Poetic Artifice," lays this out this argument persuasively. She points out that if you can take a newspaper article and break it up into verse lines, you'll read it as a poem, but not necessarily as an especially good or interesting poem.

For me poetry is a form of sophism and of rhetoric rather than of truth and sincerity.

Our terminology or typology for poetry is inadequate to the proliferating and contradictory range of approaches in the postwar years. I want to talk about hue or tone; about satire versus irony versus sarcasm versus humor; about bumpy versus smooth surfaces; about 13 ways of looking at rhythm in nonmetrical poetry; about the difference between form and its inflections. Narrative, prose poem, lyric, epic, personal, performance, long, short, elliptical, sound, visual, identitarian, disjunctive, projective, formalist, objectivist – just as "language" or "conceptual" – don't account for the wild divergences within the rubrics and unexpected affinities across them.

Jack Wiler (1951–2009)

Jack Wiler's poetry often deals with the "unmentionable" details of human experience: exactly what happens to a living body as it prepares to die, for instance, or the ways in which people ostracized by mainstream society figure out how to love one another. In the following piece from his 2006 collection Fun Being Me, *Wiler rants about the impossibility of balancing public mores with poetic honesty.*

Things I Can't Say at East Brunswick High School

First, I can't say fuck.

And I can't say motherfucker obviously and it would probably go without saying that I can't say fuck you but it occurs to me at times that fuck you is what a lot of people think when they're in school but you can't say it. At least not out loud and not in a poem and not in front of a classroom of children. I could probably talk about whether they're children or not. But I can't tell them to fuck off. Although the people that tell me what I can and can't say clearly want to be able to tell the children to fuck off or at the very least they'd like their parents to eat shit. I can't say that either. Eat shit. Or suck my dick. No way they'd let me call them cocksuckers but they are. Cocksuckers. They're also shitheads and assholes and mealy mouthed little pissants. I might be allowed to say pissants. Maybe not. It's got piss in it. You'd think their teachers would want to get up one day and walk into a classroom and tell all the little shitheads with their bmw's and suv's and rich moms and dads to fuck off but they don't and they won't let me, so fuck em. I can't say pussy. I can't say cunt. I can't say faggot. Or queer or cocksucker but I already went over that didn't I? The kids can call each other queers and the teachers can bitch about the little faggots and they can all laugh when little Jimmy in the band gets his ass kicked but they can't say it out loud. They can just think it. Or talk among themselves.

This is high school.

And since it's high school every fucking one of them has to pretend that nothing happens outside their door. They have to act like mommy and daddy are nice and the kids are okay and it's a good idea to invade various small countries and the best way to get along is go along and so we can't have any fucking, queer, poet, shithead going around saying cunt in front of the kids because god knows where that would lead.

It's fucking nuts.

But it's exactly what you'd expect in America although you'd expect it was nineteen fucking fifty fucking nine and not two thousand and three you know? It's mother fucking astounding that thirty years after I got out of all this shit it's still exactly the fucking same. Nice clean kids sitting in rows all listening to nice teachers talking about some version of history where nobody does anything but work to raise up his kids and grow old and die happy in bed surrounded by his smiling children and I hope you're noticing that I'm not even putting a woman in all of this nor is anybody in this little scenario black or Chinese or Indian or anything other than white, white, white, white to the tippy toes of their fucking little white feet. I think I could say almost all of this and get a little rise out of the attendant students and teachers if I left out the fucking little white feet.

So let's be clear.

I can't say fuck in East Brunswick, New Jersey in the poetry classroom while pretending to be an expert on poetry in front of a culturally diverse group of students who come here out of some sense of duty and a legal obligation who are overseen in this activity by underpaid employees of the state who while they may have some ideas of educating the children they teach are basically tired of them and who are in turn overseen by even more underpaid employees and all so that they will learn the essentials of American culture and history and when it's done they all go home to eat and worry and work but the one thing they can't do in this place, this classroom, this school, is to say anything that reflects the fucking world they actually live in because that's a bad, bad thing to do. It's a really bad, bad thing. So fuck them and fuck this school and God bless fucking America.

Naomi Shihab Nye   (born 1952)

In this tiny essay, from her 1996 prose collection Never in a Hurry, *poet Naomi Shihab Nye celebrates the miracle of discovering a reader, that rare person who tells the poet, "I read it – I know what you mean."*

Poetry

The library shelves opened their arms. In the library everyone was rich. I stacked my bounty, counting books, arranging their spines. Bindings of fresh new books smelled delicious.

On television Carl Sandburg strummed his guitar, his voice a honey-sweet dream of rolling, rollicking words. His white hair looked lit up from inside, like a bulb. I read every morning, every night: if you knew how to read, you could never be lonely.

If you knew how to read, it made sense that you might, one night in a Chicago hotel, ask for a large piece of pale construction paper – not the easiest thing to come by in a hotel – and write down something you felt that day when you saw the streets that were also bridges lifting up for boats to pass under. When you tipped your head back to gaze at the giant towers in which a thousand people worked who had never even *thought* of your name. It was worth saying.

You could take it to school and give it to your first-grade teacher, who didn't like you. Pretend it was a present. She would hang it on the bulletin board in the hall and weeks later, far from that trip, a girl in school who was bigger than you would pause to say, "Did you write that poem?"

"Ho! Yes. I almost forgot."

She smiled. "I read it – and I know what you *mean*," – skipping off to join her friends at the monkey bars.

She knew what I *meant*. That was something. That was a wing to fly on all the way home, or for the rest of a life.

Rita Dove (born 1952)

In a January 2012 conversation with poet Rita Dove, National Public Radio host Michel Martin asked her if she had any thoughts about writing to share with young aspiring poets who might be listening to the radio show. She responded with the following remarks, which include the reminder that "when someone tells you your poem is bad, it doesn't mean that your heart is bad. . . . So be able to separate those two."

from *Interview with Rita Dove*

by Michel Martin

Rita Dove: It's hard to be called upon to be wise. But I would say to someone who was wondering if they could become a poet, you have two things in front of you. First of all, you have your heart and the things that you want to say. Nothing is too small. Nothing is too, quote-unquote, ordinary or insignificant. Those are the things that make up the measure of our days, and they're the things that sustain us. And they're the things that certainly can become worthy of poetry.

And the other thing is your tools, which is the writing itself – the language, the way you use that language; even grammar. And so you use one in order to get to the other. And when someone tells you your poem is bad, it doesn't mean that your heart is bad, it just means that your language, the way – your tools, you have to hone them a little more. So be able to separate those two, and to work to hone the tools. To practice your scales, so to speak, in order play the symphony, is what you have to do as a young poet.

And to read. To read, read, read. If you don't love to read, if you don't get taken in by any text that you see – on the back of a cereal box or in a book – then I would say you probably won't have the right passion to write as well.

Sam Watson

(born 1952)

Poet, painter, storyteller, and activist Oodgeroo Noonuccal, also known as Kath Walker, (1920–93), was a powerful voice for the rights of aboriginal Australians. In the following transcript from a show on the Australian Radio National program Encounter, *her nephew Sam Watson shares excerpts from a play he wrote about his aunt as well as selections from her poetry and his own first novel. In the process he reveals how a poet's convictions and heritage can drive her art and shows how powerful words can be, even in the worst of situations.*

One Dreaming Stilled

a radio show hosted by Florence Spurling

Florence Spurling: I'm Florence Spurling. Welcome to *Encounter* on Radio National.

This week, "One Dreaming Stilled," an exploration of the life of Oodgeroo Noonuccal, formerly known as Kath Walker, one of Australia's most respected poets and Indigenous leaders.

Sam Watson is the Deputy Director of the Aboriginal and Torres Strait Islander Studies Centre at the University of Queensland. He is an award-winning writer and he's Kath Walker's bloodline nephew. His play, *Oodgeroo – Bloodline to Country*, was first performed in Brisbane last year. This *Encounter* explores both Kath Walker's life and something of Sam Watson's story through his play, beginning with a reminder of a traumatic experience in Oodgeroo's life which is often not recalled. Sam Watson.

SAM WATSON: In November 1974, a BOAC aircraft was hijacked in Dubai by Palestinian terrorists. The aircraft was flown to Tunisia and held on the tarmac for three days. Kath Walker, member of the Steering Committee for the Second World Black and African Festival of Arts and Culture meeting in Nigeria, was on that plane. Walker pleaded with the hijackers on behalf of the passengers, particularly a German banker who had been targeted for execution.

BANKER: Wasser! Wasser! Bitte!

OODGEROO:

Sit, obey, keep calm

The blinds shut out the landscape.

The DC10 pants on hot desert sands

Like a wounded eagle . . .

HIJACKER: Blood, I will give you blood. I have the power now! I have the gun. You must give us what we want or we will kill them all. Dogs! Pigs!

OODGEROO: Did he have to do that?

BANKER: They're going to kill me for sure.

OODGEROO: No, you'll be OK. They just want to put on a bit of a show.

BANKER: They will shoot us all.

OODGEROO: No! You'll be back home in no time. I'm sure that your government will release their friends. They've got to!

BANKER: They won't. They never negotiate. Not after Munich.

OODGEROO: Let's not think about that. Have you got any family?

BANKER: Daughter. Very young.

OODGEROO: I have two sons. I should be with them now, not here in the middle of this godforsaken hell-hole.

BANKER: You are very calm.

OODGEROO: I'm a black woman from Australia, I'm used to all this.

HIJACKER: Silence! Prisoners will be silent! We are in charge. We give the orders?

OODGEROO: Fine. Why don't you give us a cold drink too?

HIJACKER: Silence! Prisoners will stay silent! We are in control.

OODGEROO: You're a bit like a broken record, mate!

HIJACKER: Silence!

OODGEROO: Leave him alone, you can't do this!

BANKER: Let us go. We have done nothing to you. . . .

HIJACKER: Silence!!!

Sam Watson: The shock of it happening, the shock of being in a confined, compressed space with a group of young angry people with guns who were very much driven by their beliefs, by their ideology and were negotiating with various governments to bring about their demands, so she felt the shock, being so helpless in that scenario. She also bonded very quickly with the other people on the plane, the other passengers and she saw that the only way they were going to survive the experience was by staying calm, and that was very difficult, because the heat of the plane, the fact they couldn't move about very much, the fact that they had very limited supplies, limited water, and that was a very elemental force, water, right the way throughout the play, and of particular significance in the hijack scenario. So she was harking back to the importance of water around the island of her birthplace, so that carried through and that gave her some degree of strength.

Florence Spurling: So she was able to draw on the spiritual recollection of the water around Stradbroke Island to help her survive the extreme and literal deprivation of water on the aircraft, among all the other deprivations she was suffering?

Sam Watson: That's right. And I mean she wasn't totally unaware, or she wasn't totally unsympathetic to the situation of the hijackers. So she saw that they were also battling against enormous powers and she saw also that they were taking steps to address very basic needs.

Florence Spurling: Sam Watson is of the Munnenjarl and Biri Gubba peoples and through traditional adoption he has ties to the Kalkadoon and Mapoon peoples. His play, *Oodgeroo – Bloodline to Country* is also about Oodgeroo's life on Stradbroke Island in South East Queensland and her debates and differences with her son Denis Walker who co-founded the Brisbane Black Panther Party with Sam Watson in 1971. Here is the character of Denis Walker in the play.

DENIS WALKER: Off pig!
One: we want freedom. We want power to determine the destiny of our black community.
Two: We want full employment for all our people.
Three: We want an end to the robbery by capitalists of our black community.
Four: We want decent housing fit for the shelter of human beings.
Five: We want education that teaches us our true history and our role in present day society. . . .

Sam Watson: Well, Denis and I started working together and attending meetings in the late '60s, early '70s, and right the way through that process, Denis and I particularly saw that there was a need for a pure political spearhead to take to the streets, to confront the power structures of Australia, to confront the State governments, confront the Federal government, to announce our political agenda, to assert our rights as sovereign Aboriginal people. So we saw that there was a need to establish the survival services, to make sure we had legal services available for our people, to set up medical services, housing services etc., to attend to the basic bread-and-butter needs of our people. But we also saw at a higher level that nothing was going to change until we asserted our political rights. And we reached out for models and ideologies and philosophies from other oppressed groups, decolonised peoples, across the globe, and the model we particularly were impressed with was the model of the Panthers in the States, and through our comrades and friends on the waterfront, through particular unions we were given access to contraband material that was smuggled in. We were able to access books and pamphlets and speeches by the great people like Huey P. Newton, Bobby Seal, Eldridge Cleaver, H. Rap Brown and a number of others. So this is the sort of material we relied upon to adjust and change so that we could accommodate the needs and aspirations of the Aboriginal political movement here on the home front.

Florence Spurling: Can we talk about Oodgeroo's commitment to reconciliation and non-violence and, of course, Denis was working in a way in the play that's very clear, where he would have been prepared to use violence, to use arms. Can we talk about that tension both between Oodgeroo and Denis, and your own sense of comment on that?

Sam Watson: Denis at various times throughout his political career did feel very frustrated by the pace of change. He saw the needs; he travelled quite extensively throughout Australia and even in the '80s when he was working on behalf of the National Aboriginal and Islander Community Health Organisation, he was often going into communities where the needs were so glaring. Aboriginal and Islander people living in the most crushing poverty, here in the midst of one of the most affluent nations in the world. So to try to balance that with the enormous amount of money that was being produced out of stolen Aboriginal land, was always one of Denis' great dilemmas, and regardless of the advances we made, regardless of the numbers of organisations and programs we were able to establish through the '70s and the '80s, we still weren't moving fast enough. And Denis on a daily basis was continually confronted with the faces and the eyes of staring, destitute families and children and this again marked him in particular ways, and he laid the blame at the feet of the power structures – the governments and the multinational corporations that drove the economy. So this placed him on a pathway. He was driven by this sense of urgency, so it was inevitable that at times throughout his political career, he did come in confrontation with the authorities, with the State police and with the Federal Department.

> OODGEROO: Now hang on a minute, I've worked with white people and they've worked hard for us. I have so many good white friends.
> DENIS WALKER: The whites want to control everything. They're already tearing the guts out of our country. It's time, Kath. They're trying to wipe out our entire race. It's genocide. Hitler used his armies and the

gas chambers, but the Jews fought back. Look how strong Israel is now. They don't take shit from nobody.

OODGEROO: What about Gandhi? What about Martin Luther King?

DENIS WALKER: All political power comes out of the barrel of the gun. Since the first white man put his foot on our land, we've been fighting an armed struggle to survive. Only it's been the white man who had the guns. The white men do not fear us. But look at the Black Panthers. When those black men and women got out onto the streets with their shotguns, the whole world took notice.

OODGEROO: And they got arrested.

DENIS WALKER: I've done hard time before.

OODGEROO: All those months you spent in that filthy cell, you could have been doing a university degree like Pearl, or out there teaching our young ones. We need you to be talking up for us and challenging the system, not shooting it down and going to jail. We have people from all over the country looking to us for leadership. We can't afford to lose our leaders.

DENIS WALKER: If I'm going to lead, these blackfellas have to be prepared to follow. Look, onetime there, Eldridge Cleaver was talking to a mass gathering in one of the African colonies. First he asked them who was ready to kill for freedom. They all put up their hands. Then he asked them who was prepared to kill white men for their freedom. Only half of the group put up their hands. Then Brother Cleaver asked them to step to one side. And he told them that the first people they had to kill were not the white men, but their own mob who hadn't put up their hands. Do you see what I'm saying? This is business time now. We can't sit back and talk shit no more, we have to move now.

OODGEROO: So now we have to shoot our own people? Does that include me? Are you going to point that gun at me?
Denis . . . ?

Sam Watson: Aunty Oodgeroo saw that the ultimate changes had to be brought about through a shared journey, a shared journey [through] which both Aboriginal people and white Australians could appreciate each other's situation, each other's humanity, each other's culture, to share, to exchange. And it was through her work on Moongalba that I came to reach a much higher understanding of what Aunty Kath's basic ideology was. She really wanted to – she really saw the starting point as being that with children, to educate the children because in turn the children would then grow up, they'd go to universities and they would become the leaders of the community, and if she could reach them at an early age and show them how incredibly important it is to understand and empathise with Aboriginal people to develop an understanding of the way in which Aboriginal culture works, to develop understanding of how Aboriginal people could live and work within the natural environment without creating any permanent damage, I think that was one of her lasting legacies, that she tried to teach to everyone who came on to Moongalba, to minimise the human impact of our presence, of our lives, on the natural environment was of critical importance to Aunty Kath, that we had no right to mark or to scar the face of the human landscape.

Florence Spurling: Moongalba on Stradbroke Island, her school?

Sam Watson: That's right. Moongalba is taken from the Noonuccal language and it means sitting down place, and that was Aunty Kath's property which she leased from the Redlands Shire Council and she had plans to develop the Noonuccal Nughi Cultural Education Centre on that place.

Florence Spurling: Which would have involved the white community as well as the Indigenous community, sharing and educating in a way that you're describing?

Sam Watson: That's right, because when we saw Aunty Kath leading the great marches against the sand mining, again that was not only an Aboriginal struggle, that was the struggle that people from right across the social and political spectrum joined in. It was a struggle, a universal struggle for all of us, for all our children and grandchildren.

Florence Spurling: Sam Watson is Kath Walker's bloodline nephew. His play about her life, *Oodgeroo – Bloodline to Country*, was first performed in Brisbane in last year. Here in this *Encounter* on ABC Radio National we're listening to the story of poet and Indigenous leader, Oodgeroo Noonuccal, formerly known as Kath Walker, and also of Sam Watson himself. As an Aboriginal leader and writer, he has engaged in many struggles, such as late last year at a rally in the inner Brisbane suburb of West End where proposed high rise development has dismayed many in this culturally diverse and cohesive community.

Sam Watson: We are losing our place in this community. But we're not going to go down without fighting. We're saying to big business, "This is our country, this is our land," our connection to this place pre-dates Cook, it pre-dates Oxley, we have an important cultural bond with this country. Without us being here, without us conducting cultural business on this country, the spiritual energy, the spiritual heart of this land will suffer and perish. That is why it is critical that Aboriginal and Torres Strait Islander people continue to be part of this community regardless of what they do in City Hall. And we can't do it by ourselves, that's why we're reaching out to our neighbours, our friends, our colleagues and this day we have a very important community here at West End. It's worth fighting for, it is a far greater value than the sort of place they envision. They want to bring in thousands of people, they want to bring in thousands of cars. That's not the sort of world we want. This very street we're gathered upon, Boundary Street, was used during the Moreton Bay settlements to keep Aboriginal people apart from the community. Let's reclaim Boundary Street, let's reclaim West End. Let's say this is our land, this is our country, we're going to fight for it and we'll be here long after the Saabs and the Volvos and the BMWs disappear onetime. Thank you.

[*Applause*]

Florence Spurling: Where would you comment on the present with that way in which Indigenous leadership can work in conjunction with supportive white people. Is that still a living thing for you? What's your comment?

Sam Watson: I think those sort of partnerships are certainly possible but the movement generally has moved on quite a way since the 1960s, 1970s, 1980s. The way in which the Aboriginal political movement works now is this: there is not the designated space for individual leaders as there was back in the 1960s, 1970s, so whilst the 1960s created a pathway for Aunty Kath and was critical – you had people like Aunty Kath Walker and Faith Bandler, Uncle Chika Dixon and others, leading that referendum struggle forward, because of the particular gifts and the abilities and the wisdom they brought to those positions. Now largely because of their work, two to three generations of new and emerging young leaders who are coming through now, who are far better educated, far more aware of the global situation, far more able to connect and reach out to people in government etc., so the political landscape has changed dramatically. Whilst there was a need for individual, strong leaders back in the 1960s, 1970s, there's not so much the need there now, but certainly at the ground level, at the coalface, at every single rally and mobilisation we mount, we see that those partnerships are still there between black and white, between men and women, women and women etc., so there is still very much that need to reduce it to that personal level so we can talk to each other, can understand each other, can work with each other, can walk with each other.

> OODGEROO: I need a cold shower and some fresh clothes. Then a big, juicy T-bone steak and a long, cold beer. I wonder if they have any Australian beer in this part of the world?
> BANKER: Probably not. Tunisia is Muslim country.
> OODGEROO: Bugger!
> BANKER: Your brooch . . . A lizard.

OODGEROO: Lizard? No. A Sand Goanna. It's one of my totems. The gods of the dreamtime give every man and woman a spirit guardian to watch over us and protect us. They're very sacred.

BANKER: What do you do?

OODGEROO: I'm a storyteller. Maybe I should have stuck with nursing, eh? It's my writing that got me into this. I've just been in Nigeria for the Conference of Indigenous Arts.

BANKER: I'm going to a conference in Cairo. We're trying to help some of the African nations reschedule their debt. I should have been there by now. I have to present paper.

OODGEROO: You'll get there, they'll sort this out pretty soon. You'll see, my friend. These chaps won't gain anything by killing us. We're a pair of very small fish and our lives aren't worth very much to these people.

BANKER: My life is worth a great deal to me.

Sam Watson: The importance of life, I think, and the way in which Aunty Kath was very much in tune with the natural flow and the natural cycles of life; and that was very much evidenced by the way in which she would – the amount of strength she would draw from the tides, from being able to just stand on her own country and look out upon the sea and draw such incredible inspiration from the move and the flow of the waters, from the dolphins, from the birds, from the sounds, the smells, the feel of her sacred country. She was always very much just part of that eternal, perpetual cycle of life, land, country, and she would worship by just walking and being with land and country.

OODGEROO: I need to see the bay. I have to see my Quandamooka.

Look at the channel! See the gulls? There's a Fish Eagle there, cheeky fullah?

See that dark shadow. That's a school of bait fish just on this side of the shelf. If I could drag the net, we'd get a feed for sure. Out there to the north, that's Uncle Mullie in his new boat. . . .

This tide is on the turn and the dawn is at hand. It ebbs and flows. The great cycle of life.

Sam Watson [recorded at a Brisbane City Hall meeting]: . . . violent situations involving young people, so we need as a community work out. . . .

Florence Spurling: You've convened meetings where you're addressing the public street violence issues for Aboriginal people now, particularly young Aboriginal people, and there's one very strong example you gave in a recent meeting at Brisbane City Hall about the mentoring program in the southern area of Brisbane where Aboriginal Elder men were able to help younger men to cope with everyday life.

Woman participant [*at the city hall meeting*]: . . . our people are being bashed
. . . this is our country, this is Aboriginal land always was, and always will
be, and what we heard down at Woodridge the other day – our people are
scared to go out. Kids are afraid to go to school. . . .

Sam Watson: Well, at a global level there seems to be a hardening of atti-
tudes, the issues of asylum seekers being a major concern not only here in
Australia but the USA, across Europe, the UK etc., so people are hardening
in their attitudes towards people of other ethnicities who they feel are tres-
passing, invading their own spaces. And that's rather ironic because this is
how Aboriginal people feel about white Australians, that white Australians
have invaded our country, they've invaded our lands, and are still here, and
reaping an enormous benefit from stolen Aboriginal lands.

OODGEROO:
They came in to the little town
A semi-naked band subdued and silent,
All that remained of their tribe.
They came here to the place of their old bora ground
Where now the many white men hurry about like ants.
Notice of estate agent reads: "Rubbish May be Tipped Here."
Now it half covers the traces of the old bora ring.
They sit and are confused, they cannot say their thoughts:
'We are as strangers here now, but the white tribe are the strangers.
We belong here, we are of the old ways.
We are the corroboree and the bora ground,
We are the old sacred ceremonies, the laws of the elders
We are the wonder tales of Dream Time, the tribal legends told.
We are the past, the hunts and the laughing games, the
wandering camp fires.
We are the lightning-bolt over Gaphembah Hill
Quick and terrible.
And the Thunderer after him, that loud fellow
We are the quiet daybreak paling the dark lagoon
We are the shadow-ghosts creeping back as the camp fire burns low.
We are nature and the past, all the old ways
Gone now and scattered.
The scrubs are gone, the hunting and the laughter.
The eagle is gone, the emu and the kangaroo are gone from
this place.
The bora ring is gone.
The corroboree is gone.
And we are going.

Sam Watson: As we see across the world and across Australia, there are lunatic extremist fringe groups that are playing the race cards. We see that this Tea Party movement are certainly hardening in their attitudes towards their African-American President, and some of the caricatures and some of the language they're using to describe their President would never have been used during the election campaign. We see the attitudes towards asylum seekers right across Europe, and here in Australia on a daily basis we are being told about attacks on Aboriginal families, attacks on Aboriginal kids walking the streets, and this is just not acceptable, and we are regularly meeting with the police, schools, neighbourhood groups to try to calm this down. We don't want this situation to deteriorate any further. We don't want any more bloodshed, we don't want any violence and regularly we have situations where young Aboriginal men and women are feeling so frustrated by what is happening and feeling so vulnerable and exposed they want to visit payback upon the perpetrators, and again, we're doing our utmost to keep this hosed down but at some stage, our people will strike back and we have more than 200 years of being the racist targets, being the targets of these racist, genocidal attacks upon our people, upon our communities, and at a political level there is an undercurrent within the Aboriginal political movement where young Aboriginal people again are talking up the needs to get back on to the streets and perhaps start looking at far more confrontational ways in which to advance our political agendas. So unless things change dramatically, and change very soon, then our people, driven by their frustrations, may well start to take matters in their own hands.

Florence Spurling: One of the factors that came up at the City Hall meeting is that a lot of the attacks on young Aboriginal people in Brisbane are not necessarily by mainstream white Australians.

Sam Watson: Yes, because what we have here in Brisbane, is we have a situation where there are large numbers of Pacific Islanders coming in to the Brisbane and Greater Brisbane area and the authorities have created these corridors from Ipswich down to Inala and across to Logan City in which you have public housing estates, and these are areas, suburbs, groups of suburbs, clusters, where there is very high unemployment, where the mean income for the households is quite low, where there is substantial and significant overcrowding in the housing situation, where there are large numbers of young people who are locked in that cycle between school and between employment, so they hang around in the streets, and when you get young kids on the streets who are turning to drugs or alcohol, then tensions are going to rise, and authorities, communities, people have to start taking responsibility and ensuring that this Great Australian Dream, these unique economic opportunities that our politicians regularly tell us about, feed down, feed down to those people in those corridors, because like I said, places like Ipswich, Inala, Woodridge, Logan City, these places have enormous unemployment rates, and we find that a great number of the confrontations that occur between Aboriginal kids and these young people from Pacific Islands happen at a time during the day when they should be either in school or at work. So obviously, if we create the opportunities for these young people to become educated, create opportunities for these young people to take on decent jobs, then they're not going to be on the streets doing the drugs and doing the booze, or whatever, they'll have decent jobs and they'll have a whole different change in attitudes and lifestyle.

Florence Spurling: Sam Watson, writer, Aboriginal elder and academic in Brisbane, talking about the present and also about his bloodline Aunty, Oodgeroo Noonuccal, formerly known as Kath Walker, poet and leader, whose country was Minjerribah or North Stradbroke Island in South East Queensland.

> OODGEROO: Don't say that! Your name is Pearl, and you are a beautiful, strong Aboriginal woman. Some white men may have abused you and violated your body, but they have only made you stronger for the life the Old People have given you. Back in the old days the men in your family would have taken them out onto the killing ground and cut off their balls.

Florence Spurling: Sam Watson's play, *Oodgeroo – Bloodline to Country*, is at the centre of this *Encounter* on ABC Radio National. In the play, in an essay "Turning Point," and in his first novel, *The Kadaitcha Sung*, Sam Watson conveys great concern for Aboriginal women who are raped.

Sam Watson: Growing up within such a strong family that was built around the strength of our women and living and working within a community that, again, has been largely constructed around the strengths of the women, you're always very conscious of the situation and the roles and places that women hold in our community business, because right from the first meetings I used to attend, we had Aunties standing up and saying "Aboriginal men and women are held down, oppressed and denied, and we're having to fight every inch of the way," but right behind that Aboriginal man there in the background, is the Aboriginal woman. So Aboriginal women have always faced that dual burden of oppression, not only being Aboriginal but also being a woman. So Aboriginal woman has been denied her place and her rights because of her race and her gender, and she has never even found safety or sanctuary within her own community because of the high rate of domestic violence. So Aboriginal women cannot feel safe and secure within their own homes or within their own relationships with their own men because of the way in which Aboriginal men will brutalise Aboriginal woman as some sort of pay-back or – you could construct an entire program around the whys and wherefores of that – but suffice to say that Aboriginal women I've worked with have made me constantly aware of the need for Aboriginal men to respect and support our women, and that plays right through all my work and all our political business and our cultural business. We must continually enforce the need to respect and protect and secure the place of our women, our mothers, our grandmothers, our aunties, our daughters etc., because this is the only way forward and you will find across Australia that Aboriginal leaders will constantly talk about the number of Aboriginal men who are in prisons; what they don't talk about is the reasons why they're in prisons, or the victims of their crime and in a great number of those cases the victims of those crimes that have led to their imprisonment have been the Aboriginal women within their own homes or within their communities, so on one hand you have the enormous rate of Aboriginal imprisonment, on the other hand you have a silent statistic which is the number of Aboriginal women who have been brutalised and that has led to the Aboriginal men being sent to jail. So it's something that we have to deal with within our own communities, and we're trying to do that at a level of men's groups and men's networks. So slowly, but slowly, we're doing business, serious men's business, and getting our young men to understand this domestic violence has to stop, and we have to respect our women and support our women. This is the problem we have to deal with, not the white power structure, that's really, really important to us.

Florence Spurling: One of the most powerful images of rape against an Aboriginal woman is found in Sam Watson's first novel, *The Kadaitcha Sung*, where the violence is perpetrated by white men, or migloos.

> *Reader*: "Ho, Floppy Tits!" Chambers barked at Worimi, who looked up at him silently. "You fullah stay here onetime. No more walk-walk, you waitim here now."
>
> She nodded obediently, inwardly mocking the migloo's harsh-sounding chatter.
>
> Chambers and Hinds took a side of the creek bed each. The rum seemed not to have affected their skills and they stalked through the darkness in deadly silence.
>
> Worimi hunched down before the flames, her mind still beautifully alive from the meeting with the little spirit man. Jonjurrie had brought messages for her from the spirit world. Her warrior husband

and tiny daughter had sent words of love and longing to her, and she smiled at the sweet memories that flooded her.

The migloo had cut her man in half at the waist, his blood and guts spilling onto their beloved tribal land. Her daughter had only just begun to walk on her chubby little legs when the migloo had smashed her head with a club. Her daughter's brains had splattered onto her breasts as she lay almost senseless beneath the heaving loins of the white rider.

A tear coursed down her cheek and she knew that she would have to escape soon or else she would lose her mind. Jonjurrie had pledged to help her and she knew that he would. She had done the little man a great service in the dark and she had pleased him, she knew that. Now her spirit felt lighter than it had been since that day when the riders had come. She had been plunged into a world of shades. The blood and the beatings, the destruction of her land and the constant sexual degradation had almost crushed her, but now that she was back on the land her spirit was singing. The filthy, lice-ridden compound outside Brisbane had sapped her strengths, and if it hadn't been for this trip into the bush and away from the stench of the huge migloo camps, she might well have slipped into insanity. But the land had remade her and she was almost whole again. The rapes and abuse had been a further cost, but soon she would be strong enough to break away and flee back to her own people. She knew she would have to be patient, she would have to decide where she would run to. The migloo were gradually imprisoning all the great lands with their bands of steel and bitumen. Soon there would be nowhere to run.

Florence Spurling: From Sam Watson's novel, *The Kadaitcha Sung*. Returning to his play about the life of Oodgeroo Noonuccal we also return to the central motif of the play – the experience that Oodgeroo, also known as Kath Walker, had in 1974 when Palestinian terrorists hijacked the BOAC aircraft in which she was travelling. Sam Watson has already told us how traumatic and lastingly haunting this experience was for Kath Walker, who pleaded with the hijackers for the lives of the passengers, especially the life of a young German banker targeted for execution.

HIJACKER: Here, woman, here is your water.

OODGEROO: Thank you. What will happen to him now?

HIJACKER: His fate is in the hands of Allah.

OODGEROO: Well, I have never met your Allah; but I hope he's a merciful sort of fellah.

HIJACKER: Do not blaspheme, Writer Woman. Show respect.

OODGEROO: Sorry. When are you going to let us go? Surely you've made your point now.

HIJACKER: Our people are still suffering in the villages and the fields. We are fighting for our own land, for our own country.

OODGEROO: I know how you feel, mate. The white man invaded my country 200 years ago and we've been poisoned and shot and massacred. We're fighting for our lives too, you know.

HIJACKER: Maybe you are not fighting hard enough. Maybe your people should pick up the gun and fight like we are fighting. My mother was a civilian and yet she was shot down like a dog. In our own street. The Jews shot her down and killed her. I had to raise my five brothers and sisters.

OODGEROO: I'm sorry, that must have been terrible. Burt, look, the white man has killed so many thousands of my people. But hatred and violence destroy. My Aboriginal gods teach me to love my enemies and to love the land.

Come back to my land. Walk upon the sacred soil of my country and you will know peace. I promise you that.

[Water sounds and clap sticks]

OODGEROO: No . . . no . . . what have you done. . . .

HIJACKER: Do not shed tears for that pig. I shot him dead and I am pleased. Today I am a man.

OODGEROO: A man? You become a man by shooting a defenceless man?

HIJACKER: I have walked in the villages. I have seen the children starving. These dogs have no hearts. They grow rich and fat from our suffering.

OODGEROO: He had a daughter. Are you going to tell her that you have killed her father? Are you going to tell his wife that you have made her a widow?

HIJACKER: You go too far, Writer Woman. Don't think that I will not kill you too.

OODGEROO: You don't frighten me. I am an Aboriginal woman. All of White Australia couldn't keep me down. You and all your armies and all your guns and bullets won't keep me quiet.

You have the blood of an innocent man on your hands now. You have severed that man's Dreaming Line. There will come a day when you will be called on to pay for this murder. Be ready, my boy, because you will never know when or where it is going to happen. But mark my words: the dead will come for you.

Sam Watson: Within that community on the plane, she really did assume the place of the Earth Mother which was her place in her own community and across the national Aboriginal political movement, so she felt that she should be there protecting every one of the people on the plane, and also even if there had been a hijacker who'd been killed, she would have felt the same way. But it was the sheer helplessness that she felt when the decisions were made in other places not to release their colleagues from German prisons, so therefore there had to be a statement made and that statement was made by executing the banker. And she was marked by the pure, cold-blooded way in which it was conducted, it really tore at her. And again in the fact that she could do nothing to stop that.

Florence Spurling: The key line for me in the whole play is she says to him, "You have severed that man's Dreaming Line." Can you talk a bit about that?

Sam Watson: The way I've been brought up and taught cultural business by uncles and aunties in both the Aboriginal side and Torres Strait Islander side, I've come to look at my connection and my bonds to my previous generations as being a living, Dreaming Line. And that Dreaming Line travels in three ways: it travels back into the past where we connect with elders and grandparents and great-grandparents who have gone before us; it holds us in the present to our own mob here and now; it also stretches out before us into the future, down through children, grandchildren, great-grandchildren, so it's a living thing. I see it as an eternal Dreamtime cable, as it were, that carries within it – within that cable – all the knowledge, all the wisdom, all the experiences, everything we need to know or every-thing we've experienced as a people within that cable, and that's a cable that binds me like an umbilical cord, an eternal, perpetual umbilical cord that stretches back from the beginning of time and forward to the end of time, one time.

Florence Spurling: Oodgeroo says in the play to the hijackers that the dead will visit them, there will be payback, there will be consequence for having abruptly and violently severed that man's life, he's severed his Dreaming Line.

Sam Watson: That's right because one of the unique things about Aborigi-nal cultures, there's no such thing as a natural death and particularly when you have a violent act that does take life, that's very unnatural, and when you cause, when you take responsibilities for yourself to end a life, then you owe the consequence, you owe the elders, you owe the Old People because by killing that man there was a pattern created at the beginning of time for that man to do particular things, to reach out and impact on other lives, to fulfil his own destiny, the destiny that been ordained by the elders at the beginning of time. So once you cut that Dreaming Line, you'll stop that man from doing that, therefore you owe. You owe the elders, you owe the Old People for that man's undone business. Whenever a life ends, it's been ended because of a particular act from another party. So therefore. . . .

Florence Spurling: Even if someone were to die of illness or old age?

Sam Watson: That's right, again that is not a natural thing, so this has been caused by something from beyond that person's own family. So the elders will have to work out exactly why it happened and who was responsible and what needs to be done.

Florence Spurling: Oodgeroo said to me once in an interview, that death is a promotion.

Sam Watson: That's right. Because here on earth we're bound to act in a particular way and we're handicapped by the vehicle we use, the human body, and we're held back in so many ways because of the limitations of the human body. But Aunty Kath was always a woman way ahead of her time. I mean I often think of her in the same way that I think of Dr. Hawking and other great thinkers because she could see at a global level so much, and she was so in tune with the universe, and she could look at the night sky and she could talk and tell stories and sing the songs of each one of those constellations. So she really wasn't a person of our time. I just had this eerie feeling that you know, she really had been placed with us a little bit by accident, I think, because she really didn't belong there with us, she belonged at a much higher plane.

Florence Spurling: You were able to gain a lot as a writer by engaging closely with her; tell me how you feel yourself as a writer now, in your own life. In what way has your writing formed its own identity and richness for you. How would you want to talk about that?

Sam Watson: I think it's a passion that Aunty Kath took to her page, and I feel very much the same way, that Aunty Kath used her writing, her words, her poetry and her stories and her paintings, in order to record, in order to share, to unveil, to draw outsiders into her dreaming circle, and I in much the same way, put down words on the page in order to draw people, to give people a window into my world, a window into my experience so they can also walk in the same footsteps that I walked in.

Florence Spurling: You can work across the genres, you can work in different ways?

Sam Watson: That's because Aboriginal people were the original storytellers. Our culture is the oldest surviving culture on the face of the earth, and every generation, even though we now have the written page, we now have the internet, we now have so much technology available to us, the basic communication dynamic within our culture is still the spoken word, still the story, the basic engine-room of our culture is the story, And every single Aboriginal and Torres Strait Islander person across Australia is a natural gifted storyteller. No matter what happens, no matter what circumstances in which we meet, whether it be a funeral, a wedding, a christening, whatever, our mob will sit down and once the first cup of tea's been served then bang, you start talking up story and talking up yarns. And this is how I learnt at the feet of people like Aunty Kath and so many others of my elders by just sitting down and listening to the way the old people talk and the stories they told. From the time I was a child, I visited so many places across the face of Australia without leaving Brisbane, because my mob had grown up as drovers, as truck-drivers and as seasonal workers, so they travelled quite extensively throughout Australia and they took me to every one of those places they'd ever been through the beauty of those stories. So I was able to travel thousands, millions of miles as a small child without ever leaving my bedroom.

OODGEROO: Our pilgrimage as Aboriginal people is to walk upon our own tribal land, the land of our ancestors. Until we do, we find no peace. Look up into the sky. See . . . there's Mirrabooka. My Noonuccal people have a legend about that Old Man. I'll tell you that story.

Sam Watson: Aunty Oodgeroo taught me many things. She taught me the magic of words and she taught me the art of poetry. She also told me to read other poets, and in doing that I discovered a poet from ancient times, named Aeschylus, and his words have also shaped my thinking.

He wrote: "In our sleep, pain which cannot forget, falls drop by drop upon the heart until, in our own despair, against our will, comes wisdom through the awful grace of God."

A mighty shield has been taken away; her formidable spear has been laid down. That voice of thunder that pealed out against the forces of evil is now fallen silent.

Rest now, Aunty, your name has been called by the high councils of the dreamtime and a feast has been prepared for you at the fireplace of heroes. Your great deeds will be sung and your mighty battles will be danced and your story will be told.

The song that you brought with you into the world of men and women will now play in the hearts and within the spirits of all true Aboriginal people . . . that song will live within our blood and it will hold us to our sacred land, our bloodline to country.

Onetime!

Lynda Hull

(1954–1994)

In the following poem, published posthumously in her Collected Poems, *Lynda Hull takes jazz saxophonist Charlie "Bird" Parker as both her subject and the source of her poem's structure: the repeated imagery at beginning and end frame the shifts and improvisations of the internal sections. As Bird said (and Hull quotes), "If you don't live it, it won't come out your horn."*

Ornithology

Gone to seed, ailanthus, the poverty
   tree. Take a phrase, then
fracture it, the pods' gaudy nectarine shades
    ripening to parrots taking flight, all crest
and tall feathers.
                A musical idea.
                         Macaws
scarlet and violet,
                    tangerine as a song
the hue of sunset where my street becomes water

and down shore this phantom city skyline's
   mere hazy silhouette. The alto's
liquid geometry weaves *a way of thinking,*
   a way of breaking
synchronistic
   through time
              so the girl
   on the corner
                has the bones of my face,
the old photos, beneath the Kansas City hat,

black fedora lifting hair off my neck
   cooling the sweat of a night-long tidal

pull from bar to bar to night we went
    to find Bird's grave. Eric's chartreuse
perfume. That
              poured-on dress
                     I lived days
and nights inside,
              made love
and slept in, and mesh and slur of zipper

down the back. Women smoked the boulevards
    with gardenias afterhours, asphalt shower-
slick, ozone charging air with sixteenth
    notes, that endless convertible ride to find
the grave

          whose sleep and melody
                            wept neglect
   enough to torch us
            for a while
through snare-sweep of broom on pavement,

the rumpled musk of lover's sheets, charred
    cornices topping crosstown gutted buildings.
Torches us still – cat screech, matte blue steel
    of pistol stroked across the victim's cheek
where fleet shoes
           jazz this dark
                  and peeling
   block, that one.
           Vine Street, Olive.
We had the music, but not the pyrotechnics –

rhinestone straps lashing my shoes, heels sinking
    through earth and Eric in casual drag,
mocha cheekbones rouged, that flawless
    plummy mouth. A style for moving,
heel tap and
          lighter flick,
               lion moan
of buses pulling away
              through the static
brilliant fizz of taffeta on nyloned thighs.

Light mist, etherous, rinsed our faces
   and what happens when
you touch a finger to the cold stone
    that jazz and death played
down to?
        Phrases.
              Take it all
  and break forever –
           a man
with gleaming sax, an open sill in summertime,

and the fire-escape's iron zigzag tumbles
  crazy notes to a girl cooling her knees,
wearing one of those dresses no one wears
    anymore, darts and spaghetti straps, glitzy
fabrics foaming
        an iron bedstead.
                The horn's
  alarm, then fluid brass chromatics.
                Extravagant
ailanthus, the courtyard's poverty tree is spike
and wing, slate-blue
        mourning dove,
             sudden cardinal flame.
If you don't live it, it won't come out your horn.

Teresa Carson (born 1954)

This essay is poet and playwright Teresa Carson's elegy for her close friend Jack Wiler as well as an argument for the power of what she calls "astral influence" between poets who may, on the surface, seem to be entirely different from one another. Jack Wiler didn't care for the poetry of John Keats, but "soul-level influence," Carson explains, "is not a simple pass-the-baton process; we do not read our poetic ancestors and then just pick up the conversation where they left off. Rather, we are, by nature, related to particular poetic ancestors but not to others."

The Temple of Delight: John Keats and Jack Wiler

I

In spring 1819, John Keats wrote to his brother and sister: "Circumstances are like Clouds continually gathering and bursting – while we are laughing the seed of some trouble is put into the wide arable land of events – while we are laughing it sprouts it grows and suddenly bears a poison fruit which we must pluck."

In summer 2007, Jack Wiler wrote on his blog: "You know how stuff sneaks up on you. How you know something but you don't know something. Today Johanna and I got the deeply sad news that her friend Divina had died. . . . Now she won't be here except in our hearts. It's so sad that there is so little words can do when you lose a friend."

II

In the spring of 1819 Keats wrote five of his six great odes, including "Ode on Melancholy." Towards the end of the same year he wrote "This Living Hand." He died in 1821.

In the spring of 2008 Wiler put the finishing touches on his third manuscript, which was titled *We Monsters* (later changed to *Divina Is Divina*), and included two poems about Divina: "Futbol and Gowns" and "Divina Is Divina." He died in 2009.

III

Jack sent this manuscript to me in June 2008. In my e-mail response I called it "profound, yea even philosophical." I mentioned how, during my second reading of it, the following lines from Keats's "Ode on Melancholy" popped into my head:

Ay, in the very temple of Delight
Veil'd Melancholy has her Sovran shrine,
Though seen of none save him whose strenuous tongue
Can burst Joy's grape against his palate fine:

This reference was a risk on my part. Jack and I had a longstanding disagreement about the quality of Keats's poems – I worshiped at the altar of Keats while Jack dismissed him as a poet with an inflated reputation. We also disagreed about the usefulness of formal patterns of lineation, formal patterns of meter, formal anything in a poem; Jack championed free verse while I stood up for sonnets, iambic pentameter, and rhyme schemes. I enjoyed pointing out that, though he pooh-poohed formal prosody, he did indeed employ formal elements, such as anaphora, in his poems, especially the ones in *We Monsters*.

To my surprise Jack decided to use those lines from "Ode to Melancholy" as the epigraph for the book.

IV

It might be difficult for some readers to imagine mentioning John Keats and Jack Wiler in the same breath, more difficult for them to consider a strong connection between their bodies of work, and entirely impossible for them to see Keats as an influence on Jack.

I admit that, in some ways, it would be hard to find two poets more different in personal or poetic style. It might be easy to elevate Keats as a "true poet" and dismiss Jack as a "loud poseur." Keats was Apollo; Jack was Lear's Fool. Keats lived on Mount Helicon; Jack lived in Jersey City. Keats was a prophet; Jack, by his own admission, was "the jibbering monkey." One imagines Keats standing in a Greek amphitheater, intoning "Ode to a Nightingale" to hushed acolytes. One imagines Jack commanding a makeshift stage in Starr's Bar, shouting "How to Succeed in Pest Control" to heckling drunks.

I could go on and on about the differences between them, but in the end none of that matters because the persona of a poet exists only to serve the Underneath.

V

Of course, the measure of their differences can best be seen in the surfaces of their poems: Keats's orderly, iambic pentameter, end-rhyme stanzas are calm lakes with the reflections of rosy-fingered dawn slowly spreading across them, while Jack's rhythmic, slam-worthy rants are rides at Coney Island that yank the reader up, down, sharp turn left, sharp turn right, upside down.

I could go on and on about the differences between them, but in the end none of that matters because the surface of a poem exists only to serve the Underneath.

VI

When it comes to a poet's poetic influences, neither his persona nor the surface of his poems matters, though identifying those influences can be a sticky wicket. Sometimes a poet directly acknowledges a poem's connection to a particular poet, as Jack acknowledged that his "Belief Systems" was a response to Meg Kearney's "Creed." Sometimes a reader can easily spot an influence, as in Jack's poem "My Friend Asks Me to Write about Losing Things," where I see his nod to Elizabeth Bishop's "The Art of Losing." But there is a deeper layer – what I call "astral influence" – which the poet often does not acknowledge and readers often miss. The poet absorbs this influence not by choice but by similarity of soul. It has nothing to do with a poem's prosody or superficial subject matter but with a shared deeper material: with what reaches down to the Underneath.

Soul-level influence is not a simple pass-the-baton process; we do not read our poetic ancestors and then just pick up the conversation where they left off. Rather, we are, by nature, related to particular poetic ancestors but not to others. As J. D. Salinger said, "The true poet has no choice of material." We and our influences cannot help but work the same vein of the Underneath, however dissimilar our surfaces may appear. If we are persistent, honest, and loyal to that vein, then we participate in and continue the conversation of poetry – a conversation that transcends time, place, and style.

More often than one would suspect, a poet will deny his connection to his poetic ancestor. In Jack's case I don't know if he was refusing to acknowledge what he knew, in his heart, to be true or if he truly didn't see the connection between his poems and those of Keats. It doesn't matter; some of Jack's poems definitely continue the deep conversation that Keats had, in his turn, continued. Jack and Keats were most certainly working the same vein: transcendence of the dualities we perceive around or within us, such as pleasure/pain, having/losing, love/hate, male/female. They understood that these dualities are merely finite attributes of the non-dualistic infinite unknowable substance (to borrow Spinoza's term), which may be called God or nature or creativity, that is the basis of the universe. We cannot understand this substance in any everyday intellectual or emotional way, yet we can experience it, if only momentarily and incompletely, through the fusion, and thus erasure, of dualities, as can happen in great poetry.

Such an immortal poem is a rare animal. Most of us will never write one, but both Keats and Jack wrote more than one.

VII

I'm making a big claim here about Keats and Jack. Yes, I'm placing the mantle of metaphysicist on their shoulders. No, I'm not suggesting either of them approached or viewed his work in that light, though certainly Jack was not displeased when I spoke of his poems in these terms. Rather, I'm saying the metaphysical layers in their works exist because each gave his all to the subject matter that he was given. Both faced and explored inexplicable yet fundamental dualities in their lives and the lives of those dearest to them. Both unflinchingly followed the chain of dualities to the end and found that all are merely outer chambers to the awful mystery that lies at the very heart of what Keats called "the very temple of Delight": the non-duality of life/death.

Many poets write about dualities, but most do so in a distanced, self-centered, linear fashion: "something bad happened to me, then something good happened to me, then something bad, then. . . ." In this type of poem, bad things – i.e., whatever causes the speaker pain or discomfort, such as the reminder of his inevitable death – are nothing more than hurdles to overcome. From the opening line I know where this poem is headed, and it always goes there. The poem always ends with a self-satisfied platitude because that's where the poet forces it to go. Such poems are all about the belief that humans can and do have control over dualities.

Few poets have the guts to relinquish control, to look the dualities straight in the eye, to keep looking even when that focus strips away precious defenses to reveal (and I'm quoting Jack here) that "all of us rats and mice and roaches and ants," all of "us monsters," are "huddled in this mess." But both Keats and Jack had guts.

VIII

What excites me about reading Keats's poems from 1819 and Jack's poems from 2008 is being able to follow them as they leap from the paradox in Poem A ("Ode on Melancholy" and "Futbol and Gowns") of dualities existing subsequently, in a continual flip-flop, to the epiphany in Poem B ("This Living Hand" and "Divina Is Divina") of non-dualistic substance, in which dualities cease to exist as separate entities.

Because Keats and Jack have such masterly control over the structure and content of Poems A and B, the reader, in turn, hears the deep conversation; she understands, she experiences. She watches them venture into the unknowable, and she follows them.

IX

Of course, Keats and Jack were participating in an ancient unbroken conversation that began with the first poet and will end with the last poet. "Futbol and Gowns" continues the conversation that "Ode on Melancholy" continued. "Divina Is Divina" continues the conversation that "This Living Hand" continued.

To some extent, all poets participate in this conversation, but most don't add anything of note to it. Bad poets merely parrot what's been said before. Good poets restate what's been said before but in a way that catches our interest; they "make it new" or "tell it slant" or "show, don't tell"; but in the end, they simply paraphrase and go no further. This is not the process of influence.

Those who are truly influenced restate some portion of the predecessor's conversation – they follow the thread before attempting to spin – and then expand on it. Keats didn't merely restate and amplify his predecessors' themes. He went to the edge of the wild with them and then pushed further. Jack didn't merely restate and amplify Keats's themes. He, too, went to the edge with him and then pushed on.

What's fascinating is how those who are influenced will take the conversation in unexpected directions, yet those directions usually end up seeming inevitable. If we pay attention, we understand that Jack's poems go where Keats's poems would have inevitably gone.

This is not a matter of comparison, not a question of "Who is the better poet?" More than anything in this case it's a point about longevity. Let's not forget Keats was a mere twenty-four when he wrote "Ode on Melancholy" and "This Living Hand" and twenty-six when he died. Jack was fifty-six when he wrote "Futbol and Gowns" and "Divina Is Divina" and fifty-seven when he died. Keats did not survive tuberculosis and therefore did not have the chance to write from the other side of his sickness. Jack survived eight years past his hospitalization for AIDS in 2001.

X

How can we begin to eavesdrop on the Keats-Jack thread of conversation? Well, summarizing the surfaces of these poems will tell us nothing about their true poetry. Instead, in each poem we must find, and be willing to enter, a wormhole that will lead us to the very heart of the conversation.

For example, in "Ode on Melancholy" one such wormhole is "Ay, in the very temple of Delight / Veil'd Melancholy has her Sovran shrine." The reader who gives herself to this line discovers that, for Keats, the unique entity "pleasure" always transmutes to the unique entity "pain"; this is his "one-two punch" summary of human existence.

In "Futbol and Gowns," the first of two poems written in memory of Jack's pre-op transsexual friend Divina, one such wormhole is "The world is filled with tears and the song of birds." At first glance this line repeats the insight about pain and pleasure we find in "Ode on Melancholy." But as Jack always instructed me, "Pay attention." If you do, you will realize this line subtly expands on Keats's insight. Like Divina herself, who, in her very being, exemplifies the fusion of the male/female duality, pain and pleasure are not separate entities and thus do not manifest in separate moments but are integrated into and inherent in every moment. The one-two punch philosophy is smoke and mirrors; it arises from our insistence on separating what is inseparable. Pleasure always transmutes to pain; pain always transmutes to pleasure. There is no *pain pleasure* but only *painpleasure*.

XI

Neither Keats nor Jack stopped there. Each went deeper and deeper into the Underneath until he found himself in the presence of death. Though both were tremendously alive to the present moment, both were also "half in love with easeful Death." They had the capacity to experience life and death in the present moment; even more, they accepted death's presence in the present moment. Their greatness as poets lies in their ability to write about those experiences without romanticizing or demonizing death.

Keats's short life was marked by the deaths of his parents and his brother Tom. He fought TB for more than a year before succumbing to it. Yet his poems are saturated with sensual and sensory details, with the life of the moment. "This Living Hand" is a stunning example of how a simple physical detail ("This living hand"), a simple gesture ("I hold it towards you"), and a simple narrative (you'll be sorry when I'm dead) can reproduce the fusion of life and death. In eight lines – eight lines! – Keats leaps over his own death and connects his life at the moment of writing the poem to his reader's life at the moment of reading the poem. It doesn't matter if, as legend has it, these lines were written to his fiancée Fanny Brawne. Every reader of the poem becomes the *you* addressed in them. I am always surprised by the last line and in my surprise instinctively take hold of the hand that is held towards me.

We can watch Jack's dance with death change through his three collections, beginning as a no-physical-contact fast dance in *I Have No Clue*, advancing to an uncomfortable foxtrot in *Fun Being Me*, and culminating in an ecstatic whirl in *Divina Is Divina*. What opens as an almost impersonal abstract observation about "You could die / I could die" in "Thinning the Herd" (from *I Have No Clue*) progresses to the very personal experience of being "A skeleton draped with / a ready-made shroud" in "Sick of Being Sick" (from *Fun Being Me*) and then reaches the universal, hard-earned epiphany of the line "Divina is Divina" in his final collection.

Divina is Divina: male is female, human is divine, death is life. In this poem, Jack pulls Keats's individual held-out hand toward an inevitable universal truth: he fuses all life (the rising sun, the blooming flowers, Divina, us) and all death (the wilting flowers, the fall leaves, Divina, us).

Every time I read "Divina Is Divina" that last line transports me (if only for Planck time) to the non-dualistic substance. Then snap, I return to real time, exhausted, exhilarated, changed.

XII

"In poetry the answers come not as argument but as form," wrote Michael Schmidt in *Lives of the Poets*. Yes, but. . . . For differences in form are one of the reasons we are blind to the connection between the poems of Keats and Jack. For example, though both are masters at using rhetorical effects to engage the reader's attention, Keats uses rhetoric to create a vision, which the reader observes, while Jack uses rhetoric to re-create the emotional experience itself, which the reader participates in.

As is typical for Keats, the surface of "Ode on Melancholy" is formal, orderly, controlled. The heightened poetical language creates a visionary "outside time" landscape that is parallel to but separate from the real world. Though thick with sensorial and sensual details, it doesn't have a physical effect on the reader. Rather, the lushly textured surface, with its combination of hypnotic, soft soundscape and mythological imagery, puts the reader in a sort of trance that allows the poem's Underneath to speak directly to the imagination.

The landscape of "Divina Is Divina," on the other hand, is very much the real world of this time, this place. Jack grabs the reader's attention with the conversational "My beloved had a friend"; and from that point on, whether you realize it or not, you are under his control. He takes his time, builds his argument, and pretends he is just shooting the breeze. But the carefully controlled rhetoric of every line pulls you unwittingly into the complex emotional experience he's re-creating until wham, you find yourself whirling alongside him in a dervish's dance:

> Hector is Divina because the flowers bloom!
> Hector is Divina because the sun rises!
> Hector is Divina because she is.

When Jack becomes tongue-tied in his attempts to answer his own questions, his rhetoric, and you along with it, stumbles ever so slightly:

> Because we are.
> Because the sun is.
> Because we die.

Then it almost comes to a halt:

> Because.
> Because.

Here is where a lesser poet would resort to pity or self-righteousness as a device to regain his balance, but Jack has bigger fish to fry. As we fall, exhausted, to the floor, dizzy from the experience, confused about where we are, dumbstruck by the enormity, the *finality* of that repeated "because," the Underneath speaks in full voice. Dumbstruck transforms to awestruck:

> Hector is Divina because we need to hear
> Someone outside our door crying our name.
> Divina is Divina.

Those emphatic closing lines change the entire poem and reveal its inner intention.

The form of a poem doesn't matter; it exists to serve the Underneath.

XIII

Two days before his death Jack, my husband, and I were having breakfast at the Polka Dot Diner in White River Junction, Vermont. Out of the blue Jack blurted, "Teresa, did you tell me to change the title of the book or did I dream it?"

He had dreamed the conversation but, to be honest, I had never liked the title *We Monsters* – though others of Jack's closest friends did – because I didn't feel it captured the essence of the book. While I didn't have a suggestion for him, I did encourage him to find another title.

After his death, the task of finding a new title fell to Danny Shot, his friend and literary executor; Joan Cusack Handler, his publisher; and me. After much discussion we settled on *Divina Is Divina*. Those who loved *We Monsters* were disappointed. But I felt the new title was the right one, though at the time I couldn't have explained why.

XIV

Keats's physical voice stopped with his death, but his substantive voice lives in his poems. Jack Wiler's physical voice stopped on September 26, 2009, but his substantive voice lives in his poems. Their poems no longer belong to them but to Poetry. Keats and Jack are fused; Apollo and Lear's Fool are fused.

I still worship at the altar of Keats. I also worship at the altar of Jack. I miss him. I miss his physical presence in my life. I miss receiving terse "What do you think?" e-mails with his new poems attached. I miss seeing where his poems would have gone next. But I take some solace in thinking that somewhere, right now, this subject of non-dualism has chosen another poet who may or may not read Wiler, who may or may not claim to be influenced by him, who may in fact diss *Divina Is Divina*, but who will take his work further along the continuum. Maybe I'll have the good fortune to stumble upon this person's poems. Maybe I won't. Maybe someone will.

Dawn Potter (born 1964)

Even prolific poets spend most of their lives not writing; and even when they are writing, they aren't necessarily functioning "in the zone" – that wondrous state of hallucinatory intensity, so intoxicating yet so fragile. In the following essay, which first appeared in the Sewanee Review *in 2012, I consider the necessity of coming to terms with being "merely awake and alive" – that is, waiting for the poetry that we truly need to write rather than forcing ourselves to produce false poetry merely for the sake of creation.*

Not Writing the Poem

According to Henry David Thoreau, "the art of life, of a poet's life, is, not having anything to do, to do something." [See Thoreau's journal entry, p. 133.] W. H. Auden quoted from this sentence just before launching into "Making, Knowing and Judging," an essay based on a lecture he delivered after he was named Oxford Professor of Poetry and which he opened by querying the very terms of that distinguished position: "Even the greatest of that long line of scholars and poets who have held this chair before me . . . must have asked themselves: 'What is a Professor of Poetry? How can Poetry be *professed?*'"

This isn't a question that many people ask nowadays. As recently as 1948, Robert Graves was still declaring, "Though recognized as a learned profession [poetry] is the only one for the study of which no academies are open and in which there is no yard-stick, however crude, by which technical proficiency is considered measurable." Tragically, however, that long tradition has vanished. Today, poetry has become a career rather than a vocation; and at least in the United States, poets who refuse to buy a degree for the sake of a job (or, more often, the shadowy dream of a job) are generally ignored as serious artists, at least by the collegiate elite.

Yet Thoreau had it right: art doesn't require a certificate of proficiency. It requires long stretches of emptiness, not only so that artists have spans of time to produce new work but, more importantly, so that they can attend to the plain routines of living. Great art grows from the intensity of an artist's interaction with her own life. I don't mean to imply that her life has to be dramatic or even all that interesting. But the artist must make long acquaintance with her days – days that are rarely trancelike but that plod through the seasons: that strip the beds and ream out the barns and trudge through the snow to the insurance office. In this sense, then, to "profess poetry," a writer simply needs to pay attention to her hours, read the words of people who paid attention to their hours, now and then follow an urge to hammer those hours and words into her own poem, and occasionally be willing to talk about that task. As Auden said, "There is nothing a would-be poet knows he has to know. He is at the mercy of the immediate moment because he has no concrete reason for not yielding to its demands." In other words, he is merely awake and alive.

There are days when I believe that being awake and alive is the only thing I've managed to accomplish with my life. Accidentally I seem to have followed Thoreau's instructions to avoid "having anything to do." Instead, I've spent, or squandered, most of my career years in being a cook, a laundress, and an underemployed, mostly self-educated, reader and writer of small obscure books. Talking about his trajectory as a novelist, John Fowles said, "I had been deliberately living in the wilderness; that is, doing work I could never really love, precisely because I was afraid I might fall in love with my work and then forever afterwards be one of those sad, faded myriads among the intelligentsia who have always had vague literary ambitions but have never quite made it." My actions have been neither so ascetic nor so ruthless. Nonetheless, there's a selfishness about a life spent doing nothing, especially when one has growing children and a tired husband. Twenty years of well-cooked meals and clean socks are not substitutes for a paycheck.

This tradeoff seems even worse when I'm struggling to write, as I have been during the past few months. If I'm not managing to do anything remunerative, shouldn't I at least be writing? In truth, however, my problem is not "not writing" per se. Clearly, at this very moment, I'm writing this essay. Almost every morning I write a longish blog post about reading and writing. I read seriously every day, I've been steadily revising a poetry manuscript, and I've even composed a few decent poems. I've finished a memoir and written the text of a magazine photo-essay. When I stand back and look at my output, I do see that I have no right to complain about not writing. Nonetheless, something is amiss: I'm not, to borrow my friend Baron's terminology, "in the zone," and I haven't been in the zone for what feels like a very long time.

Being in the zone is rather like writing under the influence of a writing-specific drug: every step of the task vibrates with meaning, and the work seems to take charge of itself. Fowles said, "I know when I am writing well that I am writing with more than the sum of my acquired knowledge, skill, and experience; with something from outside myself." When I'm in the zone, I still produce words and revise, produce words and revise; but somehow my decision making feels sharper and more incisive. I don't plod through time, dragging at words like I'm yanking an obstinate goat up a mountain path. Weightless, I fly.

Yet being in the zone does not guarantee that what I produce is any good. As Auden pointed out, poets "cannot claim oracular immunity." The writing trance may be an intoxication, but the art that results is not dependable. Auden's example was Coleridge's famous fragment "Kubla Khan," composed, according to the author, during an opium dream in a "lonely farm-house."

> The Author continued for about three hours in a profound sleep, at least of the external senses, during which he has the most vivid confidence, that he could not have composed less than from two to three hundred lines; if that indeed can be called composition in which all the images rose up before him as things, with a parallel production of the correspondent expressions, without any sensation or consciousness of effort.

Despite historical precedent, one is not required to take laudanum or drink whiskey for breakfast in order to work in the writing zone. But drugs do add their own *je ne sais quoi* to the situation; and thus Coleridge's opium-induced zone cannot really parallel my own non-opium-induced haze. Yet his description of the experience is nonetheless familiar. "All the images rose up before him as *things*" – yes, I, too, recognize those moments, breathtaking, yet also as simple as water, when the abstractions of thought assume a swift and automatic solidity. "With a parallel production of the correspondent expressions," the words for those images appear under my fingers – easily, exactly, "without any sensation or consciousness of effort."

But trouble always looms. Waking from his dream, Coleridge "instantly and eagerly wrote down the lines that are here preserved. At that moment he was unfortunately called out by a person on business from Porlock . . . and all the rest [of the dream poem] passed away like the images on the surface of a stream into which a stone has been cast."

Oh, that aggravating person from Porlock! How well I know him. He has been sitting on the other side of my desk for about six months now, kicking the table leg, snapping his gum, and trying to interest me in political candidates and asphalt shingles. He is the anti-zone, and he interrupts every single word I write. Sometimes I manage to soldier on in spite of him, but sometimes I just give up and take him out for coffee. Coleridge, however, was unable to persevere against distraction. Daily life intruded on the trance, and "Kubla Khan" remains unfinished and unrevised. Though the author did publish the fragment, he did so only "at the request of a poet of great and deserved celebrity [Lord Byron], and, as far as the Author's own opinions are concerned, rather as a psychological curiosity, than on the ground of any supposed *poetic* merits."

Despite the poet's disclaimer, the fragment is, in truth, a wondrous piece of work; yet as Auden noted, "Coleridge was not being falsely modest. He saw, I think, as a reader can see, that even the fragment that exists is disjointed and would have had to be worked on if he ever completed the poem, and his critical conscience felt on its honor to admit this." In other words, "Kubla Khan" is a lovely scrap, but it could have been a polished work of art if the poet had been able to step outside the trance zone into the lumpish everyday world of banging words together and taking them apart, banging words together and taking them apart – a quotidian job that is rather like trying to assemble a mechanical device that seems to be missing various indispensable gears. There's nothing particularly joyous or intoxicating about the project, but it's the job that gets the work done – and a job that Coleridge knew very well he had once been able to do.

Yet there's another side to this quotidian writing story. What about the reams of work that people produce by means of prompts and "write-a-poem-every-day-for-a-month" challenges? Aren't such assignments a way to keep the juices flowing during those long tranceless droughts? Aren't these efforts both a form of education and a way of professing poetry?

To me, such force-fed production is almost too distasteful to contemplate. I don't want to write, as one literary journal's blog suggests, "a love poem in the form of a traffic ticket" or, worse yet, a "blitz poem," which is, according to another journal's blog, "a 50-line poem of short phrases and images" compiled according to specific rules:

> Line 1 should be one short phrase or image (like "build a boat")
> Line 2 should be another short phrase or image using the same first word as the first word in Line 1 (something like "build a house")
> Lines 3 and 4 should be short phrases or images using the last word of Line 2 as their first words (so Line 3 might be "house for sale" and Line 4 might be "house for rent")

Lines 5 and 6 should be short phrases or images using the last word of
Line 4 as their first words, and so on until you've made it through 48
lines
Line 49 should be the last word of Line 48
Line 50 should be the last word of Line 47
The title of the poem should be three words long and follow this for-
mat: (first word of Line 3) (preposition or conjunction) (first word of
line 47)
There should be no punctuation

The blog assures me that this is "a pretty simple and fun poem to write
once you get the hang of it." Ugh.

The prompt approach pretends that writing poetry is a pleasant activity
analogous to solving a *New York Times* crossword. It lays out the struc-
ture: all the pencil-holder does is fill in the blanks. There's no real labor
involved, no hard-won synthesis of emotion and diction, grammar and
imagination, sound and intellect. Nonetheless, a person can sit down at
her desk every day and fool herself into believing she's producing a body
of work.

These kinds of writing gimmicks infuriate me. Since when is poetry sup-
posed to be "pretty simple and fun"? Yet out there in the world today,
thousands of people may be writing their so-called poems as I sit here not
writing any poem at all. Without sweat or inspiration, they are nonetheless
making something; and we've all been taught to believe that doing some-
thing is better than doing nothing.

Which brings me back to Thoreau. If "the art . . . of a poet's life, is, not
having anything to do," then I think that perhaps we, as writers, need to ne-
gotiate better terms with nothing. In Iris Murdoch's novel *The Black Prince*,
the character Bradley Pearson, a novelist who rarely writes anything, com-
ments on "how much I was dominated during this time by an increasingly
powerful sense of the imminence in my life of a great work of art." At the
time he had no idea what his imaginary book would contain, but he felt
it as "a great dark wonderful *something* nearby in the future, magnetically
connected with me: connected with my mind, connected with my body."
Bradley is an unreliable narrator, yet his thoughts about the sensation of
"not writing" – perhaps I should say the sensation of "not writing *yet*" – re-
mind me that the trance and the labor, the mind and the body, cannot be
divorced. But neither can they be impelled. As Bradley explains, "an artist
in a state of power has a serene relationship to time. Fruition is simply a
matter of waiting."

Honorée Fanonne Jeffers (born 1967)

In this poem from her 2000 collection, The Gospel of Barbecue, *Honorée Fanonne Jeffers creates an ars poetica of sorts as she considers a subject that Thomas Wentworth Higginson (see page 145) had pondered more than a century before: the compelling pain and beauty of African-American spirituals.*

Swing Low, Sweet Chariot

And they thought we were
talking about heaven.
After all, we had not studied
the masters' poesy, we knew
nothing about central metaphors,
conceits, literary vehicles.
Chariots carrying us home
on the underground railroad.
No, we were picking cotton
or tobacco or peaches and glorifying
tragedy with our voices.
We were weeping bitter, large tears.

Brenda Shaughnessy (born 1970)

At the 2008 Association of Writers and Writing Programs (AWP) conference, poet Brenda Shaughnessy participated in a panel tribute to Lynda Hull, who had died in a car accident in 1994. In her elegy, Shaughnessy called herself one of Hull's "spiritual inheritors," though she had never met the poet or seen her read her work; for like Teresa Carson (see page 299), she recognizes how such powerful yet unexpected bonds help poets continue the conversation of poetry.

The Poetry of Danger

I'd like to start off by saying that I never knew Lynda Hull personally – that is, I never met her nor had the pleasure of seeing her read her poems. My only relation to Lynda was textual – that is, spiritual. I'm one of her readers. I'm one of her spiritual inheritors.

I feel, in this capacity, as if I am a second-born child. They say that first-born children believe they have inherited the whole world, and then, when the second child is born, that whole world is suddenly cut in half. The first child suffers, while the second child believes that the half-world she has been given is, in fact, the whole world. (I don't know who said that, but I hope someone will tell me today.)

I acknowledge how strange it must be for friends and intimates, like my co-panelists, to hear a stranger speak of such a loved person. But I am just a second child. I don't know what it was like to know Lynda Hull. I came up from the other side of the world, thinking that my precious "half" – just her poems – was the whole shebang. It's of course always good to know, in the end, that nothing that we believe is the whole shebang is ever the whole shebang.

So I begin my remarks, respectfully, from my partially obstructed view and with astonishment at how quickly time passes, and how long the dead stay dead, and yet in spite of those two facts, how intently we can hold one woman's extraordinary work so close to the heart, so close to the bone. But it shouldn't be a surprise. As Hippocrates and many others have said: Art is long, life is short.

That "life is short" part – it's the essence of danger. I want to talk a little about Lynda's work and the poetry of danger.

But I'd like to put it off a little further in favor of telling you that I first read Lynda's work in my early twenties, just after a period when I was bumming around New York City with very few coins in my shredded pockets and a certain nervous, quivering desire to be a poet, which was a vaguer idea than my much more specific, clear concept of what I was certain I did not want to be: at all costs to never, ever, be "normal" or a "sellout" or a "boring person." Oh my god – "normal" people were, like, fucking dead already – is how that goes.

As defensive stances go, it worked for a while – it was very common – but I was lucky, and it got old while I was still young, and no, I did not come across Lynda's work while I was out trolling the streets with my insane friends in the East Village. I found her work when I went to graduate school to study poetry. I certainly did not think I would find such a fireball of a poet in such a stodgy place. Both the fireball reading and the stodginess ended up being good for me. Sometimes dangerous girls find each other in the safest places.

I remember a conversation I had bunch of years ago, maybe around the turn of the century, with a dear friend of mine, who happens, now, to be ninety-seven. So at the time of this conversation she was pushing ninety. This is the great artist – and also a Graywolf poet – Dorothea Tanning. She is herself one of the most fearless, irreverent and, yes, I'd say dangerous, women I've ever met. She asked me, "Have you ever heard of a poet named Lynda Hull?" And I said of course, I'd read her work and loved it. She said, "Did you ever hear her read?" I said no. "She was" – this is Dorothea speaking – "she was this itty bitty thing, but her poems are so wild! They are amazing. I couldn't believe they were coming out of this cute little girl." How she admired Lynda and her work.

Sometimes dangerous girls meet each other and it's almost as if they are time-travelers.

But I'm avoiding, really, this idea of danger. For the real danger is the real truth, and the real truth is this: Dorothea is now ninety-seven years old, and still alive – and Lynda is not. I am myself no longer some young chick who thought danger meant oblivion and evasion and testing myself and worrying people that I love. I am alive, and I think I see now what the real danger is.

It's everywhere in Lynda Hull's poetry: the cruel characters, the rules of the street, the dark pull of substances that alter what feels like it needs so desperately to be altered.

From her beautiful poem "Fiat Lux":

> How to imagine
> those places where chaos
> holds sway, the old night where you hear scared laughter pierce
> the anesthesia dream, song
>
> of shoulders pushed rough to alley walls, torn caress, dark dress,
> song that goes
> *I'll do it for 10, for 5, I'll do it,* burnt spoon twisted in the pocket.

These lines look like danger, and no doubt what is being described is brutal, but it only alludes to the real danger. The drugs, the agony, the cruelty: those are all symptoms of the danger, but they are a part of what danger threatens, that is, life.

Lynda Hull makes beautiful even the worst moments of life, not because she re-imagines a dark patch into a glimmering sunny glade, nor does she transform the ugly into the beautiful. She allows the worst to coexist with the precious and miraculous, as if it is a normal, everyday thing, which, of course, it is. It just takes a really fearless artist to show us that. In so many poems, she was so breathtakingly fearless.

From the last two stanzas of "Red Velvet Jacket":

> God I was innocent then, clean as a beast in the streets.
> At the fringes of Warsaw's Ghetto
> stands a prison where they sorted Jews from politicals,
> politicals from homosexuals,
> where masses dispersed to nameless erasure. There's a tree there,
> lopped & blackened, yet it shines,
> enshrined in prayer scrolls, nailed icons. Oh, lucky life,
>
> I didn't understand until tonight,
> called back from the ruins in that jacket, dark stain blooming
> through the sleeve, the child squalling
> in my useless arms. I don't know what happened to the jacket
> & all those people are lost to a diaspora,
> the borough incinerated around them, nowhere in this night
> I drive through. Silk velvet and its rich hiss
> the shade of flame offering its drapery, its charm
> against this world burning ruthless, crucial & exacting.

Here, the danger looks like it's the crisis unfolding, and it is, there is real tragedy there, but the bigger danger is, of course – just so we don't lose perspective on what our sorrows and terrors are, and she puts it right out there in front of us so we can't miss it – is the Holocaust. The world horror made even more horrible for humanity's psyche because it should have been impossible.

The concept of impossibility is what danger's all about. We can't understand danger until we know what is possible. Childish fear is all about the unknown. Grown-up fear is about what we know all too well. Between the possible and the impossible, the defiance and the acceptance, Lynda's work shows us that it is all in how we posit ourselves on the continuum. If we are willing to see each detail, we get a fuller picture. If we only want to see a part of it, well, that's all we get to see – we're in denial, or we prefer to be afraid of monsters under the bed.

We know that one of the aspects of youth is an attraction to danger – perhaps this is because the very young do not understand the true nature of danger; they simply haven't been around long enough to experience the cumulative ravages. Perhaps it's because they just don't want to have to see everything so clearly.

I was twenty-four when Lynda Hull died. I had read her work and thought it brilliant, and her death a tragedy. But she hadn't seemed "young" to me then. Let's try to remember, to someone in her twenties, thirty-nine is just about middle aged, and death still seemed so far away. It still seemed impossible. Now I am approaching the same age that Lynda was when she died, and I understand, now, how very little time she had. I've almost experienced the same amount of time and suddenly, that this would be all of life allotted to me seems, well, possible, and I am bowled over with sadness for this fact all over again, and I think, she really had it right: There certainly is danger here. It's not just all a wild, painful adventure. There is harm. There is death. That is why we must grasp whatever momentary beauty we can, now, and scribble it down with as much elegance and honesty as we can muster.

She did that. Her legacy is not only an extraordinary body of work that exposes and queries, savages and relishes notions of danger and agency, hurt and healing, those stunning, inexpressible moments that somehow found their exact voice in hers. Her legacy is also that she shows us how to – if we get the chance by staying alive long enough – to grow up, how to face the dangers of this world, and not to move past them, not to ignore them, not to play it safe and be afraid, but to look always for the inevitable spark of life in all that darkness. To notice and note and say that such a spark gives darkness its pitch, and the contrast itself must exist and in that mere coexistence be beautiful. To address this danger includes being able to accept that death is in our cards and in our hands as well as in the air around us and in everyone we love.

To look for the miraculous moment of clarity in all that confusion, and give it the same treatment, give it context, let it live. Even though we die, to still let it live. It's possible. Lynda knew that to write down what is, what the mind feels and knows, what the heart hurts for, that this action is the only way to face danger bravely. There need be no battle, no struggle, no opposition when we defuse it all, face it all, with the writing of poetry. That is how we do it. She knew how. Fighting fire with fire is attractive, and certainly Lynda knew that, too. But in her work, the dangerous girl lives forever, the danger always glinting with its beauty and fever and illumination. Fiat Lux, as she might say. Let there be light.

Mike Walker

(born 1974)

In the following essay, poet, Slavist, and journalist Mike Walker considers the influence of two major writers of the Stalinist era – Anna Akhmatova and Lydia Chukovskaya – on not only his writing but his moral obligations to society. At the same time he illuminates the way in which writers' friendships can support one another personally and artistically during situations of great danger and hardship.

Anna Akhmatova and Lydia Chukovskaya: Writing under Stalin's Shadow

The cold war ended when I was in high school, when the Berlin Wall fell and the Soviet Union broke apart into the Russian Federation and numerous other nations. But even then I was drawn to that era of history, not just Russia's but also America's: to stories of the Strategic Air Command, the bombers, the missiles hidden away in silos in frigid North Dakota, the troubled looks on President Reagan's and Prime Minister Thatcher's faces as they spoke before the cameras. It was a terrible yet exciting time.

My father had been in Vietnam, but as a teenager I had no hope of such excitement. Yet I longed to be a fighter pilot and, oddly perhaps, I believed I had to understand my enemy, the Soviet Union. Thus began my study of Russian and Russia, and what wonders I discovered. Beyond the Old Church Slavonic and the impressive if disturbing application of Cyrillic to every ethnic language in the Soviet sphere, I learned to marvel at the literature that had only recently become available in the United States, literature that had in prior decades circulated in the Soviet Union only as underground *samizdat*. Horrors crept from the pages. I discovered, for instance, that Spetsburo 13 of the KGB was known in *fenya* (criminal slang) as the *Otdel mokrykh del* or Department of Wet Affairs – in other words, the department that took care of assassinations. This was harrowing news for a teenage boy barely out of middle school.

I encountered Anna Akhmatova at about the same time: by reading anthologies of poetry that presented the original Russian in an old-fashioned, serifed Cyrillic on one page and an English translation on the next. Among a wash of poets ranging from early writers of the Kievan Rus' to those working in the late twentieth century, Anna stood out immediately. There was an overwhelming sadness to her writing, but also an elegance, an Art Nouveau sense of the grand, the posh, the – dare I say it? – royal. She was nostalgic for the time of the tsars. She wrote of princes, of gardens in the moonlight, of swans, of black rivers and expansive fields of ice. She had borrowed a bucket of paint from the Romantics and had lugged it into the Communist era without spilling a drop. As the Stalinist state was bragging that nuclear power would light every home from Moscow to Vladivostok, she was putting lanterns into her poetry. That was probably high treason in and of itself.

Most of us write under some level of constraint: after a full workday as a floor nurse or a teacher, during our morning subway commute, in an overseas military barracks. Often, the very reasons we write are tied to the stressors that nearly prohibit our writing. But how would we cope with writing under the gaze of a government that not only distrusts but persecutes and even murders its citizens? If our artistic pursuit could itself motivate the government to prosecute us for supposed crimes against the state and its ideology?

Such a nightmare existence is the stuff of dystopian sci-fi movies, but it was also the reality of many writers who lived in the Soviet Union during Josef Stalin's rule. Of those writers, Anna has become the best known, both in her native Russia and worldwide. Lydia Chukovskaya, her best friend, is less well known but just as crucial. Together they endured the fear, frustration, and pain of Stalin's purges, including the murder of Lydia's husband. But during the worst years of Stalin's rule, such terror was a daily reality for millions of Soviet citizens. In that way, Anna and Lydia were typical citizens.

I've always been drawn to writers who have worked under oppression, be it sexual (Arthur Rimbaud), economic (Thomas Chatterton), gender (Kate Chopin), or otherwise. When people are forced to overcome a specific, personal mechanism of injustice, even non-writers, such as visual artist David Wojnarowicz, have turned to writing. As literary critic and philosopher Hélène Cixous has shown, writing is often the only effective – the only accessible – outlet for the oppressed, and it also allows a person to convey, in the most literal terms, what he or she is enduring.

Anna and Lydia had planned on, desired, lived for their careers as writers. Yet even if they had not been "real" writers, they would have written; for they wrote in order to survive the terror of their lives, because otherwise they would have gone crazy. Less personally, they also wrote so that the entire world might one day know how millions of Soviet citizens had coped with everything from shortages of food to the constant specter of state persecution. Both understood all too well that writers and other artists were expected to compose official dogma for the state, to celebrate its supposedly grand accomplishments – or else. It was resoundingly clear that the official story of an entire generation, of an entire civilization, would be a fraud. This was no dystopian science fiction but exactly what the Soviet state had planned on and expected. So someone, somewhere, needed to disrupt that plan. Someone needed to leave a material record for foreigners and future generations to discover and learn from. Someone needed to chronicle the lines of people standing in the snow waiting for bread, to explain that sons were barred from good universities because of the sins of their fathers, to prove that even a highly decorated colonel could be shot for a slight offense. Lydia and Anna were voices that spoke these truths. They had to write out what was being written in, to white-out the lies that were being inked in. They had a strange covert business in alchemy, these two women from Saint Petersburg.

When I first began reading Anna's poems, I learned what it meant to write while living in a society of mirrors, where even the underpinnings of the polity were in some sense fake. But the Soviets were also very fearful of the past. The orchestration of romanticism in her poetry was a powerful reminder of the contrasting world that they were ushering to the forefront and requiring their citizens to heed.

Lydia's writing I came to later, but her name cropped up in every bit of criticism I encountered about Anna. Authors would mention Lydia in passing – as Anna's friend, as her first champion, as one of the main reasons why her works have survived intact. There was no question that Lydia was important, but I never saw her books in bookstores or her works in any anthology. So who was she? Although critics claimed that she was a cornerstone of her literary era, I could not find her works in translation anywhere. As my Russian improved, I kept vowing to myself that I would read her novels and nonfiction, even if this meant going to Moscow and digging a dusty copy off a library shelf. But as it happened, a trip overseas wasn't necessary: in the library at the University of California, Berkeley, I discovered nearly all of her work that has been translated into English, plus several volumes in Russian.

At first, Lydia was not exactly what I'd expected. I'd conjured her up as a romantic, dashing, exotic figure – mainly, I see in retrospect, because she'd seemed so unobtainable. But on a first reading, her work contains none of Anna's noble romanticism. Instead, I found a long list of everyday chores. At first, this seemed to be an interesting window into the past, but it quickly became boring repetition: women bought beets and turnips (or, in too many cases, found none for sale), tended their kids, worried about their husbands, and secretly dwelt on their concerns about their supposedly perfect government. Instead of mysterious, unfiltered, exotic Anna, I had discovered a journalistic housewife.

Though at the time I was more or less blind to the value of Lydia's work, I will give myself some credit: instead of stopping after an essay or two, I charged onward through all of her corpus I could find, hoping for something less dismal. Thus, when I reencountered her a few years later, I was fairly well acquainted with her work and intentions. In the meantime, I had started researching the transition of the former Yugoslav nations away from communism toward more expansive free-market economies. Their wholesale rejection of anything Soviet – nearly anything foreign – had quickly led to those bursts of nationalism that became central to the ugly Balkan conflicts of the 1990s. Most analysts were dealing with the large issues of this situation, as they always do, but my interests lay in the actual, acute experience of the individual; and now I saw how well Lydia's work spoke to this situation.

So that is how I came to these writers – Anna with her haunting focus on a past that never really quite existed, Lydia's intense chronicle of bleak everyday life – and their work has affected my own writing in a variety of material ways. For instance, although the idea of recording simple details might not seem extraordinary, it was central to Lydia's ethos as a writer, and that centrality has stayed with me. Nothing is too small, whether I'm writing about how my grandmother raised calves on her father's farmstead or the way in which slight variants of the Ijekvian dialect surface throughout Serbia. If it mattered to someone or was part of her daily life, then it matters to history and, by extension, to our writing of history.

Anna has influenced me differently. As I have become more serious about writing poetry, her work, with its romantic overlays, its elegies for a gilded age, its nostalgic *joie de vivre*, serves as a template for much of what I want to explore in my own poems. Like Marcel Proust, who was driven to touch upon in writing every aspect of essential experience, Anna was determined to create a setting and a cast, yet she chose to use very few words to focus intently and profoundly on her characters' emotions. Place was also important to her; and as I write, I think about how she and I both recall and remedy the memory of place in our writing.

> I was not here for hundreds of years,
> But nothing changed for ages here –
> In the same way the divine lyre
> Pours bliss from the eternal crests.

Anna wrote those words in Tashkent, far from the bustle and chaos of Saint Petersburg, where she had been evacuated to escape from the city's siege during World War II. To an extent, her stanza is as literal as it is romantic. Tashkent was only starting to move into the modern world in Akhmatova's time, while Saint Petersburg – long the epicenter of Russian culture – was in the hands of uncertain fate. Anna was fascinated by the Uzbek people and how the Soviet state was changing their lives: for government control over ethnic Russians was one matter; importation of Russian language and culture to non-Russian states was another.

According to Lydia, by this point in Anna's career, she sometimes went so far as to write out poems on scrap paper to share with visitors to her apartment. After the visitors had read them, she would burn them in her stove. Now she was existing at this level of danger in Tashkent, where an entire society had been stripped of language and faith and put under the Soviet yoke. Her words were both a risk and a lament.

For most of my life I've felt a kinship to Russia and the Russian people. I listen to Russian pop and techno, I'm a huge FC Zenit fan (Saint Petersburg's leading soccer team), and I check the Russian news on the Internet every morning, only to discover I've already heard most of it from my Russian friends on Skype and VK. Despite the passage of time, Stalin's era still defines the internal and external views of contemporary Russia in so many ways. Anna Akhmatova and Lydia Chukovskaya lived and worked at this pivotal point in their nation's complex history, and despite adversity they managed to express in nuanced, emotion-laden terms exactly what was going on in their society. That effort alone is an inspiration to me, but beyond that the actual works they produced are staggering in their beauty and value.

What I've learned from these writers has changed my life not only as a poet and a scholar but also as a citizen. Once, when placing a call to an architect regarding the future of the marine hospital in Savannah, Georgia, Lydia's voice overtook my own. As the architect droned on about how much better the city would be with the building repurposed and repainted, I blurted out, "Sir, men died there . . . men in uniform. Doctors and nurses worked tirelessly there; it was part of this nation's first federal public health effort. It needs to be remembered for what it was, what happened there." A poem, a novel, a building: all are catalogs of a past that we need to remember.

Autumn McClintock (born 1976)

In this essay, poet Autumn McClintock considers the way in which we can become unwittingly responsible for our subject matter – in her case, death and the grief of death. For, as she writes, "once we experience it profoundly, grief makes itself a part of our fabric. It becomes, in the words of Psalm 139, part of 'our going out and our lying down.' We are no longer someone with; we are someone without, and that knowledge builds and sustains us as much as a great conversation, or a perfectly flawed fictional character, or our relationship with God can."

Responsible for Death

The poet Leonard Gontarek once said to me and a group of fellow work-shop students, "Poets should be able to write with elegance and grace about [Dick] Cheney." Marking the comment up to Leonard's idiosyncratic mind, I laughed but couldn't forget it. He went on to talk about the responsibility of poets to maintain conversations with not only the seemingly inappropriate (like Cheney) but with the ubiquitous elements, like nature and death. This idea of responsibility toward a subject matter stuck with me as a writer who, now solidly harnessed by adulthood in my mid-thirties, has moved through a gamut of questions about who I am as a poet and who I should or can be. I realize if I want to write (and I do), if I want to make it through my life and still call myself a poet, I can do that not by mourning the muse, but by taking onus for the way I work and the subjects I write about.

My sparse work traditionally comes even less easily in summer, so last June, in an effort to keep my brain around the practice of poetry, I began to gather pieces for a chapbook. In choosing poems, I realized easily a third of them overtly discuss death and several others were built with an implicit tone of loss. I surely was aware that my work mentioned death on occasion, but how could a third of them be overt death poems? At first, this was disconcerting, not having realized that I was a person who leans toward any specific topic, let alone this most "poetic" of subjects.

I've found that acknowledging my habits and foibles is instructive for growth and change. In hopes that this would apply to my poetry as well, I reconsidered the poems, looking for new places to channel my work. But then I remembered the notion of responsibility to the subject. What could it mean to be responsible for death? Was it as simple as wanting to understand what dictates life? The confrontation and exploration of the unknown? Fear of loss? These questions led me to the revelation that I rarely, if ever, pursue attitudes toward my own death but instead examine grief and absence.

Allow me to say this: the idea that time heals wounds and allows us to get over someone's death is bullshit. Once we experience it profoundly, grief makes itself a part of our fabric. It becomes, in the words of Psalm 139, part of "our going out and our lying down." We are no longer someone *with*; we are someone *without*, and that knowledge builds and sustains us as much as a great conversation, or a perfectly flawed fictional character, or our relationship with God can.

To take responsibility for my subject, then, I must be a warden of grief. I must care for it and employ it and share it, embrace it rather than scorn it. But here's the hard part: I don't consider myself a confessional or even a narrative poet and in fact fear sentiment. My work is image-based, sound-based, tone-based. I like to convey through subtlety and sign, not admission. (Whether or not I succeed is debatable.) So how does the contemporary poet, whose forebears have taken every advantage of death as subject matter, separate it from sentiment?

In his essay "The Serious Artist," Ezra Pound illustrated how one can move through emotion to find music and then secure music to language: "You begin with the yowl and the bark, and you develop into the dance, the music, and into music with words . . . and finally into words with a vague adumbration of music, words suggestive of music." This was where I found my answer. Making imagery driven by sound that recalls the vision of the dead or a moment of grief lets us share without confessing, talk about death without blubbering. The work requires mastery of our tools: words and their precise sounds in proximity to one another. Yes, loss can be my music. Even better, it can be my language; and as a student of that language, I want to employ its sounds and shadows precisely. As in any good art, a poet's subject takes on its own characterization and imagery: sun against a headstone, photograph of a woman in bellbottoms. Despite the overtones of my subject, I have come to see my responsibility to it not as compulsion and obligation but as desire and joy – my attempt to share and care for it: this, our collective death.

Garth Greenwell · (born 1978)

In this wide-ranging essay, first published in Fourth Genre *in 2011, poet Garth Greenwell ponders the link between a sense of alienation and a need to create art. "It seems to me now that, as surely is true of many others, I began writing poems in order to place in the world a beauty I might feel at home with, something to balance the deficiency of beauty I have always felt in my own person."*

On Beauty and Distance

The ugliest monument in Sofia stands at the northern end of the park at the National Palace of Culture (NDK), to the left as one enters the promenade from Patriarh Evtimii Boulevard. Hulking and abstract, immobile in its modernist geometry, it was raised in 1981 and began disintegrating almost immediately thereafter – though more slowly, it should be said, than the communist government that erected it. Bundled now in scaffolding, hidden in part by massive advertisements wrapped around it like so much gauze, the Monument to the Bulgarian State, which Sofians refer to fondly as the seven-angled thing with five pricks, is a reminder of the past at once imposing and somehow fairly easy to ignore. Fleeing away from it, the long central plaza leading to the Palace is lined with cafés along with, in the summer, ice cream stands, balloon vendors, and artists of all types, as well as of course the beggars unavoidable here, whatever the season. Young couples push strollers to and from the long fountains (banked, in summer, with huge beds of red flowers) that are the park's chief attraction; in winter, when the concrete basins are dry, the strollers come cocooned in plastic sheeting, antiseptic and alarming, like alien pods entering a hostile atmosphere. Nearer the Palace itself, young men ride their tricked-out bicycles or skateboards or in-line skates at ever-greater velocities over a short flight of stairs, performing tribal acrobatics for the men who watch them, waiting their turn. Sometimes, because of some misjudgment, some failure or surfeit of nerve, they send their unmarred bodies wheeling in what seem agonizing catastrophes, from which nevertheless (as though really they were impervious to ruin) they rise up again still whole. The nicest cafés cluster nearest the Palace itself, where the broad walkway branches to join with Fridtjof Nansen Street on the left and, on the right, with Vitosha Boulevard, where the latest European fashions are displayed obscenely over Roma boys begging on flattened cardboard boxes. These fashions make their way to the Palace only in the evening, where they can be glimpsed sliding into one of the concert halls I've never seen, having entered the building itself only once, and briefly, for the Christmas Fair, when it was packed with tables and booths selling candied fruits and trinkets and homemade garments of every sort.

Instead of entering the Palace, I turn, as I nearly always do, toward a long flight of stairs leading beneath the main plaza. The stairway gives out onto a subterranean plaza, the center of it (another fountain, the wall behind it an elaborate mosaic) uncovered, so that looking up one can see pedestrians pacing the main level above, or leaning over the railing to gaze down at the fountain and its pool. From here branches out an elaborate network of *podlezi*, walkways leading under the busy streets that frame the park. These corridors are crowded with clothing stores, pizza stands, little shops for alcohol and tobacco, and often enough more impromptu merchants unfold their tables to offer flowers, tomatoes, homemade wines sold in liter Pepsi bottles, carved implements of wood or little woven things the precise nature of which is hard to discern in passing. A few steps to the left are doors to the Palace basement, where the hallways are filled with shops that can afford a higher rent. There's a café inside, huge, not meant for tourists, the floors and walls carpeted with a patterned green fabric, the air unbreathable with smoke. Two mounted televisions alternate between Balkan football matches and music videos, the latter lurid pageants of heavily breasted women singing *chalga*, the pulsing and highly ornamented pop-folk music that is Bulgaria's primary cultural export. My students have told me that in more conservative countries these little films are consumed as porn. My first time in this café, sipping a painfully bitter cappuccino, I found myself unable to stop watching the strange dramas flashing so vividly on the screen, full of violence and sex, even as I listened to a middle-aged man tell me of his exhilaration twenty years ago as the world around him changed. His country seemed briefly then a land for the young, he told me, promising opportunities not so much for wealth as for the expression of a self that seemed the chief and cherishable resource of the West, filling him with an excitement that faded quickly as so little seemed changed either lastingly or for the good. The best time of his life, he said softly in an English brittle with disuse, was the two months he spent ten years ago in the States, in Madison, where he studied at a center for international journalists and where he discovered for the first time something like a viable life as a gay man. The boys there, he said quietly, half closing his eyes, the boys, and he sucked his breath between his teeth with an indeterminate sound, reliving scenes whose pleasures were locked irretrievably behind him.

Following the *podlez* past this entrance, just a dozen or so meters on the right is a narrow doorway marked by a blue sign with the letters WC printed on it in white. From here a stairway leads yet further down, and as one descends the air noticeably cools. Somehow the impression of darkness is unrelieved by the electric lights that are after all perfectly adequate, as though even after the shadows of the *podlez* one's eyes were dazzled by the shift from natural light. Or perhaps it's that excitement and dread together so distract one that it's only in memory the visual faculty seems dulled. The sense of descending into a cave, some space carved out not by human hands but by geological pressures, only increases as the air cools further and a quality of dampness pervades everything, not just the exposed pipes glistening with condensation but also the floor which pulls faintly at one's shoes; even the walls, which I always imagine perspiring just slightly, are clammy to the touch. At the end of the long stairs is a booth, from within which a dark-featured woman wrapped tightly in a shawl collects one's fifty *stotinki*, the standard fee here for such facilities. It was only after several visits that I learned to distinguish between the two women who share the responsibility of this post, and even now I tell them apart less by any distinction of appearance than by radically different affects, one smiling up at me in welcome, the other lifting a look of hostility, even disgust. From the bottom of the stairs, the women's room, which I've never seen anyone coming in or out of, is first, and then the entrance to the men's. I think it was here, at the threshold to the first of two outer chambers, when I came here for the first time – a friend and I, exploring the city on a late summer afternoon, desperate for a bathroom – that I realized the nature of this place. In the first, smallest chamber, which is typically empty, there's a mirror bolted to the wall, at which invariably I pause for a moment, adjusting whatever can be adjusted, as so little can, for greater effect. Standing at this mirror, no matter how routine these visits have become, I can't keep from feeling a certain shortness of breath, a rising excitement at the possibility of discovery matched by anxiety at what might already somehow have been missed. In the second chamber, where almost always there's someone leaning against the wall with a cigarette at his lips, advertising his availability, a line of porcelain sinks, all of them cracked and stained, offers cold water and the occasionally refilled soap dispenser. I pause here, too, heightening my anticipation, unable to tell, behind his heavy sunglasses, if I've caught the interest of my neighbor, who anyway almost certainly expects to be paid. From this second chamber one can see into the third and last room, partitioned itself into two halves, a line of urinals on the left, and, on the right, a series of stalls. Men, as many as twelve or thirteen, more usually three or four, circulate between these small rooms, and though generally it's against the wall facing the stalls that we congregate, occasionally a man will station himself at the urinals, looking furtively toward the entrance, hiding his nakedness or revealing it as interest dictates. As I enter the room on the right, I watch the little flutter of excitement at my arrival subside, like water settling after swallowing a coin. Sometimes this excitement disappears entirely, and I lean at the wall or pace nervously with the rest, waiting for new arrivals; and sometimes it lingers in one of the men, or two, and almost before I'm aware of it we've entered a stall together, sliding the little bar of the latch behind us shut.

The metro station at Vasil Levski Stadium is the first stop on the edges of the city center, and it's here, emerging through the swinging glass doors into the natural light, that I see again what was my first glimpse of central Sofia. There are better views: at the newest *metrostantsia*, at Sofia University "Saint Kliment Ohridski," one of the several entrances emerges in a beautifully groomed park, where one's first sight is of the gold dome of Nevski Cathedral framed in manicured branches. Once, not far from this park, a friend and I, searching for a particular café we never found, were astonished by an evening concert of bells coming from this very dome. We stopped in our tracks, caught by the intricate latticework of these sounds, which were governed by rules that, though indecipherable to us, nevertheless constituted an unmistakable order. I was surprised by how moved and disturbed I was by this music, and especially by the sound of the largest bells, which rang slowly enough that each of their changes was wrenching, like tectonic plates shifting beneath layered water. Looking toward the dome still gleaming in the evening light, though the rest of the building was already in shadow, I was amazed to see, just barely discernible, the silhouette of a single, apparently cassocked figure, masterfully and with all four of its limbs manipulating the elaborate system of pulleys and ropes responsible for this sound. I felt certain somehow that this figure was female, though there could be no basis for this impression from such a distance, and perhaps it was due to nothing more than memories of my mother playing handbells in a small chapel in Sonora, Kentucky, even more beautiful in her church garments than she seemed to me usually, and possessing, to my child's eyes, an inscrutable virtuosity. My friend grew impatient as the concert continued, the late summer swallows (I seem to remember) disappearing into the darkness. I stood listening until the last resonance dissolved into the air.

Nothing like Nevski Cathedral greets the traveler emerging from the Vasil Levski metro station. Across from the station is Friendship Bridge, where statues of paired men and women embrace in theatrical comradeship beside the trickle of water Sofians insist on calling a river, though in fact it's little more than a drainage ditch, its banks thick with litter picked through unceasingly by dogs. Beside these statues, along the front of a SPORT TOTO betting booth like dozens of others ubiquitous throughout the city, someone has spray-painted in huge block letters ПЕДАЛ = ПОДЧОВЕК, the sentiment of it legible to me even that first day: Faggot = Subhuman. In all the months since my arrival, no attempt has been made to remove this sign, either by the city or by the establishment, for whose clientele anyway it almost certainly constitutes an enticement. If, instead of crossing toward Graf Ignatief Street and the city center, one turns right here, a walk along the stadium reveals much more of the same, climaxing perhaps in graffiti above one of the many stairways fully visible from the street: УМРЕТЕ В МЪКИ ГНУСНИ ПЕДАЛИ: Die in pain, disgusting faggots. Violent street crime is remarkably low in Sofia (assuming one isn't part of the mafia that nearly everyone agrees constitutes a clandestine government here), and until a recent, brutal murder of a young man in Borisova Gradina, Sofia's oldest park, I hadn't heard of any assaults or raids, sanctioned or unsanctioned, against gays singly or in groups. Bulgaria's recent and still disputed accession to the EU has ensured at least silence from the government about lesbian and gay people, a silence the tenor of which was made clear when, two summers ago, the police stood by as rightist protestors threw Molotov cocktails at the few dozen marchers in the city's first gay pride parade. I remember one sleepless night in Ann Arbor, shortly after deciding to come here, searching the internet for whatever I could discover about what I thought of then as becoming my new country. On YouTube I found archived various news accounts of this event, including one from the scene itself, in which a beautiful drag queen, muscular and lean, blond, tall, speaks at once animatedly (the meaning of the words was lost to me) and with extraordinary poise, flinching only slightly at the scream of the little explosives as they sailed through the air and at their subsequent detonation. Even in this case, though, to the best of my knowledge no one was injured, and it's less the threat of physical violence than the constant barrage of casual, seemingly instinctive scorn that has marked the people I've met here.

It is a curious fact of the gay scene in Sofia, at least as I've experienced it in my first months here, that no one will admit to having anything to do with it. Such is the case with Andrey, a young colleague at the school where I teach. I met him after hearing rumors that there might be an avowedly gay Bulgarian on staff, though no one was precisely sure who this creature might be. Andrey's openness, a stance requiring not a little courage, consists largely of an absence of heterosexual pageantry and a general aura of apartness. He was quick, in our first conversations, to make clear his dislike of dance clubs, gay bars, and political or social agitation of any kind. From the beginning, curiously, there was an assumption of our fundamental differences as kinds of gay men, an assumption that I interpreted in such a way as to rankle. Only gradually did I recognize what I took for disdain as envy of attitudes I must seem to take for granted, attitudes that, however disputed, are not unforcefully promoted in America by individuals and groups some of whom are commanding of respect. Not least, of course, in the formation of these attitudes I had the resource of English-language literature, which privately, and despite all the evidence offered me to the contrary, demonstrated (in Edmund White, in Isherwood, in Baldwin) the passions of gay lives as accommodating of at least the dignity of tragedy. I've been told that there's nothing comparable in the Bulgarian tradition, no imagination of gay lives as anything but caricature. Only recently, in 2007, was a book of poems published that spoke candidly of gay male life in Bulgaria, a book written only after its author had established a life for himself in America, where he watched from afar the rather extraordinary scandal it caused. He spoke with me one morning over Skype, from the house in Florida that he owns with his boyfriend. He works delivering pizzas, writing his poems on his days off, poems only possible, he told me, because of his knowledge of English. In Bulgarian, he said, my poor internet connection causing his words to catch at times and slur, the language itself makes it impossible to articulate a basis for anything like gay rights: there's nothing in the history of the language to support it, the very words themselves don't exist. Only after learning English, or German or French, he claimed, could one have the means to resist the prejudice everywhere in the society, not least in gay men themselves. There's no gay culture in Sofia, Nikolay went on, saying that the few gay bars and clubs, which of course he hadn't visited for years, serve less to challenge the stigmatization of gay people than to perpetuate it.

Only once have I been to a gay bar in Sofia, both my schedule as a high school teacher and my temperament tending to keep me from bars or clubs of any kind, sometimes it seems from anywhere at all. It was late, and Andrey and I were with another American teacher and his girlfriend, who was visiting from the States. We had spent the evening in a park not far from the university, availing ourselves of a liquor store just opposite to get progressively more drunk. Probably only because of this drunkenness, and only after much pleading, we were finally able to convince Andrey to take us to one of the bars we had searched for on our own without success. And so we set off, on that bizarrely mild winter evening, wandering I don't remember now which streets, finding first one and then a second bar no longer where it should have been, having closed or moved without notice. On our third try, we headed to a street where a bar for gay men was located, or so we had been told, next to the city's only establishment for gay women. This bar too seemed not to exist, but before admitting defeat we decided to ask at the well-lit and clearly marked lesbian bar. A short walk down wooden stairs led the four of us into a loud, smoke-filled room in which every seat was taken. It was immediately clear, from the surprised and not particularly friendly stares we received, that only women were welcome, and I and my friend quickly retreated to the street, while Andrey and my friend's visitor (who was uncommonly beautiful) stayed to ask about our intended destination. As it turned out, the bar we were looking for was just next door, down a similar staircase the entrance to which, however, was entirely unmarked. Before we reached it, a second door at the bottom of the stairs opened and a large man stepped through, closing it again behind him. Mid-thirties, his balding hair shaved back, he had already begun the long slide to corpulence so many very muscular men suffer, a fact unhidden, even in the dim light, by the tight black t-shirt he wore. He and Andrey exchanged a few words, none of which I could understand in the quick thicket of *chalga* beating at the closed door, which the bouncer opened again now to let us pass. I was surprised by the smallness of the room, in which three or four men sat at a short bar sipping drinks. The music was too loud for conversation, but neither was anyone on the dance floor, a few squares of wooden tile between the bar and the three or four tables flanked not with chairs but with lounging couches, as is the custom here. We claimed one of these tables, taking a place next to the only other man not stationed at the bar, a muscular, young, seedily attractive guy who I suspected might be slated for the night's entertainment, dancing, once there was more of an audience, in various stages of undress on the tiny raised platform in the corner. Though he was seated no more than a foot from us and had no company of his own, this man made no attempt to greet us and may have been, for all we knew and all his demeanor could tell us, incapable of speech altogether. He stared at the television bolted to the wall just in front of him, watching as if hypnotized the football match playing there. At some point, he shifted his attention to Grace, staring at her, though she was only a foot or so away, with the same entranced fixation, entirely oblivious to our increasing discomfort and looking away only when Grace excused herself to the restroom. Probably, my students assured me later when I told them about this bizarre behavior, he had simply never seen a black woman so close before and meant no harm.

Business was slow for the first hour or so we were there, but eventually the light above the interior door, which was cued to the street entrance, began flashing more frequently, and finally the bouncer abandoned his stool at the bar and took up a permanent station in the hallway outside. By midnight every seat was full, and there were even several men moving rhythmically on the dance floor. The most energetic of these was a thirty-something, extremely fat man, who was flanked on either side by two Roma boys, no older than eighteen, who shared so uncannily the same striking, delicate loveliness they might almost have been brothers. As I sat in that crowded room, plagued by a pitch of solitude that only ever afflicts me in such places and that separated me from my friends, I wondered about the nature of their relationship, with its marked discrepancies of both age and beauty. The boys hovered about the older man, dancing seductively, and as he shook himself, his eyes clenched shut, he mouthed flawlessly the lyrics to each of the popular songs. I remember wondering to myself into what peculiar space he had withdrawn at that moment, where he could be at once such a spectacle, claiming so much of the dance floor for himself, and yet locked in some entirely untouchable privacy. At one point, over-heated, he unzipped his light fleece jacket and turned his back to one of the boys, who grabbed it at the shoulders and peeled it from his frame. I couldn't tell whether this gesture was attentive or servile, or how to read the man's attitude toward the boys, which seemed one at once of lasciviousness and disregard. When he left the floor, heading toward the bathroom, the two boys immediately closed the distance between them, dancing now with genuine heat, one lowering his face to taste the fold of the other's neck. They separated again when the man returned, resuming their awkward triangular gyrations. My attention wandered then, and when next I noticed the two boys they were alone and ministering all of their affections upon each other. As I think of them now, however, it's the fat man whose image is least dismissible, dancing ungracefully, leading behind his closed eyes (as I imagined) a life entirely different from the one in which inexplicably he found himself: a life in which the attentions he basked in were limitless, fueled by love, and not, as all of us at our table were united in assuming, something rented by the hour.

Cherokee Park in Louisville, Kentucky, is a place the geography of which I have almost entirely forgotten, as I have forgotten the name, even the face, of the man who first took me there. I was fifteen, I think, or sixteen, though I knew I had to pretend to be older, even as I knew my chief enticement was the transparency of the lie. What I do remember is the joy I felt my first time there, the sense of freedom I had, of opportunity; and, even then, the peculiar dread that still accompanies me in such places. That summer I spent whole days on that isolated hill circled by a road with no other destination, where nearly every car, you could be certain, was there for the same reason as your own. There were picnic tables we dragged beneath the tall trees stranded on the little island created by the road, where we tried to escape the terrible heat of the hottest days. From our vantage atop the hill we could look over several areas of the park, including a field, not far off, popular with families and straight couples and single men and women exercising their dogs. I remember registering, of course, the different models of affective life displayed before and around me, one open and bright and equipped with all the artillery of social sanction, the other furtive and, even at that altitude, somehow subterranean. I resented what I saw even then as the restricted possibilities available to me, who had been nursed on the dreams of romance that seemed played out in that field below, where beautiful men, often shirtless against the heat, bestowed their affections on women who seemed somehow confident of their entitlement. Always this entitlement, in either sex, has been the greatest mystery to me, and the greatest source of the resentment that seems at times almost entirely to overpower me, threatening to poison my life. Even as I felt a painfully humiliating exclusion from such scenes, however, equally I felt, especially as darkness fell and the air cooled and the park became again our privileged possession, in the same sense of apartness a kind of election. I loved nights in that park, when often I would stay until one or two in the morning, vested with what seemed like a secret knowledge, our separate life not a deprivation now, but a kind of magic second world running beneath and beside the other.

There was a community among the men who frequented the park, and I came quickly to know them, even if our acquaintance was held firmly within boundaries imposed, for most of them, by the requirements of secrecy. Closeted, married, with respectable jobs (one of them drove a school bus for the district, and asked me to ignore him should our paths ever cross), for them our little hill represented a ludic world that must at all costs be held separate from the world in which they lived. Of all the men I met, only one became – and even then only briefly – a friend. I've thought of him seldom in the last fifteen or sixteen years, and now it shames me to find that even his name is lost to me, though I can still make out his face and something like the outline of his form. He was my age, shorter than I, with fair hair and skin and a willowy build that was a marvel to me, who have always been heavy-set and broad. He seemed too fine a thing to share with me the element of earth. His life had been more vicious and traumatic than mine, and yet our experiences seemed proximate, so that we fell, somewhat to both of our surprise, into a strangely immediate understanding. He had moved out of his parents' house some time before, and lived with a series of much older men, earning money, when he needed it, by turning tricks in the park. I remember him as endlessly sweet-natured, funny, and kind, but it's clear to me now both how precarious his life was and how circumscribed his horizons. Sometimes he would dance at bars, either nearly naked or, as he preferred, in the elaborate finery that transformed him into an extraordinarily beautiful woman, a figure of absolute glamour. Only once did he allow me to watch this transformation, stripping himself naked before me and then remaking himself layer by layer. I remember lying back on the bed in the studio apartment where he was living with a forty-something army veteran, a brutish, unexpressive man because of whose occasionally violent temper my friend was on the look-out for a new patron. Lying on this bed, I watched as my friend taped back his penis and then stood with his legs tightly clasped, spreading his arms and twirling like some asexual angelic being.

He introduced me to other drag queens and gay teenagers who lived in similar arrangements, in apartments downtown that seemed worlds away from my life in the suburbs. Once we visited a young man whom my friend revered, a talented dancer who made enough of a living at the nightclubs to arrange much of the rest of his life on his own terms. It was the hottest day of the summer, a July afternoon of unremitting sun, and by the time we had made our way to the apartment my shirt was drenched with sweat. The man who opened the door came nowhere near my friend in beauty, but he was even more delicate, greeting us with a voice little more than a feminine whisper. He was dressed in a t-shirt that he wore like a nightgown, and all afternoon he gave the impression of being on the verge of disappearance. The room into which he welcomed us was entirely unlit, either windowless or with thick curtains failing to keep out the heat, and as soon as the hallway door closed behind us the room was almost entirely dark. The only illumination came from a small television, in the light of which I could make out a middle-aged man in his underclothes, sprawled in a reclining chair pushed close to the set, a can of cheap beer on his knee. He said nothing to us and never looked away from the screen. As the fey lisping man led us through the room, which I remember as surprisingly large, though it was too dark to have any real sense of its proportions, I was overcome by a sense of despondency at the sordidness into which I felt I was sinking, that hot stinking room a vision of my future.

Eventually, stumbling on who knows what debris as we felt our way forward, I could see in the darkness the outline of a door etched in light seeping past it from the room beyond. Our guide paused at this door for a moment before opening it just widely enough for us to slide through, urging us quickly inside. While it took a moment for my eyes to adjust to this new brightness, I immediately registered, with a kind of bodily happiness, the window unit aggressively cooling the air. Even in my relief, however, I felt that after a short time in the room it would be uncomfortably cool, and indeed the bed we were invited to sit on was piled thick with blankets, along with several pillows and a large number of stuffed animals, creatures of all sorts and sizes lining the edge of the bed where it met the wall. Our host lay curled in a padded enclave by the window, itself piled high with large stuffed bears, one of which he pulled close to his stomach as he spoke to us. What it was we spoke about I couldn't say, spending much of the next hour marveling at the baroque care evident everywhere in that room, which matched my own imaginings of the bedroom of an aristocratic southern debutante. Much of my amazement was due simply to how many things had been crammed into that small space. On a little dresser before a mirror were laid out layers of cosmetics, tissues, brushes and clips and combs, lipsticks and mascaras, all of the accoutrements of female adornment, accoutrements that fill me even now with the sense of suffocation I associate with my childhood. Dresses hung lushly from hooks along the walls, so that we seemed entombed in a chiffon canopy, everything softness and stale cleanliness and color. Even among so many objects there was no hint of disorder, and much of what terrified me in that room, I think, was the sense that each of these many things had been made a fetish, touchable only with reverence and inalienable from its assigned space. Always I've hated such spaces, in which the frozen quality of things that should have life takes on not a lyrical suspension but rather the unbearable weight of never-ceasing time.

Perhaps it was under the sway of this room, which he found enchanting and patently envied, that my friend told me, for the first and last time, of his desire not just to dress beautifully in women's clothes but to become in actual fact a woman. He spoke to me, as we walked through streets that seemed paralyzed by heat, the very trees wilting in their shells, of the various hormones, surgeries, and therapies he would have to undergo, and of his eagerness to begin while he had still the allurements of youth. As if in a dream, he described for me the life he imagined assuming, a life entirely at odds with his own, of indistinguishable days circumscribed by ritual and obligation and scheduled duty. How he longed to prepare meals for his husband, he said, to spend his time in domestic tasks and in the knowledge of being provided for and protected. And yet, even if he could manage somehow to amass the small fortune required for such a transformation, surgery lagged far behind the extent of his imaginings. What I really want, he said to me then, slowing to a standstill on the pavement, cupping his abdomen, rubbing the bell of his belly and contemplating the beauty that was precluded him, what I really want is to feel growing within myself a child. How can I explain why it should be now, in this landscape so different from the one I fled years ago, that the memory of this boy comes back to me, forcing upon me these remembrances that have never, until now, haunted me or troubled my sleep? Or why, despite differences of language, affect, attire, of architecture and cuisine, smells and ambient sounds, it should be this city that sends me so frequently back in my thoughts to those first years I lay grappling (as I thought of it then) with what I am, and that submerges me again in the air I breathed as a child? Regardless, this is the last clear memory I have of my friend, though I know we spent more weeks together that summer, before I left, as it turned out permanently, for boarding school and what would prove to be a new life. Nor do I remember who it was, on one of my brief trips home, that told me this friend had fallen ill and that on learning this he had disappeared somewhere beyond the reach of everyone we knew, who had seen neither hide nor hair of him for many months.

Everywhere I've lived I've sought out these places, bathrooms or bars or narrow paths in parks: in Boston, St. Louis, New York, Michigan, and now in this city so much stranger to me than those others, with its impossible language even the alphabet of which can frustrate me to tears. When I stumbled upon the bathrooms at NDK, it was with the relief of returning to a native tongue, a place where the customs and mores were familiar to me and thus affirming of the self, that strange amalgam of habit and repetition. And yet, even though much about these places seems reassuringly the same, each hangs distinct in my recollection, like rosary beads strung along their cord. So many of the moments that seem most constitutive of who I have become, as important as my encounters with poems or with the men I have genuinely loved, have been passed in these cramped, ill-lit, often unclean spaces. And in a strange way that has always been evident to me but never clear, those moments are crucial to whatever sequence of events has led to my sense of myself as a poet. How similar they are, I sometimes think, these two activities central to my life, and I feel certain that those nights in parks and bathrooms contributed to a sensibility everywhere on the lookout for the patternless muck of the world to arrange itself unexpectedly in legible signs. Often, seeking out the rumor of such places, wandering a new city, pacing its promising streets, I have a peculiar sensation of heightened sensitivity. Watching for I'm not sure what signal, attentive in all directions, I feel myself tense and receptive, like a bell waiting to be struck. The smallest detail, graffiti scratched into a wall, the darkness of a particular entranceway or narrowness of a passage, an avid, peculiarly harrowed glance, can portend access to the secrets of a place, a sudden opening up from banality to significance.

Of the poets I know, only three – Whitman, Cavafy, and Sandro Penna – write of this receptiveness in a way that feels recognizable to me, as they write also of the strange experience that is its goal, one at once of intimacy and estrangement, an experience not unlike my own of listening, through the years and languages-between us, for the particular timbre of their human voices rising just discernibly from the page. This has always been challenging for me, finding these voices that are accessible only through a kind of inner adjustment, a ratcheting up or down of the self to bring one into resonance with their particular frequency. Perhaps this explains my initial, stubborn reaction against the work of almost all of the poets who are now most important to me, a protectiveness of the self against such alteration. And yet I have always been drawn to poetry as a mode of discourse that, while public, is accessible only by means of an extraordinary and private sympathy across distances that remain finally insurmountable, these distances making only more precious whatever scrap of intelligible voice survives. Surely I was prepared for such secret meetings by those other more bodily encounters that preceded them. Contemplating this strangely dual nature of poems, at least, I have been struck by the similar nature of these places I've haunted, privacies carved out of public spaces, at once intimate and anonymous, lawless and yet inscribing their own lines that must not be crossed.

This sense of things was most forcibly brought home to me one summer night in Louisville, where I had returned from school on what would become more and more infrequent visits. I borrowed on some pretext my father's car and drove to the park alone. The hill that was my usual cruising ground was deserted, as sometimes happened, and so I drove to another area I knew was sometimes frequented by men, a little parking strip to the side of a curve in the main road. This area, too, was empty, and indeed the whole park was quiet, but I stopped for a moment anyway, turning off my lights to gaze into the dark from my air-conditioned capsule. Occasionally a car would approach, slowing as it passed, and my own would be bathed for a moment in light, my shadow, weirdly distended, sliding across the windshield from left to right. Only after some time did one of these cars pull up alongside me. I felt no particular attraction for the driver, a nondescript man perhaps in his late thirties, dressed, it's strange to remember, in a shirt buttoned all the way to the neck. He sat there, oddly formal, his hands no longer resting on the wheel but making no opening gesture, neither stepping out of his car nor looking toward me in invitation or even in greeting. I too sat there unmoving, facing forward but watching him from the corner of my eye, certain somehow that at any too sudden gesture he would startle. I'm not sure at what point or by what betrayal it became clear that, hidden in the darkness of his car and across the distance of the empty passenger seat, he was masturbating. For reasons I can't explain, among my most intimate experiences have been several, like this one, which involved no contact at all, moments of anticipation that acquired their own substance, their own intensities and satisfactions. After a few moments, still without displaying any urgency and still, so far as I could tell, without turning his head, I saw that my neighbor had lowered the window nearest me. I felt a disproportionate excitement at this act, which was the first acknowledgment of my presence or of our strange encounter. As I slid down my own window, matching his gesture, which I suspected was less overture than main act, I was overcome by the heaviness of the midsummer air, which flowed into the car like so much water, a quality of night I associate only with my childhood. No human sounds disturbed us, only the pervasive music of insects strumming themselves, crickets and katydids and the stray cicadas hatched in the wrong year. Neither of us spoke or made any sound at all, though eventually I could distinguish from the ambient noise the rustling of his clothes and, even more faintly and only intermittently, the sound of his breath. Straining for any trace of him, gauging by the acceleration and depth of his breathing his activity and arousal, the whole force of my being trained on him, I was seized by an intensity of attentiveness the pitch of which has only seldom been matched in my life. When, indeed, have I exceeded it? Nothing of his composure was lost as he finished, nor did he finally turn toward me as his car slid backward and away onto the main road.

At NDK, where I have gone more frequently as the weather has turned toward spring, already I've become acquainted with most of the regulars, and already have tired of more than a few. There is one man, however, whose beauty despite increasing familiarity has yet to lose any of its peculiar and debilitating force. The first time I saw him, early in my discoveries, he was just lowering a cigarette from his lips, standing with his back against the wall in the second of the bathroom's three chambers. He was tall, thin, young, his skin the peculiar olive complexion so striking here, his dark hair hanging greasily over his eyes. In his jeans and leather jacket he might have been imitating the neutral style of an American. He never raised his eyes, training them on the floor in front of him, as though allowing me to gaze at him in privacy. Several years ago, in graduate school, before I began to suspect the futility of searching for myself in books, I remember hoping I might find somewhere an account of the mysterious pain I feel whenever I'm confronted with great personal beauty, a pain suggestive somehow of a judgment passed against all of the circumstances and choices of my life. Thirstily I consumed accounts of the beautiful in philosophy, theology, psychology, without anywhere feeling I was nearing the essential revelation. Sometimes, overwhelmed with frustration and fatigue, I found myself responding to these texts with a vehemence inappropriate to academic inquiry. This was true of one book in particular, a slim, celebrated volume by a woman I sometimes passed in the hallways of my department. I have only vague memories of that volume now, but I recall one passage that so outraged me I hurled the book away as if at once to protect myself from it and to do it some entirely unscholarly injury. The details escape me now, but I remember that these pages concerned the welcome Odysseus receives from Nausicaa, the beauty of whose adolescent form the hero compares to a young palm tree at Delos near the altar of Apollo. This scholar explained that Nausicaa's welcome of Odysseus, with whom she conspires to win the favor of her parents, is an allegory for the welcome that all beautiful things extend to us, because (it may be that, recalling this through a certain dimness of memory, I depart from her argument here) it is in the beautiful that we find our true home.

It was here that the book and I so abruptly parted company. Never has personal beauty (as opposed to the beauty of art) extended its welcome to me, and such accounts seem always to me to be written not by those who feel welcomed as strangers by beauty, but rather by those who are certain they have always laid legitimate claim to it. For me, the experience of such beauty proceeds instead under the sign of a grand exclusion. It seems to me now that, as surely is true of many others, I began writing poems in order to place in the world a beauty I might feel at home with, something to balance the deficiency of beauty I have always felt in my own person. Perhaps this is part of what has always felt so poignant to me in the artifacts of aesthetic making, that strange, useless activity that appears at times to be our single inalienable possession. How miraculous it still seems to me, that moment when first I see the possibility of a poem and again when

I have finished it to anything like satisfaction (the moments in between often drudgery or despair), when I feel filled, as so seldom at any other time in my life, with gratitude for a beautiful thing that does not as if by necessity convey the great distances between us. It seems only slightly excessive to say that only at such moments have I felt at home in the world. Even so, these reconcilements are always transient. Sometimes, surrounded by the art I love, photographs or poems, the scores of Britten or Bach, I have the horrible suspicion that all of them, as well as the love and knowledge of them I have so ardently and at such cost cultivated, may be nothing but compensatory virtues, consolation for lacking the one great virtue in the face of which they melt away like creatures made of snow.

This, then, is the peculiar fear that made me avert my gaze from the young man at NDK, passing by him as quickly as I could, though not before noticing that in one of his ears he wore a large hearing aid, of the type used not by the hard of hearing but by the functionally deaf. This, along with his general demeanor, entirely indifferent to the goings-on around him, served only to increase the distance already purchased him by his beauty, so that at first, when he followed me into the bathroom's main chamber, I didn't recognize his intent. A short time later we entered a stall together. In some ways, much of the distance I sensed between us has remained intact: his manner of speech makes verbal comprehension between us impossible, so that in order to communicate words to me he has to type them painstakingly into his cellular phone, holding out the little screen then for me to read. After all these months, he has yet to tell me his name. And yet, for all this, my every encounter with him has reinforced my sense of the strange intimacy between us. As I knelt before him, as I would do repeatedly over the next weeks and months, running my hands over his fineness, the unearthly loveliness made somehow only more cherishable by the discovery of its flaws, I had a sense, as in some 17th century poem, that all the significance of the teeming world was amassed in the narrow stall where I uncovered him. Even in the strangely intimate space of these notes, which I intend to be public and in which nevertheless I speak as I have never spoken even to my closest friends, it would be difficult to give an accounting of the bewildering flood of emotion I feel before this man: desire, of course, wonder and gratefulness, a positive human warmth – and, in a way inextricable from the intensity of my pleasure, reverence, even dread, before a beauty that does not withdraw from me into its own distances, a beauty that does not turn its back.

Rory Waterman (born 1981)

In the following essay, poet Rory Waterman responds to Philip Larkin's "State-
ment," which appears on page 211. According to Waterman, "parts of the
'Statement' have been taken by some as evidence, straight from the horse's
mouth, of painful narrow-mindedness and lowered artistic ambition. But I
don't think Larkin meant much of what he said there – not wholly, anyway."
In other words, as Waterman demonstrates, a poet's pronouncements about
craft don't always mesh with his actual methods of creating a poem.

Almost-Instincts, Almost True:
Philip Larkin's "Statement" of 1955

Like Philip Larkin in 1955, I was asked to write a short statement on my
poetry for an anthology at what I rather hope was an early stage of my
writing career – in my case for *New Poetries V* (Carcanet, 2011). This was a
task less close to Larkin's than it might at first appear: Larkin had no idea
his "Statement" for *Poets of the 1950s* would be printed in its submitted
form, whereas I was all too aware that mine would be, and fretted over it
with farcical fastidiousness, rather too concerned that anything foolish I
said might come back to haunt me. In 1983, when his reputation as one of
our most significant post-war writers was fairly secure, Larkin allowed his
"Statement" to be reprinted in *Required Writing*, but included a footnote
making clear that he had initially submitted it on the assumption that it
would be no more than "raw material for an introduction" to be written by
D. J. Enright, the editor of the 1950s book, and was "rather dashed" to find
it instead printed there verbatim. Such details get forgotten when certain
modern critics grind their axes. Indeed, parts of the "Statement" have been
taken by some as evidence, straight from the horse's mouth, of painful nar-
row-mindedness and lowered artistic ambition. But I don't think Larkin
meant much of what he said there – not wholly, anyway.

"I write poems to preserve things I have seen/thought/felt," he claims. This
seems fair enough, though it also suggests one necessary order of produc-
tion: eureka moment followed by preservation of eureka moment in poetic

form. Of course, it isn't like this at all. At least part of finding out must be in the writing, surely – or, as E. M. Forster put it, "How can I know what I think till I see what I say?" Larkin's claim is an oversimplification, then, but it is one loaded with modesty. I am reminded of something he said about the inspiration for his great poem "The Whitsun Weddings": "It was just a transcription of a very happy afternoon. I didn't change a thing, it was just there to be written down." This just *isn't true*, and if it were true the poem would be nothing but a vivid diary entry. Larkin's method of composition was often to spend a long time rewriting the same poem, occasionally dropping it for months or even years before resuming, as the thoughts proliferated and could be harnessed and moulded. It is this drawn-out process of development that led to the creation of the seemingly effortless "The Whitsun Weddings," for instance – which was started several years before it was completed. More was going on than the simple preservation of what had been seen and thought and felt on a train one sunny Whitsun: the thinking and feeling were on-going preoccupations that enabled an idea to become a poem independent of the event that inspired it. But obviously things either seen, thought, or felt must be at the heart of any poem, to some extent. Isn't that a *sine qua non*? What on earth is a poem about something one has not thought about? Is it something like the sound of one hand clapping?

Of course, Modernist masterpieces such as T. S. Eliot's *The Waste Land* or Ezra Pound's *The Cantos* are concerned as much as anything else with the atmosphere in a particular epoch: things thought and felt and, to varying extents, seen. This isn't negated by any perceived or actual Modernist attempt at impersonality. But according to Larkin in his "Statement," the light a poem shines on experience must be pure, not refracted:

> As a guiding principle I believe that every poem must be its own sole freshly created universe, and therefore have no belief in "tradition" or a common myth-kitty or casual allusions in poems to other poems or poets, which last I find unpleasantly like the talk of literary understrappers letting you see they know the right people.

Ouch. Here Larkin was presumably railing against what he saw as the insidious influence of the Modernist "mad lads," as he called them elsewhere, whom he accused of taking poetry from the general to the specialised readership.

But the attack is ham-fisted; his comment is bile and nonsense. First of all: good luck, Philip. A poem cannot exist in a vacuum, cannot be "its own sole freshly created universe" – which is not to say that it is by necessity beholden to the strong gravitational pulls of other bodies. Secondly, and more significantly, Larkin is simply being disingenuous about his own aims, both as they had been before 1955 (the same year that his second collection, *The Less Deceived*, had been published) and as they would continue to be. A few years later, in 1962, he was happy to note that the last lines of "Absences," which is included in *The Less Deceived* and which ends "Such attics cleared of me! Such absences!," sounds like a "translation from a French formalist. I wish I could write like this more often." This is a resonance, of course, not an allusion – much less a dip into the classical "myth-kitty." But whilst he tends to leave the myth-kitty closed, a surprising number of "casual allusions" to other poems or poets *are* scattered throughout his oeuvre, not least in sardonic or ironic poem titles. For example, "I Remember, I Remember," a poem about forgotten youth written just a matter of months before the "Statement," is named after either Thomas Hood's or Winthrop Mackworth Praed's poems of the same name, both of which celebrate memories of youth much more than Larkin's poem does. The title "Sad Steps" is provided by Philip Sidney's *Astrophel and Stella*, giving an ironic twist to Larkin's speaker's own sky-gazing and the reference to "the strength and pain / Of being young." "This Be the Verse," the oft-quoted poem beginning "They fuck you up, your mum and dad," takes its title with comparable irony from Robert Louis Stevenson's "Requiem." "Annus Mirabilis" is a moniker shared with Dryden's poem about a year in the seventeenth century. "Toads," another poem written just months before the "Statement," includes the phrase "that's the stuff / That dreams are made on," an archaic construction (modern English would need "made of") consciously echoing Prospero in Shakespeare's *The Tempest*, right down to the positioning of the line-break: "We are such stuff / As dreams are made on." The list could go on. One can understand and enjoy these poems without picking up on the references, but they are nonetheless there to be noticed by, and to add a wry extra layer of meaning for, certain readers. Each of these poems isn't "its own sole freshly created universe," but it can be enjoyed on its own terms without requiring the reader to work beyond its most obvious limits – in a way that just isn't the case with, say, Eliot's or Pound's works mentioned above.

In his "Statement" Larkin makes one point I agree with unreservedly: "It is fatal to decide, intellectually, what good poetry is because you are then in honour bound to try to write it, instead of the poems that only you can write." This is in the first paragraph, before he provides what is in effect a sort of assessment by means of negation of what constitutes good poetry, with its own silly rules. But this should not blind us to the fact that Larkin broke these rules as often as he stuck to them, paying them almost no heed whatsoever. Throughout his life he said or wrote quite a lot of silly things about his writing, and in different ways some people are wont to put these things in the way of the appreciation of his poetry, as if to prove him a narrow-minded provincial – "essentially a minor poet," in the unsubstantiated words of Peter Ackroyd – with fusty sub-Georgian artistic ideals. Go back to his poems, dear reader: they are proof to the contrary.

Mthabisi Phili (born 1986)

Mthabisi Phili is a poet and visual artist based in Bulawayo, Zimbabwe, whose work reflects the tumult of Zimbabwean life under the rule of President Robert Mugabe. In the following poem, first published in 2010 on the Poetry International website, he considers the way in which economic and political trauma compromises not only physical survival but also, for better or worse, our ability to give voice to our inner selves. Phili explains the poem's political context as well as the significance of the title:

> In 2005 Mugabe exercised what he called "Operation Murambatsvina," which was a way of depopulating the urban areas that were bound to vote against him. The pretext was that he was getting rid of unplanned buildings, shacks, and squatters in Harare, Bulawayo, and the other major cities. "Murambatsvina" is a Shona word that means "we don't want rubbish." In response, the title of my poem says, "Speak out!" in three different languages: English, Shona, and Ndebele, which is my mother tongue.

The ellipses in the poem are the author's.

Operation Talk, Taura, Khuluma

There is no poetry these days
only my love for you remains
there is no poetry these days
the industrial workers walk on home . . .
there is no segregation these days (even racists are seen in queues)
no there is no poetry these days
no meat no food – even water goes on vacation
there is no nothing these days
only my love for you remains.

Ethan Richard

(born 1998)

In the spring of 2010, New Hampshire teacher Ruth Harlow asked the students in her fifth-grade class to write about what poetry has meant to them as readers. In his response to that assignment, one of those students, Ethan Richard, succinctly described the ambiguous delights and frustrations of reading a poem.

Statement

Poetry is like a very well read 3 year old, it uses terrific words, but uses them so strangely and it always spouts the truth you don't want other people to hear in public. . . . It'll act all cute and funny and make you smile for its cleverness, then keep you up all night yelling and screaming about something you don't understand at all.

About the Author

Dawn Potter directs the Frost Place Conference on Poetry and Teaching, held each summer at Robert Frost's home in Franconia, New Hampshire. She works extensively as a visiting writer in the schools and as a freelance editor for literary and academic presses.

The author of three collections of poetry, she has also published a memoir, *Tracing Paradise: Two Years in Harmony with John Milton*, which won the 2010 Maine Literary Award in Nonfiction. Twice nominated for a Pushcart Prize, Dawn has received grants and fellowships from the Elizabeth George Foundation, the Writer's Center, and the Maine Arts Commission. Her poems and essays have appeared in the *Sewanee Review*, the *Threepenny Review*, *Prairie Schooner*, and many other journals in the United States and abroad.

In addition to writing, Dawn sings and plays fiddle with a local acoustic band. She lives in Harmony, Maine, with photographer Thomas Birtwistle and their two sons.

Acknowledgments

I am grateful for permission to include the following copyrighted material in this anthology:

Lao Tzu: From *The Way of Life According to Lao Tzu*, translated by Witter Bynner. © 1944. Reprinted by permission of the Witter Bynner Foundation.

Li Ch'ing Chao: "Alone in the Night," by Kenneth Rexroth, from the original by Li Ch'ing Chao, from *ONE HUNDRED POEMS FROM THE CHINESE*, copyright © 1971 by Kenneth Rexroth. Reprinted by permission of New Directions Publishing Corp.

Marie de France: From *The Lais of Marie de France*, translated by Robert Hanning and Joan Ferrante. © 1978. Used by permission of Baker Academic, a division of Baker Publishing Group.

An Aztec Poet: "The Artist," by Denise Levertov, from *COLLECTED EARLIER POEMS 1940–1960*, copyright © 1960 by Denise Levertov. Reprinted by permission of New Directions Publishing Corp.

Sor Juana Inés de la Cruz: From *A Woman of Genius: The Intellectual Biography of Sor Juana Inés de la Cruz*, by Margaret Sayers Peden. Reprinted by permission of Margaret Sayers Peden.

Paul Verlaine: "The Art of Poetry," translated by Paul Driver, first published in *New Walk* (autumn/winter 2011). Reprinted by permission of Paul Driver.

Rainer Maria Rilke: From *LETTERS TO A YOUNG POET* by Rainer Maria Rilke, translated by M. D. Herter Norton. Copyright 1934, 1954 by W. W. Norton & Company, Inc., renewed © 1962, 1982 by M. D. Herter Norton. Used by permission of W. W. Norton & Company, Inc.

Wallace Stevens: Letter to José Rodríguez Feo, dated May 23, 1947, MS Am 1333.4, Houghton Library, Harvard University. From *LETTERS OF WALLACE STEVENS* by Wallace Stevens, edited by Holly Stevens, copyright © 1966 by Holly Stevens. Used by permission of Alfred A. Knopf, a division of Random House, Inc.

Vladimir Nabokov: From *SPEAK, MEMORY* by Vladimir Nabokov, copyright © 1978 by the Estate of Vladimir Nabokov. Used by permission of Alfred A. Knopf, a division of Random House, Inc.

Teresa Carson: "The Temple of Delight: John Keats and Jack Wiler" published by permission of Teresa Carson.

Honorée Fanonne Jeffers: "Swing Low, Sweet Chariot," from *The Gospel of Barbecue.* © 2000 by the Kent State University Press. Reprinted by permission of the Kent State University Press and Honorée Fanonne Jeffers.

Dawn Potter: "Not Writing the Poem," first published in the *Sewanee Review*, vol. 120, no. 1, winter 2012. Reprinted with the permission of the editor.

Brenda Shaughnessy: From the AWP panel discussion "A Tribute to the Poetry of Lynda Hull." Reprinted by permission of Brenda Shaughnessy.

Mike Walker: "Anna Akhmatova and Lydia Chukovskaya: Writing under Stalin's Shadow" published by permission of Mike Walker.

Autumn McClintock: "Responsible for Death" published by permission of Autumn McClintock.

Garth Greenwell: "On Beauty and Distance," first published in *Fourth Genre* (fall 2011). Reprinted by permission of Garth Greenwell.

Rory Waterman: "Almost-Instincts, Almost True: Philip Larkin's 'Statement' of 1955" published by permission of Rory Waterman.

Mthabisi Phili: "Operation Talk, Taura, Khuluma" (2010), first published on the *Poetry International* website and reprinted by permission of Mthabisi Phili.

Ethan Richard: "Statement" published by permission of Ethan Richard.

Anthologies from Autumn House Press

A Poet's Sourcebook: Writings about Poetry, from the Ancient World to the Present
Dawn Potter, Editor

New America: Contemporary Literature for a Changing Society
Holly Messitt and James Tolan, Editors

The Autumn House Anthology of Contemporary American Poetry
Second Edition, Michael Simms, Editor

Between Song and Story: Essays for the Twenty-First Century
Sheryl St. Germain and Margaret L. Whitford, Editors

When She Named Fire: An Anthology of Contemporary Poetry by American Women
Andrea Hollander Budy, Editor

Joyful Noise: An Anthology of American Spiritual Poetry
Robert Strong, Editor

Keeping the Wolves at Bay: Stories by Emerging American Writers
Sharon Dilworth, Editor

The Working Poet: 75 Writing Exercises and a Poetry Anthology
Scott Minar, Editor

The Autumn House Anthology of Contemporary American Poetry
First Edition, Sue Ellen Thompson, Editor

Design and Production

Text and cover design by Kathy Boykowycz

Cover art: woodcut by Patricia Segnan, evoking the Mesozoic ammonite fossils often seen in the paving stones of Venice, Italy

Set in ITC Giovanni fonts, designed in 1989 by Robert Slimbach

Printed by McNaughton and Gunn, Saline, Michigan, on Glatfelter Natural, an NFC certified paper

SOME THOUGHTS ON MYTH:

"... it might be useful to list some things that I think myths are *not*: myths are not lies, or false statements to be contrasted with truth or reality. This usage is, perhaps, the most common meaning of myth in casual parlance today. ... In our culture, in particular, myths are often given the shadowy status of what has been called an 'inoperative truth,' when in fact they might better be characterized as operative fictions. Picasso called art a lie that tells the truth, and the same might be said of myths" 25

"... myths do not, strictly speaking, have meanings; they provide contexts in which meaning occurs. Like other religious symbols, in Clifford Geertz's formulation, myths 'reek of meaning.' To this degree, a myth is not so much a true story as a story on which truth is based, a story which people may infuse with their truth. As the shaman replied to the anthropologist who persisted in asking him, 'What do the myths *mean*?': 'The myths signify—nothing. They mean *themselves*.' More precisely, myths have been called' 'tautegorical' rather than 'tautological': they do not *explain* themselves, but, rather, *symbolize* themselves. Myths perform what has been called 'a mating dance with meaning.'" 35

From Wendy Doniger, *Other People's Myths*

"... myths are on the one hand good stories, on the other hand bearers of important messages about life in general and life-within-society in particular. In a non-literate and highly traditional culture tales are a primary form not only of entertainment but also of communication and instruction—communication between coevals and also between older and younger, and therefore between generations. It is difficult for us, living as we do in an age of super-lteracy, but also dominated by the 'media' and by advertising, to envisage a way of life in which the only forms of mass-communication . . . are ritual on the one hand and story-telling on the other. Yet it was from that kind of life that myths emerged . . ." 28-29

From G.S. Kirk, *The Nature of Greek Myths*

Archaic Torso of Apollo

We never knew his stupendous head
in which the eye-apples ripened. But
his torso still glows, like a lamp,
in which his gaze, screwed back to low,

holds steady and gleams. Otherwise the curve
of his chest couldn't dazzle you, nor a smile
run through the slight twist of the loins
toward the center that held procreation.

Otherwise this stone would stand mutilated and too short
below the translucent fall-off of the shoulders,
and wouldn't shimmer like a predator's fur;

nor shine out past all its edges
like a star: for in it is no place
that doesn't see you. You must change your life.

Rainer Maria Rilke
Galway Kinnell, translator

"The last sentence of this remarkable poem does what some avant-garde cinema would come to do—turn suddenly toward the audience, breaking the illusion of aesthetic distance and point of view, and confide this urgent thing—"you must change your life." The poem is written in the second person, but that last line, phrased as a command, revolves its big shaggy head, eyes flashing, and issues this challenge. Ursula LeGuin has said of this poem, "When the genuine myth rises into consciousness, that is always the message. You must change your life."

(from "Whence Our Lingering Enchantment With Rilke" by Frederick Smock, *Writer's Chronicle*, Vol 41, No. 3, Dec. 2008, p. 50)

Here is a very recent and coincidentally pertinent article suggesting the continued "presence" of myth in our cultural consciousness.

Jeff Smith's fall recalls Ovid (!)

By Jane Henderson
Post-Dispatch Book Editor

Daedalus and Icarus by Frederick, Lord Leighton, ca 1869

Was it mere coincidence that the newspaper's coverage of Jeff Smith's travails this week reminded us of Ovid?

Was it mere coincidence that cynical political and crime reporters would allude to the myth of Icarus to explain a politician's downfall - just days after the newspaper's art critic wrote about the upcoming marathon reading of Ovid's "Metamorphoses"?

It could be coincidence. And maybe Smith's story is not really "a cautionary tale of flying too close to the sun." As Friday's editorial says, Greek tragedy may be too grand to explain federal election violations and commonplace lies.

But from a reader's standpoint, it also shows that myths, even Ovid, still speak to daily life. The Roman famously told the story of Icarus - the guy who used wax and feathers to fly. Icarus ignored his dad's advice to avoid extremes and boldly flew too close to the sun. The wax melted and Icarus dropped into the sea and drowned.

When Jeff Smith resigned from the Missouri Senate, he said he was sorry for disappointing his parents.

Dismiss the myth, and this weekend's "Metamorphoses" marathon, as irrelevant today? The "Metamorphoses" may seem like an unusual, eggheaded thing to read. Maybe. But when you get the urge to fly too high, don't say Ovid didn't warn you.

(Full disclosure: I couldn't say no to being a reader. The marathon event is from 10 a.m.-7 p.m. Saturday and Sunday, Aug. 29 and 30, at the Pulitzer Foundation for the Arts, 3716 Washington Boulevard.)

SUPPLEMENTAL READING

The following are titles I have found both very helpful and very challenging in my studies of myth over the years. There are, of course, hundreds, even thousands, of worthy titles that might be included, but for me, these are first choices.

Calasso, Roberto. *Ka: Stories of the Mind and Gods of India.* Knopf, 1995.

" " " *Literature and the Gods.* Knopf, 2001.

" " " *The Marriage of Cadmus and Harmony.* Knopf, 1993.

Doniger, Wendy. *Other People's Myths: The Cave of Echos.* Macmillan, 1988.

" " " *The Implied Spider: Politics and Theology in Myth.* Columbia UP, 1998.

Kirk, G.S. *Myth: Its Meaning and Function in Ancient and Other Cultures.* Oxford, 1970.

" " " *The Nature of Greek Myth.* Penguin, 1974.

Levi-Straus, Claude. *Myth and Meaning: Cracking the Code of Culture.* Schocken, 1978.

Veyne, Paul. *Did the Greeks Believe In Their Myths.* U of Chicago, 1988.